The World Computer

THOUGHT IN THE ACT

A series edited by Erin Manning and Brian Massumi

The World Computer

Derivative Conditions of Racial Capitalism

JONATHAN BELLER

Duke University Press   Durham and London   2021

© 2021 Duke University Press
All rights reserved
Designed by Drew Sisk
Typeset in Portrait Text and IBM Plex Mono by
Westchester Publishing Services

Library of Congress Cataloging-in-Publication Data
Names: Beller, Jonathan, author.
Title: The world computer : derivative conditions of racial capitalism /
Jonathan Beller.
Other titles: Thought in the act.
Description: Durham : Duke University Press, 2021. | Series: Thought
in the act | Includes bibliographical references and index. Identifiers:
LCCN 2020029359 (print) | LCCN 2020029360 (ebook) ISBN
9781478010135 (hardcover)
ISBN 9781478011163 (paperback)
ISBN 9781478012702 (ebook)
Subjects: LCSH: Mass media—Social aspects. | Digital media—Social
aspects. | Race in mass media.
Classification: LCC HM1206 .B455 2021 (print) | LCC HM1206 (ebook) |
DDC 302.23—dc23
LC record available at https://lccn.loc.gov/2020029359
LC ebook record available at https://lccn.loc.gov/2020029360

Cover art: Thomas Ruff, *r.phg.10*, 2014. Chromogenic print, 94½ ×
72⅞ inches, 240 × 185 cm. © 2020 Thomas Ruff / Artists Rights Society
(ARS), New York / VG Bild-Kunst, Germany. Courtesy the artist and
David Zwirner.

For those who are written, unwritten,
rewritten, and read

The technical subordination of the worker to the uniform motion of the instruments of labor, and the peculiar composition of the working group, consisting as it does of individuals of both sexes and all ages, gives rise to a barrack-like discipline, which is elaborated into a complete system in the factory, and brings the previously mentioned labor of superintendence to its fullest development, thereby dividing the workers into manual laborers and overseers, into the private soldiers and the NCOs of an industrial army. "The main difficulty" (in the automatic factory) "lay . . . above all in training human beings to renounce their desultory habits of work, and to identify themselves with the unvarying regularity of complex automations. To devise and administer a successful code of factory discipline, suited to the necessities of factory diligence, was the Herculean enterprise, the noble achievement of Arkwright! Even at the present day, when the system is perfectly organized and its labor lightened to the utmost, it is found nearly impossible to convert persons past the age of puberty into useful factory hands." In the factory code, the capitalist formulates his autocratic power over his workers like a private legislator, and purely as an emanation of his own will, unaccompanied by either that division of responsibility otherwise so much approved by the bourgeoisie, or the still more approved representative system. The code is merely the capitalist caricature of the social regulation of the labor process which becomes necessary in co-operation on a large scale and in the employment in common of instruments of labor, and especially of machinery. The overseer's book of penalties replaces the slave-driver's lash. All punishments naturally resolve themselves into fines and deductions from wages, and the law-giving talent of the factory Lycurgus so arranges matters that a violation of his laws is, if possible, more profitable to him than the keeping of them.

—KARL MARX, *CAPITAL*

Europe is literally the creation of the third world.

—FRANTZ FANON, *THE WRETCHED OF THE EARTH*

You fucked the world up now, we'll fuck it all back down.

—JANELLE MONÁE, "SCREWED," *DIRTY COMPUTER*

CONTENTS

ACKNOWLEDGMENTS

No book is written totally alone and today no book is informed without the aids and hindrances of machines. In the pulsing oscillation from total isolation to borg annihilation in the prison house of computation there have appeared, within the variegated cloud of machine-mediated, cut-and-mix mental life, many erstwhile recognizable but still very, very special nodes: realish folks met along the way, folks who meant and mean a lot to me and to the work here, comrades who shared their keys and who thereby sustained and sustain for me some degree of groundedness, along with some of the better instantiations of the would-be writer/code-breaker/cyborg-programmer/revolutionary who is, anyway, more modestly and in the screen-light of academic day, simply this writer. Times are hard and I admire everything you all do to make this here sphere a better place.

I'd like to thank all of you, but a partial list will have to do: Janet Jakobsen, Keisha Knight, Sara Collins, Ian McKenzie, Ian Alexander, Rongxin Zhang, Maya Meredith, Alana Ramjit, Saidiya Hartman, Samuel Miller, Minh-Ha Pham, Allen Feldman, Stephanie Boluk, Macarena Gomez-Barris, Mendi Obadike, Jayna Brown, Ethan Spigland, Ira Livingston, Maria Damon, May Joseph, Elizabeth During, Jeffrey Hogrefe, Suzanne Verderber, Paula Durbin-Westby, Drew Sisk, Christopher Vitale, Benjamin Lee, Robert Meister, Robert Wosnitzer, Dick Bryan, Rebecca Karl, Rebecca Jordan-Young, Patricia Clough, Erin Manning, Brian Massumi, Erik Bordeleau, Joel Mason, Eli Nadeau, Tina Campt, Jack Halberstam, Brian Larkin, Tavia Nyong'o, David Sartorious, Ed Cohen, David Eng, Michael Mandiberg, Nikhil Sing, Kalindi Vora, Neda Atanasoski, Mickee McGee, Nicole Fleetwood, Ana McCarthy, Nick Mirzoeff, Jasbir Puar, Mark Simpson, Marie Buck, Mara Mills, Eero Laine, Genevieve Yue, Nico Baumbach, Damon Young, Marina Otero Verzier, Nick Axel, Steven Shaviro, Chris Connery, Lucho Marcial, Anjali Arondekar, Lucy Burns, Carla Freccero, Donna Haraway, Teresa de Lauretis,

Gail Hershatter, Karen Tei Yamashita, Richard Dienst, Ariella Azoulay, J. Kehaulani Kauanui, DJ Lord Lewis, Franco Berardi, Silvia Federici, Fred Moten, Stefano Harney, Pierre Guillet de Monthoux, Alan Fishbone, Warren Neidich, Arne De Boever, Karen Irr, Paige Sarlin, Lydia Liu, David Golumbia, Daphne Dragona, Matteo Pasquinelli, McKenzie Wark, Alex Galloway, Ellery Washington, Jennifer Miller, James Hannaham, Alberto Toscano, Owen Hatherly, Jeff Kinkle, Molly Klein, John Steppling, Ruth Wilson Gilmore, Craig Gilmore, Sebastian Franklin, Paul Gilroy, Sean Cubitt, the late Randy Martin, the late José Esteban Muñoz, the late Toni Oliviero, the late Sara Danius, Stefan Jonsson, Warren Sack, Jennifer González, Mark Driscoll, Diane Nelson, Laura Marks, Cathy Davidson, Ken Wissoker, Brian Kuan Wood, Amal Issa, Simon Goldin and Jakob Senneby, Marina Grzinic, Titziana Terranova, Jodi Dean, Vicente Rafael, Dominic Pettman, Orit Halpern, Deborah Levitt, Patricia Pisters, Adam Nocek, Danielle Skorzanka, Sergei Pristas, Tomislav Medak, Petar Milat, Nicolina Pristas, Diana Meheik, Ante Jeric, Susana Nascimento Duarte, Yves Citton, the late Bernard Stiegler, Michel Bauwens, Geert Lovink, Colin Drumm, Doris Gassert, Marco de Mutiis, Akseli Virtanen, Jorge Lopez, Pekko Koskinen, Fabian Bruder, Laura Lotti, Skye Bougsty-Marshall, Sarah Raymundo, the late Edel Garcellano, Lyra Garcellano, Kiri Dalena, Sari Dalena, Raffy Lerma, Roland Tolentino, Ackbar Abbas, Emmanuel Derman, Vijay Iyer, Cecile McLorin Salvant, Lisa Nakamura, Angela Davis, Gina Dent, my mother Natalie Beller, sister Valerie Beller, my late father Barry Beller, love of my life and forever companion Neferti Tadiar, and our beloved *anak* Luna Beller-Tadiar. I bow to the divine in all of you.

I'd also like to add that this work owes a great, unpayable intellectual and indeed spiritual debt to antiracist, anti-imperialist and decolonial struggles, to Communist struggles (particularly in the Philippines, but also in Soviet, Cuban, Chinese, Central and South American contexts), to critical race theory, to black feminism, and to abolition feminism. This general debt to radical traditions is infinite and profoundly humbling. I cannot overstate the importance of these legacies of struggle and survival that open pathways where there seem to be none, and of the power and indeed beauty of certain forms of mutual indebtedness. I am aware too, at times painfully, of the fact of my own limits (if not of all of my particular shortcomings) in relation to this debt. I strove to pursue here the work that I thought was needed and that I could do, but I take responsibility for my own inability to do it better. Be that as it may, it is heartening to know that y'all are out there and that it's not over yet.

I

Computational Racial Capitalism

The Social Difference Engine and the World Computer

Power is so powerful it can afford
to pay people to speak truth to it.
—STEW

The wealth of societies in which the capitalist mode of production prevails appears as an immense collection of information; the individual bit appears as its elementary form. Or so it appears to the machines that count, the machines of account.

Moreover, the rise of information meant—in fact *is*—the ability to write a derivative contract on any phenomenon whatever. Its emergence is one with the calculus of probability and thus of risk. What price information? We will show here how information becomes a derivative on reality whose importance comes to exceed that of reality, at least for those bound by the *materiality* of information's risk profiles. Furthermore, the algorithm becomes the management strategy for the social differentiation introduced by and as information—a heuristic, becoming bureaucratic, becoming apparatus for the *profitable* integration of difference and, significantly, for any "us" worthy of that name, of that which and those who could be differentiated. The algorithm's calculative execution on information, its "procedural" problem solving, was called forth and derived from the market optimization of the socially meaningful metrics (things somehow or other worth measuring) of difference. Recursively, the algorithm and its avatars multiplied its capacities of differentiation.

With its Boolean operators, and later with pattern recognition, algorithmic execution on socially derived information effects a tranching of the world that also shatters prior social narratives and ontologies, and allows for the placing of contingent claims on any tranche whatever without regard for the rest. How much does it cost to ship a slave? Insurance policies for slave traders? Reparations for proprietors of slaves? Predictive policing? For racial capitalism, Blackness becomes a junior tranche. The third world becomes a junior tranche. The global South becomes a junior tranche. All subprime, all the lowest tranche of a security, the one deemed most risky. "Any losses on the value of the security are absorbed by the junior tranche before any other tranche, but for accepting this risk the junior tranche pays the highest rate of interest" (Curtis). The brutal divide and conquer approach, on a continuum with the separation imposed by racial capitalist pursuits from settler colonialism, factory barracks and camps, to workplace alienation and Debord's spectacle, effected the capacity to isolate certain phenomenon and then bet on the value of the outcomes while externalizing every other concern. Here too we find the distinction between signal and noise is in the first place a matter of political economy and its racism.

The slow nuclear bomb that is the COVID-19 pandemic is but a case in point in the terrible unfolding of what one may hope is still pre-history manifest as racial capitalism. It is a consequence of the convergence of the global *demos* being relegated to noise, to "the poor image" (Steyerl 2012: 31–45), to volatility by the global compute. The virus is not just information on a strand of genetic material, and should not as Ed Cohen warned us years ago, be treated fetishistically, as if it were itself the *cause* of global suffering (Cohen 2011). Viruses are everywhere—the global pandemic is symptomatic of world-systemic failure on many fronts: health care provisioning and access, economic inequality, agribusiness, social hierarchy, racism, etc. Individual bodies are made precarious by a matrix of financialized "information" that differentiates among us while externalizing whatever might be left of our pre-existing conditions that could all too briefly be summed up as our real interests or even our ecological concerns—our connection to the *bios* in the broadest sense. We are subjected to and by a continuous for-profit reformatting by the various systems of mediation that overcode us as problems to be solved—including by the regimes of all the "estates:" the fourth estate that is "the press," and particularly a fifth estate that has in fact absorbed all the others for its own calculus, namely "computation." We observe that the reigning global calculus of profit, though invented by no one in particular, everywhere seeks to extract our value and mostly benefits those who believe in theory or in practice that they are shining examples of a superior race. Those who have almost unlimited access to the social product, and to us, to our information, to our time. How does this sense of superiority, of the greatness of our oppressors, come about? From their harvesting the outputs of the rabble and their self-satisfied accession to the violence necessary to keep us down.

Most recently, the global compute has involved off-loading systemic precarity onto individuals and where possible onto entire peoples to the point, just reached in 2020, when that strategy itself created radical systemic instability: causing deaths that will likely be in the millions, and not incidentally threatening global "depression." Well, one person's, or one people's, Armageddon is another's depression—or their joy. The algorithmic optimization of society for profit, an economics that, while sometimes unconscious, is these days never too far from the conscious mind of the creators of specific programs, collectively effects a wholesale compression of the sociosemiotic into what Friedrich August von Hayek (1945: 14) precisely called "a system of telecommuncations" capacitated by what he grasped as effectively the price signal. Money, or what, in a different key, Alfred Sohn-Rethel (1978: 28) perceived as exhibit A of "real abstraction," relegates, wherever possible, everything else to noise.[1] The "noise" of course, is the source of volatility. The suppression of noise is from the standpoint of communication theory a technical matter. Here we understand it as a matter of politics and economy. Noise suppression directly correlates to people's oppression. In financial terms, volatility is a similar index—the expression, in prices, of decision making under conditions of uncertainty. Ironic then that volatility has become a major source of value creation for synthetic finance, and now for states. The U.S.'s Corona bailouts of over three trillion US dollars—responses to the volatility of the social rendered ever more precarious by the existing economy—represent more than 60 percent of the money ever issued in the history of the country.

What perhaps best characterized this period is a full-blown convergence of communication, information and financialization *as* computation; whether or not this convergence and all its incipient violence can be redesigned is an open question. This question is ultimately about a possible politics of the protocolization of these informatic networks within a literally universal system of computation that as hypostatic states looks like a virtual machine, what I here call *the world computer*, and as diachronic flow (processing) is nothing less than *economic media*. Can these formations that for their proprietors profitably collapse message and value be hacked or reprogrammed so that the command control centers that make the most (from) difference are not in the hands of racist plutocrats—do not in fact *produce* them? That question, though addressed in this volume will be taken up more fully at a later date, with a particular focus on the how and the who.[2] Here in this book we consider the various social vectors and components sedimented into machine function and then reactivated by the dire co-articulation of racial capitalism and computation—rearticulated as computational racial capitalism and its virtual machine, the world computer.

Information as Real Abstraction

Taking the notion that Capital was always a computer as a starting point (Dyer-Witheford, 2013), *The World Computer* understands the history of the commodification of life as a process of encrypting the world's myriad qualities as quantities. Formal and informal techniques, from double-entry bookkeeping and racialization, to the rise of information and discrete state machines, imposed and extended the tyranny of racial capital's relentless calculus of profit. By means of the coercive colonization of almost all social spaces, categories, and representations—where today language, image, music, and communication all depend upon a computational substrate that is an outgrowth of fixed capital—all, or nearly all, expressivity has been captured in the dialectic of massive capital accumulation on the one side and radical dispossession on the other. Currently the money-likeness of expression—visible as "likes" and in other attention metrics that treat attention and affect as currency—is symptomatic of *the financialization of daily life* (Martin, 2015a). All expression, no matter what its valence, is conscripted by algorithms of profit that intensify inequality by being put in the service of racial capitalism; consequently, we are experiencing a near-apocalyptic, world-scale failure to be able to address global crises including migration for reparations, carceral systems, genocide, militarism, climate racism, racism, pandemic, anti-Blackness, extinction, and other geopolitical ills. The colonization of semiotics by racial capital has rendered all "democratic" modes of governance outmoded save those designed for the violent purpose of extracting profits for the enfranchised. Culturally these modes of extraction take the form of fractal fascism. An understanding that informationalized semiotic practices function as financial derivatives may allow for a reimagining of the relationship between language, visuality, and that other economic medium, namely money, in an attempt to reprogram economy and therefore the creation and distribution of value—and thus also the politics and potentials of representation. In what would amount to an end to postmodernism understood as the cultural logic of late capitalism, our revolutionary politics require, as did the communisms of the early twentieth century, a new type of economic program. In the age of computation, putting political economy back on the table implies a reprogramming of our cultural logics as economic media for the radical redress of the ills of exploitation and the democratization of the distribution of the world social product. Sustainable communism requires the decolonizaton of abstraction and the remaking of the protocols of social practice that give rise to real abstraction.

Though in this section we will more narrowly address the issues of money, race, and information as "real abstraction," and their role in computational racial capitalism, we note the overarching argument for the larger study:

1   Commodification inaugurates the global transformation of qualities into quantities and gives rise to the world computer.

2   "Information" is not a naturally occurring reality but emerges in the footprint of price and is always a means to posit the price of a possible or actual product.

3   The general formula for capital, M-C-M', where M is money, C is commodity, and M' is more money) can be rewritten M-I-M', where I is information.

4   "Labor," Attention, Cognition, Metabolism, Life converge as "Informatic Labor" whose purpose, with respect to Capital, is to create state changes in the Universal Turing Machine that is the World Computer—racial capital's relentless, granular, and planetary computation of its accounts.

5   Semiotics, representation, and categories of social difference function as financial derivatives—as wagers on the economic value of their underliers and as means of structuring risk for capital.

6   Only a direct engagement with the computational colonization of the life-world through a reprogramming (remaking) of the material processes of abstraction that constitute real abstraction can secure victory—in the form of a definitive step out of and away from racial capitalism—for the progressive movements of our times. Such a definitive movement requires an occupation and decolonization of information, and therefore of computation, and therefore of money. Only through a remaking of social relations at the molecular level of their calculus, informed by struggle against oppression, can the beauty of living and the fugitive legacies of creativity, community, and care prevail.

The mode of comprehension, analysis, and transformation proposed here will require an expanded notion of *racial capitalism*. It interrogates the existence of deep continuities and long-term emergences—what one could correctly call algorithms of extractive violence—in the history of capitalism. These *algorithms of violence* include the reading and writing of code(s) on bodies, their surveillance and overcoding by informatic abstraction. Such algorithms of epidermalization or "the imposition of race on the body" (Browne: 113) are inscribed and executed *on the flesh* (Spillers 1987); and they are executed by means of codification processes that violently impose both a metaphysical and physical reformatting of bodies. As Simone Browne shows, epidermalization is given "its alphanumeric form" (99) through a vast array tools of marking, scarification, discipline, and surveillance that include branding irons, implements of torture, auction blocks, ship design, insurance policies, newspaper ads for runaway "property," photographs in postcard form and a panoply of other media of dehumanization. Executable code is imposed as social categories of race, gender, religion and property, as ideologies, psychologies, contracts, brands, communication theories, game theories, and quantities of money—these abstractions work their ways into and are indeed imposed by the machines of calculation—and their avatars. We confront a continuous process of unmaking and remaking using all means available; it is violently inscribed on bodies. Sylvia Wynter, in her post–Rodney King piece "No Humans Involved: An Open Letter to My Colleagues" writes, "Both W. E. B. Du Bois and Elsa Goveia have emphasized the way in which the code of 'Race' or the Color Line, functions to systemically *predetermine* the sharply unequal re-distribution of the collectively produced global resources; and therefore, the correlation of the racial ranking rule with the Rich/Poor rule. Goveia pointed out that all American societies are integrated on the basis of a central cultural belief in which all *share*. This belief, that of the genetic-racial inferiority of Black people to *all others*, functions to enable our social hierarchies, including those of rich and poor determined directly by the economic system, to be perceived as having been *as* pre-determined by 'that great crap game called life,' as have also ostensibly been the invariant hierarchy between White and Black. Consequently in the Caribbean and Latin America, within the terms of this sociosymbolic calculus, to be 'rich' was also to be 'White,' to be poor was also to be 'Black'" (Wynter: 52).

"To be 'rich' was also to be 'White,' to be poor was also to be 'Black.'" The real abstraction imposed by executable code—the "code of 'Race'" that "functions to systematically *predetermine* the structurally unequal redistribution of global resources" is beholden to mediating capitalist exchange while embarking on a radical reformatting of ontology. This reformatting, the supposed result of "that great crap game called life," brutally correlates race and value, but not entirely by chance, while racial capitalism embarks on imposing this calculus globally. Racial abstraction is endemic to what we will further explore as "real abstraction"; the evacuation of quality by abstract categories and quantities is, as we shall see in more detail, a "necessary" correlate to a world overrun by the calculus of money. Such algorithms of violence encode social difference, and although they may begin as heuristics ("rules of thumb"), they are none the less crucial to the calculated and calculating expansion of racial capital. Its processes and processing structures the meanings that can be ascribed to—and, as importantly, what can be done to—those of us whose data profiles constitute us as "illegal," "Mexican," "Black," "Gypsy," "Jew," and a lexicon of thousands of other actionable signs. This codification process draws from the histories of slavery, of colonialism, of state formation, of genocide, of gender oppression, of religious pogroms, of normativity, and again from the militarization and policing and the apparatuses of calculation that have developed within states and parastates in their own biometric pursuit of capital—power. Their violent destruction and remaking of the world. The *internalization* of these codes, including the struggles with them and the ways in which they license and/or foreclose various actions, exists in a recursive relationship to their perilous refinement. Their analysis, a code-breaking of sorts, will therefore demand some drastic modifications in many of the various anticapitalist, antistate warrior-stances practiced to date, particularly in a large number of their European and U.S. incarnations that until very recently remained blind to their own imperial violence and are too often complicit with hegemonic codes of masculine, unraced agency, imperialist nationalism, and default liberal assumptions in relation to questions of race, gender, sexuality, coloniality, and other forms of historically institutionalized oppression.[3]

The analytic, *computational racial capital*, would identify the field of operations that emerges around the embryonic form of the commodity and coarticulates with racial abstraction to formalize its code, code that serves as operating system for the virtual machine here hypostasized as "the world computer" and by inscribing itself on bodies and everything else. The commodity, the analysis of which famously begins volume 1 of Marx's *Capital*, expressed the dual being and indeed dual registration of the humanly informed object as both quality of matter and quantity of exchange-value, along with the global generalization of this form. "The wealth of societies in which the capitalist mode of production prevails appears as an immense collection of commodities" (125). Commodities were (and with some modifications to be discussed further on, still are) humanly informed materials with a use-value and an exchange-value—humanly informed qualities indexed by quantities. "Computational racial capital," as a heuristic device, stages an analysis of the convergence of what on the one side often appeared as universal: the economic, abstract, and machinic operating systems of global production and reproduction endemic to the commodity form and its calculus, with what on another side, sometimes appeared as particular or even incidental: racism, colonialism, slavery, imperialism, and racialization. The concept organizes this dramaturgy of analytically reunifying elements that were never materially separate in light of the study that the late Cedric Robinson conducted and recorded as *Black Marxism*. Robinson writes, "The development, organization and expansion of capitalist society pursued essentially racial directions, so too did social ideology. As a material force, then, it could be expected that racialism would inevitably permeate the social structures emergent from capitalism. I have used the term 'racial capitalism' to refer to the development and to the subsequent structure as an historical agency" (1983: 2–3). *The World Computer* takes what Robinson saw as "civilizational racism," and its central role in the development of capital as axiomatic,—and sees that this role extends to and deeply into capitalist calculation and machinery during the entire period in which the world economic system seems to have moved form the paradigm of the commodity to a paradigm of information. "Computational racial capitalism" would thus understand the generalization of computation as an extension of capital logics and practices that include and indeed require the economic *calculus* of the dialectics of social difference. These differences, both economic and semiotic, would include those plied by slavery, anti-Blackness and other forms of racism during the past centuries. *Computation must therefore be recognized as not a mere technical emergence but the practical result of an ongoing and bloody struggle between the would-have-it-alls and the to-be-dispossessed.* Developed both consciously and unconsciously, computational racial capitalism is, when seen in the light of ongoing racialization and value extraction, "the subsequent structure as an historical agency." The racial logic of computation must be pursued when considering finance, surveillance, population management, policing, social systems, social media, or any of the vast suite of protocols plying difference for capital. The local instance of computation, a specific 1 or 0, may seem value neutral, a matter as indifferent as lead for a bullet or uranium for a bomb. But we are looking at computation as the modality of a world-system. Computation emerges as the result of struggles that informed "class struggle" in all its forms, recognized or not by the often spotty tradition(s) of Marxism, including those struggles specific to the antagonisms of colonialism, slavery, imperialism, and white supremacist heteropatriarchal capitalism more generally. It is the *result* of struggles indexed by race, gender, sexuality, nationality, and ethnicity, along with additional terms indexing social differentiation too numerous to incant here but that together form a lexicon and a grammar of extractive oppression—and as we have said and as must always be remembered, also of struggle. The lexicon includes compressions that result in many of history's abstractions including a perhaps singularly pointed abstraction: "a history whose shorthand is race" (Spillers 1997: 142). The grammar for that lexicon depends upon the deployment and execution of forms of differentiating abstraction that are lived—lived processes of abstraction and lived abstraction organized by the increasingly complex and variegated calculus of profit and thus of domination.

"Real abstraction," then, emerges not just as money in Sohn-Rethel's sense, but as the codification of race, gender, sexuality, geography, credit and time—and gives rise to a "grammar," in Hortense Spillers's (1987) use of the term, that not only structures meaning and redounds to the deepest crevices of being smelted by social practices, but also, and not incidentally, prices differentials indexed to social difference.[4] "Real abstraction," as Sohn-Rethel spent his life deciphering, takes place "behind [our] backs" as the practical and historical working out of the exchange of equivalents within the process of the exchange of goods (33). For him, the development of the money-form, of the real abstraction that is money, is Exhibit A of the abstraction process mediating object exchange. This capacity for abstraction, realized first in "the money commodity" and then as money provided the template for further abstraction, not least in the conceptual formations of Western philosophy itself (1978). Sohn-Rethel develops this argument that practices of exchange precede the abstraction of value in *Intellectual and Manual Labour*, providing the full quotation from Marx: "Men do not therefore bring the product of their labour into relation with each other as value because they see these objects merely as the material integuments of homogeneous human labour. The reverse is true: by equating their different products to each other in exchange as values, they equate their different kinds of labour as human labour. They do this without being aware of it. (Marx 1990: 166 in Sohn-Rethel 1978: 32). Here is Sohn-Rethel's commentary:

> People become aware of the exchange abstraction only when they come face to face with the result which their own actions have engendered "behind their backs" as Marx says. In money the exchange abstraction achieves concentrated representation, but a mere functional one—embodied in a coin. It is not recognizable in its true identity as abstract form, but disguised as a thing one carries about in one's pocket, hands out to others, or receives from them. Marx says explicitly that the value abstraction never assumes a representation as such, since the only expression it ever finds is the equation of one commodity with the use-value of another. The gold or silver or other matter which lends to money its palpable and visible body is merely a metaphor of the value abstraction it embodies, not this abstraction itself. (33–34)

Exchange-value is "in our heads" but is not the creation of any individual. Alongside use-value it is the other, abstract component of the "double being" of the commodity-form. Like Norbert Wiener's (1961: 132) definition of information but, strictly speaking, emerging long before the idea of information proper, real abstraction is "not matter or energy." There is not an atom of matter in exchange-value, or, as Marx puts it, "Not an atom of matter enters into the objectivity of commodities as values; in this it is the direct opposite of the coarsely sensuous objectivity of commodities as physical objects" (1990: 138). And a bit on, "So far no chemist has ever discovered exchange-value in a pearl or diamond" (177). But unlike in Wiener's naturalist definition of information, exchange-value *is* an index of a social relation, an historical outcome. It indexes "abstract universal labor time," a third term that forms the basis of comparison between two ostensibly incomparable and therefore incommensurable commodities, and, because common to both, creates the ratio of value that renders them quantitatively commensurable. This distinction between the social basis of exchange-value and the universal character of information should give us pause. As we shall have occasion to observe, information, as it is today (mis)understood, is thought to be a naturally occurring additional property of things—neither matter nor energy—rather than a domain of expression constituted by means of a technological and economic repression of its social dimension. Notably, Sohn-Rethel "set[s] out to argue that the abstractness operating in exchange and reflected in value does nevertheless find an identical expression, namely the abstract intellect, or the so-called pure understanding—the cognitive source of scientific knowledge" (34). For him, it gives rise to the abstract capacities of the subject of philosophy as well as the quantitative capacities of the subject of science and mathematics that in the twentieth century move toward a paradigm of information. Echoing Sohn-Rethel, we could say then that information is in our machines but not the creation of any individual machine. *Not an atom of matter enters into information, though, like value, it is platformed on matter and requires energy for creation.* This thesis will take on particular importance as we consider social differences whose descriptors, it turns out, are executable in a computational sense, at least from the point of view of financial calculus, but platformed on matter, and indeed, on living matter, on life.

Beyond the intention of any individual, abstraction as "exchange-value" in "money" occurs in and as the process and processing of exchange in accord with an emerging standard. This standard, which economists call "exchange-value," and which, in Marx is based on abstract universal labor time (the historically variable, socially necessary average time required to produce a commodity), persists alongside and within the specific qualities of the commodity (its use-value) and creates the commodity's dual being. Though without chemical or material basis, this standard, exchange-value, is a social relation—a social relation as an abstraction—that inheres in the commodity-form itself and is formalized with the rise of the money commodity. The money commodity, in becoming a general equivalent, standardizes and thus renders fully quantifiable the exchange-value of commodities—exchange-values denominated in quantities of money. The quantification of value in a measure of money is an abstraction enabled by money itself which, as we have seen, is a real abstraction. It is a calculation that has occurred behind our backs, and indeed produces what Hayek (1945) identifies as the price system. When we recognize the differences in wages among people who are raced, gendered, nationed, and classed by various matrices of valuation, we also recognize that the calculus performed by and as real abstraction includes racial abstraction and gender abstraction. It is part of the calculus of capital that provides it with an account of and discounts on the rate of exchange with the labor power of marked people(s)—by discounting people(s) (Beller 2017b; see also Bhandar and Toscano 2015: 8–17). Racial abstraction provides capital with an index that measures a deviation from the average value of human life (itself historically driven down by the falling rate of profit). In this, computational racial capitalism is not merely a heuristic or a metaphor for the processes of a virtual machine; it is a historical-material condition.

As we shall see, and as is obvious at least in the general case to anyone who has thought seriously about it, whiteness (and the fascist masculinity endemic to it) is not only operating where one finds "race": it is operating everywhere in the imperium that it can be imagined (by some) that race is *not* a factor—in medicine, in science, in statistics, in computation, in information. As I wrote—resituating Bateson's (1972) definition of information—in *The Message Is Murder*, information is not merely "a difference that makes a difference"; it is a difference that makes a *social* difference. This slight difference in expression situates information historically. While in keeping with Bateson's far reaching ideas regarding an ecology of mind ("If I am right, the whole thinking about what we are and what other people are has got to be restructured"; 468), ideas that at once problematize any distinction between inside and outside and that make him dubious of any thought that presupposes sovereign subjectivity, my interpolation of "social" in his formulation "a difference that makes a social difference" shifts the emphasis somewhat by insisting on the always already sociohistoricity of any possible knowledge. Bateson believed that his understanding of information and systems ecology promised a new mode of thinking that he himself, as a twentieth-century bourgeois white man, did not feel capable of really embodying. Thus our interpolation, in keeping with Bateson but made compatible with Marx is, in keeping with Marx, designed to "transform . . . the problem of knowledge into one of social theory" (Postone 2003: 216). Such a transformation situates knowledge and now also information in the socio-historical milieu, the ecology such that it is, of racial capitalism, and therein finds information's historical conditions of possibility.

Here we advance the argument for the ultimately determining instance of social difference (and up the ante for the bet against whiteness) by proposing that information is the elaboration of real abstraction, of abstraction that results from collective practices of economic exchange and therefore from the general management of value as a social relation. I argue that set out in logical sequence, information is posited by, then posits and then presupposes the human processes of exchange that Sohn-Rethel, following Marx, argues are the practices that first give rise to the money-form and to real abstraction. For Sohn-Rethel the result of the activities of comparison, adequation, and trading of specific things that have qualities—which are, strictly speaking, incomparable—resulted over time in a process of finding a relation of equivalence and then general equivalence indexed to abstract labor time, what was in effect socially average human labor time. Exchange-value was a quantitative measure of that abstract time—the average socially necessary time to create commodity X denominated in money. This real abstraction was no one's invention but was the practical result of exchange—of people's activity—and thus emerged as a nonconscious result that nonetheless interceded on conscious process. Consequently, real abstraction was for Sohn-Rethel also the precursor to conceptual abstraction, including philosophy, science and mathematics. He writes:

> The essence of commodity abstraction, however, is that it is not thought-induced; it does not originate in men's minds but in their actions. And yet this does not give "abstraction" a merely metaphorical meaning. It is abstraction in its precise, literal sense. The economic concept of value resulting from it is characterized by a complete absence of quality, a differentiation purely by quantity and by applicability to every kind of commodity and service which can occur on the market. These qualities of the economic value abstraction indeed display a striking similarity with fundamental categories of quantifying natural science without, admittedly, the slightest inner relationship between these heterogeneous spheres being *as yet* recognizable. While the concepts of natural science are thought abstractions, the economic concept of value is a real one. It exists nowhere other than in the human mind but it does not spring from it. Rather it is purely social in character, arising in the spatio-temporal sphere of human interrelations. It is not people who originate these abstractions but their actions. "They do this without being aware of it."[5]

The practical rise of a form of abstraction indifferent to particular qualities is key here and is to be understood as a precursor to the content-indifferent abstractions of a variety of types. As Simmel notes in *The Philosophy of Money*, law, intellectuality, and money "have the power to lay down forms and directions to which they are content indifferent" (441–2). Without doubt, such power informed the racial categories of the Humanism of Ernst Renan, Roger Caillois, and others so brilliantly excoriated by Aimé Césaire in his *Discourse on Colonialism*. We add here the hypothesis that the rise of information as the content-indifferent assignation of numerical index to any social relation whatever, is a development of the abstraction necessary for economic exchange to persist under the intensive "developmental" pressure of global racial capitalism—information is derived from the increasingly complex things that people do through and as exchange and as such is both precursor and corollary to financialization—the social conditions that sustain what is fetishistically apprehended as "finance capital" and its seeming capacity to derive wealth from pure speculation and risk management in ways that (incorrectly) appear to be fully detached from labor and labor time.

In this light, information reveals itself as neither naturally occurring nor the creation of anyone in particular, but, in keeping with Sohn-Rethel's Marxian formulation of real abstraction, is likewise invented "behind our backs" as a result of "man's" practical activity. Information enables a complexification and further generalization of what will turn out to be monetary media, media that would be adequate to, and indeed are adequate (from the perspective of capital) to contemporary forms of exchange—what people do when they interact with one another in what is now the social factory. In brief, information is the extension of a monetary calculus adequate to the increasingly abstract character of social relations and social exigencies. It is an interstitial, materially platformed, calculative fabric of abstraction that through its coordinated capillary actions orchestrates social practice and provides interface for the uptake of value production. Once this idea is fully grasped, it becomes pointless to look for any other origin to the information age.

Just as for Marx there is not a single atom of matter in exchange value (1990: 138), we say that there is not a single atom of matter in information.[6] "All the phenomenon of the universe, whether produced by the hand of man or indeed by the universal laws of physics, are not to be conceived as acts of creation but solely as a reordering of matter" (Pietro Verri 1771, cited in Marx 1990: 133; note 13). Value is the socially valid *informing* of matter, so too is information.

Economy then is society's matter compiler and, approximately simultaneously with the advent of "man," "history," and "the world market," "exchange value" emerges as a quantitative measure of the social value of material state changes indexed to human labour posited as "abstract universal labour time." Marx's famous example of the simple wooden table in Chapter 1 of *Capital*, which "transcends sensuousness" when leaving the clear-cut framework of use value and becoming a commodity and thus an exchange value, registers as "fetishism," the "metaphysical subtleties," "theological niceties," and "grotesque ideas" (1990: 163), endemic in the table's computability as value. In brief, just as discreet states of matter embodying value as a network of commodities mediated by markets and tied to labor give rise historically to the discrete state *machine*, otherwise known as the computer, exchange value gives rise to computable information and then to computation itself, becoming interoperable with it. Even before the rise of information proper, exchange value operates as information (and thus, necessarily information processing)—and then, as synthetic finance and contemporary forms of computer-mediated accounting and production readily testify, by means of it. Computation is the extension, development, and formalization of the calculus of exchange value—the ramification of its fetish character—and becomes in spirit and in practice, a command control layer for the management of the profitable calculus of value. Platformed on states of matter, information, not matter but rather *difference* between and among states of matter, extends, grammartizes, and granularizes the calculus of value regarding the organization of matter. Commodities and computation thus run the same basic operating system—state changes in matter driven by human practices—the value of which in any given state is expressed in the context of an informatic network and indexed to labor time. As such, information is the processing power of money itself and is inexorably beholden to abstract labor time and thus to racial capitalism. It is, in brief, an outgrowth of the money form. The cost of computation, the arrival at a discrete state, is a derivative operation, indicating an investment, that is explicitly a risk on the future value of an underlier, that is, on value itself.

This argument for understanding the social as the ultimate referent and ground for any and all information, further advanced in chapter 1, is not content to serve as a mere heuristic for cultural theorists to express a modicum of suspicion with respect to truth claims backed by statistics and information. It is a thoroughgoing indictment of information as a *technique* of value extraction, racialization, and instrumental social differentiation. As a first approximation, actually existing information, like actually existing money, can indeed be said to be the root of all evil—in as much as the fact of its existence is a symptom of a far more complex historical process than what would seem to be discernible from the fact of the coin or the bit. The problem, of course, is that your metabolism (and mine), cannot easily extend into the future without access to both. I develop this idea here to say that *everywhere computation operates, so too does racial capitalism*—at least until proven otherwise. The repressive apparatus of capital clearly *assumes* this role for information, even if it does so at a level that most often exceeds ordinary default "human" (white) understanding: the net result to date of the number crunch of "the world computer" is a hierarchy of valuations inseparable from the violence of racialization and its attendant dispossession, and inseparable again from what Ruth Wilson Gilmore (2007: 28) in her classic and statistically attuned definition of racism calls "the state-sanctioned or extralegal production and exploitation of group-differentiated vulnerability to premature death." Today, we argue, no calculation, networked as it is with the world computer, is fully separable from informatics and its basis in racial capitalism. We will argue for this logical and also horrific history of abstraction in more detail below as we explore the interoperability of digital systems and their colonization of the semiotic, corporeal and material domains. The global learning curve of revolutionary praxis must attend to this modal innovation of systemic oppression, an oppression which is at once beyond all calculation and one with it.[7]

The fundamental premise of this book, which then gives rise to the rest, is that what we today call digitization began more than seven centuries ago with commodification, that is, with wage labor and the rise of private property along with money of account. Private property, recall from Marx, was not the cause but the result of alienated labor (though later the relationship becomes reciprocal). In Marx's words: "Private property appears to be the source, the cause of alienated labour, it is really its consequence, just as the gods in the beginning are not the cause but the effect of man's intellectual confusion. Later this relationship becomes reciprocal" (Marx 1978: 79). The alienation of labor and the accumulation of value as private property are of a piece: private property, for Marx, is no more natural than is avarice. Some seven centuries ago, the commodity-form, which allowed for the denomination of use-values in terms of exchange-value, and wage labor, which denominated human creativity in terms of the same exchange-value quantified by means of the money-commodity (e.g., gold), inaugurated the universalizing conversion of all qualities into quantities. This emergence, indexing quantities of money to amounts of abstract universal labor time, like that of private property itself, was a result of man's "practical activity" (76). We might call this emerging domination of production, exchange, and social life by the money commodity and its capacity to mediate a quantifiable yet content-indifferent value-form present in all other commodities Digital Culture 1.0 (DC1). As materials and persons recursively passed through the expanding production cycles of capital and were increasingly caught in the warp of private accumulation enabled by the institution of capital's unequal exchange with labor by means of the wage (itself an abstraction machine, a calculus), and of private property's systems of accounts, so began an incipient digitization of the life-world through the generalized inscription of all existing use-values and of all imaginable use-values in terms of quantities of exchange-value. Money's operating system permeated the world. Under capitalist expansion and its highly varied methods of accounting, qualities became increasingly treated quantitatively, and therefore become supplemental to and subjugated by the calculus of profit; the rest is world history. It is also the history of the intensive *development* of real abstraction—the rise from social exchange of money-denominated numbers indexing social activity and social relations attained increasingly complex forms.

Without doubt, capital was not and is not the only organizational force that gives form and systematicity to inequality—racism is "civilizational," as Cedric Robinson argues and forms of gender oppression predate capitalism—but capital expansion depended upon utilizing existing inequalities, developing new ones, and legitimating that development. It was and remains a social difference engine. Legitimation of differentiation is a means to monetization. This is not to say that racism was not and is not often its own motivation. However, to abstract here from Robinson's vastly understudied work, capitalism was not only always racial capitalism, it was always a social difference engine. It operated by means of differentiation, abstraction, and exploitative extraction: the imposition of fungible units and forms, as well as the excision, stifling, and oppression of counterclaims to the "law" of value. As Marxist feminism and Black Marxism have shown, and as white Marxism has resisted, the value-form always was and yet remains raced and gendered. Indeed it depends upon the fungibility of these abstracting categories. Capital offers recognition through remuneration to some types of labor while depending upon other forms of coerced (enslaved, feminized, or otherwise discounted) socially mandated labor (domestic labor, indentured servitude, disposable) and upon a large, often deadly, gray area stretching along social differentiation ranging from full citizenship to second and third class citizenship to social death to murder for its expansion and generalization. Put another way, money—as vanishing mediator of exchange by means of value abstraction—was also a system of representation. The money commodity, in being able to represent value, was also an instrument for the enforcing of systemic bias. Its very circulation and pricing mechanisms legitimated hierarchies of social differentiations as it utilized them and their capacity to format the social. This systemic bias of the content indifferent money-form became increasingly true with sovereign monies.

Monetary systems of representation, invisible, pure or natural as they may seem thanks to their ability to deracinate quantities *for all "practical" purposes* are nonetheless always platformed in an instance of the social order. This platform, for example, can be the sovereign state, the interstate system, an institutionally and ideologically upheld regime of truth, or distributed computation. These platforms have their advantages in that by assuming and naturalizing their institutionality and thus their sovereignty, they can compress heterogeneous values into information. Price, as Hayek theorized at the dawn of the computer age, condensed social complexity into a single number and rendered other considerations external and/or redundant. All social signals were collapsed into the "telecommunications" of the price signal that, like Shannon's mathematical theory of communication, was "content-indifferent" (Hayek 1945: 519–30; Shannon 1948). It is the argument here that such content indifference depends not just on monetary abstraction but on a matrix of abstraction—including commodity abstraction, racial abstraction, and gender abstraction—and that these forms of abstraction impose lived abstraction on social relations that have themselves become abstract (in time that itself has become abstract [Postone: 186–225]), while naturalizing or otherwise normalizing and thus enforcing, their platform sovereignty. The media of content indifference have cutting edges. Such cuts are everywhere felt; here we must assemble them and interrogate their digitality to decode their deeper logic and their grounding in violence.

We observe that within the economy of DCI, and certainly within that of contemporary digital culture—or Digital Culture 2.0 (DC2), in which the digital computer or discrete state machine becomes the primary medium of social exchange—the quantification process, like everything else that might matter in economics, always passes through "monetization." That is, everything else that will matter will pass through monetization if its capillary processes in science, engineering, mathematics, informatics, war, housekeeping, cottage industry, demography, and every other domain are to be valorized and thus assured both continuing relevance, and thereby, an existence fully conferred. Some platform somewhere will find interest in extracting your information, and you must "consent" to survive. Quantified processes as well as the quantification process itself must provide an ROI—return on investment—to databanks, computers and cloud computers. Such a rationale is rigorously applied both to human processes and to human-machine processes in an intensive development of metrics and systems of account. This development of vertical and horizontal systemic integration around the requisites of the value-form must be clearly understood as "the computational mode of production." It optionalizes and optimizes value extraction and, in what may be a surprising result, has rendered social processes themselves as investible derivatives—financial positions that structure risk in relation to the volatility of valuation. This generalization of a direct relation of cybersocial processes to finance is accomplished vis-à-vis computation and results in derivative conditions, or what, following Randy Martin's (2015a) understanding of both the financialization of daily life and the social derivative, I sometimes refer to as "the derivative condition."

Nowhere perhaps is this general and thoroughgoing recasting of the character and calculus of interactive nodes by capital more clearly stated—at least early on—than in Foucault's analysis of "human capital" in his lectures on neoliberalism in *The Birth of Biopolitics* (2008). There, recapitulating Irving Fisher, Foucault asks what is a wage—and replies, "It is an income." He continues: "How can we define an income? An income is quite simply the product or return on a capital. Conversely we will call 'capital' everything that in one way or another can be a source of future income" (2008: 224). From this brilliant and (for the humanist) devastating treatment of the wage, which becomes merely, that is, generically, "an earnings stream" (224), Foucault remarks upon the shift of economics form an analysis of "process" to the analysis of "activity": "Economics should not consist in the study of these mechanisms [production, exchange, or consumption data], but in the nature and consequences of what they [economists] call substitutable choices" (222). Foucault (224) quoting Lionel Robbins: "Economics is the science of human behavior as a relationship between ends and scarce means which have mutually exclusive uses." Thus, as human capital, the worker becomes an entrepreneur of the self who manages his human capital, "being for himself his own capital, being for himself his own producer, being for himself the source of earnings" (226). The wage becomes an income stream derived from the risk taken with one's own human capital. As a structured form of risk management, it becomes a derivative position on the activity of a network:

> So we arrive at the idea that the wage is nothing other than the remuneration, the income allocated to a certain capital in as much as the ability-machine of which the income cannot be separated from the human individual who is the bearer. How is this capital made up? It is at this point that the reintroduction of labor or work into the field of economic analysis will make it possible, through a sort of acceleration or extension, to move

on to the economic analysis of elements which had previously totally escaped it. (226)

This "reintroduction of labor or work" allows Foucault to take the formerly social elements—education, healthcare, parenting, genetic makeup—as variables in the composability of human capital that can then be submitted to cost-benefit analysis. "What type of stimuli, form of life, and relationship with parents, adults, and others can be crystallized into human capital? . . . Migration is an investment; the migrant is an investor. He is an entrepreneur of himself who incurs expense by investing to obtain some kind of improvement" (230). Foucault thus identifies in the rise of neoliberalism and the shift to the analysis of human capital, "the internal rationality, the strategic programming of individual's activities" (230). Here we may observe the generalization of a computational economic calculus to the neoliberal subject—an "internal rationality," a "strategic programming" bent on ROI. This optimization strategy is of course not the sole province of the individual and is, even in Foucault's analysis, transposed from an understanding of the corporation and the firm. Indeed, just as with corporate or investment bank management, social and now digital composability allows for multiple strategic programs to compete for the processing power of the "ability machine" under the worker's charge, making the worker, the entrepreneur of the self, a portfolio manager engaging in relationships that are always posited as contractual or informal forms of risk. For reasons that will become apparent later on, we could say that the worker manages a portfolio of derivatives and is themself a derivative in as much as they derive an income stream from a composable financial architecture designed for the timely management of contingent claims.

Here we glimpse an element of the social processes that will be formalized as a credit system acutely attuned to social difference, aspects of which are rigorously explored in Ivan Ascher's *Portfolio Society* (2018), and also as forms of derivative finance that allow for exposure to the volatility of underliers by means of structured obligation and the off-loading of risk rather than traditional forms of ownership. We understand these ramifications of the price system and its emerging complexity in and as synthetic finance as the development of a banking, credit, and financial system by informatics seeking the capability of representing anything whatever (that is, anything that counts for or can be counted by capital) and of assessing risk on the modes of accounting in the form of credit scores, interest rates, liquidity premiums, or other predictors of ROI. These informatic and computational assessments indexed to race, gender, zip code, age, and a million other data points, formalize contracts referring to such risk indices in the content-indifferent systems language not only of digital computation but of money. As we shall see, in these terms at least, any representation as information is a capital investment, and information is a form of money, indeed a *development* of money. Its operations by means of quantification, shot through sociality and through what we understand as computation (ubiquitous computing), continue to ramify every and all appreciable appearance with ever greater resolution and granularity to this day.

Foucault casts the neoliberal insight as a response to both Marx and to classical economics which, because of their theoretical standpoints, only perceives labor as abstract labor rather than in "its specification, its qualitative modulations and the economic effects of these modulations" (222). With this corrective to what, for him, is Marxism's coarse optic, Foucault seems to embrace neoliberal rationality (and the individualization of agency) as the price of rendering his analysis, and of describing the economic approach elevated to the high level of discernment involved in and necessary to making "substitutable choices." It is as if "the scribe of power," as Edward Said once called Foucault, did not register contradiction, ontology, or a teleology in neoliberalization, and was agnostic at best on metaphysics, ethics, and the revolutionary goals of social movements. His mode of analysis—his sublime comprehension, which looks at the world synchronically and lucidly tells it like it is—demurs and indeed refuses the production of an outside, of a space of appeal, of an alternative to history, and registers only what can be represented in the representational terms that an "episteme," here that of neoliberalism, provides. This is the great power but also the political failing of Foucault, the writer, who will not deign to work in the name of anything but, in telling it like it is, would rather put on the mantel of an episteme and be the master of names. In this, Foucault seems tacitly but fully to accept the subjugation of competing traditions, alternate analytic strategies, and discrepant futures by the dominant discourses he so astutely mimes.[8]

So we will continue with the analysis of the abstraction process, of money, of racial abstraction, of information as a continuous reformatting of inside and outside, and this process's connection to present, past, and future—its connection to *the historically contested processes of social differentiation*. The sublime of the cultural dominant cannot be allowed to stand nor can criticism embrace the antiseptic aesthetics of fascism. We understand real abstraction as a result of the practical and practiced computation of social difference begun in the exchange of distinct objects possessing incommensurable qualities (objects that would, over time, become commodities) and developing over time into money, finance, mathematics, statistics, communication, and computation. In other words, we understand that the status quo, elaborated by this abstraction process everywhere testifies to the dominion of the avatars of capital's AI—the alienated processing power of what has been called our species. But we will take our inspiration from the struggles of the global oppressed and endeavor to understand how our efforts might provide a currently existing, antiracist, anti-heteropatriarchal, anticapitalist, decolonial emergence with insight and opportunity in its *refusal* of objectivity, fungibility, and capitalist abstraction—its refusal of what in an earlier time might have been considered the realism imposed by capitalist domination (but today, in a world riven by derivative logics, would have to be called the hegemony of the deconstructive state). In this view, the calculative process itself, as an abstraction feeding on and creation abstractions, is limited in discernment, collapsing as it does difference into the executed computation performed as exchange. Difference is lost in differentiation; information provides an instrumental approach to life by collapsing its dimensions. Life becomes more abstract when a computation resulting in exchange is taken as a sign and then as a reference for future exchange. In this *programmatic* abstraction, computation as monetization and monetization as computation has totalizing and universalizing tendencies. But the entire process and processing is nonetheless materially tied to the qualitative, concrete specificity being processed—and it is here, in its radical exclusion of a diverse remainder from its methods of account, that we may discern the violence of abstraction. The scaling of real abstraction in capitalism, its formalization in material process that will include institutions and computational machines, never exhausts difference or annihilates conflict even as it sheers off noise, reduces variance, and renders objects, money, commodities, and people fungible. Such contradictions are endemic, unresolved, and—under racial capitalism—irresolvable. "Private property," Marx taught us, is "not the cause but the effect" of alienated labor (1978: 79), and, as this book shall demonstrate, as with private property, so too with "digitality," "race," and "information."

Of course, the properties of private property, as well as the ways in which matter is informed by what was called labor are in a process of transformation. We will explore the expansion of labor to processes of generating information that utilize attention, cognition, perception and metabolism. The collapse of all such activities into information, into a "universal monoculture of informational naturalism" (Steuer: 29), is the general elaboration of real (monetary) abstraction, and as such implies the shift in the mode of production that we call computational. Understanding information not as a discovery but as an invention, a *technique*, reveals that its capacity for conversion accomplishes the injection of a sociohistorically mediated system of valuation into any domain whatever. This claim that information is in effect financialization, a response to racial capital's systemic need to configure new assets and assess risk while at the same time endeavoring to capture all knowledge, semiotics and sociality for the purposes of production, is to be explored in greater detail throughout this volume. As an invisible hand with infinite digits, what information is announces the universal generalization of ever more granular accounting. In this, it is—in itself and in what it enables—the development of the logistical dynamism of the money-form, its calculus of all things differentiable: skin color, nose size, carbon emissions, property. Because of the generalization of sociocybernetics, a calculus of risk and reward now accompanies all knowing. And all unknowing. All appearing and all disappearing. Information serves as an instrumental proposal for the universality of accounting and for the rendering accountable; it serves as the medium of computational racial capital—the means to generate an income stream through a cybernetic interface with any phenomenon whatever. The rest is technology, which is to say, social relations, or, more precisely, the abstraction and reification of social relations and their sedimentation and automation in machinery. Despite the somewhat shocking acknowledgment that "information is information, not matter or energy" (Wiener 1961: 132) information has nonetheless been assumed—incorrectly—to be an effect of things' mere or sheer existence, an ontological component of things. Here we argue that information is a real abstraction, in short, a consequence of what people have done and do when they produce and exchange their goods, when, historically, they compile matter to combat the falling rate of profit and thereby "innovate" to arbitrage the cost of labor. Information is not, as has been long held, a natural property of things. Information is precisely an extension of the logic of property, a social result, *a capitalizing way of knowing and doing*, that is now intelligible as a derivative instrument indexed to an underlier—a generalized means for the pricing of investible risk in a field of contingencies that has its local meaning in the marketplace and an overall consequence that is beyond all price.

Syed Mustafa Ali's scholarship further demonstrates the consilience of white supremacy and informatics. In a significant essay, "Race: The Difference That Makes a Difference" (2013), Ali wagers: that "cybernetics and informatics should be considered racial formations and the allegedly 'abstract' and impartial/neutral stance associated with them should be understood as masking the operation of racism or white supremacy" (102).[9] Turning to the work of Charles Mills (1997) on the systemic and contractual aspects of racism, this allows

Ali to consider both the conscious and non- or unconscious aspect of the racism endemic to the function of information.

While sympathetic to cognitive accounts of racism, Mills insists that racism can—and *does*—exist in a purely structural (or pattern-based) capacity, that is, in terms of differentially-embedded power relations that are at least not explicitly intentional, that is, dependent on consciousness for their continued existence. Put another way, racism can exist in the absence of inform*ed* subjects who are conscious of their racist beliefs and practices, although subjects who *are* conscious of their racist beliefs and practices—racist inform*ers*—are necessary for the production of racism in the first instance. This is possible because Mills maintains that patterns of discrimination and/or domination associated with racial difference— that is, racism—should not be understood as the *exceptional* behavior of *individuals* deviating from a non-racist social norm, but rather, as a global socio-political *system* (30) that is both historical and material in nature. On Mills' view, racism—more precisely, global white supremacy—is a political system, a particular power structure of formal or informal rule, socioeconomic privilege, and norms for the differential distribution of material wealth and opportunities, benefits and burdens, rights and duties. Crucially, Mills maintains that white supremacy can be theorized as a "contract" between whites—a Racial Contract—which he proceeds to define as follows: The Racial Contract is that set of formal or informal agreements or meta-agreements (higher-level contracts about contracts, which set the limits of the contract's validity) between the members of one subset of humans, henceforth designated by (shifting) "racial" (phenotypical/genealogical/cultural) criteria $C_1, C_2, C_3 \ldots$ as "white", and coextensive (making due allowance for gender differentiation) with the class of full persons, to categorize the remaining subset of humans as "nonwhite" and of a different and inferior moral status, subpersons, so that they have a subordinate civil standing in the white or white-ruled polities the whites either already inhabit or establish or in transactions as aliens with these polities, and the moral and juridical rules normally regulating the behavior of whites in their dealing with one another either do not apply at all in dealings with nonwhites or apply only in a qualified form (depending in part on changing historical circumstances and what particular variety of nonwhite is involved), but in any case the general purpose of the Contract is always the differential privileging of the whites as a group with respect to the nonwhites as a group, the exploitation of their bodies, land, and resources, and the denial of equal socioeconomic opportunities to them. All whites are beneficiaries of the Contract, though some whites are not signatories. (Mills 1997: 11, quoted in Ali 2013: 99–100)

Ali concludes here: "To the extent that information is concerned with differences that make a difference (Bateson 1972) and involves a process of *informing*—that is, transmission of meaning (Baeyer 2003)—which can turn out to be a process of *mis/dis*informing, it might be argued that the 'signing' (establishment) and subsequent 're-signing' (maintenance, expansion and refinement) of the Racial Contract of white supremacy constitute informational processes" (Ali 2013: 100).

We have argued this here and something more. The global institutionalization and formalization of white supremacist programming in racial capitalism, wherein "the Racial Contract of white supremacy" is written, signed, and resigned, is not an incidental outcome of informatics, rather it constitutes the material history of the rise of information and its foundation in social difference and profitable social differentiation. Ali's "critical information theory" of race deepens our exploration of the co-evolution of racial abstraction and information. The coherence is even more powerful when racialization, the "signing" and "re-signing" of the racial contract inherent in the ongoing development of code, is considered in the context of both labor and financialization.

As the emergence of codes and contracts that can be formally and informally applied in the profitable organization of dissymetrical exchange between labor and capital, "the Racial Contract of white supremacy" generates data and management requisites that become formalized as what Safiya Umoja Noble calls "algorithms of oppression" and Ruha Benjamin (2019: 1) calls "the new Jim Code." Computation is invested in and vested by racial capitalism and the resultant fractal fascism of computational racial capitalism is in our faces every day. Its development occurs in lockstep with oppression. These algorithms, formal and informal, are not incidental emergences in a general system of computing that can also be used to run the economy. They are rather foundational and decisive strategies of emergence and control, evolving codes that would include, for example, the southern "black codes" prevalent in the United States post-1865, that seemingly automate and render autonomous so many types of binding contracts. These "contracts," vertically and horizontally integrated planet-wide, are a fundamental part of the still developing extractive paradigms of computational racial capitalism and its profitable management of value extraction and dispossession through strategies of social differentiation that allow for the creation of tranches that must be inhabited and if possible survived. Additionally, information *processing* has become the paradigmatic uptake for what elsewhere I have called informatic labor and the programmable image, in which denizens of racial capitalism provide additional information to platforms for capital accumulation in exchange for currencies that allow us to survive. This computational colonization of the semiotic domain further renders semiosis productive for capital, while demanding the re-signing of its code: minimally, a utilization of and participation in the logistical capacities of racial capitalism. These contracts, and all the others expressed as information and platformed on the virtual machine of the world computer function through the build out of real abstractions by means of informationalization, turning money into finance, value into risk, and bodies into races and genders to the point where, in the bloodless halls of Google, everything appears (and disappears) in a content indifferent common denominator: information. A result toward which we, who inhabit the bloodied world, cannot remain indifferent.

The Factory Code

The World Computer endeavors to address the moment when "the factory code," as described in the quotation from Marx that fronts this volume, has become—that is to say, has developed or morphed into, been subsumed by—computer code. In so doing, the ramifications of codification imposed by sociological metrics, financial accounting, and racial abstraction that give rise to "the computational mode of production" have turned society itself, and with it nearly all of semiotic activity, into a distributed factory. This factory, in its relentless pursuit of value-extraction, mercilessly drives the semiotic capacities of planetary life—its heteroglossia—toward the normative monologue of the value-form, policed by the disciplinary rationale of profit. Don't be fooled by the fancy accommodations and sleek ergonomics, the first-person shooter interfaces, the health monitors, the VR, the AR, the fetching AI, the panoply of apparent choices. And don't be fooled by the apparently nontechnical conditions of global slums, forced migrations, detention centers, and camps. In, on, and within this, the planetary factory floor, now rendered n-dimensional by the world computer and its screens, we encounter the unprecedented extension of the colonization of space, time, discourse, mind, and the imagination by means of algorithms that operationalize historically produced categories of social difference as so many inflections of class—so many instances of access and rights to (or the barring thereof) the global-social product. The informatic matrix and its compute becomes the means for regulating and integrating the mesh of income streams, the access to money, and the capacity to convert ones life-products into goods. All denizens of the world computer are cybernetically locked in a machine-mediated competition for liquidity.

The general tendency of cybernetics to become a tool of capitalist competition was observed by Norbert Wiener as early as 1947:

> It has long been clear to me that the modern ultra-rapid computing machine was in principle an ideal central nervous system to an apparatus for automatic control; and that its input and output need not be in the form of numbers or diagrams but might very well be, respectively, the readings of artificial sense organs, such as photoelectric cells or thermometers, and the performance motors or solenoids. . . . Long before Nagasaki and the public awareness of the atomic bomb, it had occurred to me that we were in the presence of another social potentiality unheard of for the importance of good and for evil. The automatic factory and the assembly line without human agents are only so far ahead of us as is limited by our willingness to put such a degree of effort into their engineering. . . .
>
> I have said that this new development has unbounded possibilities for good and for evil. . . . It gives the human race a new and most effective collection of mechanical slaves to perform its labor. Such mechanical labor has most of the economic properties of slave labor, although unlike slave labor, it does not involve the direct demoralizing effects of human cruelty. However, any labor that accepts the conditions of competition with slave labor accepts the conditions of slave labor, and is essentially slave labor. The key word of this statement is competition. (1961: 26–27)

Sounding like more of a Marxist than a Keynesian, Wiener continues:

> Perhaps I may clarify the historical background of the present situation if I say that the first industrial revolution, the revolution of the "dark satanic mills" was the devaluation of the human arm by the competition of machinery. There is no rate of pay at which a United States pick-and-shovel laborer can live which is low enough to compete with the work of a steam shovel as an excavator. The modern industrial revolution is similarly bound to devalue the human brain, at least in its simpler and more routine decisions. (27)

Speculating on the solution to the problem endemic to cybernetics and to what we may grasp as the colonization of life and labor by information, Wiener writes, "The answer, of course, is to have a society based on human values other than buying or selling. To arrive at this society, we need a good deal of planning and a good deal of struggle, which, if the best comes to the best, may be on the plane of ideas, and otherwise—who knows?" (28). Seventy-five years since the writing of these lines, the best, unfortunately, has not come to the best, and the competition endemic to the automation of racial capital that accepts and competes with the conditions of slave labor has pushed us all the way to "who knows?"

"Any labor that accepts the conditions of competition with slave labor accepts the conditions of slave labor, and is essentially slave labor" (Wiener: 27). That's the bottom line. With the calculus of social difference firmly in mind, *The World Computer*, in its titular concept, hypostasizes the operations of computational racial capitalism. Racial capitalism sets machinic efficiencies against the socius and in competition with slavery, and casts these integrated operations as a vast machinic assemblage mediated by real abstraction (information) for the ordination and therefore coordination of operations that can be divorced neither from finance, computing, representational media, or from social difference and differentiation, nor from the bio- or ecospheres. As an idea, "the world computer" expresses not the capacities of Ethereum virtual machine running atop its blockchain,[10] but the algorithmic computing of global domination occurring at unprecedented speed and scale and running on top of the *bios*.

This generalized and granular domination is busily at work not just in what W. E. B. Du Bois (2015) called, in his brilliant work of speculative fiction "The Princess Steel," the "Far Great" and the "Near Small," observable with telescopes and microscopes, respectively, but in what he called the "Great Near."[11] Dr. Hannibal Johnson, the black professor of sociology in "The Princess Steel" (originally titled "The Megascope: A Tale of Tales"), explains his efforts to reveal the otherwise invisible "shadowing curves of the Overlife" (823) with his great *megascope*: "You know, we can see the great that is far by means of the telescope and the small that is near by means of the microscope. We can see the Far Great and the Near Small but not the Great Near" (823). In their introduction to *W. E. B. Du Bois's Data Portraits Visualizing Black America*, Whitney Battle-Baptiste and Britt Rusert (2018) explain that "the vision produced by the megascope . . . is generated in part by data contained in a massive set of volumes lining the wall of the laboratory, a vast set of demographic studies collected for over '200 years' by some kind of 'Silent Brotherhood'" (8). They describe the vision and the subsequent allegory of the story this way: "When hooked up to the megascope, users are able to view the 'Great Near,' Du Bois's term for the always present but usually invisible structures of colonialism and racial capitalism that shape the organization of society" (7). Here, taking inspiration from Du Bois's megascope, we assemble the data of the counterfactuality, among which we find what Shaka McGlotten (2016) might call "Black Data." We call out and make visible the virtual machine that is the world computer, along with its generalization and elaboration of the factory code to administer the protocols of computational racial capitalism. As we shall further explore, the invisible structures of colonialism and racial capitalism extend not only into society, but into the knowledge society produces and can produce with respect to the Far Great and the Near Small as well.

The world computer thrives on the production of difference and differentiation to produce ever more of the same: wealth and dispossession, that is, more wealth and more dispossession. In the name of efficiency its algorithms and algorithmic effects seize upon and would developmentally ramify all forms of historically worked-up social difference for the purpose of arbitrage on labor power even as they occupy and format our technologies and machines. They are programmed by the constant drive to get the same thing—in this genuinely tragic case, a quantity of the value-form—for less. Driven by the falling rate of profit and the subsequent cheapening of life, the result of this generalized arbitrage on the value of labor-time is unprecedented social hierarchy and a general devaluation of labor power—or what elsewhere I have called "attention" and Neferti Tadiar, in her recent work (2012), calls "life-time." This devaluation creates both a surfeit of discounted concerns along with the discounted people who may embody them.

Though generally devalued, we humanoids are nonetheless essential, though not in the ways we might choose to be. Our inability to choose our essential qualities results in large part from the fact that capital can only measure innovation in terms of its accumulation of surplus value. And, the larger the ratio of fixed capital to variable capital, says the law of the falling rate of profit, the greater the degree of exploitation (of the worker, of attention, of life-time) required, if the rate of profit is to remain constant. In other words, as labor power makes up an increasingly smaller proportion of the total value of capital outlay in the expanding production cycles of commodities, the return on the cost of labor power must increase in order to keep the proportion of profit relative to the total capital costs constant. If not, the rate of profit falls. Thus, the drive to innovation is a drive to increase the efficiency of labor and thereby the ratio of value-extraction (unpaid "surplus" labor) to the paid time (necessary labor) of the working day. (For the sake of this example, assume that the length of the day and the daily wage here, are held constant.) Over time, capital must keep an increasingly larger proportion of each worker's value production, on average, if it is to valorize itself at the general rate of return and remain capital. Capital drives down what it pays per hour (it pays only for necessary labor) and takes the increasing proportion of unpaid time (surplus labor) for itself. As Moishe Postone puts it in *Time, Labor and Social Domination*, "Increased productivity leads to a decrease in the value of each commodity produced because less socially necessary labor time is expended. This indicates that the total value yielded in a particular period of time (for example, an hour) remains constant. The inversely proportional relationship between average productivity and the magnitude of value of a single commodity is a function of the fact that the magnitude of total value produced depends only on the amount of abstract human labor time expended. Changes in average productivity do not change the total value created in equal periods of time" (193).

From this we understand that innovation, driven by the falling rate of profit due to the increasing proportion of fixed capital to the value of labor in production that pushes capital to pay less and less for labor, is effectively a devaluation of the worker, since the worker is paid for less and less of the working day. We also mark clearly that this relationship between the proportion of fixed capital and the amount of labor that results in a falling rate of profit that can only be combatted by driving down the price of labor converts innovation under racial capitalism into an arbitrage on human time. The simple math driving down the proportion of the worker's necessary labor (necessary labor is the amount of working time necessary for a worker to reproduce themselves given a certain level of social and technological development, which is what they are actually paid for and no more) with respect to their surplus labor (surplus labor is the amount of time the worker works for free and thus yields their productive power to capital) reminds us, as we regard the vast build-out that was once thought of as the human species, that Benjamin's dialectical flash is still true: "Every document of civilization is simultaneously a document of barbarism." We should recall this formulation when regarding the great scientific, cultural and technical achievements of our time—from the megacities to the cloud-connected microelectronics, to the great advances in capacity and efficiency such as the one that can be viscerally perceived as an F-35 fighter plane comes from nowhere and shatters the sky. Today, the vast communications infrastructure that links all together—an infrastructure which is at once computational in function and composed of fixed capital—requires massive amounts of input in exchange for minimal and often no direct remuneration to turn its profits at a competitive rate. Both point-and-shoot cameras and point-and-kill F-35s must provide ROI. Algorithms operating on phones, missiles, stock markets, and everywhere else manage the uptake as well as most of the payoffs such as they are, while states and other hegemonic formations—themselves managed by a business calculus—police the externalities and the malcontent. Migrants and those seeking reparations are incarcerated, left to die, executed; Jair Bolsonaro, practicing his own brand of investment genocide, burns the Amazon and its peoples in order to graze cattle. Financial balance sheets require daily settlements and therefore returns for the short-term benefit of owners and externalized costs to the denizens of the image and the inhabitants of the unrepresented and the unthought. Through these algorithms of extraction—machinic and embodied, increasingly formalized, sedimented, formatted, and absorbed into computational digital infrastructure—and the representational system they drive, we directly confront the instrumentalization of thought, perception, action, and event.

This instrumentalization makes every act or expression into a wager of some consequence—a contingent claim on a share of the social product. It is characterized by a desperate war of each against all for access to income streams, to social currencies, to convertibility, to liquidity. Such is the derivative condition, where organization and expression are inexorably forms of a calculus that composes "positions" on value in conditions of global volatility. These positions are speculative and their claims are contingent on outcomes. Such a relentless globally integrated compute requires its data visualizations. Many formerly extra-economic activities—activities of "superintendence" otherwise to be understood as watching machines and making adjustments in accord with the protocols the machines put forth such that their operations may be valorized—are now value-productive for capital. Our superintendence has grown more complex since we were forced to supervise machines, arguably having come to encompass what today is called "visual culture." Since the inauguration of what I called the cinematic mode of production and the bringing of the industrial revolution to the eye, we have been watching and are still watching, if not exactly watching over, machine-mediated production. Today we still are being extracted from; and we are being watched, by the very machines we watch and some we can neither watch nor see. In the interface we read and are written by social codes that allot rights and access that include forms of ownership and citizenship, and that also license violence, secure impunity, and enforce genocide by means of networks. In ten thousand or a million ways, we survey and are surveilled. All these control mechanisms—and their throughput—have a stake in violence, a violence that some may benefit from while others are forced to endure or die. They undertake an encoding of all appearance and engage in a writing on the world, turning being into a surface of inscription. They orchestrate what Kathryn Yusoff (2018: 2) calls, when referring to White geology in *A Billion Black Anthropocenes*, "colonial earth writing"—inscriptions on the materiality of the planet that include both the geo- and the bio-. Life and earth become surfaces of inscription, recording, and memory storage archiving capital's wagers and facilitating its grand compute.

While computational racial capital may appear in the guise of its many instances (e.g., the state form, fractal fascisms, institutional entrenchment, ambient social media, carceral systems, military-industrial complexes, a fleeting affective dispensation, a click, any datalogical event), *the world computer* endeavors to name the highest order abstraction of the transnational and indeed transspecies and multiversal historicomaterial logic that coordinates—and in reality (such as it is) ordinates—the planetary *bios*—at myriad levels of scale and with vast, increasingly integrated systems. Because of the planetary— and from an epistemological standpoint, *cosmic*—scope of this encroachment, along with the physical and metaphysical consequences thereof, it will also be demonstrated here that computational racial capital, as the world computer, commands the value-extractive reprogramming of ontologies—a reformatting of life, time and cosmos by means of information. This reformatting is practical-material, representational, physical, and metaphysical, but above all, political-economic.

As a concept, the world computer is an abstraction that names a system of abstraction, a stack (Bratton 2016). This system of abstraction(s) is beyond the control of any individual and functions instrumentally and materially to structure the value-productive reconfiguration of ontologies. As *Star Trek*'s epic intonation, "Space, the final frontier," intimated for the childhood of some members of my generation, enterprising imperialism embarks upon a project of cosmic proportions. Today, with the conquest not only of reality but of virtual reality, we might add "Time, the final frontier," or "Neuronal processing, the final frontier," or "Ontology, the final frontier," the point being that these are all frontiers being readied for the extractive practices enabled by their informationalization. Information becomes the secret ingredient that liquefies ontologies by rendering them computable, while providing liquidity by making their now-informatic being into work-sites; computational racial capital is, among other things, the processor of our time and times, our thought and thinking, our metabolic unfolding in relation to information— our becoming cyborg that results in our "being," such that it is. Computational racial capital's informatic computing is the practical extension of our senses—or rather "our" senses, since property, colonization and possession, never simple matters, have grown far more complex. Nonetheless, despite its cosmic colonization of subject and world, the world computer is at least as difficult to perceive as is the medium of a message, precisely because its theater of prosthetic operations stretches both to the geographic and the epistemic horizon: with the near fatal capture of representation by computational racial capital, the convergence of all media with computation and of computation with financialization, one looks *through* computational racial capitalism even if one wants to look *at* it. In its very operations of constituting an object and perception, computational racial capitalism also ordains (and indeed intensifies) a project of unparalleled violence. Our apprehension of the world is therefore an apprehension by means of violence.

This system of leveraged abstraction—with its half-Hegelian, half-Heisenbergian property of only being able to be perceived through its own emergent process, and thus only perceivable from particular points of view—is most often reductively understood as if it were two distinct components: most commonly as "computation" and, in a somewhat more sociological register, as "finance." As we shall further demonstrate, these ostensibly separate registers of computation and finance have a deeper unity. What is called "social difference"—is at once precondition and result of their operations;—its elaboration is at once the result of an increasingly global struggle for liberation *and* a homogenizing strategy of global subsumption.

Despite philosophers' claims and, in some cases, their vain hopes, and despite economists' disavowals, we have not (yet) escaped the dialectic of capitalism as "simultaneously the best and worst." We may hope that one day computational racial capitalism will remain the worst thing that ever happened but will no longer also be endemic to what counts as "the best," but hope alone will not be enough to make that day arrive. All modern achievements, or what in the capitalist world one might want to call progress, beauty, refinement, and liberation, are to be measured against violence, violence that includes the middle passage, colonial encroachments, climate injustice and "environmental" racism, modern modes of enslavement, camps, slums, sexisms, wars, carceral systems, murders, pogroms, and genocides all endemic to this self-same (post)modernity. To this tragic, "all-too-'human'" (in the colonial sense) list of atrocities and its formations of violence, we might add to the consequences of abstraction-extraction techniques that form the bedrock of postmodernism: the blanket militarization, widespread securitization, endless competition, implacable xenophobia, neoapartheid, border walls, white supremacist heteropatriarchy, drone warfare, fractal fascism, inescapable precarity, global psychosis, the colonization of time, perception and semiotics, and the endemic, widespread generalized unfriendliness unfolding with a computationally driven racial calculus that motivates bio- and necropolitics. We will make an attempt to understand these phenomena in the wake of colonization and slavery, and to understand the dissolution of traditional cultural form(s), as further consequences of the cut-and-mix derivative condition imposed by the world computer—as consequences of the world computer, its merciless calculus of profit and its suppression of noise.

Computational racial capital as an operative process or metaprogram—presiding, I am obliged to report (pace Flusser), over the photographic program as well as over some premature pronouncements of the arrival of some postcapitalism—endeavors to constitute the horizon of our historical imagination. It presides over the disavowal of its own imposition of such limitations on the imagination. Indeed, the world computer's enclosure of futurity is sometimes presented as an opening toward freedom. As if to hide its own function, the AI that colonizes planet Earth must disguise the fact that it is AI; or, when it does appear, it appears in philosophy, cinema, fiction, and, yes, even critical theory as a transcendent and sublime fantasy. The thrill of these various genres is that the AI-sublime leaves the specific form for the socially necessary reconstitution of the ego, postencounter, posteuphoria, seemingly open (things can never be the same, we will never be the same, I am not the same), while also seeming to render the fate of the so-called human irrelevant. May as well shop on, then! But if the people are to be the companion species to AI, we, like Haraway's dogs, might require a manifesto of our own—a political statement that respects our historically arrived-at position. Though we cannot say whether or not AI "intentionally" hides its invisible hands and digits, as well as its habitation of bodies and minds (an undecidability that correctly suggests that systemic instrumentalization and real abstraction partake of a logic of a different order than does everyday understanding and subjectifcation), this writing endeavors to rupture the containment of the imagination by the overdetermining logic of computational capital and frame out the Great Near consequences of the colonization of the life-world by machinic fixed capital as if these consequences matter.

Machine logic posits and increasingly presupposes subordinated human metabolic processes as value productive. Given the world computer's capacity for profitable semiotic absorption, this book therefore must endeavor to create a rupture in its function in part by rendering the global compute legible as a concept—as "the world computer"—and in part by doing so in what can only be an incompletely digestible mode. The fugitivity of contemporary political theory is a necessity, as full legibility within "capitalist realism" is tantamount to capitalist production and systemic cooptation. To be clear (without being too clear), the text's sometimes unconventional "style," as well as its "speculative" claims, are part of its theory and practice—a form of *budo* that would be opposed to the computational operations of the colonizer, resident to varying degrees in nearly all lands and heads.

In relation to problems of periodization, the concepts constellated as computational racial capital, the social difference engine, the world computer, and the computational mode of production are wrought to comprehend and thus also recast a number of terms created over the last forty years or so, terms coined in pursuit of intellectual adequation for emergent structures of domination and exploitation beginning in the last century. This aging terminology includes *postmodernism, posthumanism, post-Fordism, cognitive capitalism, virtuosity, neuropower, biopolitics, necropolitics, necrocapital,* and my own earlier efforts, *the cinematic mode of production* and *the attention theory of value.* The breaking of these forms is also subject to the dialectical advance of the world computer. Computational racial capitalism emerges in and through the computational mode of production, which, as will be shown here, itself institutes and develops "informatic labor," "networked commodities," and new techniques of abstraction whose summation can be given in the phrase *the world computer* and whose result is not only the financialization of everyday life but "the derivative condition," in which any and all instantiations of form can be taken as positions on the generalized volatility of the market—because they are, unavoidably.

Digital culture and what we recognize as digitization (DC2) emerges within the framework of instrumentalization and what Seb Franklin (2015) and before him Alex Galloway (2004) and James Benninger (1986) call "control." Control is the organization of society by capital, but it is often imagined in a first instance as society, science, governance, or cybernetics, and only secondarily as having to do with capital and capitalist informatics. Deleuze saw an intimate relation between capital and control, with control opening a new phase of capitalist organization. I take a new tack here in order to propose an analysis of informatic protocols from a Marxist theory of *techné.* In practice, the term *information* is both the means by which the generalized digitization of all that appears is first posited as a possibility, and the name for this process of universal digitization; information is understood as a historically emergent "always already" that ascribes to every aspect of the multiverse a quantitative component that is neither matter nor energy. It's dead labor. This becomes apparent as soon as we recognize that information is only gathered and processed by apparatuses of our own making. We also recognize that despite appearing natural or eternal, information historically instantiates a new domain or property to cosmic being and effectively posits the universe as a standing reserve for the epistemological emergence of quantitative metrics—a domain of infinite sites of infinite accumulation and volatility. This information can be meshed with human inputs to become capital. The informationalization of the cosmos is the meshing. Dead labor can be affixed and indexed to everything that appears in a way that informs matter, that is, machines, that are then ready to further interface with human process.

Just as computation emerges in the footprint of racial capitalism, its medium—namely, information—emerges in the footprint of the value-form, and specifically from price as a number that when attached to a denomination quantifies the value of anything whatever. In different ways (to which we will devote some passages further on), both price and information are means for capital to get from M to M': both are measures of states of negative entropy, that is, of a type of value-creating order imposed on matter by intentional social process, but what is forgotten or for the most part not understood at all, particularly in the latter case of information, is that both have their ultimate, determining instance in social relations. Just as capital posits quality as quantity, computation posits material organization as information. This latter—organized matter or energy, legible (by observation) as information—is precisely what the digital physicists tell us about the very structure of the multiverse: it is numbers all the way down, quantities—discrete states. No one stops to think (and it sounds almost impolite, if not insane, to suggest) that they, *Solaris*-like, as they look out to the cosmos, are gazing into their own unconscious—an alien(ated) world nonetheless inseparable from their own history and thus, irreducibly, tainted by traces of their own making. As we shall see in chapter 1, they are gazing into the computational unconscious. Numbers are organized by and as material arrays; they are practical, material, computational. By attaching a technical cost to all knowledge, computational methods of account and accountability measure information flow in what amounts to a financialization of the observable world. That's the cosmic ecology—bets can be placed on the various outcomes. It is perhaps less surprising that the "DNA" of the cosmos turns out to be the same as that of exchange-value when we recognize that the apparatuses of capture, the machines that extend human perception to information at any scale imaginable, are also machines of capitalization—that computational systems of account are themselves always mediated by the vanishing mediator known as money. But we are saying more, namely, that they are also the thinking of money, its calculus. Such conditions and means of production extend the operating costs of the logistics of perception into all phenomena and seek a return on their investment, and thus they are always already functioning in the marketplace. In short, the infrastructure for the appearance of "information," as such and at all, is inseparable from the developmental expansion process of exchange-value and the history of generalized commodification; this history is the result of a process occurring behind the scenes of any particular exchange, but it is no less social for all that. Just as exchange-value is in our heads and yet not the creation of any particular individual, information is in our computers and yet not the creation of any particular computer. It is inscribed in the social totality. And as with exchange-value before it (historically speaking), information, as a seemingly natural appurtenance of all things, a second nature, is, in fact, an extension, symptom, and means of the expansive logic of commodification—an extension of its operating system—the OS of racial capitalism.

Just as, through double-entry bookkeeping or derivative pricing models, capital "perceives" value, computation "perceives" information,—whether by means of punch cards or digital sensors. The entrepreneur of the self, with its "internal rationality and strategic programming," is a nodal point in the fabric of valuation analogous to the role of the computational machine in the fabric of information. Capital, we could say, is the metabolism of value while computation is the metabolism of information. Value mediates social wealth while information mediates the cosmic, yet the cosmic is known through the framework of the social and is incorporated in the sociality of wealth, which is to say that "the cosmic" is mediated by value and thus capital.

The unity of value and information appears with the concept and capacities of computation, and can be grasped with the concept of computational capital. This concept then provides explanations for the capacity of processes it identifies. Suspicious that information is a means of capitalization, we could ask whose metabolism provides the motor force? We begin to suspect that capital and computation are not two things but one, now that, *in practice*, they can no longer be considered separately and, furthermore, that their metabolisms depend upon yet another level of metabolic processes near the bottom of the stack: ours. Information, like value, and computation, like capital, is always already cybernetic. Understood *without* the historical apparatuses of perception, capture, and manipulation that not only make information useful but indeed *constitute* it, "information" remains a mere fetish. In common usage it is such a fetish. When we grasp the fact of the appurtenances that surface and record information, we also posit the totality of their infrastructure, their history, and their cybernetic integration with human practice. Information then appears as a real abstraction, an essential practice of capitalist production; it is a means to price. The world computer puts a price on knowledge that is the price of the risk of its cost. Finance, ordinarily hidden from view in the pure sciences and the oh-so-discrete disciplines, now emerges as being all about the various methods of account that have grown up like mushrooms in every field of endeavor. Learning Outcomes Assessment, anyone? Like everyone else, scientists, no matter how ascetic they may be, are entrepreneurs of themselves and their computations, managing as best they can their highly mediated portfolios in the same sordid marketplace—of knowledge.

Some of these methods, ventures, and adventures, scientific or otherwise, became highly specialized and—because highly mediated by vectors that mystify or dignify their relation to capital—seemingly autonomous. But like the endeavors of colonial settlers and frontier prospectors, and even like those of Foucault's migrants who invest some (or all) of their human capital on the possibility of reparations to get a higher return on their "life-time" (Tadiar 2012), all endeavors must ultimately demonstrate their sustainability in the market or face severance. Thus, we understand Jodi Melamed's (2019) take on administrative power—"Policing is the power to administer capitalism to the point of killing"—as indicating the totalitarian scope of capitalist administration by the factory code, the same code that would organize social difference, access and profits. Today even the rhizome is subjugated to the market; ask your local mushroom farmer, Deleuzian adjunct professor, struggling architect, or Israeli military strategist.

The standard clerical methods of bureaucratic organizations, streamlined as flowcharts, heuristic devices, and algorithms and then encoded and sedimented into discrete state machines known as computers, turned out to have even more applicability than was at first imagined in the nineteenth-century parameters that defined the organization of workflow and commercial value transfer. No surprise, really, at least so long as we keep in mind Charles Babbage's steam-driven mechanization of calculative thought, or Alan Turing's (2003) notion that machines can surprise us even if we think we grasp the rational principles of a program, or Phillip Mirowski's (2002) analysis—based upon John von Neumann's view of market emergence as the computational effect of cellular automata—of economics as a "cyborg science." Mere unaccommodated humans cannot run all the logical permutations of a program with the rigor and thoroughness of calculation engines. Automate thought, animate it as Deborah Levitt (2018) suggests, and the unpredictable emerges from the seemingly predictable—to the point of ontological disruption. We could add here that ontological disruption by means of programming and animation creates new opportunities for interface. From this insight alone—specifically, that information interfaces as a medium of value production and transfer (to be further demonstrated in the following pages) and that increasing complexity emerges from the automation and autonomization of value—one begins to grasp that the sense organs capable of the requisite orders of informatic perception and participation are cultivated, and cultivated *cybernetically*, over the long term. It takes a lot of work *not* to see all this. The making of the five senses requires the entire history of the world down to the present, as Marx said. This nineteenth-century insight, hailing from the days of the steam engine and its early industrial products, was already a theory of technics and cybernetics. The ever more refined, ever more global, and ever more granular detection and parsing of value in a network of commodities is one with the further development of the senses. Real abstraction, beyond becoming the basis of abstract thought (Sohn-Rethel) requires the transformation of perception, the ability to sense and think value; indeed its evolution requires the constant revolutionizing of perception. Dialectically, these senses—human senses for a world that is the result of human labor, a humanized world—remake the world through an immense number of productive and reproductive iterations with it. The early Marx understood the senses to be undergoing reorganization by capital but nonetheless locked in a struggle to perceive a humanized world. This world in which the hidden social dimensions impacted in objects (commodities)—as well as in categories, abstractions, ideologies, genders, and sexualities—became visible in what could only be the immanence of the communism of species creativity and emergence. It is (or should be) troubling that the techné of the value-form—as well as its regime of perception historically worked-up by means of reification to conform to the protocols of alienation, private property, and individual agency—is grafted so seamlessly to the techné of what seems to be a subsequent and succeeding form, information. Particularly as we are *experientially* coming to understand that computation is an intensification of capital, and that computation has infiltrated all matter of appearance and therefore all (known and knowable) matter. The calculus of each moment and all things becomes an affordance of the human-machine, the cyborg, and these assemblages grow new organs with which to measure the world with ever increasing granularity and, when deployed in concert, with ever increasing totalization. This calculus is ultimately one of life or death, or as Jasbir K. Puar (2017) theorizes, of capacitation and maiming. Computation *emerges as* the development of capital, its ramification of the life-world, its intensification of extraction, its automation of management strategies, its strategic apportioning of an increasing palette of resources, its insidious mechanics of colonization, its multiplication of modes of capacitation and maiming, its totalizations and its totalitarianism—its practice and its thought. It emerges as nothing less than a harness for the processing power of the "human capital" from which the entrepreneur of the self is to derive their revenue stream, Foucault's "ability machine."

Of course, this explication of the general expansion of the factory code constitutes an argument. Understanding, from our current vantage point, that capitalism, with its calculus of profit, was always already a computer—as Nick Dyer-Witheford (2013, 2015), drawing on Hayek (1945), has brilliantly pointed out—would allow for a thorough reimagining of world history along with a complete rethinking of the meaning, emergence, and indeed sociohistoric function of computation. Here the wager is on the *conceptualization* of the emergent and historical relations endemic to capitalism and computation, and on revealing their mutual imbrication as computational racial capital executing its programs as the world computer, all the while imposing increasing volatility, financial precarity, and derivative conditions.

Derivative Computing, Read-Write Ontologies, Financialization of Deconstruction

The notion of computation currently dominant is that it is an information management tool that helps to reveal the inner workings of nature whether in the analysis of cognitive function, markets, or galaxy formation: scientific tools reveal nature's ontological character. Simulation helps us understand reality. Information science, like other sciences and like "reality itself," is presumed to pertain beyond the merely social, even if it turns out that "reality itself" is a simulation. In the thought experiment that is *The World Computer*, the aim is to understand that *this thinking of information as being everywhere*—and thus, as everywhere legible, at least in principle, *is a direct extension of the colonial project* and carries with it the legacies of slavery, wage labor, heteropatriarchy, and proletarianization. Modern computation, rather than revealing a standalone truth in things, is foregrounded here as always already the bureaucratic thought of capitalism—and thus also its practice, its practical organization of production. It is the alienated and alienating thought of the *bios*. Computation is the thought of finance capital in the same manner that, for Lukacs in *Reification and the Consciousness of the Proletariat*, Kant's categorical thought was the thought of reification and of the consequent spatialization of time imposed by the commodity-form and wage-labor, respectively. And again, computation is for finance capital just as, for Sohn-Rethel in *Intellectual and Manual Labor*, the real abstraction known as "money" was for the social act of commodity exchange. Sohn-Rethel argues that real abstraction opens the space for the transcendental subject of philosophy—the subject of and for the exchange of equivalents who was represented—we might say formatted—as the owner of their commodity to other commodity owners, similarly formatted. In our day, the real abstraction that is the computationally mediated process of exchange develops the complex relationship between market and subject by opening the space for AI and the social derivative. We interface as nodal points on a distributed network—a network that constitutes us as agents for exchange, and we assemble our relationships as best we can to wager on an income stream for our activity machine.

In considering computation as the alienated and alienating thought of the bios, an autonomization of the thinking of racial capitalism that all of us, perhaps without exception, are forced to game, it is useful to recall Postone's account of abstract time, or what is effectively, the alienation of time and its consequent conversion to a real abstraction. Postone notes that antecedent, "concrete time" was a dependent variable whose character was determined by the concrete relations of a given society, but the emergence of socially necessary labor time converted time into "abstract time," an independent variable.

> Because abstract human labor constitutes a general social mediation, in Marx's analysis, the labor time that serves as the measure of value is not individual and contingent but *social* and *necessary* [190]. . . . As a category of the totality, socially necessary labor time expresses a quasi-objective social necessity with which the producers are confronted. It is the temporal dimension of the abstract domination that characterizes the structure of alienated social relations in capitalism. The social totality constituted by labor as an objective general mediation has a temporal character wherein *time becomes necessity* [191]. . . . In capitalism, abstract temporal measure rather than concrete material quantity is the measure of social wealth. This difference is the first determination of the possibility in capitalism that, not only for the poor, but for society as a whole, poverty (in terms of value) can exist in the midst of plenty (in terms of material wealth). Material wealth in capitalism is, ultimately, only apparent wealth [194].

Examining the process by which "time becomes necessity" Postone takes his readers thorough an account of the standardization of time in Europe by the systemically coordinated need to measure labor time, that included factory discipline, the organization of village life and the development of clocks. "Variable hours" became invariable, and abstract time became "the uniform, continuous, homogeneous 'empty' time . . . independent of events" (202). "The temporal forms have a life of their own and are compelling for all members of capitalist society" (214). As opposed to the dependent variable that was concrete time situated in various communities and their particular, seasonal temporalities, "abstract time is an independent variable; it constitutes an independent framework with which motion events and actions occur [and can be measured]. Such time is divisible into equal, constant, nonqualitative units" (202). Postone writes, "The abstract form of time associated with the new structure of social relations also expressed a new form of domination (214). "As a result of general social mediation, labor time expenditure is transformed into a temporal norm that not only is abstracted from but also stands above and determines individual action. Just as labor is transformed from an action of individuals to the alienated general principle of the totality under which the individuals are subsumed, time expenditure is transformed form a result *of* activity into a normative measure *for* activity. Although . . . the magnitude of so-cially necessary labor time is a dependent variable of society as a whole, it is an independent variable with regard to individual activity. This process, whereby a concerte, dependent variable of human activity becomes an abstract inde-pendent variable governing this activity is real and not illusory. It is intrinsic to the process of alienated social constitution effected by labor" (215).

The independence of time from concrete situations, "real and not illu-sory," is a historical result, a consequence of production. Abstract time is a real abstraction, a social relationship embedded in a new form of time that con-fronts humanity as both alien in its independence and as necessity in its indif-ference to all qualities. This of course is the same objective, homogeneous time that allows for the development of modern physics, calculus and computation.

Categoricality, abstraction, computability, and the horizon of omni-science become the basic architecture of capitalist planning and perception—the ever finer granularity of computation means precisely the capillary ramifi-cation and reorganization of the life-world, of space, time and consciousness, by means of the modular affordances of objective and objectifying content—indifferent 1s and 0s. These two numbers were and are of course ideologically neutral because content-indifferent—unless, of course, content indifference is itself an ideology, naturalized in the same manner that so many have natural-ized abstract time. Is such a degree-zero view of number a blindness to the message that is its medium? Simulation, as Baudrillard (2004) powerfully in-tuited, was not just an effect of political economy; it was in effect a praxis, and thus a (quasi-) philosophy—of a kind that meant the end of traditional notions of both. It also meant a new period of capital and a new mode of production. "Today abstraction is no longer that of the map, the double, the mirror, or the concept. Simulation is no longer that of a territory, a referential being, or a substance. It is the generation by models of a real without origin or reality: a hyperreal. The territory no longer precedes the map, nor does it survive it" (365). In theorizing hyper-reality, he almost could have written, "All that is solid melts into information." Computability liquifies the solid in accord with the requisites of capital. Just here in the informatic flux, we can see, alongside its vast achievements, computation's intimate link, in the alienation of the territory by means of the map, to the colonial project, the industrial project, and globalization in the derealization of traditional forms of space and time. Capital's ability to infiltrate, organize, and predict, to simulate a model *and to impose it*, to abstract and to subsume difference in accord with its own code (and, where necessary, to generate difference and distinction to serve the expansion and development of this code), to operationalize and then self-optimize, provided and continues to provide the conceptual, material, and existential basis, along with the urgency, for the further *development* of computation. Tragically, it also provides the urgency to transform its process, its processors, its processing. Compounding the tragedy of this millennium, those who are or might be in a position to best interrogate computational process most often view it as a ratification of their assumptions about nature by relegating the material conditions of computation and *of their thought* to the unthought.

In sharp contrast, we view computation as a strategy of efficient risk management—a cost-benefit analysis of the "substitutable choices" for the essential program of capital. It opens new ways of apportioning resources and does so in keeping with the potential profitability of new sites of value extraction necessary in order to stave off the falling rate of profit. In this respect, computation has the structure of a derivative on any activity whatever, opening up a market for risk management and liquidity preservation to wager on an exposure to the underliers of any calculation whatever. Engineers, scientists, and coders manage their portfolio of interests to create their income streams. "Create needs, then help," writes Trinh T. Minh-Ha (1981), summarizing the colonial logic of "development." Thus, as with the development of colonial banking, analyzed by Rosa Luxembourg, that puts colonies and colonial labor in the service of capital—first by making them service an ever increasing debt incurred on their purchases from the colonizer of the instruments for the modernization of production, and second by making them compete each against the other in debt servicing—the development of computation, despite the democracy-themed PR that accompanied the rise of the desktop computer, further pits each against all. "Yes, but email," some will exclaim, or, "FaceTime!" "The Higgs Boson!" We can't help but wonder if the creators of Slack and Zoom savored the irony of their platform names. No more slacking off while zooming in on the requisites of the value form! Let's intensify the production and invisibility of our own off-screen death in pursuit of pure production! Long live the factory code.

Innovation organized by entrepreneurs of the self, of the cyberself, creates possibilities for arbitrage on those super-sets of labor-time, attention and life-time; and all the while, everyday risk management is underpinned and indeed anchored by the calculus of genocide. From the binary of the A-bomb to IBM's punch-carding of the Nazi Holocaust, from the calculus of sovereign debt to that of social media, the lives of people (in Nagasaki, in Auschwitz, in Furguson), become the substrate that registers the meaning of the compute—at least the meaning as far as they may have been concerned. So many are posited as but renewable pawns in an endless game, and the game goes on. Dispossession and genocide, and the capacity to wreak these, guarantee the liquidity of the financial system by guaranteeing that there will always be some billions willing or forced to do anything for its money and the access to information, to informed matter and therefore to life that it provides. In our era, we see clearly that, under capital, the "stability" imposed by systemic integration and its programs of finance, surveillance, security, mediation, and so on produces ever greater volatility, and we see that this volatility risk can be bought and sold; it can be cut up, bundled, bought, and resold, priced as content-indifferent numbers based upon volatility indices. Meanwhile the markets roil, dispossession rages, and the planet boils.

As history could confirm, by the mid-twentieth century, the complexity of the techniques for the management of societies, from markets to warfare, from media to cybernetics, and now from social media to the derivatives created by synthetic finance, all required discrete state machines to store and manage the pertinent inventories, schedules, and programs—their valuable information. Though usually thought of as properly belonging to the history of science, communication, mathematics, or computation, the socioeconomic endeavors composing the history of the discrete state machine and its ever more supple functionality are to be thought as part of the increasing complexity of capitalist abstraction and thus the abstraction of social relations. They are the elaboration of real abstraction, the expansive formalization of the field of exchange taking place "behind the backs" of living people. These socioeconomic endeavors such as Google, Facebook, the security state, are the effective occupation of space and time at all scales by the logistics of exchange and its expanding field of production.[12]

Datalogical representation is already risk management. Management, efficiency, optimization; Foucault's entrepreneur of the self; and even Brian Massumi and Erin Manning's "more than human of the human" all recognize a technological paradigm of control operating in and through (and as) the individual (Massumi 2018). We may also observe that the techno-logic of capitalism bent upon efficiency—the maximum exploitation of the laboring substrate to meet the demands of the falling rate of profit—prevails across all organizational scales, from the individual to the laboratory to the university to the jail, the township, the state, and the nation-state. In "cultural" spaces, representative agents (a.k.a. subjects) manage and aggregate resources, offering themselves as profiles or brands that are themselves not only marketable, but marketable as derivative exposure to their underliers: their audiences, networks, assets, and currencies. I "friend" you to add you to me, to gain exposure to your network, to add you to my portfolio. I am an "influencer." "Culture," too, understood as a semi-autonomous domain separable from materiality and technology, can today only be a fetish—another case of platform fetishism—because the generalization of computing means that culture as the connective, communicative tissue of the sociosemiotic is ever more subject to the granularization and grammartization of commodification on the "object" side (and, its other aspect, the fractalization of fascism on the "subject" side) in what, from a global standpoint, is a racial capitalist sociocybernetic bio-techné. Such is "culture" today—an expression of an overall informationalization of social relations subject to historically imposed computability. Cultural form, computable because inseparable from computation, heretofore always a way of connecting to (or disconnecting from) a multiplicity of networks, is now itself a derivative—a social derivative. Its derivative condition explains what was known as "the postmodern condition," and is instituted by the universal expansion of the factory code toward the total colonization of space, time, representation, and mind: sociality itself in the largest sense.

That the principles of the ordination of matter, being, time, and value by number (or of publics by statistics, and/or of opinions by likes) were perceived to be universal, that is, generally applicable to all phenomena, was more than convenient. It was, as we have said, colonial. It was racializing and gendering. It was capacitating and maiming (Puar 2017). The math, though famously "content-indifferent," was never value free. Nor were the devices, from desktops to mainframes, from bombers to smartphones, that it spawned. As Diane Nelson (2015: 56) writes in *Who Counts?*, her astonishing ethnography of Mayan number systems and genocide and, also and as importantly, her scathing ethnography of Western mathematics and genocide, "Double-entry bookkeeping is *also* an 'ethnomathematics,' but one with an army." Double-entry bookkeeping was also a proprietary technique; its truth claims, in the form of accounts, implied pathways of control and functionality that served as conduits for capitalization and colonization. It was a system of representation that repressed noise (context) to clearly resolve the value signal called price in a calculus of profit and loss. In our own period, where we see very clearly (simply by looking at the business pages or, for that matter, the culture pages in any newspaper) that contemporary global capitalism is in lockstep with computation, we might expect that the politico-economic meaning of computation as an emergent order of proprietary organization is becoming clear. As new and powerful terms such as *platform sovereignty* (Bratton 2016), *algorithmic governance*, and *the society of metadata* or *"metadata society"* (Pasquinelli 2018) indicate, it appears that it is the information itself that has (or indeed *is*) value. But the argument here is that it is only valuable within the framework of computation, and indeed within the framework of computational racial capital—at least thus far. Information is the result of that framework; it is an *ethno-graphic* (not just anthropocentric) instantiation composed from, in, and on states of matter. The framework, a computational infrastructure that is also primarily fixed capital, emerges in conjunction with the myriad phenomena that are now treated informatically; the apparatus is the other side of the supposedly raw material of information. Information is and can only be a relation. The clear implication of this argument is that, just as a DVD presupposes a technical world that can record it and make it play, the very presence of "information" implies the background armature of computation as a mechanism of perception and organization that is fundamentally social and historical. This background armature of perception and organization further indicates the background armature of racial capital as the primordial condition—the meta-machine architecture—of the present social system of accounts. We note, and not only in passing, that this way of narrating the epic poem of AI puts anti-Blackness, slavery, settler colonialism, indentured servitude, imperialism, sexism, proletarianization, racial capitalism, and the active organization of oppression for profit at the epistemic center of a compute that could be called world history. It is computation that perceives information, and it is capital expansion that requires the perceptual-instrumental processes endemic to quantification, digitization, and computation. The entire system has its conditions of possibility and derives both its significance and its character from the history of capital accumulation, that is itself theft and only theft, and which is, to defer again to the chorus: colonialism, slavery, white heteropatriarchy, imperialism, globalization, financialization, and genocide.

Let us not romanticize the awesome capacities of so-called civilization. Sadly, indeed tragically, with the encroachment of value thus described, to value something, anything, threatens to be a mode of evaluation for capital. Odds are, anyway. And so much has been swept away, repressed, annihilated. In this book we will also have occasion to dwell on the remainder, on what Neferti Tadiar calls "remaindered life," a category I understand as designed to demarcate the domains or haecceities of experience that fall outside of system-atization—a dialectical category for that which is beyond the resolution of the dialectic. Remaindered life—a social derivative on capital whose market value went to zero but that nonetheless persists as lived experience, existence, or survival beyond the horizon of capitalized representation. As I understand it, remaindered life is the disavowed context and condition of relations for any and all value creation. However, despite our adherence to an "immanent out-side" (Massumi) in this volume and everywhere, the dominant and dominating principles organizing value and evaluation have been colonized by what Randy Martin called "the financialization of daily life" in the "society of risk," cen-turies in the making. This financialization structures representation, and the structuring of evaluation—internal to the elaboration of the value-form and to the universe of information—gives renewed meaning to this longstanding and recurrent theme in my own work adopted directly from Marx and already in-voked here: again, the forming of the five senses is a result of the entire history of the world down to the present. As Marx's observations themselves imply, and as this text is at pains to elaborate in a sociocyborg vein, our senses have been further informed—by/as information and informatics—since he wrote that line. The urgent and perhaps ultimate question of whether or not we might use these emerging perceptual capacities to reprogram the *socius* echoes Marx's abiding stake in revolution and what today (at least before Spring 2020) for many seems even more unthinkable than ever before—the abolition of private property and the withering away of the state. However, in the key of Marx in *The Communist Manifesto*, we hasten to add that this abolition and this withering has already been achieved for more than 2 billion people—that is, for twice the living population of Earth during the time Marx wrote. We must take courage from the fact that much of what "we" might claim to value has already been lost for two planetfuls of people. For that allows us to see that what would like to pass as "our values"—which in one way or another might include an allegiance to the enduring virtues of the nation state, of private property, of "liberal" soci-ety and its pleasures—have fallen into the black hole of self-contradiction and self-negation. As the shiny and pleasant other side of dispossession, they are never to be resurrected or redeemed, for beneath their veneer they are literally the expressions of hell on Earth. And this adherence to their bloody privilege is why the "liberals" of today are closet fascists, and why at the time of revising the copyedits for this book, Joe Biden, a racist, misogynist white man, is the liberal candidate for President of the United States.

Therefore, the event horizon of this book is the end of capitalism, a hori-zon that forcibly, it must be admitted, exceeds the horizon of contemporary common sense—at least it did when I began writing it. Witness Stanford economists who, dismissive of the very possibility of revolution, blithely suggest along with the *Daily Telegraph* writer James Bartholomew (2015) that we "learn to love economic inequality." But as Gramsci (1971: 170–171) reminds us in *The Modern Prince*, "Anybody who makes a prediction has in fact a programme for whose victory he is working," and this without doubt includes today's self-proclaimed realists, as well as a more reactionary faction in open pursuit of profits from the volatility of racial war. Another aspect of the topos of the argument here is that not only have the imaginary and symbolic been transformed by capitalist informatics, but a corresponding transformation of (human, but not only human) being itself has been instantiated. It is thus unsurprising that those with the big paychecks (economists at Stanford) uncritically parrot the logic of computational racial capital, even if they may be partially unconscious of its basis in slavery and murder-by-numbers, and even if they refrain from explicitly demanding that we lick the bottom of their boots. But people get the unconscious they can afford. Most can no longer afford to build our egos on such self-serving ignorance—if they ever could.

But are fascists really people? We demand the right to wonder if anyone is left in there after being fully colonized by computational racial capital's AI. Capital's realization and generalization of simulation by digital logic—as, for example, with spectacle in the aesthetic register, or by means of statistical modeling in the computational register, and with multiple grids of intelligibility and evaluation (algorithmic governance) in various other academic and social disciplines—allows for the machine-(re)thinking of ontologies *in general* in terms of the effects of processes of instrumental inscription and codification. Metaphysics itself is under siege. Is there any remainder in the fascist?

Thus, when considering the recent interest in ontology, Fredric Jameson's "Always historicize!" comes to mind (1981: 9). Machine-thinking, which is one with execution, entails a reconfiguration of ontologies. As Alex Galloway (2012) taught us, the medium of computing, which instantiates its objects via programming, is metaphysics. And as Allen Feldman (2015) brilliantly demonstrates in analysis ranging from South Africa to Guantánamo to drone warfare, metaphysics is a medium of war. However, in a classic disappearing act of the medium, this fact of the instantiation of executable ontologies by computation, as well as their ascription to physical forms, most often goes unremarked—despite the fact that the reformatting is "the message." The question is whether or not it is possible to critique this computational, capitalist ordination of phenomena and thought—and the stakes here are far higher than what is generally meant by "academic." Ontological claims, such as "*x* is *y*," always have an addressee. The ontological layer, what something *is*, is an artifact of data visualization—in short, an inscription, an act of writing, and a speech-act—and never a neutral endeavor. Simulation deconstructs objects into distribution patterns; it makes us skeptical about who or what is present, both objectively (as we regard the perceptible) and subjectively (in ourselves as consciousness). It ordains "a tremendous shattering of tradition" (Benjamin: 236). Fake news! Data teaches us that we, as subjects, may not be the privileged addressee. The reign of simulation is everywhere imposed as antecedent forms of subjectivity are garbled, shattered, reformatted, and placed on a continuum with informatic throughput. Through an inversion of the priority between world and data visualization, the digital simulation of the world by concepts encoded in apparatuses at once reveals the stakes of intervention in the protocol layer of computation and raises the pointed and possibly still political question of what may remain of so-called humanity beyond the purview of a now fully financialized knowing that is a kind of doing—and here again, we glimpse the remainder. It does so by posing the question of the possibility of a "beyond" to (contemporary) simulation, particularly in a world—and in keeping with current physics, a cosmos—in which simulation has overtaken the place of truth as ground, and has done so in a way that both implies and corroborates the insight that number, deeper than matter or energy, is the fundamental component of All. I'm not sure, but it seems that some of us have an awareness of remaindered life and its possible alternative futures, and others not at all. It is no wonder the oppressed called Pinochet's brutal fascist supporters "mummies."

This appeal, in the face of foreclosure, to alternate strategies of account—to ontology, otherwise—would be the place to reflect for a moment on the fact that a marginal strand of thought, namely, deconstruction, has today become the dominant mode of state power, practiced on a massive scale by what Feldman (2017) calls "the deconstructive state." Ironic that this intervention in the protocol layer of language function was introduced by philosophers, but then again, none of us really know whose thinking we are doing. The incredible grammatical and conceptual innovation that Derrida used to dramatize *differánce* was first developed and utilized to intervene in the axiology of the extant colonial, imperial, and patriarchal epistemes. These knowledge formations supported the hegemony of various Western regimes, sustaining a broadband governance that functioned by producing and mobilizing a contiguous, persistent, dominant reality, along with its attendant objects and subjects. Derrida's technique of shattering these state-supported knowledge formations ostensibly grounded on axiology with a kind of accuracy that combined the skills of diamond cutter and watchmaker, disassembled seemingly—inviolable metaphysical first principles such as the superiority of Western civilization, or of men over women, and other forms of "truth" like "God" or "Man" or Truth. At the time deconstruction was a highly specialized strategy and toolkit developed by certain forms of feminist and postcolonial theory: Hélène Cixous, Luce Irigaray, Judith Butler, Gayatri Spivak, and Homi Bhabha, to name only a few. The appropriation and inversion of these strategies of deconstruction for the disruption of ontology by hegemonic actors who now deploy it tactically, if without subtlety or study (there is an analogy to be made with a hatchet somewhere), to scramble *marginal* ontologies is shocking, yet it must be seen as another example of the right-wing appropriation of left political techniques. Deconstruction has been financialized—it's a volatility inducing accumulation strategy. When the United States and Israel defend freedom of speech and democracy, when pinkwashing enables embarking on the representational and practical deconstruction of the individuals, families, homes, organizations, and nations which are their targets and victims, we must observe that there has been a sea change in both the calculus of dominant representation and the status of its objects. The discursive *overturning* of local reality now occurs by means of an executable language backed by media platforms and military power, by a formalization and calculus of what, almost twenty years ago, Sarah Ahmed (2004) called "affective economies." By a strange inversion, "reality" has gone from an independent variable to a dependent variable. It has become dependent upon the information that produces it and that allows stakeholders to bet on its outcomes. It is information itself that is now the independent fact and has the status previously held by "reality." It, information, is now the necessary condition, ground and medium for any wager on the future. Google's and Facebook's recent forays as defenders of privacy against the state's encroachments on our information is a similar result illustrating the priority of information over any specific reality: it is not a defense of "us" but only a proprietary strategy, a narrative and datalogical exploit for control over the means of production of on-demand realities. The organization of affect driven by the profit motive, depends upon the deconstruction and recomposition of read-write ontologies.

In gesturing toward the situatedness of even this world of total and indeed quasi-totalitarian computation, a totalized world that, whether by means of finance, physics, or the screen most often has the force of a (rewritable) fact, we observe that the deracinated, ascetic world of computational racial capital's dollars and sense is simultaneously the world of financial derivatives. Computation writes options on reality. Derivatives, as it turns out, are only more elaborate and more structured schematizations of the liquidity risk endemic to financial contingencies present in the very process of commodity forma-tion (production and consumption) through what was always distributed pro-duction and sale. The financial derivative allows for the breaking apart of an asset or bundle of assets to sell off its various components in pieces, so that it become possible for example to structure risk and trade it without owning the underlier. The risk management necessarily engaged in, one way or another, by all participants in a capitalist economy can now be managed from above by a specialized cartel of market makers offering specialized products—executable contracts of new types—all to the greater benefit of financiers. Additionally, as we shall further demonstrate, advertisers and politicians become the au-thors of social derivative compositions, semiotic forms of risk and information management. These derivatives formalize the contingencies bearing on their liquidity and are operative everywhere in both formal ways as financial instru-ments and in informal ways as advertising and social media currencies of af-fect such as likes and votes, and, like most everything else today, these instru-ments best succeed through data analysis and can only do their accounting with computers—they are extensions of computer programs. By a process that the brilliant new work of Robert Meister (2021) defines as collateralization, packages of risk may be rigorously defined and (Gramscian) bets made on the contingent outcomes of events. Derivatives are thus liquidity premiums that would in principle allow exposure to the upside of any asset whatever while limiting the downside by clearly structuring risk. The last chapter of this book treats this question of the derivative directly, moving in a direction suggested by Randy Martin's understanding of the social derivative as a strategy that was social before it was formalized by finance, and in accord with Bob Meister's key question "Is justice an option?" It partially accepts the historical shattering of ontologies and endeavors to offer a way forward—one that neither mandates nor fully excludes forms of historical return, for example, to the subject/ob-ject or to experiences of truth. Because colonial "invasion is a structure not an event" (Wolfe: 388), and because we recognize that economy is a network of networks, it will be argued here—and this may be a hard pill to swallow—that a successful revolution capable of sustaining a postcapitalist sociality, will have to have, in addition to all other requirements, a new financial imaginary.

Financial derivatives are sustained by ambient computation, although they nonetheless also have their own psychotropic, experiential, aesthetic, metaphysical, and behavioristic affects and effects. We shall see here that the explicitly financial derivative is only the most obvious form of what, culturally speaking, has become a general case in relation to the acceleration of compu-tational calculus that iterates recursively and consequently induces volatility as it pursues its arbitrage on labor-power through the articulation of social difference and capacity. The result is unending (e)valuation in every domain and continuous risk management—in Randy Martin's term again, the financialization of daily life. Such is the situation for the implantation of the cognitive-linguistic and such is the situation for the image and for the body—navigating a volatile world of increasing precarity. Logically this situation extends to any people who may be involved—more or less everyone. Indeed, we know now (or at least are in the position to know) that there is no semiotics (to speak of, much less to tweet about) without media platforms, and we also have begun to openly suspect that, with "convergence"—another way of saying the general absorption of mediation by digital computing—these platforms, whatever they may have been in the past ("natural language," "writing," "humanism") have been more or less completely subsumed and thus "denatured" by full financialization.

As the factory code morphs into social codes and computer code and into "the New Jim Code" (Ruha Benjamin 2019: 1–48), and as institutions migrate into platforms, the meanings we may most easily produce and transmit are those in some way consonant with and therefore supportive of racial capital. If capital has its way, these meanings that conform to capitalist production and reproduction would, very generally speaking, include all of them—even the ones that as noted by Stew and quoted in the epigram that opens this Introduction "speak truth to power." The everyday disavowal of the capture of expressivity by platform-based mediation is also a disavowal of the derivative condition of knowledge. The deeper significance for semiotics—of the content indifference of the mathematical theory of communication and of racial capital—is the full colonization of meaning, representation, and consciousness. Consciousness is instrumentalized by a vertically integrated background order that delimits the significance of any expression whatever to an option on the value form. Paradigmatically, social media profits from anything and everything you can say or photograph, but this case is just the most obvious one in a system in which representational media have been captured and subordinated wholesale by computational logistics. Thus, we should not be the least bit surprised by the effective if not also actual racism of a Mark Zuckerberg or, similarly the fascism of a Jeff Bezos. By means of informatics, the logic of capital has been combined with the very substance of things and of expression at the level of their appearance—we confront a logistics of perception and simultaneously an instrumentalization of the objects of knowledge organized by computation and capital and the exploitation of social difference. Psychologically, many experience a balancing act between "reality" and psychosis, between

abjection and megalomania, that informs everyday violence, domestic terror-
ist gunplay, melancholia, and the insane oscillations between murderous rage
and delusional mastery. Critical poetics dances on the high-tension lines and
in the borderlands linking what appears with what could be; it calls for a resto-
ration of politics through an abolition-feminist reclamation of the power of expression (and economy) and seeks sustainable practices of anarchocommunism
in ungovernable and utopian pursuits of the not-yet.[13]

Cybernetic Ontologies and Derivative Conditions

We could say that the concept of computational capital allows us machine-
thinkers to understand how, by the time of postmodernity, the financialization of culture renders culture as both a means of capitalist production and
an economic calculus. Culture—with a capital "C"—becomes a grammar of
extraction, and cultural work becomes a wager on a future: the condition of
art and the artist in a nutshell. We may understand postmodern culture as
production and calculus precisely because we grasp that in myriad ways cultural production is networked to machinic mediation, and we recognize that
these machines, including discrete state machines and the infrastructure that
supports them, are fixed capital: Marx's "vast automaton" in the form of the
world computer. Cultural practices, which include epistemological transformations, the strategic codification of representations, and read-write ontologies are computer-mediated and parametrically ordained; the "human" inputs
are thereby subsumed as necessary and surplus labor in the calculus of production cycles. Some of this labor—which, truth be told, includes that of critical
theory—is locally leveraged within the field of computational capital for personal and political survival and perhaps gain, even as it is part of an arbitrage
structure to stave off the falling rate of profit. With computing, writing is no
longer typing but proto-typing.

The production of culture, like the production of everything else today, is
necessarily, then, a position on the market. It is a risk management strategy—a
derivative position organizing, as best it can, a set of contingent claims. Of
course, this book directly delivers on only a very small portion of what may
be the ultimate affordances of its specific derivative position, wagered as it is
as a critical-poetic, political-economic concept of computational racial capital
and its world computing. I hope to propose outlines for a clear-cut analysis
and critique of computational racial capitalism's expropriation of the general
intellect, its brutal liquidation of (in)human resources, and its violent reordination of the material world. The book's primary purpose is to establish the

concept, broadly suggest its possibilities and implications, and then use the concept as a heuristic to rethink a very limited number of inflection points for political theory, media theory, critical race theory, and decolonization. In the short term, it would provision tools for the ongoing revolutions that are the other sides of universal subsumption by information—the immanent outsides. In the long term, it would be part of creating a position on the capital markets that will destroy them. I think I have made my peace with the fact that this book will not make any money. I hope my publishers have too.

Though I have, perhaps unavoidably, presented some of the above conceptualizations and claims as if they were deracinated abstractions emerging directly out of the rarefied conceptual tick of the dialectical clock, the book is committed to sounding the *material* histories of the formation of social practices becoming real abstractions and in turn becoming concepts and computation. The text is grounded in and—to work up its concepts—mobilizes an abiding commitment to the investigation of historically produced social difference and of the instrumental production and organization of inequality endemic to contemporary forms of social mediation. The codification of social difference—particularly but not limited to racialization; gender differentiation; and religious, national, linguistic, and other cultural forms of difference and the anti-Blackness, racism, sexism, and Islamo-, homo-, and trans-phobia that these feed—becomes the fodder for the emergence of a computational nascency in what Cedric Robinson identified as racial capitalism. Computational racial capital, like prior forms of racial capital, is built upon—which is to say, functions by means of—the production, codification, and recodification of social difference and the abstraction of the media of differentiation. It is a racial formation that is itself an engine for the mutability and profitable (re) deployment of racism, what we called some pages ago, a social-difference engine. Whatever else they are or have been or may have been, today race, gender, sexuality, and class are also technologies that both objectify and subjectify oppression. "Class difference" is but one form of social difference, and the loss of class as a privileged analytic only testifies to the economic functionality of race, gender, nation, and so on, as well as the struggles made from those quarters and the ever more granular fractionalization, and subsequent factionalization, of the social—that is, the wholesale economization of social differentiation. "Race is the modality in which class is lived," as Stuart Hall and colleagues (1978: 394) wrote—and other forms of social difference comprise a matrix of oppressions that inevitably have an economic component (see Singh 2015).

These vectors for the development of social difference are elaborated by and as algorithms—some formalized and some effectuated—that also function as financial derivatives: strategies of risk management that allow capital to discriminate, to securitize, and to bet on the aggregation of difference in synthetic products including mortgages, insurance, security, and other forms of debt and credit, as well as in military, police, and surveillance technologies designed to control variously marked populations for the purpose of capital preservation. The proposed analytic extends the powerful notion of "racial formation" proposed by Omi and Winant (1994) beyond the curated imposition of identities and ethnicities to abstractions and to machines. It sees "society" in places where it is usually thought to be absent: namely, operating in and as abstract machines; in and as what we refer to simply as machines, software, programs, and code; and on and in visuality and thought itself. This claim—that elements and functions formed within the domain of racial capital are racial formations—includes discrete state machines. As has already been noted, where Gregory Bateson famously defined information as "a difference that makes a difference," what cannot be overemphasized is that what "makes a difference" is always already social. By this I mean that the context in which any difference might make a difference—in any (and all) meaningful way(s)—is always already social; the rest is idealism, a domain of deracinated abstraction, indeed, an ascetic ideal, as Nietzsche says, a *ressentiment*-driven will to power, concocted to imagine a world without oneself, without an "us" or without "humanity's" petty concerns.

We recognize that, for some, this self-serving asceticism which makes ego, masculinity, and whiteness disappear in the very medium of its fabulations produces comforting thoughts. The scientist, who insists that his biology, chemistry, or physics contains truths that exceed "man" and exist before and after, addresses himself *to* man. With his grandiose statements, he humiliates man—at times not without provocation and often not without dire results. Nonetheless and despite their seeming indifference to an Other, the ontological pronouncements, the ontological claims, are always triangulated; they are speech acts—a something for someone, a signifier for another signifier. They are also fetishistic, ways of knowing and not knowing, ways of preserving the phallus man in the face of his castration. The child-man killing the traditional father-man to marry mother nature and consummate truth: this becomes science the universal man whose power is now expressed in sublime technologies that in the next generation threaten man with further castration. Such hand wringing about "technology itself" becomes a mansplaining complex as deadly as it is schematic and even absurd—though one nonetheless dangerous for its libidinal-economic logic, its patho-logic. Among the stakes in the analysis of computational racial capital, therefore, is a critique of this very sense of disembodied mind, of the "us" that is supposedly without us. The imperial, Oedipal "us," to be sure, the psychotic, the sociopath, the fascist. One clearly grasps the problem: god or cyborg—and, in this, Donna Haraway's materialist answer still resonates: "I'd rather be a cyborg than a goddess."

Cybernetics as the now unavoidable ontology of ontologies must become the ground for anarchocommunist becomings, sociocybernetic becomings. Information as physical process bound to alienated, deracinated labor, is itself a cyborg formation. Janelle Monáe, as if building on the Fanonian analysis of the impossibility of Black ontology, makes answer to both the prohibition of all but cyborg ontologies and the violence of abstraction. With her brilliant musical and video work, most recently, the song "Screwed" and the "emotion picture" *Dirty Computer*, embodied and desirous, dynamic, assertive, affecting, sexual and creative dirty computing becomes a kind of answer embracing queer, Black, and non-normative alternatives to being constituted and commanded to perform by the deracinated abstractions that colonize bodies. And the emotion picture changes the way we are screwed (together): "You fucked the world up, now we'll fuck it all back down." This *détournement* of the activity machine that is the body, dancing, musical, thinking suggests that we can and perhaps must occupy computation differently, using the resources of our bodies, of our musics, and of our histories. Since everything runs on us, since we are the substrate at the bottom of the stack, Monáe proposes and actualizes a creative utilization of the immense reserves of capacity in music, dance, movement, song, experience, and embodied knowledge. Such an embarkation is not a total answer but a strategy that suggests alternative kinesthetic ways to process information. One thinks also here of Erin Manning's (2018) work on neurodiversity and Black life, the living taking place beyond the confines and perceptions of institutions: "The urgency of these undercommons cannot be ignored. We are moving through them, but are we proliferating enough? Are we inventing at the speed, in the duration, of the movements of thought that move us to ask what else it can mean to know?" (5).

As societies move from cultural hegemony to computational hegemony machine-instituted forms of abstraction and computing become colonial enclosures, worksites, and camps—lived, embodied experience. Computers and their programs are thought to be technical deployments of mathematical concepts and mechanisms that up until now have most often been perceived as value-neutral, that is, as technical or scientific or objective. This misunderstanding provides those vested by the current technocracy with an alibi. An additional purpose of this book is to permanently disrupt the very notion that concepts and machines occupy or could ever occupy such a neutral zone, a kind of degree zero of technicity, untouched by histories of social difference and the practices of inequality. It is as foolish to think that machines are neutral as it is to think neutrality is neutral. "The ruling ideas are nothing more than the ideal expression of the dominant material relationships" (Marx, 1978: 172–3). Thus, today we might say that the ruling thinking machines are nothing more than the informatic expression of the dominant material relationships, the dominant material relationships grasped as technologies and therefore the machines of their dominance. As opposed to the various quasi-ontological instantiations of dominant informatics (e.g., "the self," "greed," "human, "~~white~~"), we glean that consciousness is at once material and distributed, relying upon a whole set of substrates, machines, images, and codes as well as upon the visible living beings—and, what's more (much more), the beings disappeared—among them.[14] In view of such distributed systems, therefore, you are not the locus of your thought, even if the functionality of "your" thought simulates you as such; the locus of your thought is the world computer and its material implantation in the bios, what Benjamin Bratton (2016) poetically and indeed accurately conceives as "the stack." You is a node. Nodes of the world, remake your networks! The only thing you have to lose is your algorithms of oppression (Noble 2018).

Despite not being able to write in the key of Marx any longer, it is possible to politicize social relations that are naturalized, technologized, or buried in abstraction, in machinery, and in the unthought. Social difference, the profitable maintenance and elaboration of social differentiation fundamentally but not exclusively along "racial" and monetary lines is inherent in information itself. Learning from Hortense Spillers, this critique of information extends itself to the *grammar* of social differentiation and to the increasing granularity of that grammar. It is impossible to write in the key of Marx because of the historical materialist recognition that both the writer and the reader are distributed cybernetic agents who are themselves caught up and constituted in the traffic of information and must therefore decolonize themselves as they work to decolonize the world. No single perspective is adequate to such a task. We observe that the situation of difference and differentiation, inseparable as it is from histories of violence, is, in fact, the deeper meaning of what is called "the world market." The world market is the real-time computational processing of the evaluation of everything—and from which today (next to) nothing escapes—by the relentless calculus of the value-form endemic to profit under the historical system of racial capitalism.

By looking at specific machine histories and processes of grammartization we shall demonstrate that modern machines themselves are racial formations.

They are formed by actual practices of racialization and are informed by them as these relentless and for the most part remorseless activities crunch money into more money. But how could they not be? Indeed how could we not be? Machine-mediated hegemony continues to posit (if less and less convincingly) autonomous individuality and value-neutral machines, while at the same time facilitating a disavowal of the fact that "we" think what we think because of our cybernetic relation to machines and to objectified bodies (ours or others) consigned to what in *Get Out*, Jordan Peele (2017) brilliantly configures as "the sunken place." It is these sunken places that provision liquidity for those who put folks in them, and if they run dry, if we die, more have to be created. When we consider the social totality in this way, when the integrated information machines of social mediation are designed to confer life to some and social death, debility, or disposability on others, it should really be no surprise that racist encodings sedimented into institutions and machines organized for value extraction reencode racism. But for some it is, and for some, no matter how clear the argument—this singular fact in an instrumentally postfactual world, namely, that capitalist technology is a racial formation, will remain unintelligible.

By 2019, readers will no doubt have seen that, despite various forms of public knowledge about racism, and despite the mostly unpublicized yet mass experience of racism, today's journalistic commentators are nonetheless surprised when it is pointed out that facial recognition software or linguistic search functions recapitulate, reenact, and reinscribe the racism of the social. Shock has been expressed at the suggestion that Google or Facebook are racist—at least by those who don't know from experience that all the games are rigged. Few want to draw the obvious conclusion that there are algorithms for racism, for this admission would mean that racism has been encoded and sedimented into machines and that they are racist in their function. Images, it is hastily explained when the facts emerge, contain human prejudices—the implication is that racism may be in the images or in the selection process, but not the computers. Time and again someone will say, yes, people can be racist, but *technology* is value-neutral. Most often, these iterators and their explanations hew closely to the idea that one can get beyond the pedestrian concerns of the social, that technical form is based in scientific research and that with a few responsible correctives, given the appropriate input and the rigorous weighting of results, the machines, their learning, and their neural nets will work neutrally again and without prejudice. What is forgotten is that the images and word clusters, corrected and adjusted or not, are not just *of* the machines; they are *parts* of the machines—they *are* the machines. The image is no longer a freestanding entity if it ever was—like the word, it is a component in a network, at once of the machine and itself a machine. These machines, authored in strife, are machines of extraction and are themselves social relations in every aspect of their functionality. Like every other part of the computer, signs—linguistic, numeric, and visual—are encoded abstractions operating on a complex set of networked material substrates that include the technical image (Flusser 2000), feminized labor in the production of circuitry and devices (Nakamura 2007), rare earth blood metals (e.g., the coltan wars), the general conditions of cultures, and the many histories and practices—including censuses and holocausts—necessary to constellate and incarnate computation. Acts of computing are moments in a planetary process of encoding and valuation that runs on inequality and that has *already* coded the visual and semiotic domains with the perceptual and ideological, not to say *material*, logistics of race, gender, nation, and class. Not only is consciousness distributed through, by, and *in* these machines—a result of distributed computation accumulating and intensifying over seven centuries or more—but so too are racism, sexism, ableism, cis-heteropatriarchy, and the like endemic to the world computer. It is politically and historically necessary for us to learn to see the social basis operating at this level of abstraction—as *in*formation—in order to see the image, the word, or even the machine or platform not as a stand-alone formation but as what, in a similar context, Régis Debray (1996: 22) described as follows: "To speak of the videosphere is to be reminded that the screen of the television receiving signals is the head of a pin buried in one home out of millions." Then we perceive that the default functionality of the machine, like that of information, is racist and capitalist. The only real hope beyond poetry is a revolutionary attack on the racial capitalist order of things, its ordering of things. This attack requires a materialist, informatic, cultural, and economic strategy.

Technology, as Joel Dinerstein (2006) once argued, has long functioned in the United States and beyond as a "white mythology" (570). It allows racial thinking to masquerade as technical thinking. We can go a step further. The history of racialization and gender differentiation is sedimented into machines, machines that in turn organize our thought, and all of that recursivity is part of a financial calculus in which—increasingly and ever more rapidly and thoroughly—absolutely everything we may know, think, or do undergoes, with ambient computing, a leveraged background monetization to produce both the massive accumulation of capital and the massive distribution of dispossession. Such is the factory code. The computational matrix that extractively abstracts every utterance and act as information presents an inordinate problem, one that—though mostly unthought, both in our everyday interfacing and indeed everywhere, all the time—is nonetheless the most diabolical problem of our time: society and the bios as incorporated by the world computer running the operating system of racial capitalism.

Digitization, parallel processing, the Hayekian market, informatics, financialization. The problem that is computational racial capitalism is known mostly by its scattered symptoms: burnout, ADD, psychosis, genocide, famine, border walls, camps, interminable war, settler colonialism, carceral society, climate injustice, militarized policing, state terrorism, plutocracy, Apple, Google, tech boosterisms, business innovation, high school shootings, bail bonds, megalomania, neo-Fascist grandstanding, Lamborghinis, super yachts and the like. Like our words, images, and thoughts, our problems do not exist in isolation, even though atomization, separation, and social alienation may seem to render them modular. Though ostensibly disparate and unevenly distributed, these problems and too many others to name here are profoundly integrated in and through their striated differentiation. *The World Computer* endeavors to offer a partial description of the rise and function of this matrix of extractive abstraction that results from the historically imposed conversion of any and every thing whatever into an informatic asset that is, in one way or another, a derivative exposure to risk; a description of the abstract machines of differentiation and integration, separation and accumulation, profit and dispossession—machines that, though abstract, function in an integrated fashion. They function concretely by crunching information, shattering life, and shedding blood.

Is it possible to invert the process? Through the visceral and in many respects subaltern calculus of "dirty computing"? Through cybernetic communism?[15] Through the embodied calculus of social derivatives wagered on a better world fucked all back down? Through distributed computing and the crypto-economic creation of new social architectures? Such a reparative informatics might radicalize finance by redesigning the protocols of money and credit to reconfigure economic media, and do so in such a way that a fully expressive postcapitalist medium becomes capable of abstraction without extraction. It might thus allow for the collective authoring of futures and sharing risk to create radical solidarity. On the way to really asking these questions well, the chapters that follow would derive and elaborate several other significant ideas and concepts from the notion of the world computer. These new formulations are put forward to both substantiate and give amplitude to the central concept. To list the main ones here: the computational unconscious, the programmable image, computational racial capitalism, informatic labor (a redefinition and refinement of the labor theory of value and of the attention theory of value), the computational mode of production, advertisarial relations, the advertisign, derivative living, the fourth determination of money (beyond the classic three: measure, medium of exchange, store of value), economic media, and platform communism, cybercommunism—or, perhaps better, derivative communism. Though each of these ideas might themselves offer materials for book-length projects, the aim here is to generate a new conceptual armature and its necessary terms, such that the new tools can be utilized and refined in multiple domains by the ongoing critics of and revolutionaries against the everyday compute of racial capitalism, by those who have been and who remain bound to struggles for social justice, reparations, and emancipation. Fuck the police!

The Computational Unconscious

Technology as a Racial Formation

God made the sun so that animals could learn arithmetic—without the succession of days and nights, one supposes, we should not have thought of numbers. The sight of day and night, months and years, has created knowledge of number, and given us the conception of time, and hence came philosophy. This is the greatest boon we owe to sight.

—PLATO, TIMAEUS

Without community there is no liberation. . . . But community must not mean the shedding of our differences, nor the pathetic pretense that these differences do not exist.

—AUDRE LORDE, THE MASTER'S TOOLS WILL NEVER DISMANTLE
THE MASTER'S HOUSE

The Sedimentation of Social Practice

The term *computational capital* posits the rise of capitalism as the first digital culture with universalizing aspirations *and capabilities*, and it recognizes contemporary culture, bound as it is to electronic digital computing, as Digital Culture 2.0. Rather than seeing this shift from Digital Culture 1.0 (DC1) to Digital Culture 2.0 (DC2) strictly as a break, we consider it as one result of an overall intensification in the practices of quantification. Capitalism, says Nick Dyer-Witheford (2013), was already a digital computer, and historical shifts in the quantity of quantities led to profound shifts in the quality of qualities. If capitalism was a digital computer from the get-go, then "the invisible hand"—as the nonsubjective, social summation of the individualized practices of the pursuit of private (quantitative) gain thought to result in (often unknown and unintended) public good within capitalism—is an early if woefully incomplete conceptualization of the computational unconscious.

With the broadening and deepening of the imperative toward quantification and rational calculus, one posited then presupposed during the early modern period by the expansionist program of capital, the process of the assignation of a number to all qualitative variables—that is, the *thinking in numbers* (discernible in the commodity-form itself, whereby every use-value was also encoded as an exchange-value)—entered into our machines and our minds. Over "the succession of days and nights," this penetration of the digital—rendering early on the brutal and precise calculus of the dimensions of cargo holds in slave ships, the sparse econometric accounts of ship ledgers for insurance purposes during the Middle Passage, double-entry bookkeeping, the rationalization of factory production, the categoricality of time and wages in the assembly line, and, more recently, global assembly lines, cameras, and modern computing—leaves no stone unturned. The collapse of difference into quantity to make a difference in quantity. Sight teaches reason, says Plato, and under capital reason teaches sight to see race; capital uses racial differentiation to collapse difference into more of itself. From Sohn-Rethel's "real abstraction" to racial abstraction, to Georg Lukács's critique of reification and the categoricality of Kantian thought to Hayek's understanding of commodity "telecommunication" by the price signal, there is ample evidence for the thoroughgoing collapse of qualities into quantities by capital.[1] Today, as is well known from everyday observation if not necessarily from media theory, computational calculus arguably underpins nearly all productive activity and, particularly significantly for this argument, underpins those specific activities that together constitute the command-control apparatus of the world system and that stretch from writing to image-making and, therefore, to thought.[2] My contention is not simply that modern computation is on a continuum with capitalism, but rather that computation, though characteristic of certain forms of thought and recognizable as such, is also the unthought of modern thought. This is to say that the content-indifferent calculus of computational capital ordains the material-symbolic and the psychosocial even in the absence of a conscious, subjective awareness of its operations. As the domain of the unthought that organizes thought and feeling, the computational unconscious is structured like a language, a computer language that is also, and inexorably, an economic calculus. This thought that is unthought, because automated in and as fixed capital, is externalized and sedimented into discrete state machines whose programs and programmable environments, though ostensibly constituted in number, nonetheless carry elements of racial abstraction and gender abstraction down to the metal.

The idea of "the computational unconscious" allows us to propose that much contemporary consciousness ("virtuosity" in post-Fordist parlance, but also the Jamesonian "waning of affect" that indicated a generalized flattening of affective ground precisely and remarkably at the moment when affect studies began their rise to prominence) is a computational effect—in short, a species of artificial intelligence. Our thought is AI (the reader may here place the words *our* and *thought* in quotation marks as they see fit). A large part of what "we" are has been conscripted, even as "thought" and other allied metabolic processes are functionalized in lockstep service to the ironclad movements of code. This conscription is part of what Paolo Virno (2004: 110) calls "the communism of capital," or what Guy Debord (1995) calls "the false community of the spectacle," under which social differences are exacerbated and exploited on the one side (labor/production) and shed and sheared away through the subsumption of these differences in the universal value-form on the other side (accumulation/capital). While *ironclad* is now a metaphor and *code* is less the factory code described by Marx and more the computer code of the deterritorialized factory of the silicon-driven screen, recognizing that the logic of industrial machinery and the bureaucratic structures of the corporation and the state have been abstracted and absorbed by discrete state machines—to the point where in some quarters "code is law"—will allow us to pursue a surprising corollary: The structural inequalities endemic to capitalist production— categories that often appear under variants of the analog signs of race, class, gender, sexuality, nation, and so on—are also deposited and thus operationally disappeared into our machines. Nonetheless they continue to do their work.

Put simply and perhaps, in deference to contemporary attention spans, too soon: our machines are racial formations. They are also technologies of gender and sexuality.[3] Computation, as an extension of capitalism, is thus necessarily racial capitalism, the *longue durée* digitization of the logic and logistics of racialization—as well as, not in any way incidentally, of regimes of gender and sexuality. In other words, the inequality and structural violence inherent in capitalism also inhere in the logistics of computation that process economic production and exchange and that consequently also inhere in the real-time organization of semiosis, which is to say, our practices and our thought. The "servility" of consciousness, remunerated or not, aware of its underlying operating system or not, is organized in relation not just to sociality understood as interpersonal interaction in the footprint of the master-slave dialectic but in relation to digital logics of capitalization and machine-technics in service of the same master-slave relations. For this reason, the political analysis of post-modern and, indeed, posthuman inequality must examine the materiality of the computational unconscious. That, at least, is the hypothesis, for if it is the function of computers to automate thinking, and if dominant thought is the thought of domination, then what exactly has been automated?

Already in the 1850s the worker appeared to Marx as a "conscious organ" in the "vast automaton" (1990 [1867]: 502) of the industrial machine, and by the time he wrote the first volume of *Capital* Marx was able to comment on the worker's new labor of "watching the machine with his eyes and correcting its mistakes with his hands" (1990: 496). Marx's prescient observation with re-spect to the emergent role of visuality in capitalist production, along with his understanding that the operation of industrial machinery posits and presup-poses the operation of other industrial machinery, suggests what was already implicit if not fully generalized in the analysis: that Dr. Ure's notion, cited by Marx, of the machine as a "vast automaton," was scalable—smaller machines, larger machines, or entire factories could be thus conceived, and, with the increasing scale and ubiquity of industrial machines, the notion could well describe the industrial complex as a whole. Historically considered, "watching the machine with his eyes and correcting the mistakes with his hands" thus appears as an early description of what information workers such as you and me would do on our screens. To extrapolate: distributed computation—its in-tegration with industrial process and the totality of social processes—suggests that not only has society as a whole become a vast automaton profiting from the metabolism of its conscious organs but that, furthermore, the confronta-tion or interface with the machine at the local level ("where we are") is an isolating and phenomenal experience that, while still a form of work, is not equivalent to the perspective of the vast automaton or, under capitalism, the perspective of capital. Given that here, while we might still be speaking about intelligence, we are not necessarily speaking about subjects in the strict sense; we might replace Althusser's relation of S–s (Big Subject [God, the State, etc.] to small subject ["you" who are interpellated with and in ideology]) with AI-ai (Big Artificial Intelligence [the world system as organized by computational racial capital, or, the world computer] little artificial intelligence ["you," as or-ganized by the same]). "Yes, it is really me—an entrepreneur of the self." Here subjugation is not necessarily intersubjective, and it does not require "mutual" recognition. The AI does not need to speak your language even if it is your op-erating system. With this in mind (haha), we may at once understand from our own experience that the space-time regimes of subjectivity (point-perspective, linear time, realism, individuality, discourse function, etc.) that once were part of the digital armature of "the human," have been profitably shattered, and that the fragments have been multiplied and redeployed under the requisites of new management. We might wager that these outmoded templates or protocols for meaning and care despite their cannibalization by the ruling borg may still also meaningfully refer to an affective register that can take the measure of historical change—if only for some kind of species-remainder whose value is simultaneously immeasurable, unknown, and hanging in the balance among the various futures. Is there a meme for that?

Ironically perhaps, given the progress narratives attached to technical advances and the attendant advances in capital accumulation, Marx's hypothesis—in chapter 15 of *Capital*, "Machinery and Large-Scale Industry" (1990: 563)—that "it would be possible to write a whole history of the inventions made since 1830 for the purpose of providing capital with weapons against working-class revolt," casts an interesting light on the history of computing and its creation and imposition of new protocols of relation. (We are perhaps only now, as I put the finishing touches on this book begun many years ago, seeing rebellion that will challenge these.) Let us say that from the moment Charles Babbage, the inventor of modern computing, wanted to use a steam engine to drive calculations once thought to be possible only in the domain of thought, computing emerges as just such a weapon against working-class revolts—delimiting and channeling pathways to community and/or liberation such that they are always rendered productive for capital. Computing absorbs the intelligence of labor and sets it against labor. As Matteo Pasquinelli puts it, "Babbage provided not just a labor theory of the machine but a *labor theory of machine intelligence*. Babbage's calculating engines ('intelligent machines' of the age) were an implementation of the analytical eye of the factory's master. Cousins of Bentham's panopticon, they were instruments, simultaneously, of surveillance and measurement of labor. It is this idea that we should consider and apply to the age of artificial intelligence and its political critique, although reversing its polarization, in order to declare computing infrastructures a concretion of labor in common" (Pasquinelli 2019: 54).

Not only have the incredible innovations of workers been abstracted and absorbed by machinery from the earliest moments of industrialization; so also have many of their myriad antagonisms toward capitalist domination—all roads have lead to capital, or almost. Machinic perfection meant the imposition of continuity and the removal of "the hand of man" by fixed capital or, in other words, the absorption of know-how and the foreclosure of many forms of disruption—both by means of automation (Marx 1990: 502). Thus the repression of individual moments of resistance to mechanization and computation, the *disciplinary* aspect of production and reproduction, results socially in a generalized repression of the understanding of machine intelligence as the alienation of the general intellect. This repressed history of domination results in a symptomatic fetishism around AI that indicates the unknown history of this alienation—the computational unconscious.

Dialectically understood, subjectivity, while having its arsenal of anticapitalist sensibilities and capacities, is also a consequence and a force of the laws of the market. Modern subjectivity, itself an abstraction (as is clear from the radical skepticism of Descartes's "I think therefore I am" on), was the result of the generalization of a mandatory exchange of equivalents in the marketplace—in which each person, as a representative of their commodity, brings their commodity to market in a relation of equivalence and computes the quantity of its value. In collapsing particular differences into exchange-values, the market allowed for the exchange to take place among "equals," albeit along a highly reduced bandwidth of language and sensibility. "Some semantics for 'yes' and 'no,' for pointing to this or that, and to indicate quantity, is sufficient to the essentials of a transaction of exchange whether it is carried on between two village gossips or between two strangers who do not speak each other's language. Ethnologists are acquainted with the incidence of 'silent trade.' To put it in the words of Bertrand Russell it is 'that all my data, in so far as they are matters of fact, are private to me.' Thus one can justifiably say that commodity exchange impels solipsism[:] The doctrine that between all people, for every one of them, *solus ipse* (I alone) exist" (Sohn-Rethel 1978: 41–42). Individuation, for Sohn-Rethel as for Marx, is at once a result of commodity abstraction and a collective phenomenon, "the action is social, the minds are private" (44), as Sohn-Rethel says. Here too we see that even in basic exchange that presupposes and performs alienation, an unconscious dimension emerges along with the creation of the subjective agent.

> What the commodity owners *do* in an exchange relation is practical solipsism—irrespective of what they think and say about it. This practical solipsism does not need to coincide with self-interest. Someone who takes part in an act of exchange on behalf of another must obey exactly the same principles. If he does not, then the resulting relation is no longer exchange, but one that is qualitatively different, for instance charity. The principles which concern us here belong to the form of interrelation of commodity exchange, not to the psychology of the individuals involved. It is rather

this form that molds the psychological mechanisms of the people whose lives it rules—mechanisms which they then conceive of as inborn, human nature. This makes itself apparent in the way that those in subservience often act to the advantage of those above them. They consider themselves to have acted in self-interest although in fact they have merely obeyed the laws of the exchange nexus. The practical solipsism of commodity exchanging owners is nothing but the practice of private property as a basis of social relations. And this is not by people's choice but by the material necessity of the stage of development of their productive forces. (42)

The unconscious of market discipline goes to the core of the subject form and has its basis in the computation of exchange-value. As a way of talking about the conditions of possibility for subjectivity, the high price of conformity and its innumerable discontents, and also about nonconformity, antisociality, the violence of abstraction, the idea of the unconscious still has its uses. The conscious organ in Marx's (502) "vast automaton" does not entirely grasp the cybernetic organism of which it is a part; nor does it fully grasp the rationale of its subjugation. If the unconscious was formerly mercantile, machinic, or cinematic (Beller 2006b), emerging, when theorized, as a bourgeois fall-out of the late industrial revolution that expressed itself as linguistic and corporeal dysfunction, it is now computational—and if it is computational it is also the residue of an historical, dialectical and *technical* struggle with capitalism.

Alternatively, if what *now* underlies perceptual and cognitive experience is the automaton, the vast AI, what I refer to as "the world computer"—the totalizing integration of global practice through informatic processes—then *from the standpoint of production, "we" constitute its unconscious*. We are the unconscious of capital. We revolutionaries. However, as we are ourselves unaware of our own constitution, it is specifically as the unconscious of individuated and now dividuated producers that we exist in relation to what Paolo Virno calls, as previously noted and in what can only be a lamentation of history's perverse irony, "the communism of capital." If the revolution killed its father (Marx) and married its mother (capitalism), it may be worth considering the revolutionary prospects of an analysis of its unconscious, along with its Oedipal blindness. Of course, such an analysis can only take us so far, as it operates within gender constraints that, while revealing the character of hegemony for a certain form of historical neurosis, nonetheless require disposal. We are precariously close to saying that there can be no revolutionary subject—but we are not saying that there can be no revolution.

Machine-History: Protocols of the Computational Unconscious

Beginning with the insight that the rise of capitalism marks the onset of the first universalizing digital culture, this chapter develops the insights of *The Cinematic Mode of Production* (Beller 2006b) regarding the proliferation of screens as work-sites in an effort to register the violent digital subsumption of the lifeworld by computational racial capital that the (former) "humans" and their (excluded) ilk are collectively undergoing. This subsumption and enclosure occurs both as *Aufhebung* (the cancellation and preservation endemic to subsumptive absorption) and in a manner generative of sites of counterpower, of—just to name it here while leaving the explanation to the end of this volume (and to a future book-length study)—derivatives of counterpower, or derivative revolutions. To this end, this section offers a reformulation of Marx's formula for capital, Money–Commodity–Money' (M–C–M'), which accounts for distributed production in the social factory and by doing so hopes to direct attention to zones where capitalist valorization might be prevented or refused. For if attention has long been captured, bundled, and sold by capital and thereby converted into a force of oppression, its reclamation and redirection are key components of revolutionary culture. Capital's self-valorization must be prevented or refused not only to break a system which itself functions by breaking the bonds of solidarity and mutual trust that formerly were among the conditions that made a life worth living, but also, as we shall see in a later chapter, to posit the redistribution of our own power toward radical ends—ends that for me are still best described by the word *communist*, though antiracist, decolonial, feminist, queer, and anarchic struggles must be fundamental to the understanding and practice implied by this word for it to have any relevance or meaningful future. This thinking, political in intention, speculative in execution, and concrete in its engagement, also proposes a revaluation of the aesthetic as an interface that sensualizes information. As such, the aesthetic is both programmed and programming—a privileged site (and indeed mode) of confrontation in the digital apartheid of the contemporary.

Along these lines, and similar to the analysis pursued in *The Cinematic Mode of Production*, I propose to defetishize a medium—computation itself—that can only be properly understood when grasped as a *means of production* embedded in the bios. History is not only the history of the emergence of computation; it is the dialectics of its emergence. Computation is often thought of as being the thing accomplished by hardware churning through a program (the programmatic quantum movements of a discrete state machine). However, it is important to recognize that the universal Turing machine was (and remains) media-indifferent only in theory and is thus justly reconceived of—media-theoretically, as it were—as an abstract machine in the realm of ideas and indeed in the realm of *the ruling ideas*. The Turing machine is an abstract machine that, like all abstractions, evolves out of concrete circumstances and practices; which is to say that it is itself an abstraction subject to historical-materialist critique and is, furthermore, a real abstraction. It is, in short, an idealization of real abstraction—a practical idea. Turing machines iterate themselves on the living, on life, reorganizing its practices through the conversion of life energy into machine states, into information. One might situate the emergence and function of the universal Turing machine as perhaps among the most important abstract machines in the last century, save perhaps that of capital itself. However, both their ranking and even their separability are here what we seek to put into question. Was it the mere passage of days, or was it the passage of working days that gave rise to all those numbers?

Without a doubt, the computational process, like the capitalist process, has a corrosive effect on ontological precepts, accomplishing a far-reaching liquidation of tradition that includes metaphysical assumptions regarding the character of essence, being, authenticity, and presence. And without a doubt, computation, like capital, has been built even as it has been discovered. It is pure ideology that informatic abstractions are substrate indifferent and are thus unaltered by their substrate or do not really even need one. Is it really the same information if it is archived in silicon or on human skin? The paradigm of computation marks an inflection point in human history that reaches along temporal and spatial axes: both into the future and back into the past, out to the cosmos and into the subatomic. At any known scale, from Planck time (10^{-44} seconds) to yottaseconds (10^{24} seconds) and from 10^{-35} to 10^{27} meters, computation, conceptualization, and sense-making (sensation) have become inseparable. Computation is part of the historicity of the senses as well as of embodiment, the organization of the built environment, communication, the psyche . . . ad infinitum. Just ask that baby using an iPad.

The slight displacement of the ontology of computation itself implicit in saying that it has been built as much as discovered (that computation has a history even if it now puts history itself at risk) allows us to glimpse, if only from what Laura Mulvey calls "the half-light of the imaginary" (1975: 7) (because what Stefano Harney and Fred Moten call "the general antagonism" [2013: 10] is feminized when the apparatus of capitalization has overcome the symbolic), that computation is not, so far as we can know, the way of the universe *per se*, but rather *the way of the universe as it has become intelligible to us vis-à-vis our machines.* The understanding, from a standpoint recognized as science, that computation has fully colonized the knowable cosmos (and is indeed one with what is known as knowing) is a humbling insight, significant of us in that it allows us to propose from the half-light that seeing the universe as computation, as, in short, simulable, if not itself a simulation (the computational effect of an informatic universe), may be no more than the old anthropocentrism, the old *ethnocentrism,* now automated by conscious organ-driven apparatuses. We see what we can see with the senses we have; autopoiesis. The universe as it appears to us is figured by—that is, is a figuration of—computation. That's what our computers tell us. We build machines that discern that the universe functions in accord with their self-same logic. The infinitely receding recursivity effects the God trick. When the ruling ideas begin to explain the cosmos, we encounter their *Weltanschauung*—their worldview or ideology. But here ideology, rather than being a necessary component of a particular social arrangement as it was with, say, religion and nationalism, is only an afterthought regarding a material entrenchment that no longer really requires ideology. Think what you want, says the computational cosmos, the operating system has already been switched on.

For those prone to such afterthoughts, parametrically translating the resonant account of cosmic emergence as computational process into the domain of history before overtaking it, reveals a disturbing allegiance between computational consciousness organized by the computational unconscious and what Silvia Federici calls the system of global apartheid. Let's confront hostile intelligence, the expropriation of the general intellect. Historicizing computational emergence pits its colonial logic and optimizing comprehension schemes directly against what Stefano Harney and Fred Moten (2013: 10) identify as "the general antagonism" (itself the reparative antithesis of the general intellect as subsumed by capital). As computation naturalizes itself, it also erases its history and with that the history of the violence from which it emerged and upon which it depends. The procedural universalization of computation is a cosmology that attributes and indeed enforces a sovereignty tantamount to divinity—and externalities be damned. Its process of real abstraction, inexorably tied to the informatics of financialization and exchange, appear foundational, axiomatic, axiological. Dissident, fugitive planning, Black study, decolonial aspirations, liberatory practices, anarchist communiqués—a studied refusal of optimization, an abiding refusal of computational colonialism—may offer some ways out of the current geo(post)political and its computational orthodoxy: a detournement of the antihistorical protocols of computational racial capitalism.

Computational Idolatry and Multiversality

In the new idolatry cathected to inexorable computational emergence, the universe is itself currently imagined wholesale as a computer. Here's the seductive sound of the current theology from a conference sponsored by the sovereign state of New York University:

> As computers become progressively faster and more powerful, they've gained the impressive capacity to simulate increasingly realistic environments. Which raises a question familiar to aficionados of *The Matrix*— might life and the world as we know it be a simulation on a super advanced computer? "Digital physicists" have developed this idea well beyond the sci-fi possibilities, suggesting a new scientific paradigm in which computation is not just a tool for approximating reality but is also the basis of reality itself. In place of elementary particles, think bits; in place of fundamental laws of physics, think computer algorithms. ("Rebooting" 2011)

Science fiction, in the form of "the Matrix," is here used to figure a "reality" organized by simulation, but then this reality is quickly dismissed as something science has moved well beyond. *The Matrix* was just a movie, while science shows that computation *really* underpins the cosmos and its universe of appearances. However, it would not be illogical here to propose that this deeper "reality" is itself a science fiction—a fiction whose current author is no longer the novel or Hollywood but science and computation. It is in a way no surprise that, in a manner consistent with "digital physics," the MIT physicist Max Tegmark claims that consciousness is a state of matter: consciousness as a phenomenon of information storage and retrieval is a property of matter described by the term *computronium*.[4] Humans represent a rather low level of complexity. In the neo-Hegelian narrative in which the philosopher-scientist reveals the working out of the world (or, rather, cosmic) spirit, one might say that it is as science fiction—one of the persistent fictions licensed by science— that "reality itself" exists at all. We should emphasize that the trouble here is not so much with "reality"; the trouble here is with "itself." To the extent that we recognize that colonial poiesis, or world making, has been extended to our machines, and to the extent that it is through our machines that we think and perceive, we may recognize that reality is itself a product of their operations. The world begins to look very much like the tools we use to perceive it, to the point that "reality itself" is thus a simulation, as are "we." As science outcinemas cinema, ontology has become the orchid in the land of technology.[5] Here it is a pure simulation, given that everything is computation all the way down. The only piece of the picture left out is everything that makes such a picture what it is: computational technology and its history—its *historicity*. The conclusion that ontological forms are but computation concurs with the notion of a computational universe but somehow seems (conveniently) to elide the immediate (colonial, racial capitalist) history of its emergence. The emergence of the tools of perception is taken as universal or, in the language of a quantum astrophysics that posits four levels of multiverses: multiversal. In brief, the total enclosure by computation of both observer and observed is either reality itself becoming self-aware or tautological, waxing ideological, liquidating as it does historical agency by means of the suddenly a priori stochastic processes of cosmic automation.

Well! If all is total cosmic automation, then no mistakes are possible—and so we may as well take our time-bound chances and wager on fugitive negation in the precise form of a rejection of informatic totalitarianism. Plucking this orchid in the land of computation, we might see that cosmic communication and cosmic community were perhaps created through the forced shedding and structural collapsing of differences. Let us sound the sedimented dead labor inherent in the world-system, its emergent computational armature, and its iconic self-representations. Let us not forget that those machines are made out of embodied participation in capitalist digitization, no matter how disappeared those bodies may now seem. Marx wrote, "Consciousness is . . . from the very beginning a social product and remains so for as long as men exist at all" (1978: 178). The inescapable sociality and historicity of knowledge—in short, its *political* ontology—follows from this, at least so long as humans "exist at all."

The notion of a computational cosmos, though not universally or even widely consented to by scientific consciousness, suggests that we respire in an aporiatic space, in the null set (itself a sign) found precisely at the intersection of a conclusion reached by Gödel in mathematics (Hofstadter 1979)—that there is no sufficiently powerful logical system that is internally closed such that logical statements cannot be formulated that can neither be proved nor disproved—and a second conclusion reached by Maturana and Varela (1992), and also Niklas Luhmann (1989): that a system's self-knowing, its autopoiesis, knows no outside; it can know only in its own terms and thus knows only itself. In Gödel's view, systems are ineluctably open, there can be no closure, complete self-knowledge is impossible and thus there is always an outside or a beyond; while in the latter group's view, our philosophy, our politics, and apparently our fate is wedded to a system that can know no outside since it may only render an outside in its own terms—unless, or perhaps, even if or even as that encounter is catastrophic.

Let us observe the following: 1) there must be an outside or a beyond (Gödel); 2) we cannot know it (Maturana and Varela); 3) and yet. . . . In short, we don't know ourselves and all we know is ourselves. One way out of this aporia is to say that we cannot know the outside and remain what we are. Enter history, enter emergence: multiversal cosmic knowledge, circa 2017, despite its sublime simulation, turns out to be pretty local. If we embrace the two admittedly humbling insights regarding epistemic limits—on the one hand, that even at the limits of computationally informed knowledge (our autopoiesis) all we can know is ourselves, and on the other hand Gödel's insight that any "ourselves" whatsoever that is identified with what we can know is systemically excluded from being all—then it is axiomatic that *nothing* (in all existential valences of that term) fully escapes computation (for us). Nothing is excluded from what we can know except that which is beyond the horizon of our knowledge, which for us is precisely nothing. This is tantamount to saying that rational epistemology is no longer fully separable from the history of computing—at least for any of us who are, willingly or not, participant in contemporary abstraction. I am going to skip what could be a rather lengthy digression about "fugitive nothing" as precisely that bivalent point of inflection that escapes the computational models of consciousness and the cosmos, and instead I just offer its conclusion as the next step in my discussion: We may think we think—algorithmically, computationally, autonomously, or howsoever—but the historically materialized digital infrastructure of the *socius* thinks in and through us as well. History, the unthought and unthinkable externality of computation is nonetheless its necessary supplement. The impossible, the fugitive, the socially dead, the colonially or informatically erased, the land haunts the reigning simulation of life and of being. Or, as Marx put it, "The real subject remains outside the mind and independent of it—that is to say, so long as the mind adopts a purely speculative, purely theoretical attitude. Hence the subject, society, must always be envisaged as the premises of conception even when the theoretical method is employed" (1986: 38–39).[6]

This too is a theory of the unconscious. The "subject, society," in Marx's terms, is present even in its purported absence—it is inextricable from and indeed overdetermines theory and, thus, thought: in other words, language, narrative, textuality, ideology, digitality, and cosmic consciousness. This absent structure informs Louis Althusser's (1971) Lacanian-Marxist analysis of ideology (and of "the ideology of no ideology" as the ideological moment par excellence: an analogous way of saying "reality" is simulation) as well as his beguiling (because at once necessary and self-negating) possibility of a subjectless scientific discourse. This nonnarrative, unsymbolizable absent structure—

akin to the Lacanian "Real"—also informs Fredric Jameson's (1981) concept of the political unconscious as the black-boxed formal processor of said absent structure, indicated in his work by the term *History* with a capital "H." We will take up Althusser and Jameson in due time. For now, however, for the purposes of our mediological investigation into the *apparatus* of computation, it is important to pursue the thought that precisely this functional overdetermination, which already informed Marx's analysis of the historicity of the senses in the 1844 manuscripts, extends into the development of the senses and the psyche. As Jameson put it in *The Political Unconscious* forty years ago: "That the structure of the psyche is historical and has a history, is . . . as difficult for us to grasp as that the senses are not themselves natural organs but rather the result of a long process of differentiation even within human history"(1981: 62). Visual and computational media as the prosthetic and *cybernetic* extension of the senses have not yet escaped this paradigmatic difficulty.

The evidence for the accuracy of Jameson's claim, built from Marx's notion that "the forming of the five senses is a labor of the entire history of the world down to the present" (1978: 89) has been increasing. There is a host of work on the inseparability of technics and the so-called human (from Marcel Mauss to Gilbert Simondon, Deleuze and Guattari, Donna Haraway, and Bernard Stiegler) that increasingly makes it possible to understand and even believe that the human, along with consciousness, the psyche, the senses and, consequently, the unconscious are historical formations. My own essay "The Unconscious of the Unconscious" from *The Cinematic Mode of Production* traces Lacan's use of *montage, the cut, the gap, objet a*, photography and other optical tropes and argues (a bit too insistently perhaps) that the unconscious of the unconscious is cinema and that a scrambling of linguistic functions by the intensifying instrumental circulation of ambient images (images that I now understand as derivatives of a larger calculus) instantiates the presumably organic but actually equally technical cinematic black box known as the unconscious.[7] In this account psychoanalysis is the institutionalization of a managerial technique for emergent linguistic dysfunction (think literary modernism) precipitated by the onslaught of the visible. The inevitable failure of psychoanalysis—inevitable for all the reasons that Fanon recognized in Algeria—leads to the generalization of psychopathology everywhere evident today. Saying that formal computation and discrete state machines were developed to process all that insanity for the benefit of racial capitalism is perhaps crude, but right in the main, particularly as it suggests that decolonial resistance and the general antagonism drove computational innovation.

The early-twentieth-century rise of psychotherapy, and the collateral rise of the antipsychotherapy known as advertising, indicates linguistic responses to the rise of technical images and moreover their calculus. More recently, and in a way that suggests that the computational aspects of the unconscious surfaced here by historical materialist critique are not as distant from the Lacanian Real and the Unconscious, as one might think, Lydia Liu's *The Freudian Robot* (2010) shows convincingly that Lacan modeled the theory of the unconscious from information theory and cybernetic theory. Liu understands that Lacan's emphasis on the importance of structure and the compulsion to repeat is explicitly addressed to "the exigencies of chance, randomness, and stochastic processes in general" (2010: 176). She combs Lacan's writings for evidence that they are informed by information theory and provides us with some smoking guns including the following:

> By itself, the play of the symbol represents and organizes, independently of the peculiarities of its human support, this something which is called the subject. The human subject doesn't foment this game, he takes his place in it, and plays the role of the little pluses and minuses in it. He himself is an element in the chain which, as soon as it is unwound, organizes itself in accordance with laws. Hence the subject is always on several levels, caught up in the crisscrossing of networks. (quoted in Liu 2010: 176)

Liu argues that "the crisscrossing of networks" alludes not so much to linguistic networks but to communication networks, and precisely references the information theory that Lacan read, particularly that of George Gilbaud, the author of *What Is Cybernetics?* She writes, "For Lacan, 'the primordial couple of plus and minus' or the game of even and odd should precede linguistic considerations and is what enables the symbolic order" (179).

"You can play heads or tails by yourself," writes Lacan, "but from the point of view of speech, you aren't playing by yourself—there is already the articulation of three signs comprising a win or a loss and this articulation prefigures the very meaning of the result. In other words, if there is no question, there is no game, if there is no structure, there is no question. The question is constituted, organized by the structure" (quoted in Liu 2010: 179). Liu comments, "This notion of symbolic structure, consistent with game theory, [has] important bearings on Lacan's paradoxically non-linguistic view of language and the symbolic order" (179).[8]

Let us not overly distract ourselves here with the question of whether or not game theory and statistical analysis represent discovery or invention.

Heisenberg, Schrödinger, and information theory formalized the statistical basis that one way or another became a global (if not also multiversal) episteme. Von Neumann and Morgenstern's game theory informed the politics of both nuclear detente and the economies of decision making under conditions of uncertainty. Norbert Wiener, another father, this time of cybernetics, defined statistics as "the science of distribution" (1989: 8). We should pause here to reflect again that—given that cybernetic research in the West was driven by military and, later, industrial applications, that is, applications deemed essential for the development of capitalism and the capitalist way of life—such a statement about the essence of statistics calls for a properly dialectical analysis. Distribution is inseparable from production under capitalism, and statistics is the science of this distribution—which indeed is the superset? Indeed, we would want to make such a question resonate with the analysis of logistics recently undertaken by Harney and Moten (2013) and, following them, link the analysis of instrumental distribution to the Middle Passage as the signal early modern consequence of the convergence of rationalization and containerization—precisely the "science" of distribution worked out in the French slave ship *Adelaide* or the British ship *Brookes* as they averaged the size and cost of bodies (see also Browne 2015: 43–50) and echoed in Gilmore's (2007) classic definition of racism. For the moment, we underscore the historicity of the "science of distribution" and thus its historical emergence as a sociosymbolic system of organization and control—*an elaboration of the processes of exchange.* Keeping this emergence clearly in mind helps us to understand that mathematical models that are elaborations of exchange quite literally inform the articulation of "History" and the unconscious—not only homologously as paradigms in intellectual history but materially, as ways of organizing social production in all domains. Whether logistical, optical, or informatic, the technics of mathematical concepts, which is to say programs, orchestrate meaning and literally constitute the unconscious. Note that the "literal" constitution of the unconscious by mathematics, finance, and computation is not a metaphor. I refer explicitly to the logistics of literacy and modalities of inscription that inform the semiotic universe of data visualization.

———————————

Perhaps more elusive even than this historicity of the unconscious—grasped in terms of a digitally encoded matrix of materiality and epistemology that constitutes the unthought of subjective emergence—may be that the notion that the "subject, society," extends into our machines. Vilém Flusser, in *Towards a Philosophy of Photography*, tells us,

> Apparatuses were invented to simulate specific thought processes. Only now (following the invention of the computer), and as it were in hindsight, it is becoming clear what kind of thought processes we are dealing with in the case of all apparatuses. That is: thinking expressed in numbers. All apparatuses (not just computers) are calculating machines and in this sense "artificial intelligences," the camera included, even if their inventors were not able to account for this. In all apparatuses (including the camera) thinking in numbers overrides linear, historical thinking. (2000: 31)

This process of thinking in numbers, and indeed the generalized conversion of multiple forms of thought and practice to an increasingly unified systems language of numeric processing, by apparatuses, digital computers, and capital markets, requires further investigation. And now that the edifice of computation—the fixed capital dedicated to computation that either recognizes itself as such or may be recognized as such—has achieved a consolidated sedimentation of human labor at least equivalent to that required to build a large nation (a superpower) from the ground up, we are in a position to ask in what way has capital-logic and the logic of private property—which, as Marx points out, is not the cause but the effect of alienated (wage- and otherwise quantified) labor—structured computational paradigms? In what way has that "subject, society," unconsciously structured not just thought but machine thought? Thinking, expressed in numbers, materialized first by means of commodities and then in apparatuses capable of automating this thought. Is computation what we've been up to all along without knowing it? Is AI the unconscious of computational racial capital, or are we the unconscious of that subject, society operationalized by AI? A reading of Flusser might suggest as much through his notion that 1) the camera is a black box that is a program; and that 2) the photograph or technical image produces a "magical" relation to the world in as much as people understand the photograph as a window rather than as information organized by concepts. This amounts to the technical image itself, along with its disruption of linear time and its dissolution of logical thought, functioning as a program for the bios, and it suggests that the world has long been unconsciously organized by computation vis-à-vis the camera. As Flusser has it, cameras have organized society in a feedback loop that works toward the perfection of cameras. If the computational processes inherent in photography are themselves an extension of capital logic's universal digitization (an argument I made in *The Cinematic Mode of Production* and extended in *The Message Is Murder*), then that calculus has been doing its work in the visual reorganization of everyday life for almost two centuries.

Put yet another way, thinking—expressed in numbers (the principles of optics and chemistry) and materialized in machines—automates thought (thinking expressed in numbers) as program. The program of, say, the camera, functions as a historically produced version of what Katherine Hayles has recently called "nonconscious cognition" (2016). Though locally perhaps no more self-aware than the sediment-sorting process of a riverbed (another of Hayles's computational examples), the camera nonetheless affects purportedly conscious beings from the domain known as the unconscious, as, to give but one shining example, feminist film theory clearly shows. We could then say that the function of the camera's program organizes the psychodynamics of the image-maker and spectator alike in a way that at once structures film form through market feedback, gratifies the (white-identified) male ego, and normalizes the violence of heteropatriarchy—and does so at a profit. Now that so much human time has gone into developing cameras, computer hardware, and programming, such that hardware and programming are inextricable from the day-to-day and indeed nanosecond-to-nanosecond organization of life on planet Earth (and not only in the form of cameras), we can ask, very pointedly, which aspects of computer function, from any to all, can be said to be conditioned not only by sexual difference but, more generally still, by structural inequality and the logistics of white supremacist masculinity as the paradigmatic expression of subjectivity in capitalism? In such a computational extension of the repressive hypothesis, subjugated bodies express their desires for liberation in ways that extend their subjugation. Which computational functions perpetuate and enforce historically worked-up, highly ramified social differences? Structural and now infrastructural inequalities encode social injustices—what could be thought of, and indeed *is*, algorithmic racism, sexism, and homophobia, as well as the programmatically unequal access to many things that sustain life. They legitimize murder (both long and short forms, executed by, e.g., settler colonialism, police brutality, carceral societies, and drone signature strikes) and catastrophes both unnatural (toxic mine-tailings, coltan wars) and purportedly natural (hurricanes, droughts, famines, ambient environmental toxicity). The urgency of such questions, resulting from the near automation of geopolitical emergence along with a vast conscription of value productive agents, is only exacerbated as we recognize that we are obliged to rent or otherwise pay tribute (in the form of attention, subscription, student debt) to the rentier capitalists of the infrastructure of the algorithm in order to access portions of the general intellect from its proprietors whenever we want to participate in thinking—a thinking that is subservient to the photographic universe and hence to computation and hence (pace Flusser) to racial capital.

For it must never be assumed that technology (even the abstract machine) is value-neutral, that it merely exists in some disinterested ideal place and is then utilized either for good or for ill by free men (it *would* be "men" in such a discourse). Instead, the machine, as in Ariella Azoulay's understanding of photography, has a political ontology: it is a social relation, and an ongoing one, whose meaning is, as Azoulay says of the photograph, never at an end (2012: 25). Now that representation has been subsumed by machines, has become machinic (overcoded as Deleuze and Guattari would say), everything that appears, appears in and through the machine, as a machine. For the present (and as Plato already recognized by putting it at the center of the *Republic*), even the sun is political. Going back to the opening epigraph, the cosmos is now merely a collection of billions of suns—an infinite politics.

But really, this political ontology of knowledge, machines, consciousness, and praxis should be obvious. How could technology, which of course includes the technologies of knowledge, be anything other than social and historical, the product of social relations? How could technologies be other than the accumulation, objectification, and sedimentation of practices and subjectivities that are themselves a historical product? The historicity of knowledge and perception seems inescapable, if not fully intelligible, particularly now, when it is increasingly clear that it is the programmatic automation of thought itself that has been embedded in our apparatuses. The programming and overdetermination of "choice" and of options—by a rationality that was itself embedded in the interested circumstances of life and continuously "learns" vis-à-vis the feedback life provides—has become ubiquitous and indeed inexorable. To universalize contemporary subjectivity by erasing its conditions of possibility is to naturalize history; it is therefore to depoliticize it and therefore to recapitulate the violence endemic to its formation in the present. For the record, if anyone is keeping one, I dismiss "object-oriented ontology" and its desperate effort to elide its own white, male subjectivity thusly: there are no ontological objects, at least not for them—there are only instrumental epistemic horizons.

Nor, we must almost regretfully add, can we abide by the subject-oriented ontology of the New Hegelians. I will not name names. A locus of total comprehension neither contains nor exhausts all perspective that it would include, and nothing but material governance and the repressive fantasy it enables secures its preeminence. Even, said Adorno, "if the Hegelian synthesis did work out, it would only be the *wrong* one" (Adorno, quoted in Sohn-Rethel 1978: 16).

The short answer to the question regarding digital universality, then, is that technology (and thus perception, thought, and knowledge) can only be separated from the social and historical—that is, from racial capitalism—by eliminating both the social and historical (society and history) *through its own operations*. It is not "technology" that takes the bios as standing reserve; it is capital.

While computers—if they were taken, along with a few of their most dedicated biotic avatars, as a separate representative constituency and then pressed for an opinion—might once have agreed with Margaret Thatcher's view that "there is no such thing as society," one would be hard pressed to claim that this postsociological (and post-Birmingham) "discovery" is a neutral result. Thatcher's observation that "the problem with socialism is that you eventually run out of other people's money"—while admittedly pithy (if condescending, classist, and deadly)—subordinates social needs to the protocols of existing property relations and their financial calculus at the ontological level. As if to say: with respect to the masses, money always is and always will be other people's money! In a naturalizing gesture, she smugly valorizes the status quo imposed by sovereign money ("you are ontologically poor") by positing capitalism as an untranscendable horizon, since within it the social product is by definition always already "other people's money." But neoliberalism has required some revisioning of late (which is a polite way of saying that fascism has needed some updating): the newish but by now firmly-established term *social media* tells us something more about the parasitic relation that the cold calculus this mathematical universe of numbers has to the bios. To preserve global digital apartheid requires *social* media, the process(ing) of society itself cybernetically interfaced with the logistics of racial-capitalist computation. This relation—a relation of production—is a means of digital expropriation presumably aimed to profitably exploit an equally significant global aspiration toward planetary communicativity and democratization. It has become the preeminent engine of capitalist growth. Society, at first seemingly negated by computation and capitalism, is then directly posited as a source of wealth for what is now *explicitly* computational capital and *actually* computational racial capital. The *attention economy, immaterial labor, neuropower, semiocapitalism*: all of these terms, despite their differences, mean in effect that society, as a deterritorialized factory and space of distributed production, is no longer disappeared as an economic object; it is now merely disappeared as a beneficiary of the dominant economy that is parasitical on its metabolism. The social revolution in planetary communicativity, a revolution that emerges precisely as a response to the foreclosure of society by representation, is defeated by being farmed and harvested by computational capitalism.

Oh Westworld! For biologists it has become au courant, when speaking of humans, to speak also of the second genome—one must consider not just the twenty-six chromosomes of the human genome that replicate what was thought of as the human being as an autonomous life-form but also the genetic information and epigenetic functionality of all the symbiotic bacteria and other vectors without which there are no humans. Pursuant to this thought, we might detect the rise of and ascribe to ourselves a third genome: information. No good scientist today believes that human beings are free-standing forms, even if few (or really, none) make the critique of humanity or even individuality through a framework that understands these categories as historically emergent interfaces of capitalist exchange. Most scientists just don't think capitalism is that big a deal and do not believe that it manages all their accounts. However, to avoid naturalizing the laws of capitalism as simply an expression of the higher (Hegelian) laws of energetics and informatics (in which, e.g., adenosine triphosphate [ATP] can be thought to function as "capital" and AI emerges as world spirit), this sense of "our" embeddedness in the ecosystem of the bios must be extended to that of the materiality of our historical societies. In particular it must be extended to their systems of mediation, systems of representational practices, archivization, knowledge formation, and communication—including the operations of textuality, visuality, data visualization, and money—which, with convergence today, means precisely: computation.

The collapse of the ecosystemic diversity of cultures, languages, histories, and life-forms into a single digital substrate presupposes countless acts of violence—a thoroughgoing reformatting of ontologies by content-indifferent media. As we shall show, this violence of abstraction not only makes what was formerly differentiable like, and therefore exchangeable, but the imposition of a content-indifferent calculus on the cosmos also makes each act of imposition into a financial derivative—a position on the future. In their cancellation and preservation as web pages, for example, ancient Sumer, the Harlem Renaissance, or Shintoism all become pathways for the extraction and aggregation of attention. The recognition of human faces becomes but another product sold to security states along with arms, drones and walls. If we want to understand the emergence of computation (and of the Anthropocene), we must attend to the transformations and disappearances of life-forms—of forms of life in the largest sense. And we must do so despite the fact that the sedimentation of the history of computation would neutralize certain aspects (the extra-economic, the noncomputable) of human aspiration and of "humanity"—including, ultimately, even the referent of that latter sign—by means of law, culture, border walls, drones, derivatives, what have you. What was resonant in the human and what was abominable have been flattened into a single appliqué. Convergence, consolidation, homogenization—the installation of a single operating system depends upon the exclusion and foreclosure of a near infinity of possible worlds. In the car, even the rock and roll sounds corporate when mixed by Sirius.

The biosynthetic process of computation and human being gives rise to post-humanism only to reveal that there were never any humans here in the first place: we have never been human—and we know this now. The human too was a technical effect, and "humanity," as a protracted example of instrumental *méconnaissance*—as a problem of what could be called the humanizing-machine or, better perhaps, the human-machine of the Renaissance—is on the wane. Naming the human-machine is of course a way of talking about the conquest, about colonialism, slavery, imperialism, and the racializing, sex and gender norm–enforcing regimes of the last five hundred years of capitalism that created the ideological legitimation of the unprecedented violence in the so-called humanistic values it spat out. Aimé Césaire (1972) said it very clearly when he posed the scathing question in *Discourse on Colonialism*: "Civilization *and* Colonization?" What I am calling "the human-machine" (a very specific kind of cyborg) names precisely the mechanics of a humanism that at once resulted from and were deployed to do the work of humanizing planet Earth for the quantitative accountings of capital while at the same time divesting a large part of the planetary population of any claims to the human (Wynter 2003). Following David Golumbia, in *The Cultural Logic of Computation* (2009), we might look to Hobbes, automata, and the component parts of the Leviathan for "human" emergence as an explicit formation of capital. For so many, humanism was in effect more than just another name for violence, oppression, rape, enslavement, and genocide—it was precisely a *means* to violence. "Humanity" as symptom of The Invisible Hand, AI's first avatar. Thus stated, it is possible to see the end of humanism not as a tragedy but as a result of centuries of decolonization struggles, a kind of triumph. The colonized have outlasted the humans. But unfortunately so have the capitalists: against the general antagonism and in direct response to a desire for global self-knowledge and autopoietic communication, a more capacious hostile intelligence has emerged and the terrain of struggle (its terms and symbols) has shifted.

This posthuman turn is yet another place where recalling the dialectic is particularly useful. Enlightenment humanism was a platform for the linear time of industrialization and the French revolution with "the human" as an operating system, a meta-ISA (Ideological State Apparatus) emerging in historical movement, one that developed a set of ontological claims that functioned in accord with the early period of capitalist digitality (DCI) that was commodification, colonialism, and industrialization. The period was characterized by the institutionalization of relative equality for some—Cedric Robinson (1983) does not hesitate to point out that the precondition of the French Revolution was colonial slavery—along with institutions of privacy and property. Not only were humanism's achievements and horrors inseparable from the imposition of logics of numerical equivalence, they were powered by the labor of the peoples of Earth, by the labor-power of disparate peoples, imported as sugar and spices, stolen as slaves, music, and art, owned as objective wealth in the form of lands, armies, edifices, and capital, and owned again as subjective wealth in the form of cultural refinement, aesthetic sensibility, and bourgeois interiority—in short, colonial labor, enclosed by accountants and shaped by the whip, was expatriated as profit and collapsed into price, while industrial labor, also expropriated, was itself sustained by these endeavors, including the cheap calories produced by the cheaper labor of the sugar plantations. The accumulation of the wealth of the world and of self-possession for some in the form of nominal equality, as representative of one's commodities and as citizen, was organized and legitimated by humanism, even as those worlded otherwise by the growth of this power of wealth struggled passionately, desultorily, existentially, partially, and at times absolutely against its oppressive powers of objectification and quantification. Humanism was colonial software, and the colonized were its outsourced providers—the first content providers—conscripted to support the platform of so-called universal man. This platform humanism is not so much a metaphor; rather, it is the tendency that is unveiled by the present platform posthumanism of computational racial capital. If "the anatomy of man is the key to the anatomy of the ape," as Marx so eloquently put the telos of man, we may ask, "Is the anatomy of computation the key to the anatomy of 'man'?"[9]

So the end of humanism, which in a narrow (white, Euro-American, technocratic) view seems to arrive as a result of the rise of cybertechnologies, must also be seen as having been long willed and indeed brought about by the decolonizing struggles against humanism's self-contradictory and, from the point of view of its own self-proclaimed values, specious organizational principles. Making this claim is consistent with Frantz Fanon's insight that people of the third world "literally" built the European metropoles. Today's disappearance of the human might mean, for the colonizers who invested so heavily in their humanisms, that Dr. Moreau's vivisectioned cyberchickens—all the mutants and aliens created by the brutal science of colonialism—are coming home to roost. Fatally, it seems, since Global North immigration policy, internment centers, border walls, police forces, camps, and military appropriations give the lie to any remaining pretense to Western humanism. It might also be gleaned that the revolution against the would-be humans has also been fostered by the machines. Caliban-like, they too have risen to curse old Prospero. First reduced to the Wizard of Oz on the gold standard, and now reduced to a naked, Tweeting, orange clown on the digital finance standard, in the digital revolution the human figure has lost its pizzazz. However, the jokered-POTUSian defeat of the so-called humans by cyborgs and aliens is double-edged: as if the digital revolution against humanism has won the battle but lost the war. The dialectic of posthuman abundance on the one hand and the posthuman abundance of dispossession on the other has no truck with humanity, but the violence conducted at this former humanity's behest is unabated. Today's mainstream futurologists, when they look out their windows, mostly see "the singularity" and apocalypse. Among academics, only critics of the "human" and the "posthuman" periodization who have commitments to antiracist world-making have clearly understood that the dominant discourse of the posthuman is not the end of the white liberal human subject but, when left in the hands of those liberals who are not committed to an antiracist and decolonial project, becomes precisely a means for its perpetuation, a way of extending the unmarked, transcendental, sovereign subject (of Hobbes, Descartes, C. B. Macpherson)—effectively, the white male sovereign who was *in possession* of a body rather than forced *to be a body* (Hayles 1999). Sovereignty itself must change (in order, as Giuseppe di Lampedusa taught us, to remain the same), and "digital culture" (DC2) has been the expropriation of a revolutionary transformation.

If one sees production and innovation on the side of labor, then capital's need to contain labor's increasing self-organization and self-communication has driven capital into a position where the human has become an impediment to its continued expansion. Even human rights, though oftentimes along with "democracy," serviceable as a means to further expropriation, are today, with the end of neoliberalism, in the way. Let's say that it is global labor that is shaking off the yoke of the human from without, as much as it the digital machines built from that self-same labor that are devouring it from within. The dialectic of computational racial capital devours the human as a way of revolutionizing the productive forces. The global explosion in computational communications, which introduces social media cybernetics and vitiates humanism, is simultaneously democratizing and a democratization of the means of expropriation. Weapons-makers, states, and banks, along with Hollywood and student debt, invoke the human only as a skeuomorph—an allusion to an old interface technology that helps facilitate adoption of the new. The human being that was previously a useful double standard has become a barrier to production; it is no longer a sustainable form. The human, and those (human and otherwise) falling under the paradigm's dominion, must be stripped, cut, bundled, and reconfigured in derivative forms. All hail the dividual. A cheer for the politics of affect! Again, female and racialized bodies and subjects have long endured this now-universal fragmentation and forced recomposition. "Dividuality" which describes a precapitalist, precolonial interface with the social that appears again in the posthuman, postsubjective moment as a name for discontinuous points of the subjective.

Thus we are obliged to point out that this, the current dissolution of the human into the infrastructure of the world-system, is double-edged, neither fully positive nor fully negative—the result of the dialectics of struggles for and against liberation distributed around the planet. As a sign of the times, posthumanism may be, as has been remarked about capitalism itself, among those simultaneously best and worst things to ever happen in history. We see on the one hand the disappearance of presumably ontological protections and quasi-religious legitimating statuses for some (including the promise of rights never granted to most) and, on the other, the preservation of a modality of dehumanization and exclusion that legitimated and normalized white supremacist patriarchy by allowing its values to masquerade as technological (and cultural) universals. However, it is difficult to maintain optimism of the will when we see that that which is coming, that which is already upon us, may also be as bad or worse—in absolute numbers, *is already* worse—for unprecedented billions of concrete individuals. Frankly, in a world where the cognitive-linguistic functions of the species have themselves been captured by the ambient capitalist computation of social media and indeed of capitalized computational social relations, of what use is a theory of dispossession to the dispossessed?

For those of us who may consider ourselves thinkers, it is our burden—in a real sense, our debt, living and ancestral—to make theory relevant to those who haunt it. Anything less is betrayal. It must also be relevant to those present, and those to come. The emergence of the universal value-form (as money, the general form of wealth), with its human face (as white maleness, the general form of humanity), clearly inveighs against the possibility of extrinsic valuation since the very notion of universal valuation is posited from within this economy. What Cedric Robinson shows in his extraordinary *Black Marxism* (1983) is that capitalism itself has become a white mythology. The history of racialization and capitalization are now inseparable, and therefore the treatment of capital as a pure abstraction deracinates its origins and functions—its *materiality*. This deracination pertains both to its conditions of possibility as well as its operations in and by means of racialization—pointedly including those conditions of possibility of the internal critique of capitalism that, in ignoring racism, has nonetheless been the basis of much of the Marxist tradition. Both capitalism and its would-be negation as Marxism have proceeded through disavowals of racialization. The quantitative exchange of equivalents, circulating as exchange-values without qualities, are the real abstractions that for Sohn-Rethel give rise to (Western) philosophy, science, and white liberal humanism wedded to the notion of the objective. Therefore, when it comes to exchange-values, there is no degree zero, only perhaps nodal points of bounded equilibrium: a "degree zero" within the framework of a particular polity and its practices of recognition. To claim neutrality for an early digital machine—say, a national monetary system—that is, to argue that money as a medium is value-neutral because it embodies what has (in many respects correctly, but in a qualified way) been termed "the universal value-form," would be to miss the entire system of leveraged exploitation—of violence—that sustains any money system in capital. In an isolated instance, money as the product of capital might be used for good (building shelters for the homeless) or for ill (purchasing Caterpillar bulldozers) or both (building shelters for the homeless in Seattle using Caterpillar machines), but not to see that the capitalist system sustains itself through militarized and policed expropriation and large-scale, long-term universal degradation is to engage in mere delusional utopianism and self-interested (might one even say psychotic?) nay-saying. It is to imagine (disingenuously) community through the instrumental(ized) shedding of differences and "the pathetic pretense that these differences do not exist" (Lorde 2007: 112).

Will the apologists for science and liberalism calmly bear witness to the sacrifice of billions of human beings so that the invisible hand may placidly unfurl its abstractions in Kubrickian sublimity? The cold long shot, when bone became starship, in *2001* (Kubrick 1968) of the species life span as an instance of a cosmic program is not so distant from the endemic violence of postmodern—and indeed posthuman—fascism he depicted in *A Clockwork Orange* (Kubrick 1971). One could argue that *2001* rendered the cosmology of early posthuman fascism while *A Clockwork Orange* portrayed its psychology. Both films explored the aesthetics of programming. What we beheld in these two films was the annihilation of agency (at the level of the species and of the individual)—and it was eerily seductive: Benjamin's (1969) self-destruction as an aesthetic pleasure of the highest order taken to cosmic proportions and raised to the level of art.

So what of the remainders of those who may remain? If for Kubrick the holocaust echoes not only through *Dr. Strangelove* (1964) and its depiction of nuclear holocaust, but throughout the cosmology and psychology of fascism, what of all the other holocausts? Here, in the face of the annihilation of re-maindered life—to borrow a powerfully dialectical term from Neferti Tadiar (2016)—by various iterations of techné, we pose the following questions: How are computers and digital computing, as universals, themselves iterations of and management tools for long-standing historical inequality, violence, and murder? And what are the entry points for an understanding of a computa-tion society in which our currently prehistoric (in Marx's sense of the term) conditions of computation might be assessed and overcome? This question of technical overdetermination is not a matter of a Kittler-style antihuman-ism in which "media determine our situation," nor is it a matter of the post-Kittlerian, seemingly user-friendly repurposing of dialectical materialism which, in the beer-drinking tradition of "good-German" idealism, offers us the poorly historicized neoliberal idea of "cultural techniques" (Cornelia Vismann (2013: 83–93) and Bernhard Siegert (2013: 48–65). This latter is a conveniently deracinated way of conceptualizing the distributed agency of everything tech-nohuman without having to register the abiding fundamental antagonisms, the life-and-death struggle, in anything. It leads to decidedly conservative scholarship because it fails to recognize that the real abstractions it identifies as cultural techniques are endemic to socioeconomic organization and there-fore to social conflict. In contrast, the question I want to pose about comput-ing is one capable of both foregrounding and interrogating violence inherent in abstract machines, assigning responsibility, making changes, and demand-ing reparations. The challenge upon us is to decolonize computing.[10] Has the waning not just of affect (of a certain type) but of history itself brought us into a supposedly posthistorical space? Can we see that what we once called history, and is now no longer, has *really* been prehistory, stages of prehistory? What would it mean to say in earnest, "What's past is prologue?" If the human has never been and should never be, if there has been this accumulation of negative entropy first via linear time and then via its networked disruption, then what? Postmodernism, posthumanism, Flusser's posthistorical, and Be-rardi's *After the Future* notwithstanding, can we take the measure of history?

Technohumanist Dehumanization

I would like to conclude this foray into the unthought and the unconscious of computational racial capitalism with a few examples of technohumanist dehumanization, moments that were themselves building blocks of modern computing and finance. In 1889, Herman Hollerith patented the punch card system and the mechanical tabulator that was used in the 1890 censuses in Germany, England, Italy, Russia, Austria, Canada, France, Norway, Puerto Rico, Cuba, and the Philippines. A national census, which normally took eight to ten years, now took a single year. The subsequent invention of the plug-board control panel in 1906 allowed for tabulators to perform multiple sorts in whatever sequence was selected without having to be rebuilt—an early form of programming. Hollerith's Tabulating Machine Company merged with three other companies in 1911 to become the Computing Tabulating Recording Company, which renamed itself IBM in 1924.

While the census opens a rich field of inquiry that includes questions of statistics, computing, and state power that are increasingly relevant today (particularly taking into account the ever-presence of the NSA), for now I only want to extract two points: 1) humans became the fodder for statistical machines; and 2) as Vicente Rafael (2000) has shown regarding the Philippine census and as Edwin Black (2001) has shown with respect to the Holocaust, the development of this technology was inseparable from racialization and genocide.

Rafael shows that, coupled to photographic techniques, the census at once "discerned" and imposed a racializing schema that welded a historical "progress" narrative to ever-whiter waves of colonization in the Philippines, from Malay migration to Spanish colonialism to U.S. imperialism. Racial fantasy meets white mythology meets Manifest Destiny meets world spirit. The census and photography are not only used to tell the story of the progressive whitening of the Philippines; this racist notion of uplift finds its expression in and as these technologies. Their expressive powers are not just evidence but the occasion for the performative self-evidencing of Philippine ascendance toward sovereign nationhood. The census was not just an exercise in early computing; it used the Philippine socius to encode colonial meaning and colonial aspiration on the bodies of Filipinos. For his part, Edwin Black writes:

> Only after Jews were identified—a massive and complex task that Hitler wanted done immediately—could they be targeted for efficient asset confiscation, ghettoization, deportation, enslaved labor, and, ultimately, annihilation. It was a cross-tabulation and organizational challenge so monumental, it called for a computer. Of course, in the 1930s no computer existed.
>
> But IBM's Hollerith punch card technology did exist. Aided by the company's custom-designed and constantly updated Hollerith systems, Hitler was able to automate his persecution of the Jews. Historians have

always been amazed at the speed and accuracy with which the Nazis were able to identify and locate European Jewry. Until now, the pieces of this puzzle have never been fully assembled. The fact is, IBM technology was used to organize nearly everything in Germany and then Nazi Europe, from the identification of the Jews in censuses, registrations, and ancestral tracing programs to the running of railroads and organizing of concentration camp slave labor.

IBM and its German subsidiary custom-designed complex solutions, one by one, anticipating the Reich's needs. They did not merely sell the machines and walk away. Instead, IBM leased these machines for high fees and became the sole source of the billions of punch cards Hitler needed. (Black 2001)

The sorting of populations and individuals—by forms of social difference including "race," ability, and sexual preference (Jews, Roma, homosexuals, people deemed mentally or physically handicapped) for the purposes of sending people who failed to meet Nazi eugenic criteria off to concentration camps to be dispossessed, humiliated, tortured, and killed—means that some aspects of computer technology (here, the search engine) emerged from this particular social necessity of segregation sometimes called Nazism (Black 2001). The Philippine-American War, in which Americans killed between 10 and 16 percent of the population of the Philippines, and the Nazi-administered Holocaust are but two world-historical events that are not just occasions for but part of the meaning of early computational automation. The socius was the substrate. These genocides were the concrete circumstances from which abstract ideas of communication gained form and substance. Humans watched and helped to encode the less-than humans. Computers bear this legacy of imperialism and fascism—it is inscribed in their operating systems.

The mechanisms, as well as the social meaning, of computation were refined in its concrete applications. The process of abstraction hid the violence of abstraction—what it took to make people into numbers—even as it integrated the result with economic and political protocols and directly effected certain behaviors. It is well-known that Claude Shannon's landmark paper, "A Mathematical Theory of Communication" (1948), proposed a general theory of communication that was content-indifferent. This seminal work created a statistical, mathematical model of communication while simultaneously consigning any and all specific content to irrelevance as regards the transmission method itself. Like use-value under the management of the commodity-form, the message became only a supplement to the exchange-value of the code. In

Message I wrote about the fact that some of the statistical information Shannon derived about letter frequency in English used as its ur-text *Jefferson The Virginian* (1948), the first volume of Dumas Malone's monumental six-volume study of Jefferson. This work was famously interrogated by Annette Gordon-Reed in her *Thomas Jefferson and Sally Hemings: An American Controversy* (1998) for its suppression of information regarding Jefferson's relation to slavery (see also Beller 2016a, 2017b). My point here is that the rules for content indifference were themselves derived from a particular content, *as well as a particular form of indifference*, and that the language used as a standard referent was a culturally specific deployment of language. The representative linguistic sample did not represent the whole of language, but language that belongs to a particular mode of sociality and racialized enfranchisement—an "American grammar" (Spillers 1987). Shannon's deprivileging of the referent of the logos as referent, and his attention only to signifiers, was an intensification of the slippage of signifier from signified ("We, the people . . .") already noted in linguistics and functionally operative in the elision of slavery in Jefferson's biography—to say nothing of the same text's elision of slave narrative and African-American speech. Shannon brilliantly and successfully developed a reconceptualization of language as code (sign system) and now as mathematical code (numerical system) that no doubt found another of its logical (and material) conclusions (at least with respect to metaphysics) in poststructuralist theory and deconstruction, with the placing of the referent under erasure. This recession of the real (of being, the subject, and experience—in short, the signified) from codification allowed Shannon's mathematical abstraction of rules for the transmission of any message whatsoever to become the industry standard even as they also meant, quite literally, the dehumanization of communication—its severance from a people's history. A people's history haunts the mathematical theory of communication—another meaning of the computational unconscious.

In a 1987 interview, Shannon was quoted as saying, "I can visualize a time in the future when we will be to robots as dogs are to humans. . . . I'm rooting for the machines!" (1987: 61). If humans are to be the robot's companion species, they (or is it we?), like the dogs who went before us, need a manifesto. The difficulty is that the labor of our "being"—such that it is or was—is encrypted in their machine function. And "we" have never been "one." But we see what readers of Haraway already know: that a companion species manifesto for whatever remains is necessarily a trans-cyborg manifesto.

In the context of the machinic absorption of forms of human being and human exploitation, Tara McPherson (2012) has brilliantly argued that the modularity achieved in the development of UNIX has its analog in racial segregation. Modularity and encapsulation, necessary to the writing of the UNIX code that still underpins contemporary operating systems, were emergent, general sociotechnical forms, what we might call technologies, abstract machines, or real abstractions. "I am not arguing that programmers creating UNIX at Bell Labs and at Berkeley were *consciously* encoding new modes of racism and racial understanding into digital systems," McPherson argues. "The emergence of covert racism and its rhetoric of colorblindness are not so much intentional as systemic. Computation is a primary delivery method of these new systems and it seems at best naïve to imagine that cultural and computational operating systems don't mutually infect one another" (30–31).

This is the computational unconscious at work—the dialectical inscription and reinscription of sociality and machine architecture that then becomes the substrate for the next generation of consciousness, ad infinitum. In an unpublished paper entitled "The Lorem Ipsum Project," Alana Ramjit (2014) examines industry standards for the now-digital imaging of speech and graphic images. These include Kodak's "Shirley cards" for standard skin tone (white), the Harvard Sentences for standard audio (white), the "Indian Head Test Pattern" for standard broadcast image (white fetishism), and "Lenna," an image of Lena Soderberg taken from *Playboy* magazine (white patriarchal unconscious) that has become the reference standard image for the development of graphics processing. Each of these examples testifies to an absorption of the sociohistorical at every step of mediological and computational refinement (Roth 2009).

More recently, as Chris Vitale (2015) brought out in a powerful presentation on machine learning and neural networks given at Pratt Institute in 2015, Facebook's machine has produced "DeepFace," an image of the minimally recognizable human face. However, this ur-human face, purported to be the minimally recognizable form of the human face, unsurprisingly turns out to be a white guy. This is a case in point of the extension of colonial relations into machine function. Given the racialization of poverty in the system of global apartheid (Federici 2012), we have on our hands (or rather, in our machines) a new modality of automated genocide. Fascism and genocide have new mediations and have not just adapted to new media but have merged. Of course, the terms and names of genocidal regimes change, but the consequences persist. Just yesterday it was called neoliberal democracy. Today it's called the end of neoliberalism. The current worldwide crisis in migration is one of the symptoms of the genocidal tendencies of the most recent coalescence of the "practically" automated logistics of race, nation, and class. Today racism is at once a symptom of the computational unconscious, an operation of nonconscious cognition, and still just the garden variety self-serving murderous willed stupidity that is the legacy of slavery, settler colonialism, and colonialism.

Thus we may observe that the statistical methods utilized by IBM to find Jews, Gypsies, and queers in the shtetl are operative in Wiener's antiaircraft cybernetics as well as in Israel's Iron Dome missile defense system. The prevailing view, even if it is not one of pure mathematical abstraction, in which computational process has its essence without reference to any concrete whatever, can be found in what follows. As an article entitled "Traces of Israel's Iron Dome Can Be Found in Tech Startups" for *Bloomberg News* almost giddily reports: "The Israeli-engineered Iron Dome is a complex tapestry of machinery, software and computer algorithms capable of intercepting and destroying rockets midair. An offshoot of the missile-defense technology can also be used to sell you furniture" (Coppola 2014).[11]

Not only, it seems, is war good computer business, it's good for computerized business. It is ironic that the Iron Dome is likened to a tapestry and now used to sell textiles—almost as if it were haunted by Lisa Nakamura's (2014) recent findings regarding the (forgotten) role played by Navajo women weavers in the making of early transistors for Fairchild, the eerily named company of Silicon Valley legend and founding father—as well as infamous eugenicist—William Shockley. The article goes on to confess that the latest consumer spin-offs, which facilitate the real-time imaging of couches in your living room and drive sales on the domestic front, exist thanks to the U.S. financial support for Zionism and its militarized settler colonialism in Palestine. "We have American-backed apartheid and genocide to thank for being able to visualize a green moderne couch in our very own living room before we click 'Buy now.'" (Okay, this is not really a quotation, but it expresses the essence of the article.)

Census, statistics, informatics, cryptography, war machines, industry standards, markets—all are management techniques for the organization of otherwise unruly humans, subhumans, posthumans, and nonhumans by capitalist society. The ethos of content indifference, along with the encryption of social difference as both mode and means of systemic functionality, is sustainable only so long as derivative human beings are themselves rendered as content providers, body and soul. But it is not only tech spin-offs from the racist war dividends that we should be tracking. Wendy Hui Kyong Chun (2004) has shown in utterly convincing ways that the gendered history of the development of computer programming at ENIAC (Electronic Numerical Integrator and Computer), in which male mathematicians instructed female "computers" to physically make the electronic connections (and remove any bugs), echoes into the present experiences of sovereignty enjoyed by users who have, in many respects, become programmers (even if most of us have little or no idea how programming works, or even that we are programming).

Chun notes that "during World War II almost all computers were young women with some background in mathematics. Not only were women available for work then, they were also considered to be better, more conscientious computers, presumably because they were better at repetitive, clerical tasks"(2004: 33). One could say that programming became programming and software became software when commands shifted from commanding a "girl" to commanding a machine. Clearly this puts the gender not just of the machine but of the commander in question.

Chun suggests that the augmentation of our power through the command-control functions of computation is a result of what she calls the "Yes sir" of the feminized operator—that is, of servile labor. Indeed, in the ENIAC and other early machines, the execution of the operator's order was to be carried out by the "wren" or the "slave." For the desensitized, this information may seem incidental, a mere development or advance beyond the *instrumentum vocale* (the *speaking tool*, i.e., the Roman term for *slave*) in which even the communicative capacities of the slave are totally subordinated to the master. Here we pose the larger question: What are the implications for this gendered and racialized form of power exercised in the interface? What is its relation to gender oppression, to slavery? Is this mode of command-control over bodies and extended to the machine a universal form of empowerment, one to which all (posthuman) bodies might aspire, or is it a mode of subjectification built in the footprint of domination in such a way that it replicates the beliefs, practices, and consequences of "prior" orders of whiteness and masculinity—that is, of male and female and of master and slave—in unconscious but nonetheless murderous ways?[12] The question is complex. Recall here that when speaking of automated "mechanical labor," Wiener said that "any labor that accepts the conditions of competition with slave labor accepts the conditions of slave labor, and is essentially slave labor (1961: 26–27). Is the computer the realization of the power of a transcendental subject? Or of the subject whose transcendence was built upon and is still built upon a historically developed version of racial masculinity based upon slavery and gender violence that was then automated? The computational unconscious also implicates the unconscious processes at the interface.

Andrew Norman Wilson's scandalizing film *Workers Leaving the Googleplex* (2011), the making of which got him fired from Google, depicts poor workers, mostly people of color, leaving Google's Mountain View campus during off-hours. These workers are the book scanners, and they shared neither the spaces nor the perks of white-collar workers, had different parking lots and entrances, and drove a different class of vehicles. They were the repressed and indeed the unconscious of the digital scan. Wilson has also curated and developed a set of images that show the condom-clad fingers (black, brown, female) of workers next to partially scanned book pages. He considers these mis-scans a new form of documentary evidence. While digitization and computation may seem to have transcended certain humanistic questions, it is imperative that we understand that its posthumanism is also radically untranscendent, grounded as it is on the living legacies of oppression and, in the last instance, on the radical dispossession of billions. These billions are disappeared, literally utilized as a surface of inscription for everyday transmissions. The dispossessed are in fact the disavowed substrate of the codification process by the sovereign operators commanding their screens and waging their data visualizations. The digitized, rewritable screen pixels are just the visible top side (virtualized surface) of bodies dispossessed by capital's digital algorithms on the bottom side, where, arguably, other metaphysics still pertain. Not Hegel's world spirit—whether in the form of Ray Kurzweil's singularity or Tegmark's computronium—but, rather, Marx's imperative toward a ruthless critique of everything existing can begin to explain how and why the current computational ecosystem is cofunctional with the unprecedented dispossession wrought by racial computational capitalism and its system of global apartheid. Racial capitalism's programs continue to function on the backs of those consigned to servitude. Data visualization, whether in the form of selfie, global map, digitized classic, or downloadable sound of the Big Bang, is powered by this elision. It is, shall we say, inescapably local to planet Earth, fundamentally historical in relation to species emergence, inexorably complicit with the deferral of justice.

The Global South, with its now worldwide distribution, is endemic to the geopolitics of computational racial capital—it is one of the extraordinary products of the world computer. The computronics that organize the flow of capital through planetary materials and signs also organize the consciousness of capital and with it the cosmological erasure of the Global South. Computers organize the whips and chains while humans watch and help. Thus the computational unconscious names a vast aspect of global function that requires analysis, protest, activism, and revolution. Here we sneak up on the two principle meanings of the concept of the computational unconscious. On the one hand, we have the problematic residue of amortized consciousness (and the praxis thereof/remaindered life) that has gone into the making of contemporary infrastructure—the structural repression and forgetting that is endemic to the very essence of our technological build-out as stolen, dead labor. On the other hand, we have the organization of everyday life taking place on the basis of this amortization, that is, on the basis of a dehistoricized, deracinated abstract relation to machines that function by virtue of the fact that intelligible history has been shorn off of them and the legibility of stolen, dead labor purged from their operating systems. Put simply, we have the forgetting—the radical disappearance and expunging from memory—of the historical and technical conditions of possibility of what is. As a consequence, we have the organization of social practice and futurity (or lack thereof) on the basis of this materially encoded, functionalized absence. The capture of the general intellect by such machines means also the management of the general antagonism and the general rendering unconscious of the lived price of complicity with computation. Never has it been truer that memory requires forgetting—the exponential growth in memory storage means also an exponential growth in systematic forgetting—and the withering away of the analog, of history, of tradition, of feeling. As a thought experiment, one might imagine a vast and empty vestibule, a James Ingo Freed global Holocaust memorial of unprecedented scale, containing all the oceans and lands, real and virtual, and dedicated to all the forgotten names of the colonized, the enslaved, the encamped, the statisticized, the read, written, and rendered in the history of computational calculus—of computer memory. These too, and the Anthropocene itself (the "billion Black Anthropocenes"), are the sedimented traces that remain among the constituents of the computational unconscious.

II

The Computational
Mode of Production

M–I–C–I'–M'

The Programmable Image of Photo-Capital

The camera (like all apparatuses that followed it) is computational thinking flowing into hardware. . . . To be in the photographic universe means to experience, to know and to evaluate the world as a function of photographs.

–VILÉM FLUSSER, *TOWARDS A PHILOSOPHY OF PHOTOGRAPHY*

Interface as Work-Site

With the computational unconscious in mind we now have an expansive way of thinking about the repressed of computational representation, of data-visualization. This chapter begins by taking the selfie as a paradigmatic example of the production, extraction, and monetization of expression by means of the interface of the screen. The selfie vernacular, as an attention aggregation effect, is also understood as a symptom of fractal fascism—a form of appearing that, in general, tends to depend upon the subsumption of the subjectivity of others. The movement from image to code to a transformed image (Image–Code–Image') replaces the "C" that stood for commodity in Marx's general formula for capital, in which commodity production for wages mediated the movement from money to more money. The selfie is a wager, a projection of one's "human capital" to return to Foucault, as a digital object offered on the attention market. It is, in brief, the conversion of ones life energy into information as a means to accumulate more information produced by the attention of others. This wager within the image can be shown to describe the general case of capitalist production—a new paradigm. Additionally, this total relation between image and code can itself be abstracted as Information (I), and thus—as we shall demonstrate more fully—the general formula for capital can be rewritten as M–I–M'.

What if the selfie and fractal celebrity have become the spectacular obverse of the world system organized by and as the world computer—the obverse of what Sylvia Federici calls the system of global apartheid? Such historically precipitated dispossession, the condition and result of a financialized attention economy, indexes a shift in the character of both labor and the commodity-form toward screen-mediated code work and networked valorization. The screen interface is essential in the organization of both what appears and what does not appear. In this chapter, we will consider more thoroughly the extent to which we can rewrite the labor theory of value in relation to image and code and the new forms of labor entailed in their processing at and beyond the machine-body interface of the screen. The goal here is two-fold. First, to identify financialized social media as a form of economic media that dialectically signals the convergence of communications media and monetary media for the production, transmission and extraction of value. Monetary media (money) and communications media (computational media) converge as economic media. Second, to lay the groundwork for the argument that this relation of semiotics to money to production mediated by information also and indeed already inheres in monetary media and finance. This latter would demonstrate that the standpoint of production and reproduction best explains what might be thought of as the perception of the sensual laborer (a.k.a. content provider) and best reveals the sociohistorical practices and consequences of modern finance, and furthermore, that in racial capitalism, the abstraction and extraction of the sensual laborer's activity, whether as factory work, domestic labor, digital content provision, or surface of inscription still underpins all value creation. While traditional ontologies—some of which belong to older notions of "labor"—are devoured by the new order of value production and extraction, remainders that may be resources for transformation, exit, and defense persist everywhere. We shall explore aspects of such remainders as well.

Pixel Programming and the Geopolitics of the Selfie

The megalomania, abjection, and fractal celebrity ascendant alongside digital platforms such as Facebook, Instagram, Tumblr, YouTube, and many others, are practically familiar—we have felt the repercussions of their practice. The younger people are, the more immersed, the more affected they are: primarily but by no means exclusively in the Global North, students and nonstudents are driven to physical and psychic extremes to manage and perchance control the information throughput. Race, gender, body image, clothing, homework and course selection, community, career, politics, futurological imaginaries, sexualities, music, dance moves, fashion, and psychic worlds are all renegotiated, networked as they are with flesh wounds, anorexia, washboard abdominals, Bentleys, $200K watches, brutal beatings, catastrophic accidents, two-headed animals, alt-right memes, and thigh gaps.[1] No one is left untouched. For the more than two billion users of these platforms, new currencies have emerged—domain-specific forms of wealth, measured in "likes," that not so surprisingly turn out to be convertible.[2] As U.S. college students are hired for their "friend" lists and people trade Instagram microcelebrity for versions of modeling careers and "influencer" roles, we recognize that the fractal logic of celebrity offers a payoff to successful pixel programmers up and down the food chain.

But as with classical factory work, dissymmetrical exchange still determines the payoffs offered to content providers by the big image-combines in return for their shareholders' ownership of the background monetization of the photopolitical social metabolism. In the reigning future now current, everyone may be famous for fifteen minutes a day, but the billionaires, though few and far between, are billionaires practically forever. POTUS, as the reigning symptom of social media capitalism organized by the world computer, expresses the logic of the deconstructive state while reinforcing the hegemony of the billionaires made by racial capitalism. POTUS, the Twitter president and, as Benjamin Lee remarked, "the volatility president," is capital incarnate—the principle cybernetic figurehead of its AI.

Navigating a present in which, as Vilém Flusser presciently told us almost forty years ago, all activities aspire to be photographed entails a radical reprogramming of not just subjectivity but also of social relations, including forms of connectivity, community, solidarity, and the state; as well as the climate and the linear time of what was known as history. The effects of the photograph run from the psychological to the Anthropocenic, from Adorno's quip that advertising is "psychoanalysis in reverse" to Sean Cubitt's thoughtful definition of mediation as "the primal connectivity between human and non-human worlds" (2014: 276).[3] This terrain of the "technical image" is also that of attention economy, here attention economies that would turn everyone else into a means for one's own celebrity. Justin Bieber's infamously insensitive remark upon his visit to the Anne Frank house in Amsterdam—"Truly inspiring to come here. Anne is a great girl. Hopefully she would have been a Belieber" (Williams 2013)—is an eloquent testimony to the one-dimensionality and historical disarticulation that oftentimes comes with fractal celebrity's dissymmetrical, narcissistic, and megalomaniacal absorption of attention.[4]

Fortunately, from Tahrir to Madrid to Taksim to Ferguson to Palestine, and more recently with the Extinction Rebellion, the Chilean uprising, and even perhaps the potentials of #AOC, Ilhan Omar, and Rashida Tlaib we can observe other modes of pixel programming besides those composed in the key of fractal versions of charismatic fascism—and therefore other ways of organizing the attentional product. "Black Twitter"—including @Nettaaaaaaaa (Johnetta Elzie), @Tefpoe (War Machine III), @deray (DeRay Mckesson)—Jewish Voice for Peace, and the BDS movement are among countless examples of folks working to change the way the United States understands racism and the everydayness of the legacies of slavery: by focusing critical attention on the diurnal experiences of racism and police violence. On the academic front, intellectuals and activists make their marks and assemble the ranks, challenging settler colonialism, carceral society, police brutality, imperialist war, structural violence, homophobia, heteropatriarchy, transphobia, racial capitalism, and other matrices of violence even as they face penal threats, lawsuits, institutional ostracism, and alt-right blowback (Canary Mission!). Among the ways these challenges are posed is the demonstration that status quo violence is presupposed and perpetuated by the knowledge base and ways of knowing. These ways of knowing, once considered cultural, institutional, and ideological are increasingly to be understood as also technological and mediological—algorithmic. The focus, solidarity, documentation, community building, pedagogy, outcry, and organizing of protest, new knowledge, and counteraffect made possible by numerous activists using social media, broadly understood, cannot be underestimated. Here, in the spirit of Negar Mottahedeh's and Jodi Dean's more affirmative takes on selfie dialectics, we sense that the cybernetic outgrowth of social media is also an outgrowth of the commons, of something like what the early Marx might have called species life and species consciousness—a welling up "from below" of liberatory aspirations, or, more dialectically perhaps, a repository of modes of struggle and a transmission of subaltern becoming: a postliterary "world literature."[5] One can in fact participate in platforms like Instagram, Tumblr, YouTube, and others to help create a sustaining environment for, for example, gender-queer becoming, anti-Zionist activism, #BlackLivesMatter, and much else.[6] These scenes of cultural production have their own specific and often alternative relation to the logistics of attention economy. However, there is a war over the utility, meaning, potentials, and proprietary control of these technologies and performances (to say nothing of the conversion of all semiotic exchange into a medium of advertising or other types of value-extraction). My point is obvious: present media technologies of value extraction and creation are also social, historical, and biosynthetic outgrowths; they are part of political economy and thus sites of struggle. In this respect, they are *economic media*.

But the content indifference of communications platforms, as well as the fact that these potentially common spaces are privately owned, reveals the way the deck is stacked. We must not forget, then, that alongside the new modes of fandom and personality or community generation, the planet—overlaid with social media that threatens to turn the sociosymbolic, the semiotic, and the political into a subroutine of capital accumulation—is increasingly blighted by too many recent and ongoing apartheids, genocides, and holocausts. Of course I am thinking about Palestine, Darfur, Rwanda, Congo, Afghanistan, Iraq, Central Syria, Yemen, and various countries in the Americas, the global situation of refugees, and also about the dispossessed population of what Mike Davis (2006) called, more than a decade ago, "the planet of slums" (a billion people living in slums, two billion people living on less than two dollars per day—most of them young). This form of radical dispossession—itself the dialectical antithesis of celebrity for the subject—is not an accident, and no amount of "liking" is going to fix it. Silvia Federici (2012: 70), in a significant revision of Davis's notion of the planet of slums, has, as previously mentioned, invoked "the system of global apartheid" to describe this situation in which a dispossessed population equivalent to the population of planet Earth in 1929 stands as a new type of historical achievement. This pointed reformulation, invoking "apartheid," underscores the econometrics, cartographics, mediations, and modes of *racialization* that actively and concertedly—systematically—constitute one third of the people on "our" planet as simultaneously a global underclass *and* a *racial* Other in relation to "the Free World." For me, the system of global apartheid names a postindustrial, postcolonial, postmodern, and "postracial" form of dispossession in which all of these words following "post-" still function under forms of disavowal and erasure. In imagining an alternative future that can break with a ubiquitous new modality of classification and the new forms of racialization and racism that function through restructured economies of dispossession and disappearance (evolving in direct relation to new economies of possession and appearance), we must do far better than (re)assuring ourselves in our own fractal celebrity (if you have any) that, were things otherwise, the two billion or more dispossessed members of the media platform Earth, reduced in one and the same movement to media of signification for the meanings of others and to invisibility to the point of extinction, would also have been "beliebers" in our best media-selves. The sad truth is that things are as they are in part because we have way too many beliebers—beliebers in the celebrity-form itself.[7]

One could indeed wonder: Is "the selfie" the other side of global apartheid?

Toward the practical end of producing critique within the infrastructure of belief sustaining both Global North–style "believers" and global apartheid, I am interested in what I think of as the archive of the visible and the logistics of visualization. The selfie as attention aggregator and as distilled model for the logistics of contemporary personality provides a form of data visualization consistent with computational racial capitalism—it is, in short, a program. The expression that it affords relies upon certain protocols of value aggregation that are endemic to its form and beyond the selfie's power to recompose. It is easy to post a selfie today, far more difficult to adjust the protocols for its monetization. Noting clearly the structural boundedness of its attention aggregation and celebrity creation within a system of value extraction will help us cast doubt on "the good Americans," "the good Europeans," and "the good cosmopolitans" in the same way that Nazism casts doubt on the goodness of "the good Germans." Tragically yet ineluctably today, the consequence of the very fact that the communications infrastructure is fixed capital and fully integrated into the operating system of global apartheid is that the message is murder, whatever else it may want to say. Corporeal life is stolen and rendered a substrate for inscription, for the dissemination of messages. We struggle for survival as we are written and read—for too many this is an everyday matter of life and death. While the older modes of visualization persist (meaning the history of visuality as organized by print, painting, photography, cinema, mathematics, optics, the built environment, and the commodity-form, as well as the today inseparable vectors of race, gender, class, colonization, industrialization, and imperialism), it is paramount to interrogate the dual emergence of digital culture and the omnipresence of the screen-image itself alongside global apartheid. Despite recent suggestions regarding the decreasing importance of visuality in the face of computation, the omnipresence of the visual interface that is the screen-image as mise-en-scène for social becoming is at once incontrovertibly occasioned by the development of digital computers, along with their mathematical and semiotic codes, and their structural, infrastructural, and geopolitical inequalities.[8] Even as modes of visual literacy and modulation shift, visuality remains an indispensable feature of the command-control functionality of computation—and, as argued in the beginning of this volume, establishes itself through violence and *remains* a seeing through violence.

Although digital-visual technologies continue to structure data visualization along psychoanalytic, fetishistic, classist, racist, sexist, and nationalist spectacular lines, no analysis of this increasingly complex relation between image and code—a relation which has encroached, fatally perhaps, on self and world—could ever be complete without an understanding of *digital culture as itself an extension of the logic of financialization*. This new computational matrix I have identified here (somewhat unimaginatively) as Digital Culture 2.0, since the first globally aspiring digital culture—and this is an argument—was that of capitalism itself. In the span from mercantile capital to finance capital we move from Digital Culture 1.0 (DC1) to our present Digital Culture 2.0 (DC2). One result among many in this long history of economic and computational convergence—which places the rise of visual culture in parallel with the rise of modern credit and synthetic finance—is that financialization has given us the derivative pathway called the selfie: a specific mode of commodity calculus amid a new calculus of commodities. Understanding that commodities have a calculus, are a form of calculation, helps us to deepen our understanding of their essential nature as conferred by the economic network of racial capitalism. The commodity, like the selfie and like the image in general, is, we must now recognize, itself a contingent claim, a derivative on the underlier that is value.

Generalizing from the trend that turns the computer interface into a work-site of financial and cultural programming (and content provision into a contingent claim on the social, on social currency), we may observe that today the bios is confronted by the programmable image—the selfie is but one example, albeit one that puts the face back in the interface. Facial recognition and other biometric forms of access and surveillance will keep it there for a while at least. The long twentieth century has been characterized by the penetration of the life-world by images, the restructuring of linguistic function by the image, the machinic ramification of the psyche, and the reordination of fundamental vectors of social participation (sociality), and power. The visual turn meant that images and then computers became the dominant mnemotechnical devices, overcoming language-based archives and what Kittler called precisely "the bottleneck of the signifier" (1999: 4). But it has been a mistake to imagine (if anyone really has) that all the agency of social transformation resides in the development of media technics. Photography, cinema, and computation were themselves developments of capital, and this in a *dialectical* way. To invoke dialectics here means that visual and computational culture developed in a context of social struggle (sociality) over the means (and meanings) of production, caught between what might be hypostasized as opposing vectors of expropriation, domination, and control on the one hand and pursuits of pleasure, community, welfare, justice, liberation, autonomy, and plenitude on the other. Today's instrumentalization of the subject-function (as consumer, gamer, drone pilot, debtor, citizen, national, alien, and so on, *ad infinitum*), along with the pulverization of psychic life that results from multiple fragmentary, fractal instantiations of "subjective" agency induced and required by broad-spectrum dividuating networks, is both symptom and result of a Digital Culture 2.0 in which images have become, in addition to a kind of antilinguistic *vernacular*, also archive, calculus, work-site, and code. (Post) Modern consciousnesses, such as they are, bear the signature features of these technical transformations that are themselves part of a history of struggle for liberation and autonomy while also being part of the apparatus that secures domination, precarity, and radical unfreedom. Consciousness itself, integrated in myriad ways with the fixed capital of digital media, is at once entrepreneur, work-site, toxic externality, and resource. Caught in the double bind that is signification and thought itself, aesthetic, kinesthetic, and semiotic dimensions now accompany some moment of nearly every transaction with "the environment"—a technically produced externality, that as Sean Cubitt (2014) teaches us, was centuries (of colonialism) in the making. Or, as Derrida (1997 [1967]: 44) put it, "The outside is the inside," where "being," or more precisely, being, is the effect of *différánce*, the difference and deferral of meaning created by the movement of the code itself such that an impossible break between an ostensible "inside" and "outside" (inside and outside) is operationalized.

The general form of the new calculus is as follows: the accelerated mathematics of capital that have long been mapping and then generating real abstractions (the basic money-form but also more advanced forms of money) out of the materiality of living formations (forms of life) today number-crunch not only behind and beyond but also *in and through* the screen-image. The processing of abstraction is the metabolism of real, material, sociality that infuses material infrastructural and structural emergence—it is the real accounting of social praxis requiring the contingent yet continuous hypostasization of networks. The screen-image has become the paradigmatic means by which capital bioprocesses its programs, although the corporate-sponsored state—with its law, police, military, borders, walls, and banks—clearly continues to have a part to play as medium and screen infrastructure. The commodity-form and capitalist production have evolved in terms of complexity, but, as we shall see, the intervals between the discrete moments of production that induce movements in discrete state machines, still require "human" input, or what was once paradigmatically thought of as labor.

"The image of capital" is not a single image—neither Marilyn Monroe, the American flag, a Jackson Pollack, apple pie, nor a UNICEF poster child—not even the ugly mug of 45. If capital had its way, "the image of capital" would be all of them. Capital would position labor power within the media enclosure that is the generalized encroachment of capitalized images on all aspects and moments of life, within the general movement of social relations *en toto* toward the image—that is, within a formation already immanent and brilliantly analyzed in 1967 in Guy Debord's *Society of the Spectacle*: "All that was once directly lived has become mere representation" (1995: 12). It would place us within, in short, the becoming-imaginary of the world (the bottomless overlays of imaginaries) and the virtual-ization of reality that seems to forever place the Real in quotation marks. It is in and from such a condition—a condition that, in marginalizing linear thinking and linear time, in short-circuiting the ability to frame contradiction à la Orwell, Vilém Flusser would call "magical"—that we wage our struggles. Even violence often appears magical, irrational because beholden to the rationality of another, abstract domain. Therefore, it is within the emergent totality that Flusser calls "the universe of technical images," here being taken to another level by ubiq-uitous computing and the rise of the world computer iterating the program of photocapital, that we receive our programming and wager our counterprograms.[9] These wagers, the struggles with capitalist informatics, are everywhere, but the results are nonetheless desperate, mournful, bloody, or material for all that.

Famously, Marx discerned what was effectively and literally the calculus of the commodity-form when he showed that the commodity was the sum-mation of the value of labor time (the summation of labor, per unit time, times time) plus the value of the raw materials required to produce it. This allowed him to demonstrate precisely that profit came from the expropria-tion of labor time through its unequal exchange as labor power for the wage. The commodity had more labor time in it than the worker was paid for—it has both "necessary" and "surplus" labor, while the worker was only paid for necessary labor—the amount required for the worker to reproduce themselves. While *circulation* meant the exchange of value equivalents in the realm of com-modities, *production* was the production of commodities by means of the dis-symmetrical exchange between labor and capital, where capital underpaid for labor time and extracted surplus value. Marx made the distinction between C–M–C (commodity-money-commodity) and M–C–M (money-commodity-money): in other words, the distinction between the exchange of equivalents in simple circulation (C–M–C) and the movement of capital accumulation in production—where the latter formula, which was really M–C–M' (in which M'>M), contained within it profit, the dirty secret of the dissymmetrical exchange between capital and labor by which surplus value is extracted through wage labor during commodity production. Within the relation known as "wage labor," workers brought *their* commodity (their labor power) to market and received less value from capital than they produced *for* capital.

The workers' unpaid labor time (surplus labor) became the capitalists' profits, generating M' from the original M when the commodity produced by wage labor was sold on the open market. The worker went home with subsistence wages, the capitalist went home rich.

This relation of alienation, along with the commodity-form itself, was, in retrospect, already a mode of digitization, the translation of qualities into quantities, of subjective, sensual labor and use-values into exchange-values, of subjective time and objective qualities into numbers. Under this process of the expansive and indeed viral digitization that included the rise of the money economy, the countryside was emptied as the urban proletariat grew; cities expanded along with factories and tenements as vast fortunes were created; traditional societies were liquidated as peasants, dispossessed of land and in need of money (for food, taxes, shelter, education) became urban proletarians and lumpen; colonial states erected; spices, gold, and slaves shipped; armies conscripted; people slaughtered. To coin a phrase: "All that was solid melted into air, everything that was sacred was profaned." Much ink has been spilled over the consequences of emergent capital's evolutionary if not revolutionary transformation of the human species during the five or six hundred years leading up to the twentieth century. Colonization, industrialization, imperialism, modernity, world wars, the great metropoles—while profits and corpses mounted, material life was besieged by its inexorable conversion into a numerical denomination in the money commodity known as price. In brief, this global recomposition of the relations of production is the bloody, brutal, and mostly unspeakable history of the first great phase of quantification: Digital Culture 1.0, with "humanity," particularly those who were excluded from it, consequently positioned as standing reserve under the apotheosis of "the human" of humanism. *Vive la France!*

With post-Fordism, virtuosity, attention economy, cognitive capitalism, semiocapitalism, and the like, another evolutionary (if, again, not authentically revolutionary) moment is underway. In writing about these changes in the biomechanical interface with capital (the movement from factory to screen), first in terms of the cinematic mode of production and more recently as "Digital Culture 2.0," I have contested the ruling idea that simply because commodification no longer exclusively incarnates itself in industrial objects, value has become "immeasurable." I have suggested rather a distributed, screen-based, cybernetic interface with fixed capital—it being understood today that the logistics of value extraction are increasingly ambient, informatic, and, in a certain sense with respect to the harvesting of metadata, metabolic.

The case for the immeasurability of value has not been so much argued as assumed. Here is Antonio Negri's early and highly influential formulation:

"My first thesis, a deconstructive and historical thesis, is that measuring labor, and thus ordering it and leading it back to a theory of value, is impossible when, as today, labor-power is no longer either outside or inside capitalist command (and its capacity to structure command)" (2010: 80). Negri continues,

> We have thus far posed a number of affirmations: (1) that the measure of labor-value, grounded on the independence of use-value, has now become ineffectual; (2) that the rule of capitalist command that is imposed on the horizon of globalization negates every possibility of measure, even monetary measure; and (3) that the value of labor-power is today posed in a non-place and that this non-place is *s-misurato* (immeasurable and immense)—by which we mean that it is *outside of measure* but at the same time *beyond measure*. (83)[10]

Digital metrics had not evolved to their current levels of granularity when Negri first wrote this article in 1999, so he can be forgiven for thinking for a moment that "labor power is no longer outside or inside capitalist command (and its capacity to structure command)." But we should not allow autonomist Marxism (or any Marxism) to imbibe the value-imaginary of financialization wholesale. Indeed, Negri's own analysis (unconsciously?) forecasts the emergence of a new metrics of subjectification:

> The latent recognition that political economy gives to the fact that value is now an investment of desire constitutes a real and proper conceptual revolution. . . . This revolution in political economy is revealing in that it involves dominating the context of the affects that establish productive reality as the superstructure of social reproduction and as the articulation of the circulation of the signs of communication. Even if the measurement of this new productive reality is impossible, because affect is not measurable, nonetheless in this very productive context, so rich in productive subjectivity, affect *must* be controlled. Political economy has become a deontological science. In other words, the project of the political economy of conventions and communication is the control of an immeasurable productive reality. (87)

While this view of the immeasurability of productivity became the accepted one in "post-Marxist" and autonomist circles (and an unnecessary detour in what appeared obvious to rampant internet boosterism), some of us always saw measure in monetization itself—as did Marx, as I show in this chapter. Even John von Neumann and Oskar Morgenstern (1944), in their classic work on game theory, posited and mathematically demonstrated the possibility of the pricing of affects, which they called "preferences" in marginal utility theory. And then there is the relatively unexplored work of Gabriel Tarde

(Latour and Lépinay 2009) that understands intersubjectivity as the very basis of quantification and scientific thought. As shown in the introduction to this volume, all of these heuristic devices, along with their metrics, enter into the general expansion of "the factory code." For his part, Negri correctly describes a shift in the form—one could say the identity—of labor, locating productivity in affect. This is a key observation and represents an essential transformation in the organization of production and in what Negri identified from Marx as "social cooperation." As an increasingly central feature of political economy— by which the formally external productive capacities become internal to po- litical economy and formalized within its domain—this shift toward affect (what in my earlier work I called and still sometimes call *attention*) marks a change which made it immeasurable by existing criteria. However, as we shall see, *the positing of a field of valuation already posits and over time effects the emergence of metrics both of measure and of extraction*. In the form of ratings, "likes," finan- cial derivatives on volatility, and metadata parsable by algorithmic sorts, *new currencies are created* and the measuring of "affect" becomes the pathway to its financialization and computability. The transformed status of labor, now as affect, attention, cognition, somatic function, virtuosic capacity, and metabo- lism became, in short, the situation of labor consecrated by a higher order of abstraction that posited it as generative of information. This labor was paid for in new forms of currencies—social currencies.

We add here that part of the confusion arising from the intensification of the role of affect and linguistic command in postmodern capitalism stems from a category mistake regarding the nature of the commodity in the context of post- Fordism or what we've been calling Digital Culture 2.0. Because all that was solid melted into pixels, it was a mistake to persist in imagining that, because the in- dustrial object was comprehended as a commodity, the commodity-form is prop- erly (necessarily) an object—and that the value of anything that is not strictly speaking an object (or can be objectified in the form of an object) is immea- surable. The digitally composed assets of synthetic finance directly contradict this idea of a commodity object and reveals its emergent "truth." The object, as it turns out, was, like "labor" in the classical sense, a *moment* in the historical development of the commodity-form. Today we might say that the object was a node in a network of relations, or an *interface* with general sociality that appeared as an object. To speak thusly about the nodality of an object as a composed *posi- tion*—a wager—on value, is merely a rewording of the critique of reification in the context of computational racial capitalism and its financialized networks. The corollary confusion accompanying the movement from the commodity object to the dispersed, disbursed, distributed commodity—the digital object—regards the movement from factory production, in the case of the former "objectivity" of the commodity, to distributed production of the network-commodity in the social factory in the case of the latter. Industrial production created commodified objects in the factory to be sold at markets, while distributed (digital) production creates digital objects, what are effectively derivative "objects" in the social factory—*network derivatives* that are also "commodities"—to be sold on attention markets. They are also produced via attention in distributed fashion, meaning to say they undergo distributed production in a society that has literally become a factory of the imaginary. The new, distributed image-objects are mediated and indeed inseparable from franchises, platforms, brands, and other modes of associative transmission. Owning a piece of a network, whether as stock, infrastructure, or as token, or even as a "commodity" can be considered to be a network derivative because it provides revenue (even if negative at times in the case of cryptotokens) on an underlier: the traffic that is the utility of the network as a whole. A commodity is also a piece in a network of relations—a node or, in normal parlance, an object. But, in light of today's digital composability, even the traditional commodity object is nonetheless a derivative, a structured, composable position on the tradable exchange-value, its underlier, in the market. Your tofu is an interface with the Monsanto platform, its momentary cost a specific wager towards your net-positive cash-flow.

Rather than saying that value has become immeasurable, we should say that a mutation of objects and subjects, and of labor and money, has been a requirement imposed by the scaling of capitalist production driven to innovate by the falling rate of profit. If anything has disappeared beyond the ostensible solidity of the nodes and interfaces that were moments in the capitalist networks of yesteryear, it is the anyway always problematic strict distinction between circulation and production. The network for circulation multiplies interfaces for and occasions of value production. Networked relations have colonized the social field, created "digitality" and the "social factory," and maximally extended the working day to create a near total occupation of life. This condition—in which network commodities function as network derivatives and invade the semantic field, such that practically all social activity is dedicated to maximizing the return on one's capital, small as it may be—describes the mediological shifts required to bring about Autonomia Operaia's post-Fordism, Foucault's "entrepreneur of the self," and Randy Martin's "financialization of daily life." The computational mode of production gives rise to "the derivative condition." A key interface is the programmable image.

As financial markets have long presumed through options, commodities can be constituted through derivative (in all senses of that word) forms of enterprise and still be treated as the commodity-form by capital. What is effectively being priced in every instance is a social relation, one summed up in the idea of risk. The commodity, like the products of synthetic finance is a risk profile. Indeed, as indicated above, it is arguable that the derivative was always implicit in the commodified object—from the moment that its dual identity of use-value and exchange-value was posited by capital, it was in point of fact a social relation that was being priced: the production and purchase of a commodity was a calculated risk at every instant and its price was a strike price on all the knowledge compressed in its information. Its information signals the potential for transaction, and any and indeed in principle all transactions affect its information. As Marx was highly aware, risk was always endemic to sale, the valorization process of the commodity, for one exchanged the general form of wealth for a particular asset, both of which were subject to volatility, that is, value fluctuation. The intensification of capitalist production has meant the multiplication of forms of risk and of strategies of risk management. We might say that the history of the logistics of the commodity-form is one first of composition and then of decomposition, one of integration and then of derivation. We are most familiar with the integration of labor in the production process (the summation over time of the labor time in an object), since the commodified object, as site of proprietary intelligibility, sale, and therefore of valorization of capital's profit in money, naturalized while marginalizing the derivative component in the form of the object itself (a denomination of value that itself has an exchange-value and indeed an exchange rate) in the moment of price. The derivative on the going market price of labor power—offered by a particular commodity purchased at a particular time—was immanent but repressed. However, following the moment of the commodity's composition (as object), the value (quantity of abstract universal labor time) as price in money of a particular commodity was indeed *derived* from the integral that was the summation of values contained in that commodity. If the *cost* of a production run of commodified objects was the summation of the cost of labor time (the integral of cost of work over time times time) plus the total cost of raw materials and fixed capital (machine) amortization, then the object's price was the derivative price of the *value* of the total amount of labor time inherent at the moment of (which is to say, "in") a particular object, over the total number of objects produced, plus that of the appropriate fraction of raw materials and machine amortization utilized per object. In the same sense that, in basic Newtonian mechanics, an object's displacement is a derivative of its velocity, the price of the commodity as object was itself a derivative of the general movement of capitalized object production (the fluctuating price of labor inherent in the commodity) at a particular point (an evaluation of a particular moment of value in the fluid movement of values in general), and only in this way was it possible for the market to compute the relative price of an object in relation to the general equivalent. Or rather, this is what market practices effected relative to labor and price—effected, that is, as real abstraction resultant from practices of exchange. At first, perhaps, money "itself" seemed like enough to manage this complexity, later marginal utility theory credit and debt instruments, and derivative finance provided more precise ways of managing risk by securing liquidity. Such mathematics were *practiced* before they became conscious, as for example in von Neumann and Morgenstern and later in Fischer Black and Myron Scholes, where the volatility of price was formalized (and itself priced) by options traders. One paid to secure a future price for x in a volatile market, and the price paid was a hedge against volatility, a liquidity premium.

The rise of modern financial derivatives and the metrics of attention represent the developing conceptualization and cognition of relations that were already practical and practiced. Just as the ancient Romans didn't need Newton to have an adequate sense (a sense adequate to their times) of how long it took to get a chariot from point A to point B, buyers of Model T's did not need financial derivatives to pay for their cars. Henry Ford's statement, "You can have any color you want so long as it's black," was an acknowledgment of the possibility of options and of the necessity of limiting options for the purposes of market heuristics and their imposition of limits on production. Options in consumption practice—and hence options allowing for risk management with respect to sales (on the consumer side, commonly called preferences)—were in this case effectively reduced to near zero for consumers (or more precisely, two: buy it or don't). The introduction of variation on brands and specifications, as well as the introduction of credit, increased the number of options. From the perspective of the purposeful delimitation of options in a world in which options were becoming immanent, marginal utility theory, which proposed that a particular commodity would be worth slightly more to one buyer than to another, was already a theory of derivatives that acknowledged a secondary market of risk management in the domain of social difference (aesthetics, taste, necessity, and the semiotics thereof, along with other aspects of "utility"); it was an acknowledgement that, unlike abstract labor time, which homogenized productive labor (either as production effect or as representation), affect was not socially uniform. The development of options (in commodities trading, fashion, and finance) allows for purchasers to make a bet on the currency of their own *read* of market value: their "desires," in Negri's terms above. This read includes a calculus of their particular needs amid the play of values and implies a pursuit of tailor-made contracts. The metrics follow these wagers, but the calculus is not free—it requires work and demands a program. The tailor-making of options posits the domain of the social as a huge space of innovation by market-makers—a space for the production of new needs and for arbitrage. The structural and historical point here is that the development of the calculus of commodification, which has moved away from factory and object as paradigm to that of the deterritorialized social factory and distributed consumption, dialectically transformed the possibilities of both spatial and economic movements beyond the optionless Model T. From the space-time of the Model T and the industrial factory has emerged the space-time of spacecraft and the virtuosity of the social factory: Google, nanotechnologies, satellites, drones, fiber optics, hedge funds, ambient computing, algo-trading, cryptocurrencies, and the like run the myriad options so that the products of the social factory can be efficiently distributed and consumed to produce . . . capital.

Financial derivatives and digital media platforms—monetized on bank and shareholder speculation (shadow banking) and facilitated by attention metrics—are among the new calculi of value.[11] They are not as different from the speculative leap into buying early commodity-forms as we may imagine. These digital metrics—media of risk management that are also modes of extending the logistics of quantification *and* valuation—emerge directly from, and in turn facilitate, new distributed forms of commodity production in the social factory. They extend not just the logic of the market but the cultural logic—part of their "meaning" is that they themselves are tools for the navigation of capitalist culture, of risk. Thus "meaning" becomes market making. The new metrics adequate to distributed processes of production and value accumulation (from Apple's global commodity chains and networks to Mechanical Turk's cellularized labor, Walmart's product tracking, Facebook's social interface, and Ethereum's cryptocurrency) are far more complex than, say, the assembly-line output counts on the factory floor, and more complex again than the consumption of labor power objectified in what appeared as a clear-cut "object" (purchased with money received in exchange for what appeared as a clear-cut "wage"); ultimately they require the movement of the exponentially more complex pathways and calculations of capital into the (nano) second-by-(nano)second operations of discrete state machines, that is, digital computers—as well as the new modes of sociality that post-Fordist theory has been at pains to describe. Society has become more abstract in practice, that is, in the recursive interactions with its real abstractions. This convergence of the calculus of value production with new modes of sensual interface and with the provision of sensuous labor—and thus with production itself—made possible by computation marks the rise of a new phase of the capitalist mode of production, the computational mode of production. *The computational mode of production describes the dynamic function of a regime of creation and valuation programmed by computational racial capital and functioning as a world computer.* This shift in the mode of production takes us beyond the bourgeois era—and indeed beyond the cinematic one as well—toward a convergence of the computations of capital with the operations of the universal Turing machine and the ramification and codification of social difference. It turns commodities into derivatives (which is to say it elaborates the derivative aspect always already latent in the commodity form) and forces all economic participants to manage market volatility, that is, risk.

Elsewhere in this text, I have endeavored to show that computational capitalism finds its lineage directly in racial capitalism. As my examples above about the negotiation of social difference as an informatic enterprise would imply, this relation to racialization and social difference is not ancillary but central, since a matrix of affective relations structured by concrete circumstances imposed differently on various bodies structure processes of valuation (of time, of product, of life) and access to liquidity (Beller 2016a, 2016c). I will develop this argument further in subsequent chapters. Here, however, to attend, if only briefly, to another conversation situated in a different quarter and finally to answer those who claim that in post-Fordism value has become immeasurable, one need go no further than Marx's discussion of "the price-form" in chapter 3 of *Capital*, "The Circulation of Commodities." He writes, "Things which in and for themselves are not commodities, things such as conscience, honour, etc. can be offered for sale by their holders, and *thus acquire the form of commodities through their price* [emphasis added]. Hence a thing can, formally speaking, have a price without having a value. The expression of price is in this case imaginary, like certain quantities in mathematics. On the other hand, the imaginary price-form may also conceal a *real* value-relation or *one derived from it*" [emphasis in original] (1990: 197).

It was the great contribution of Marx—one on par with those of Newton and Leibniz—to derive some of the rules by which a calculus of value could be configured. Marx's comparison of the relation of price to value with both real and imaginary numbers tells us that, as in mathematics, whether a value is "real" or "imaginary" (i), it can be treated according to mathematical rules; that is, it is subject to mathematical operations that yield practical results. It is worth recalling that, utilizing imaginary numbers, made acceptable by Leonhard Euler in the eighteenth century and developed by Carl Friedrich Gauss in the nineteenth, mathematics predicted the existence of the Higgs boson and, lo and behold, equipment designed by the same mathematics found it. Whether the Higgs boson is real or not is somehow beside the point, since mathematics mediated by technics of its own design stages "nature" to produce mathematical effects that are internally consistent—verifiable in their own terms (and then photographed, of course). Here we say that the derivation of value in finance is both an instrument of measure and a means of production; mathematicians use imaginary numbers to produce real (or is it virtual?) solutions. No doubt these solutions work, but as Gödel and Derrida both have shown, internal consistency is not "truth" in the classical sense. Bringing things back to Earth, we might say simply that, in the context of capital circulation, the price-form posits the commodity-form. From the perspective of racial capital your conscience is but one substitutable choice among a variety of options and pathways for getting things done. The price-form allows the mathematics of the commodity-form to operate even in the absence of classical rational(ized) production—it posits a social process and thus organizes an imaginary. When, for example, capital buys off someone's conscience, it does so for a reason—that too is a cost of production. Capital says: "I'll budget an extra $10,000 a year to buy off your conscience." Today perhaps the same could be said about a situation when capital buys off someone's *consciousness* wholesale as well—or indeed a large portion of that of an entire society.[12] These are costs of production and have a *systemic rationale*. In the mesh of the rationale, and in the crunch of its execution, such ramifications may restructure the ontology of that which is rationalized while reformatting the way it is imagined. Getting rid of your conscience (or consciousness) is then posited as a form of labor—one pathway (among many other possible pathways) to create a particular result. If there is a cheaper way to produce the same result, it will likely be discovered in the next production cycle. Hence the falling rate of profit not only implies a decrease in the cost of labor over time, but a falling rate of conscience.

When Marx wrote *Capital*, conscience and consciousness were not the obvious market products of what today have come to be known as disciplinary societies, control societies, or mediological ones—despite the fact that Marx lucidly grasped German idealism's notion of consciousness as, unbeknownst to the German idealists themselves, being at once precisely the *product* of alienated labor and the *disavowal* of the material basis of socioeconomic organization of material practice as the social basis of bourgeois idealism. In *The German Ideology*, Marx writes a phrase often quoted throughout this volume, "The ruling ideas are nothing more than the ideal expression of the dominant material relationships, the dominant material relationships grasped as ideas . . . and hence the ideas of their dominance" (1998: 67). Today, however, there can be no doubt that those once presumably divine, biological, organic, psychological, or quintessentially human properties—the "ideas" composing the general intellect—are inexorably bound up in the material exigencies of regimes of production; indeed, as we are at pains to demonstrate, the colonization and financialization that is digital culture presupposes the productive capacities of cognitive, neurological, and attentional practices as cybernetic forms.[13] Given this massive shift toward the computational ramification of the general intellect as part of the intensive development of prior machine-body interfaces, it seems imperative to derive the "real value relation" priced by the market of diverse modes of attention gathering, social media practice, linguistic practice, and other human activities that fall outside of traditionally recognized forms of formal wage-labor but that are nonetheless required for social production and reproduction. The (re)organization of the productive powers of the general intellect requires the integrated organization of many moving parts: matter, consciousness, computation, money, and, as you will have already guessed, the programmable screen-image.[14]

M-I-C-I'-M', The Programmable Image, M-I-M'

In recognition of the paradigm shift in the character of both labor (toward attention, affect and neuronal process) and the commodity-form (toward integrated distribution based upon a rentier model of the general intellect and network derivatives), which, when put thus, is an analytically strategic way of invoking the shifting character (sublation) of subject and object in post-Fordism, I'd like to take this opportunity to reintroduce a slight modification into the general formula for capital: $M-C-M'$.[15] As noted, the value that will generate this second, greater quantity of money is classically acquired in the production process, that is, in capital's dissymmetrical exchange with labor through the medium of the wage. As we have seen, it is the worker's unpaid labor that provides surplus value to capital and thereby creates the increase from M to M' during the cycle of commodity production culminating in market valorization.

Let's now rewrite the general formula for capital as $M-I-C-I'-M'$—where M is still money, but I is image and C is code. C, as code, is to be understood here not as a stable entity but as a discrete moment in the movements of the discrete state of a computer—we could say, of all networked computers and, with a nervous nod toward the emergent integration of the totality of computation, the world computer. By replacing Marx's commodity "C" with $I-C-I'$ (which together reduces to commodity "C" at Fordist speeds by a process in which an object is simply informed by the material manifestation of the information laboriously imposed upon its materials as it is given form), we register the sublation of the commodity-form as object by the matrix of information. At 55 mph, a car looks like a car, but at the speed of light (as displayed on your phone, for example) it is a node in a vast distributed network of social relations. Indeed such image relations stick to your actual, material car like an appliqué. Thus I–C–I' indexes the movement between appearance, praxis, and digital-informatic substrate, as when, for example, one uploads an image on Insta, tweets, makes a purchase on Amazon.com, trades a stock, "likes" the red Ferrari, or accesses GPS while driving it. In reality, I–C–I' might represent many iterations of I–C–I'–C'–I''–C''–I'''–C''' . . . and so on—state changes driven by attentional, cognitive, metabolic, or other types of inputs. Holding those types of units fixed for a moment, it now appears that value production may take place anywhere in the circuit or network that mediates between M and M'—the interval formerly indicated by the commodity "C". That is, at any moment along the circuit from monetized capital investment to monetized profit, a value-productive transaction is possible—each movement or modification generates new data and each new state is a potential interface with productive labor, affect, and attention. Access to this data, from a particular point with designable rights, may be priced, and a price may be denominated in money or in other kinds of inputs such as personal information or metadata. Important for this discussion is the argument that automated "labor," that is, work done by computational machinery alone (or even ordinary machinery), is not labor—it is never labor—but machine amortization. Machine amortization too is a cost of production, but it is not in itself a source of profit. Ultimately, liquidity depends upon the liquification of people and societies, the rendering of them for sale. It is in the sale of people and what matters to them that capital's money is "redeemed." Labor and, more to the point, surplus labor—what Marx understood as the "living labor" provisioning both necessary labor and also the surplus labor that gets abstracted and extracted as value and surplus value in the profitable waged production of commodities—now appears to have multiple forms and insertion points: there are today many more ways not to pay for labor. Recall that profit from the portion of unpaid factory labor, namely "surplus labor," objectified in the commodified product, provided profit in money when sold. Surplus labor is extracted over networks of employment and by other means, just as necessary labor is paid for in low wages and discounted by racism, sexism, and colonialism, as well as by new kinds of social currencies resembling company scrips. The labor of production is, in short, distributed across multiple sites: for example, hundreds of thousands of software writers, tens of millions of historically devalued (mostly female, mostly Asian) hands, billions of screens attended to by billions of operator-functionaries such as ourselves, and finally the whole media ecology and economy of images and information broken down into the ever smaller and more granular units that structure perception, proprioception, and even the very conditions of planetary survival and the widespread premature death that is a consequence of the world computer. Boiled down, innovation is merely arbitrage on the labor-cost per informatic bit. Commodities, now fully algorithmic in that they seamlessly integrate use-values and exchange-values and script the realization of use-values as means for the production of further exchange-values (except when they don't), are constructed through the juridical and practical organization of proprietary pathways through the vast database of the world computer (the sum total of all code, all the infrastructure, and all else that runs it—the stack).

The emergence of the world computer, already "superintelligent" (Bostrum 2014) and effectively "self-aware" (even if difficult to recognize as conscious by one of its "conscious organs"), is the result of the absorption and mobilization of distributed life activity—alienated dead labor, that is to say, alienated subjectivity and thus alienated intelligence—by the calculus of capital.[16] At every (infinitesimally small) moment, the universal Turing machine that contains—not simply in theory, but indeed as is *posited* both in theory and by alienated theory thinking as capital to contain—all actually existing or possible discrete state machines is itself necessarily in a discrete state. "This special property of digital computers, that they can mimic any discrete state machine, is described by saying that they are universal machines" (Turing 2003: 54). We say that the modification of each state is the direct or indirect result of social process just as these social processes are inseparable from its emergence. As discussed in chapter 1, the technical elaboration of the logistics of informatics in the medium once known as life is the necessary other side of capital's absorptive accumulation of life activity as value. Using computational technologies, capital can now write futures contracts on life, in effect writing a derivative on a partitioning of the network. This structure, precisely, can be found in the market capitalization of Facebook, or sovereign debt.

In the movement from the factory to the social factory, commodities no longer have to be materialized as goods in object form (although they still can be, though even these "goods" are now combinatories of brands, images, franchises, and other financialized informatic-semiotic vectors); they exist and are produced as *integrated* value formations. Some of what is bought (by us) with our screen labor is the use of the platform itself (its utility is our payment, our social currency), but, as we saw with the branded self and fractal celebrity, the utility and the logic exceed the domain of any particular platform and compose a *cultural logic*—"the cultural logic of computation," as David Golumbia (2009) puts it. The branded self, fractal celebrity, and other platform affordances are part of the control exercised by "digitality as cultural logic," in Sebastian Franklin's (2015) terms. The rest of our labor, beyond that for which we get some return in social currency, is also sedimented as data but not returned to us either as utility or proprietary stake; it is absorbed, gathered, captured, scraped, accumulated—in short, stolen through the primitive accumulation of metadata—and then bundled and sold to angel investors, shareholders, or advertisers, or seized by governments, police and secret police forces, and so on. Our modification of the discrete state of the global computer—remunerated at work, unremunerated as dispersed life activity (but actually remunerated *at a discount* in "soft" social currency: viability, know-how, stupefaction, connections, likes etc.)—generates modifications of what I am calling the code through our use, indeed through our inhabitation, of networked media machines. Since this enclosure by new-media capital posits and extracts forms of labor that are also now explicitly forms of intersubjective communication, the expropriation of labor is also an expropriation of communication and hence an expropriation of individual consciousness, semiotic capacity, collectivity, and democracy. From the days of Proudhon's "property is theft" to industrialized wage labor and then on to the computerized expropriation of the cognitive-linguistic, the institutionalized computational theft of the creative product of individuals has always been antidemocratic. Today technological logic is a carceral logic of enclosure, a settler-colonial logic that posits consciousness as standing reserve. Communication is theft. Given the present context, in which everyone is enjoined to participate and add their voice, it is arguable that capital, "the communism of capital" as the antithesis of what is usually meant by "democracy," has never functioned more contradictorily than it does today. Consciousness is theft. The institution of consciousness is a product of theft and a form of theft; it is active stealing. Consciousness today, organized by I-C-I' in the circuit from M-M' cannot but choose oppression because enclosure and theft are posited in its very function in and through the media that are fixed capital. There may be democracy, but not for us, or so says capital's current foreclosure of (and on) history and the historical imagination. Politics would require the disaggregation of the infrastructure of thought and imagination from racial capitalism. It would demand, in Ariella Azoulay's (2012) terms, "the right not to be a perpetrator."

In the formula M-I-C-I'-M', the expanded notation I-C-I' represents the integrated productive activity formerly denominated by "C." Image-code, the network commodity, replaces what was formerly understood as the commodity on the way from M to M', from money to more money. This description, befitting of the shift from the paradigm of the factory to that of the distributed screen-based social factory, understands both that material objects pressed into the service of capital are themselves *media* and, furthermore, that networked mediation required for production and exchange—that is, productive exchange—is cybernetic and extractive. It recognizes that the very function of these mediations of M–M' enacts the computational *colonization* of the subject, the human, and the bios. It also asserts, in an extension and Marxification of Flusser's notion of the universe of technical images, that in Digital Culture 2.0, commodity production, mediated as it is by images, really data-visualization, has now become paradigmatically a transaction in the movement from money to image-code and back.[17] As already indicated, this mediation is not a linear process as with the assembly line, or even simply a global process as with "the global commodity chain" paradigmatically signified by Nike in the late 1980s and 1990s. It is a networked process of vectoral connections, presided over by what McKenzie Wark (2012: 72) deftly calls "the vectoral class"—those best able to extract value from its flows. (See also Wark's *Capital Is Dead* [even though it's not].)[18]

One immediate consequence indicated by this formula M-I-C-I'-M' is that the image became and remains a paradigmatic work-site of capitalism. With respect to the technological reproduction of images, print—as Walter Benjamin pointed out almost a century ago in the "Work of Art" essay—is here only "a special case, though a particularly important one" (1969: 220). Your reading of this text, very possibly on a screen, is a special case of image processing, and even if you are reading on paper, the character of paper media and what appears on it has been radically transformed by the media ecology in which it now resides. This sentence is the result of the history of computation down to the present. Furthermore, taking Flusser's surprising example in *Towards a Philosophy of Photography* of the shoe as a form of encoded information, we can see even more clearly that the social product itself, to say nothing of the commodity-form, has—at least from a present mainstream perspective in which information is an ontological reality accompanying all—always had both an image component and an informatic component. These components have been nascent even if the senses had not yet undergone sufficient dialectical development to recognize negative entropy in these terms (that is, to recognize and thus constitute order itself as image and information)—even if the senses had not yet become, as Marx might say, "theoreticians."[19] The commodity object was a protoimage and protoinformation. Though in reality we should say that information grew out of the image of the commodity in the correlation that was price, we can now say that image is an aspect of information. Whether it was some purportedly Platonic form of the shoe guiding the shoemaker to encode that information in the leather and then allowing that information to be recognized in the medieval shop and consumed by means of the leather until the medium gave out on the cobblestone street, or whether it is some ultraprovocative media-hyped aesthetico-ballistic property of a gender imaginary guiding an aspirant selfie-maker to wager yet another possibly sexy skin-shot for fractional-collective valorization, the relation between image and code/commodity is here implicitly operative. Gaming information, one creates appearance and utility. To this McLuhan might have responded, "The differences are a matter of media, and of the sense ratios! Leather was tactile, it facilitated walking and perhaps agrarian labor, while digital images are virtual and haptic, facilitating corporeal organization by visuality, electrified consumption, and variants of masochistic lust." Correct Marshall but, from the standpoint of political economy, also incomplete: the differences from the informatic treasure trove that was the medieval shoe to post-Fordist, informatic "booty" are also a matter of an intensive programming of behavior—the sociohistorical process of making the senses receptive to information—in as much as the regime of images is part of the developmental program of racial capitalist expansion. Two further points:

1   This program of racial capitalist expansion works its way through the psyche and the built environment toward cybernetics and the bio- and necropolitical in order to stave off the falling rate of profit and augment capital's self-valorization—its autonomy and impunity. It is capital's "answer" to revolutionary attempts to throw off its yoke, the strategic planning of racial capital's AI. AI is the dialectical outcome of the struggle for the liberation of production from capital and capital's endeavor to enslave it. Here then with new media, we find the makings of a new order of imperialism—a kind of computational colonialism characterized by omniveillance, scripted behavior, and its own specific distributed practices and mentalities.

2   Flusser's notion of the early yet undetected presence of information raises another claim pursued in this volume, the claim that information is not ontological but is instantiated as the ur-medium of fixed capital. I simply flag these points here to mention and underscore that their emergences are not mere domination, but the concatenated result of historical contradiction— which is to say, struggle.

———————————

Our efforts here are to conceptualize the informatic absorption of social practice necessary to postindustrial capitalist expansion that goes back at least to the mid-twentieth century. I'll give a historical example to better concretize what I have so far set forth. In a brilliant essay entitled "Italian *Operaismo* and the Information Machine," Matteo Pasquinelli (2015: 52) rediscovers the work of Romano Alquati, "one of the first authors of Italian operaismo," and finds "a conceptual bridge to connect Marx with cybernetics" in Alquati's 1963 text.[20] In his discussion of the rise of cybernetics and information, Pasquinelli convincingly shows that a passage of "Alquati could be understood *avant la lettre* as the very first postulate of cognitive capitalism that *operaismo* will start to develop only many decades later" (55). Building a powerful argument that the current conjuncture of capitalist informatics should be properly understood as a "society of meta-data" (64), Pasquinelli, with a Marxist theory of value firmly in mind, explains: "Alquati introduces the concept of *valorizing information* to describe the flow running upstream and feeding the cybernetic circuits of the whole factory. Such a valorizing information is continually produced by workers, absorbed by machinery, and eventually condensed into products" (54). His essay offers us a few tantalizing passages from Alquati's text, including the means to understand Alquati's term *valorizing information*. As Alquati's essay is otherwise untranslated into English, I reproduce Pasquinelli's translation here:

> Information is essential to labour-force, it is what the worker—by the means of constant capital—transmits to the means of production on the basis of evaluations, measurements, elaborations in order to operate on the object of work all those modifications of its form that give it the requested use-value. (Alquati 1963: 121; quoted in Pasquinelli 2015: 54)

> The productive labour is defined by the quality of information elaborated and transmitted by the worker to the means of production via the mediation of constant capital, in a way that is tendentially indirect, but completely socialized. (Alquati 1963: 121; quoted in Pasquinelli 2015: 55)

> Cybernetics recomposes globally and organically the functions of the general worker that are pulverized into individual microdecisions: the "bit" links up the atomized worker to the figures of the Plan. (Alquati 1963: 134; quoted in Pasquinelli 2015: 55)

As Pasquinelli summarizes,

> In other words, operating as a *numerical interface* between the domain of labour and capital, cybernetics transforms information into surplus value. . . . Alquati's important insight is a continuum merging management,

bureaucracy, cybernetics, machinery and the division of labour: cybernetics unveils the machinic nature of bureaucracy and, conversely, the bureaucratic role of machines as they work as feedback apparatuses to control workers and capture their know-how. With Alquati we visit the belly of an abstract machine that is a concretion of capital no longer made of steel. (55, emphasis added)

A concretion of capital no longer made of steel. Here we have an image of an abstract machine with components of flesh, mind, architecture, bureaucratic organization, habit, and machinery. It is not lost on us that Alquati was observing Olivetti's computer factory, wherein information became the medium for both the machine's operating system and its production of surplus value for capital. Information is transmitted in a way that is "tendentially indirect but completely socialized." While information may concern itself with any number of things, it is always already social. What is left out of this astonishing account, and what is absent more generally from the writings of Italian operaismo is *the history of the industrialization of visuality* as an equally significant—and in my view historically necessary—pathway for the direct cybernetic absorption of cognitive and affective activities by fixed capital. This absorption of "the labor of superintendence" (Marx 1990: 549) is where we find an important part of the history of information, for *it was the necessity of the more granular absorption of labor power in the form of cognition, "oversight," and attention to stave off the falling rate of profit that gave rise to informatics.* That is, on the side of production. So too with the visual turn, which was, in retrospect, a means for the rapid absorption of what would be information, a preparation of its machinic and cognitive ground. The labor of superintendence was extended to watching over components of the distributed "abstract" machines that included others and oneself. As I have shown elsewhere and will develop further below, on the side of consumption, information develops in the footprint of the strike price on the value-form, that is, in the footprint of price.

We note that the cursory treatment of visuality by many of the theorists of cognitive capitalism is closely related to the mistaken notion of value's immeasurability discussed earlier. Contra Rousseau and Foucault, the labor of superintendence of the machine was imagined without oversight. As I argued in "Cinema, Capital of the Twentieth Century" (1994) and in *The Cinematic Mode of Production* (2006b), cinema brought the Industrial Revolution to the eye. This technology marked the real beginning of the industrialization of the visual—of sight and the oversight of sight—which was then placed in a financial feedback loop with the social on the way to becoming information. Notions found in

Christian Metz's (1982) discussion of the three types of cinematic writers that together with the audience formed a feedback loop between the cinema and the spectator's metapsychology, or in Jean-Louis Comolli's (1980) view that the queues around the block invented the cinema, offered early testimony to the cybernetic role of visual culture in the increasingly financialized integration of bodies and machines. This reformatting of the visual field, as well as its general conversion into a work-site during the cinematic mode of production, prepared the ground for the massive dissemination of colonization by informatic machines and the computational mode of production.

The understanding that looking became labor—that looking was in fact employed—also means the buildup of fixed capital from its harvest of new forms of attentional labor and suggests that the history of visual technologies constitutes an open archive capable of documenting the real subsumption of cognition, perception, and sociality by capital. Such were the technologies that organized "the grammar of the multitudes." Capital does not capture the cognitive-linguistic without industrializing vision (along with the other senses to varying and increasing degrees, with sound as a kind of repressed of the visual, and haptics on the horizon), and it does not achieve its current level of complexity without turning all aspects of this industrialization into processes of informatic, that is mathematical, communication. Thus, to redeploy Pasquinelli's phrase in relation to visuality, screen-images were already and for a long time "concretions of capital no longer made of steel." With the image as interface—as programmed and programmable—the industrialization of visuality can be understood both to drive and to complement the industrialization of ratiocognitive processes, from Charles Babbage's "Analytical Engine" (contemporary with the birth of photography) to Norbert Wiener's account of cybernetics as the machinification of low-level decision-making and "discrimination" (contemporary with the birth of television), through to Olivetti mainframes (precursors to the birth of the internet) and the now more obvious convergence of visual and discursive cognitive processes today in informatic social-media capitalism.

Virtuality and "Remaindered Life": The Labor of Watching, the Factory Code, Autonomization, and De-Ontologization

Norbert Wiener: "The new industrial revolution which is taking place now consists primarily in replacing human judgment and discrimination at low levels by the discrimination of the machine" (2003: 71).[21] As the recent work of Joy Buolamwini (2017), Safiya Umoja Noble (2018), Ruha Benjamin (2019), Charlton D. McIlwain (2020), and others shows, "discrimination" was the right word, but also only the tip of the iceberg. The father of cybernetics, at the twilight of the industrial era and the dawn of the digital one, could just as well have been thinking, as Flusser did only a few decades later, about the automation of certain aspects of thought and of perception in the visual domain by means of the quantum functions of the camera. Indeed, given Flusser's theory of the apparatus of the camera turning society into a feedback loop—one with the program of photography and with those who fed it posited as functionaries—it is not certain that the camera was not thinking Wiener. Paul Virilio (1986) has shown that Exhibit A of cybernetics—Wiener's antiaircraft gun, a fusion between human operator and machinic weapon, with precalculated trajectories enabling targeting—was already a kind of camera. As drone signature strikes based upon pattern recognition today attest, replacing human judgement and photo-discernment was a program for a far-reaching liquidation. We have already remarked that even the discursive "virtuosity" of the locuter, theorized by Paolo Virno (2004) as an extension of social cooperation scripted by capital, emerges in a media ecology equally dependent upon the production and absorption of cognitive-affective processes prescribed by programmatic visualization and strategically calculated decision making. In a reformatting that is also an expropriation, these machinic and linguistic reformations, organized by visual protocols, mark the capture and displacement of human agency as well as a reorganization of cultural terrain first registered as a full-blown sea change in the notion of postmodernism and here understood as endemic to computational racial capitalism and what Ruha Benjamin (2019) calls "the new Jim Code" (2019: 1).

However, the thoroughgoing reorganization of culture and ground (superstructure and base) by capital's transformation of the senses, where the "hyperreal" was a symptom of an ontological shift—one that accompanied what Fredric Jameson, when viewing a work of Nam June Paik, experienced as "the imperative to grow new organs"—has been a long time in the making. As early as the mid-nineteenth century, in the "Production of Relative Surplus Value" chapter of the first volume of *Capital*, Marx observed the emergence of new industrial jobs that—remarkably—consisted in watching the machinery:

> In many manual implements the distinction between man as mere motive power and man as worker or operator properly so called is very striking indeed. For instance, the foot is merely the prime mover of the spinning-wheel, while the hand, working with the spindle, and drawing and twist-

ing performs the real operation of spinning. It is the second part of the handicraftsman's implement, in this case the spindle, which is first seized upon by the industrial revolution, leaving to the worker, in addition to *his new labour of watching the machine with his eyes, and correcting its mistakes with his hands*, the merely mechanical role of acting as the motive power. (1990: 495–96, emphasis added)

Notably, this emergence of visual labor in "the fragment on machines," in which industrial manufacturing is conceived (borrowing from one Dr. Ure) as a "vast automaton," for which the workers become but its "conscious organs," rests upon the discipline and regimentation imposed by the increasing automation of steam-driven industrial capital. Again, this time in "Machinery and Large-Scale Industry," Marx writes,

The *technical subordination* of the worker to the uniform motion of the instruments of labour, and the peculiar composition of the working group, consisting as it does of individuals of both sexes and all ages, gives rise to a barrack-like discipline which is elaborated into a complete system in the factory and *brings the previously mentioned labor of superintendence to its fullest development....* "To devise and administer a successful code of factory discipline, suited to the necessities of factory diligence, was the Herculean enterprise, the noble achievement of Arkwright!" ... *In the factory code the capitalist formulates his autocratic power over his workers like a private legislator and purely as an emanation of his own will,* unaccompanied by the division of responsibility otherwise so approved by the bourgeoisie, or the still more approved representative system. *The code is merely the capitalist caricature of the social regulation of the labor process and becomes necessary in co-operation on a large scale and the employment in common in instruments of labor.* (549–50, emphasis added)[22]

The code is merely the capitalist caricature of the social regulation of the labor process. Software studies might pause here and take a deep breath, particularly as code is derived from "the labor of superintendence" and the requisites of "oversight." Since the mid-nineteenth century, the labor of watching, of making adjustments with one's hands, and the emergence of what was already the recognizable outlines of executable code, were, we could say, in the works. Already here we witness the labor of superintendence, the labor of machine-mediated cooperation organized by code. The requirements were there; it was a matter of formalizing the mechanism. In the 1844 manuscripts Marx wrote that "industry was the open book of human psychology." Is it any wonder then that just over one hundred years later Turing suggested in "Computing, Machinery and Intelligence" the high likelihood that the laws of human behavior were governed by a rule set?

From the standpoint of capital, the role and indeed the fate of the two formerly distinct sensory tracks, the visual and the verbal, is combined in the reprogramming of behavior by the labor process. This process, from plantation to computation, is coordinated by the calculus of capital—organized by the requisites of the value-form that includes capital's self preservation. Their integrated emergence as computational modes of oversight for the organization of value-productive activity is bound together just as is their social codification through juridical prescription, scientific inscription, and police/state execution. These are inseparable again from the histories of money and credit, imperialism, labor relations, class, gender, sexuality, and racialization that consciously or not informed the organizational development of visual and verbal cognition by means of their encryptions, transmissions, and valuations. This history, then, is one of a broad-spectrum colonization of and by media, one that makes clear that by the time the medium is the message, the message is capitalist exploitation, which is to say cybernetically assisted discrimination and statistically distributed murder—known in the vernacular merely as "information."

For criticism, we note in passing, it is perhaps only vis-à-vis such a broadband, interdisciplinary, and indeed antidisciplinary approach (a version of which is practiced above and throughout this volume) that one might fully glimpse the modality of the network of encroachments of informatics, of code, and of programmable images on the life-world. To avoid platform fetishism (and to begin to decolonize media studies), it should become discursively impossible to separate the above terms fully and render any one of them autonomous. No race without class, no cinema without gender and imperialism, no computation without capital, no value without murder. And no information without the whole shebang. Logically, it is thus also impossible to extract these "objects" of analysis from historical process or to separate any of these from violence: the violence of abstraction, of codification, of low-level discrimination, is not merely metaphorical. An argument for the full autonomy of any of these discursive sedimentations amounts to a disavowal of the violent history of their formation as interoperable with one another, and hence amounts to *an automated (and often automatic) reproduction of that violence*. Media studies bound to platform fetishism leads to a processing of data in the fascist sense, as do strictly disciplinary approaches more generally. The twenty-first century reveals that the disciplines themselves are the disciplines—the discipline—of fascism. Their pedagogy educates their disciples to plan and staff the camps.

The cybernetics that are the very condition of digitality and computational capital place us not only in a post-Fordist but, as noted previously, also a posthuman moment. And once posthuman, always already posthuman because always already cyborg. If biopolitics (necropolitics) and the technics thereof have become the measure of all things formerly social, then "man" most certainly is not. Neither can "man," nor "woman," as Donna Haraway clearly indicated in her 1985 "Cyborg Manifesto," remain the gold standard of Marxism, socialism, or socialist feminism. We emphasize that this demotion of "man," "woman," and "the human" is not necessarily a bad thing for all constituents. It is significant not only as a symptom of a mammoth dialectical transformation of the mode of production and reproduction to computation in the cybernetic interpenetration of image, code, and financialization, but also because "the human" (along with God, Gold, and Truth) no longer appears available to function as ground (see Haraway 2000, but also Sylvia Wynter 1994a, 1994b, 2003). During the twentieth century the dollar went off the gold standard, representation went off the reality standard, and capital went off the human standard—three outmoded interfaces that were at the same time metrics (methods of account) rendered clunky if not obsolete by informatics and digitization. Today, in a near total degrounding of metaphysical assurances by information, standards are ones of protocol interoperability, and old terms like *the subject*, *the object*, and *the human* are reduced to forms of user-interface, what N. Katherine Hayles (1999) calls "skeuomorphs." Indeed, as Allen Feldman (2015) has brilliantly shown, metaphysical reformatting as an operational effect of the strategic programming of a calculus of power allows for an on-demand restructuring of ontologies and is a medium of (permanent) war. Read-write ontologies are a product of warfare characteristic of the derivative condition.

In the triumvirate of gold, reality, and human as standards, the last, it should also be admitted, seems irredeemable (despite its continued currency), given that "the human" is an idea built upon the racial exclusion of colonized and enslaved peoples. Some might argue that the jury is still out, but racism, colonialism, apartheid, and genocide were part of the human operating system of Digital Culture 1.0, and, as I've argued elsewhere, the enslaved and the colonized were the first content providers for the buildout of the platform of capital known as "humanism." The oppressed were long caught between aspiring to the status of the human and overthrowing it as an oppressive ideology of exclusion and a legitimating alibi for racist (and sexist) violence. Nowadays, with the continuation of these value-extractive programs by other means (though the "old" means, in the form of the plantation, the sweatshop, etc., certainly persist), the distributed, transspecies, and in fact in the broadest sense transmedia cybernesis that characterizes the computational mode of production blurs the neat distinctions between human and technology, between biology and semiology, between inside and outside—for better and for worse. As mentioned at the outset of this chapter, these mutations in the protocols of valuation are themselves the result of struggle, of class war, just as the earlier essentialist algorithms (Human, God, Gold, Reality) were both forcibly imposed and forcefully resisted (by, e.g., skirmish, witchcraft, alchemy, fabulation)—were at once the products of struggle and means of production. With the antiquation of these once ostensibly ontological systems of value, value does not become measureless, as we have shown, but the impositions of the dialectical developments of the hegemony of the value-form break up the received ontologies of prior modes of life as they ordain, impose, and legitimate new orders capable of orchestrating universal exploitation by means of totalitarian abstraction for the purpose of infinite accumulation.

Given some clarity on the macrological character of the dialectic of capital accumulation and radical dispossession, it seems obvious, even trivial, that the new computational metrics being put in place have a bearing on "representation" and "politics," domains that are themselves no longer conceivable as autonomous (if they ever were), to the degree that they are being subsumed by the operating system of computational capital. Informatic metrics have a derivative function relative to their semiotic underliers; in the new economy, they provide exposure to the financial upside of any meaning whatever—that is, to the futurity of semiotic and informatic practices.

Some questions arise: With the real subsumption of humanity as a standard of value, how to confront the full autonomization of capitalist valuations? With looking and indeed survival posited as labor, abstract universal labor time becomes struggle with/in abstract time and the moral, formerly based on humanistic values, gives way to the political. With the shattering of the sovereign subject in multitasked distributed production that deploys ontologies as executable algorithms (American; male; Chinese; female), we are forced to ask exactly who or what is exploited in the social factory? If not humanity, than in whose name and on whose behalf are we making the revolution? What figures community? *Suddenly, the configuration of communitarian agency appears as a speech act and a program,* a political and *economic* strategy of survival in a field stratified by vectors of extraction. Looking toward the horizon one must also ask: Is there a communist computing?[23] Is there a way of creating communities, by drawing on their historical experiences and claims, that will *sustainably* retake the means of production and reproduction without reproducing the extractive logic of capital? In my view, these questions are equally questions of poiesis and of programming—and they must be answered in theory and practice with a *decolonization of computation*, which here means a decolonization of the real abstraction organized and executed by computer mediated exchange, a decolonization of I-C-I' that would be, in fact, an interruption in the circuit from M-M' and as we shall see, *necessarily*, a decolonization of money.

With these questions in mind, we may perceive that it is not value that has become immeasurable, as Negri thought, but rather the immeasurable is that which Neferti Tadiar (2012: 796) calls "remaindered life": the fragments and dimensions of persons and peoples, of experience and aspiration that literally fall out of an economy (and its representations and political programs—all of which have become financialized) in which, over the past century, product, semiotic, measure, and value are increasingly systematized and unified.[24] Remaindered life is immeasurable and unaccounted for because the metrics of account are themselves instruments of capitalization through the financialization of the schema of information. This immeasurability, this being beyond number—what's lost in information—is what Negri was probably reaching for (and what Tadiar is able to name) in his mistaken claim that value had become immeasurable. The corollaries of remaindered life, "life-times" and "life-times of disposability," become the basic functions within the black box of production and the production of liquidity. It is life-time that must be politicized, but in a "language" ("languages") or protocol (protocols) not bound to capital.

With respect to what is immeasurable, the words that conclude Borges's 1941 "The Garden of Forking Paths," a story about encryption if there ever was one, seem prescient. Knowing that the newspapers will pick up his story, the spy Yu T'sun murders an Englishman, who could have taught him much about his own history, to send a message to German military intelligence: the Englishman's surname, Albert, is that of the town to be bombed. Incarcerated and bearing witness to the remnants of informatic war, and writing from his English cell, he melancholically reflects on his deeds, his losses, and his relation to his German commanding officer for whom he foreclosed his alternative life paths in order to send a message—"He does not know (no one can know) my *innumerable* contrition and weariness" (Borges 1964: 29, emphasis added).

Subsumption is the measuring; the remainder, the innumerable, is what is not subsumed. It is tempting to say that this remaindered life, already present in Borges and the result of the logistics of communication in the context of global war, is a new antithesis that is and will be the resultant form of the synthesis of capital and labor in the network of M–I–C–I'–M'. Capital which, with its colonization of the life-world and of the semiotic, would put labor, capital, and meaning in lock-step ordained by the value-form itself and simultaneously would externalize noncapitalist experience beyond the horizon of representation. Everything representable would be *of* capital, everything nonrepresentable would be externalized as waste, noise, heat. We—those of us and those parts of us—who live in the remainders, who are wasted, who are noise, who are heat, are being pushed toward a nonproductive fugitivity and toward forms of endurance and survival *within* the confines of the prison-house of information. We are not the first and we may find community there.

This remaindered life—clearly in relation to what Tadiar earlier observed in her title *Things Fall Away* (2009), and more recently registered in Harney and Moten's *The Undercommons* (2013)—suggests a systemic unassimilability that dialectics may only approach with caution: outsides that are at once inside but also really outside, or what Brian Massumi (2018) might call "the immanent outside." The insistent call of and for a politics beyond politics (since "politics" is now a subroutine of financialized semiotics) results from the near total colonization and capture of sign systems by a formation of capital that is increasingly autonomous in function and cosmic in scope—as if language itself had become a platform for capital. A beyond politics dwells in the borderlands, in space-times that demur from the drama of value. This beyond, a hauntology, a feel, a music, an unevenly distributed subalternity, calls on knowing to shift its resolution—its resolution of object and their subjects. It calls for shifts in mode, mood, affect, and tone. And not just in poetry, theory, or journalism but in science, digital imaging, and statistics. It calls for an awareness that life-time is at stake as we signify on the dead and the dispossessed—as we must.

Such awareness has to be opposed to the autonomization of the value-form:

> In simple circulation, the value of commodities attained at the most a form independent of use-values, i.e., the form of money. But now, in the circulation of M–C–M, value suddenly presents itself as a self-moving substance which passes through a process of its own, and for which commodities and money are both mere forms. But there is more to come: instead of simply representing the relations of commodities, it now enters into a private relationship with itself, as it were. . . . Value . . . now becomes value in process, money in process, and, as such, capital. It comes out of circulation, enters into it again, preserves and multiplies itself within circulation, emerging from it with an increased size, and starts the same cycle again and again. M–M, "money which begets money." Lastly, in the case of interest-bearing capital, the circulation M–C–M′ presents itself in abridged form, in its final result without any intermediate stage, in a con-

cise style, so to speak, as M–M', i.e., money which is worth more money, value which is greater than itself. (Marx 1990: 257–58)

Capital's "concise style," its interest, is precisely the occlusion of the dialogue with producers, the repression and attempted foreclosure of our claims and aspirations that renders us spectral. Capital's colonization of the life-world, its artificial intelligence that results from and indeed is the autonomization of the value-form allows us to observe two things. First, money's shimmering presence, its pyrotechnics, its metaphysical, psychotropic, cybernetic effects (which might be abstracted and understood as the financializing precondition for the processual unfolding known as the identity of identity and nonidentity) are the effects of its "concise style" and are consequences of its role in structuring, which is to say *programming,* the *metabolism* of society—the latter word is Marx's. Fetishism (be it of money, computing, freedom, or any value whatever), its affects, and its requisites result from the gradients of value's churn. Second, what has happened in the past long century, particularly with the visual turn, the capture of the cognitive-linguistic, and the consequent evisceration of classical metaphysics (an imposition of the same "concise style" that ultimately required the placing of "being" under erasure [being] and, along with the rise of simulation and virtuality, required the evisceration of traditional metaphysical essentialisms by the screens of capital, such that truth [truth], and we might as well add philosophy [philosophy], could themselves only ever be simulations), is that, under the authority of the autonomization of the value-form, the number and type of intervals from M to M' have undergone an exponential expansion. *All interests have been subsumed by interest.* The wholesale rewiring of space-time and semiotics—at all operative levels, by the concise style of the protocols of a unified operating system (originally the invisible hand, now sporting the infinite digits of AI) that is synonymous with and indeed authored by capital logic in deadly struggle with revolutionary innovation from below—withers away old-world metaphysics (as well as the old world itself), utilizing methods of ramification and incorporation through enumeration, the assignation of number to any quality whatever. All representable interests become a means to interest, a means to move from M to M'.

The computational mode of production has encroached upon the world. The general procedure required to move from M to M' was and is the recursive loop of computation's image-code, though at an earlier stage in capital development this was simply called commodification. This procedure, along with the ability to reverse-engineer a desired effect (affect) back to a fragmentary process, could be traced back to Gutenberg, and the scientific revolution, and industrialization—all of which, whatever else they were, pace McLuhan, were vehicles of capital expansion (including print media). The expansion and intensification of this procedure of image-code-financialization—where image was a desired image (say, a printed page), code was the executable script for its production and circulation, and finance was the cost-benefit analysis beholden to the value-form that experimented with options on both on the way from M to M'—strove at once locally and systemically to encompass both the macro- and micro-infinities of space-time. The image as data-visualization is both worked up and worked on—it is a worksite for the modification of code, for the absorption of negative entropy on the road from M to M'. We interface with images and are taken as images by both psychic and machinic technologies of racial abstraction, gender abstraction, and so on. As we have seen, with computational capital's exponential growth of the circuits from M to M', through the organization of image and code and the development of these as work-sites, this colonization of space-time-meaning transfigures the forms of the commodity and the forms of labor along with the very mode of the presencing (or nonpresencing) of the human, of being and the cosmos.

We are in a better position here to once again state a fundamental thesis of this volume: information is not a cause but an effect of the history of capitalism. It is alienated sociality. Later, as Marx would add, the relationship between cause and effect becomes reciprocal. As such, its emergence depended upon the development of machines by means of which a gradual encoding and decoding could function socially as a general equivalent. In a first phase, the subject develops with the object through material expansion: then, as the machines for the perception of information advanced and extended themselves, information became widespread, and, as we have seen, subject and object went through their metamorphosis. Subjects, first constituted by real abstraction became dividual and cybernetic, objects, likewise constituted as objects of exchange, became digitally composable. And because we know from Marx and so many others that wage labor, industrial machines, money-forms, and the like were globally imposed by force, we must also recognize that the same is true for the making and unmaking of subjects and objects but also for information and the material practices that make it what it is. It's apparent autonomy, *the autonomy of information*, is the consequence of a long history of violence, class war and genocide in racial capitalism. Any understanding of the nature of information must recognize this condition of the emergence of information as an expression of the value calculus or must fall into fetishism and mystification.

Amid all the semiomaterial reordination that characterizes the rise of visuality and of informatic society, a reordination that Flusser names the universe of the technical image, in which the informatic program of the camera presides and thus overwhelms the rational thinking and linear time characteristic of a discursive world, two fundamental conditions remain. They remain as dialectical results of the photopoliticization characteristic of the increasing autonomization of the value-form as program, an intensification that underscores the fact that photocapital is ultimately computational racial capital. Designated hypostatically these results are the premises of historical alienation: private property (the accumulation of capital) and structural violence (the accumulation of dispossession). As Marx wrote in *Capital*, "There is not one single atom of . . . value that does not owe its existence to unpaid labor" (1990: 728), even as he clearly recognized that value had no atoms of matter. Today we might understand that these "atoms" of value are life-quanta, bits, stolen moments of "life-time" (Tadiar 2012) that result from capitalist class war and the antithesis of democracy—they are units of information, the aggregated alienation of what the young Marx called "species being" bent to the assemblage of matter, its informing. We red-flag in passing the symptomatic rise of interminable war, climate racism, worldwide precarity, and everyday fascism along with its fractalization on social media as inescapable aspects of capital's broad-spectrum, increasingly fine-grained photographic-informatic praxis of command-control that liquidates ontologies, narrative, reason, and time. And, with Tadiar, we gesture toward the remainder, that which falls away from the calculus of capital and from its informatic domination, as a direction of insurgent investigation.

The programmable image, then, is at once programmed and programmable—a data-visual site for informatic transaction in photocapitalism. People find their currency there, their social liquidity, but at a great price. And, as with the selfie, the basic structure is protofascist if not fractally fascist, running as it does on the aggregation of the attention of others disappeared into the selfie/image. In the next chapter I will reconsider the space of the interval from M to M'—along with the politics, such that they are, of the production of "interest," a term that, as noted, itself indicates a convergence in accord with the new calculi of value operative within the domain of images and codes (Beller 2016b). The interval from M to M' is the interval of speculation, creativity, exploitation—and also and always of struggle. It is an interval mediated by information and information's interface with social process. Capturing imagination and interest, M-M' is an interval in which the programmable image emerges as the paradigmatic template for labor. It is anything but static. Thus, we now know that we can specify this dynamic interval, once figured by the commodity ("C") and here analyzed as "image-code" under the term *informa- tion* ("I"), and write the general formula for capital as M–I–M'. We do not yet know if that sovereign interval that has presided over so many nightmares can be meaningfully transcended or only momentarily suspended. Any viable reprogramming will require detournement of language, images, social media platforms and money itself.

M–I–M′

Informatic Labor and Data-Visual Interruptions in Capital's "Concise Style"

Commodity as Information, Information as Commodity

In this chapter I will be committed to interrogating some of the new pathways from M to M′. We examine the movements by which money becomes more money, movements that—as we saw in the conclusion of the preceding chapter—Marx described, with reference to interest-bearing capital, as capital's "concise style" (1990: 257–58). From the depositor's point of view, M simply becomes M′. What are the mediations of interest at work beneath this concision?

The term *informatic labor*, further developed below, implies that the "human" metabolic modification of the status of information—its state—is both the paradigmatic form of value-uptake by capital and the paradigmatic form of labor imposed by capital. As we saw in the previous chapter, capital's "concise style," by which money becomes more money (M–M′), is in effect the organization of "interest" in all senses of that term. The provisioning of information can thus be understood to occur in accord with such interest. I will, however, partly undertake this investigation into what is, in effect, the production of interest by providing negative examples: examples in which hegemony is effectively challenged by acts and processes that are disinterested in or antagonistic toward profit—and capital is therefore, at least to a certain extent, divested. In such examples capital valorization is deflected or refused and the price of peace is raised.

Fortunately, many people have divergent interests from those of capital. It is as if by intervening in the logistics of the image and/or the linguistic sign it were possible to interrupt the circuit from M to M′ and in doing so open up pathways for the reconfiguration of the informatics of racial capitalism in order to forestall or transcend them. Certain elaborations and ramifications of the relationship between image and code serve as a space of politicization and anticapitalist praxis, rather than as a practice of capitalist valorization—at least at first. Radical practices—forms of counterculture designed to have an impact on political economy—may not break the paradigm of information, but they play against its regime and produce statistically unpredictable results, results that in one way or another are open to the masses and to antistate or anarchist mass action. They also feel different. Not in all cases considered in this volume, but in many, the practice of resistance, refusal, détournement, or reprogramming will further schematize the dominant while generating critique, counterculture, and counterhistory by means of hacks. It would be remiss not to mention here that such destabilizing efforts do not guarantee a politics particularly as they have been used by the right to accelerate fascism.

However, before moving to examples of interest to revolutionary sensibilities and of disinterest to capital (at least in their first instance), it is important to assess clearly that the penultimate formula for capital arrived at in the last chapter (M–I–C–I′–M′) can be expanded, without any natural limit, as a process of M–I–C–I′–C′–I″–C″–I‴ . . . (n) . . . —M′. The point is that the oscillation between image and code, or indeed any form of data-visualization and codification, is not necessarily linear in the movement from M to M′ but is more often varied, and networked. Indeed, as I indicated at the end of the previous chapter (and as I argued in *The Message Is Murder*), we can ultimately abbreviate any of these possible pathways through image and code simply as "I" (where "I" is information). Thus "I" replaces the nineteenth-century "C" that stood for the commodity—and we now write the general formula for capital as M–I–M′.

It follows from this reformulation that changes in the state of the matrix of information, here posited as a universal Turing machine, are necessary for M to become M′. Information is now platformed not only on discrete state machines but on all materials of interest to the socius. Let us momentarily embark on a flight of fancy to a world in which clear divisions pertain and things may be simply understood. We may then observe that changes in the universal discrete state machine posited here come about by many means but that these means may be separated into two basic categories: those that add value to M and those that do not. For the latter set of factors (those that do not add value to M), modifying the state of the world computer, or cosmic discrete state machine, we have the churn of nature along with machine function. The first is like the water turning the mill, and the second is like the paddle wheel, axle, and millstone that grind the wheat. In this pastoral, the water flows in indifference, while the millstone wears itself out. Both can be used to transform the form of value, but neither in and of itself *produces* value. Only living labor does that, or only, to take the most extreme reduction of this Marxian notion, "life-time." What Neferti Tadiar (2012) calls "life-time," a development of the notion of living labor that is attuned to the dynamics of the global matrix of extraction and the functioning of financial logics even in phenomenologically nonfinancial domains, can be harnessed to tend the mill. Composed of matter and life-time themselves, the millworks, in their amortization, additionally give some of their stored value to the grain as it is ground, but it is the miller that feeds the mill, just as the farmers grow the wheat and peasants or other, perhaps migrant agrarian laborers, harvest it, and it is there—on the plantation and along with the miller's labor—that people oversee state changes in matter and new value is added to the product. If these are waged workers, then the labor market that uses historical dispossession and competition to leverage down the price of their labor power allows for the payment only for their necessary labor time (the time the worker needs to work to reproduce themself) while their surplus labor (their "surplus" time that is stolen in the wage relation) becomes profit for the various owners of the means of production.

What then of the generalization of information, the positing of information in relation to any underlying phenomenon whatever? This notion—though really more than a notion, in fact a generalized *treatment* of the cosmos by some Earthlings—indicates a formal subsumption of the cosmos by capital. Information is a technique of capture, a technique of harnessing cosmic flux for the computational mill. Everywhere information is harvested the computer-millstone is engaged. These millstones, sensors and processors, are investments for reaping the flux. The real subsumption of the cosmos has indeed been launched; however, it requires the computational armature that is extended into life and matter as an extension of our very senses and interests to make the cosmos the grist and information the product—the modality of all appearance. This means that the cosmic flow may be treated as information, but the machines to gather it, measure it, and optimize its use must be built. The computational millworks may give value to its products through machine amortization (our computers wear out), but it is we who (like the serfs, slaves, or wage-workers on the land) supply the computers and who (like the miller tending the mill) tend the computers with our own metabolic processes. We are the ones that help turn those 1s and 0s, and it is in this activity that we generate new value.

We remark in passing that—just as streams can do and be other things besides energy flux to turn a mill—so too can the cosmos be more than informatic flux to drive changes in machine states. And so too can we denizens of the planet be more than information providers. Or so we must assume. But the universalization of this *treatment* of the cosmos as informatic is what is key. Here, with an understanding that informatic perception is nothing more than the financializing perception of capital—an investment in instrumental knowledge—we have reached a point where we can write the general job description for the universal employ offered by capital:

> Wanted: humanoid information processor capable of converting I to I′. Tasks may include manual, mental, attentional, cognitive, screen, and metabolic labor and making yourself infinitely available as a surface for the inscription of information. All interfaces with the social armature accepted. Only the yet living need apply themselves.

What was formerly called living labor, and is now understood in terms of work, attention, cognition, affective capacity, life-time, and the like now drives the state changes in discrete state machines, and these changes, the creation of socially useful information, are at the core of the transition from M to M′. Every case of value production, even the most traditional cases of food or object production, can be thought in these terms, for this case is the most general case. Informed matter is securitized in a system of access rights that are accumulated by capital and withheld from the living, only to be accessed in exchange for the leveraged production of more information, as money or whatever acceptable form.

We have seen from this analysis as well as from the recent history of finance that among the myriad intervening subroutines in the movement from money to more money in capital, that is, from M to M′, is the subroutine known as the financial derivative. Even the Indian farmer, subject to the volatility of price fluctuations on the world market, becomes a portfolio manager with respect to their crops. Rather than growing for the local miller in our example, each crop represents for this farmer a position in relation to the world market (Seth 2017). Each crop is an exposure to volatility, and the growth of several different crops is a way of hedging volatility. Thus, what seems to be the most traditional of activities can be understood to have been simultaneously financialized and informationalized. Growing a particular food is nothing less than launching a program in a world of programs—together the farmer's plantings represent a portfolio of contingent claims, a profile of risk. The financial derivative, as part of the contemporary era characterized by "financialization," is Exhibit A of what is sometimes termed "synthetic finance," as it bundles existing financial products together, securitizes these bundles, tranches the risk, and sells them off. Derivatives offer various options on the future. Most economists will tell you that the rules of "value creation" in derivative finance are of a different order than that of the old or traditional economy, and they will oftentimes speak as if derivatives create value out of thin air, "notionally," by bypassing the rules of traditional economy in what is yet another and greater discrediting of the labor theory of value—which is held in contempt and, in mainstream economics, is beneath mention. This last remark, that derivative finance, by creating an industry that profits directly from risk management, has transcended the Marxist account of value is of course never stated, since it is common knowledge that capitalism has already shown that Marxist value theory and its account of worker exploitation is not only defunct but dead wrong. Just look at all that growth! And how many rich people there are! Marginal utility, anyone?

What is not taken seriously is information asymmetry and access rights to partitioned networks, or what amounts to different levels of enfranchisement by computational racial capital. But even in the mainstream, not everyone is happy. As the late Randy Martin (2013: 85) tells us, the derivative is often seen (even by non-Marxists) as an economic formation that, by general consensus, broke the economy in 2008, wantonly making "something out of nothing" and allowing "a greedy few [to take] advantage while regulators looked the other way." Martin observed the following:

> While derivative principles have been applied in economic settings for thousands of years, albeit without the materiality or impact they presently exercise, their logic has a presence in many fields. Despite entering august dictionary listings and public discourse only in the past decade, derivatives actually have a long history and complex genealogy that incorporates meanings from law, medicine, geology, engineering, chemistry, music, calculus and grammar. In all these senses, derivatives are a transmission of some value from a source to something else, an attribute of that original expression that can be combined with like characteristics, a variable factor that can move in harmony or dissonance with others. (85)

The derivative emerges in modern finance as a risk management tool and had resulted in offloading risk onto the precariat who do not have the financial tools or the wealth to insure themselves against it. For example, if, say, a U.S.-based business enters into a contract to make a purchase six months from now for one million euros, it can also purchase an option—that is, a contract—to buy those euros at a set price (say, $1.10 per euro) to hedge against the risk of a large price fluctuation that might make euros more expensive. Such a contract offsets risk; the price of such a contract is called a liquidity premium and guarantees its purchaser the right to buy a set amount of euros for a set amount of dollars on a certain date. In fact, it represents a stochastic relation to the market, a weighted bet on one set of results within a statistical range of outcomes. Thus, it requires—and in fact is—a reading of market forces, including the psychology of all players. It is, in short, a wager on the movement of the totality of the market, a wager regarding how market movements may affect the pricing of a particular commodity that delimits the risk of contingency for a price. It is a hedge against the risk of decision making under conditions of uncertainty. Derivative pricing is done in real time using the Black-Scholes equation, which is based on Brownian motion and thermodynamics (see chapter 5). The financial derivative becomes a way of organizing information and creating a rigorous program of fixed outcomes based upon the probabilities of a set of possible variations in a structurally limited informatic matrix. That the strike price of risk regarding a particular outcome adjusts moment to moment demonstrates both the usefulness and the limits of the prediction model. Ordinary folk, whose lives (salaries and savings, if any) are denominated in local currencies such as the Philippine peso, the Argentine peso, or the Venezuelan Bolivar cannot hedge their holdings in this way and are totally exposed to the volatility of the world market.

Understanding the instrumentality of such a product as the financial derivative, one that can be used as a speculative instrument or as a hedge to guarantee a return on investment (as with the example of dollars and euros above), allows us to remark and indeed make the case that advertising can be viewed as another instrument of risk management, one whose various forms have, like those of the financial sector, grown into an "industry." The comparison of these two entities is mutually revealing. Like the financial industry which applies mathematics to psychology, the advertising industry applies psychology to mathematics to make the case to investors for its own legitimacy and productive potential. As I show in the next chapter, advertising too formalizes "social cooperation" and endeavors to leverage it by means of its calculus of codes for the benefit of its investors. And of course, for the benefits of the market makers—here the attention brokers. With advertising, however, the wager on market forces directly depends upon a formalized (and increasingly algorithmic) organization of the psyche and of semiotics via the programmable image. Just as the various derivatives of commodity circulation open up spaces of transaction within a transaction (transactions which themselves can be bundled and sold, as in the price of euros in dollars or the securitization, tranching, and resale of home loans), we can demonstrate that this logic of the derivative—itself a calculus of multiple transactions that reduces a complex process to a price (per eyeball over time, yes, but increasingly *which* eyeball over *what* time)—pertains specifically to image function. These new "industries" involving various combinatories between the mathematics and the psychology of finance have long troubled a Marxism that—with some brilliant early exceptions, including Dallas Smythe, Guy Debord, and Jean Baudrillard—was in large part capable of only a rudimentary, quasi-Newtonian conception of the commodity-form as object, and thus of productive labor as remunerated work. We saw in the last chapter the pathways of networked emergence beyond these subject-object paradigms. The Newtonian conception of the commodity only as object (a form that, as I tried to indicate in the previous chapter, was itself a derivative on the underlier "exchange-value," though not understood as such) was relatively unable to perceive the incipient networking of either the commodity-form or of its composition by networked forms of productive labor, some remunerated and some not. We might even say that it was this relationship of risk to liquidity spanning social production and reproduction networked by money that Marx was trying to explain. Be that as it may, as early as the late 1960s, in his famous "Blindspot" essay, Dallas Smythe (1977) recognized the productive role of audiences in the valorization of commodity pricing and—in making a case for the concept of "the audience commodity" by arguing that audiences do the work of learning to consume—introduced a networked model of valorization that factored in the productive value of tapping psychology, perception, desire, imagination, and the like, the very capacities that I endeavored to describe as the basis of the attention theory of value through an expansion of Marx's notion of sensuous labor (Beller 2006b). Smythe's effort, like my own, was to conceptualize what was transacted (and indeed produced) in the network. It was a theorization of the evolving logistics of the market—always already a network, even if not conceptualized as such. It was, in short, a reconsideration of "the problem of the road," of circulation itself, the paving of its pathways, as a space of production.

This brief comparison of these two "industries," derivative finance and advertising, securitizing pathways for M to M', reveals that risk management techniques account for the vagaries of subjective actors and intersubjective social dynamics by creating a spread. They are instruments priced to manage volatility, calculi of informatic capture networked via screens converted into various types of contracts. They are nothing less than new techniques of capital for the harvesting of the social product and, as such, are to be seen in relation to the plantation, the factory, and the deterritorialized factory of mass media. The plantation had institutionalized slavery and the whip, the factory added the imperial state, its police, and the clock, and social media added delirium, frenzy, generalized psychosis, the credit system, metadata, and the screen. Cotton and sugar required different methods than washing machines and automobiles, and images, too, demanded a redesign of the protocols of organization, control, and value extraction—all shaped by economies of scale and rising market volatility, as the ramification of inequality and the falling rate of profit pushed ever deeper into the flesh of the world. Thus, we see that monetary media and the development therein for the structuring of credit/ debt and contingent claims, and social media with the development of new metrics of attention and attention markets, are convergent as computation and thus as *economic media*. "Economic media" here means the convergence of monetary and semiotic media as computation orchestrated by the world computer of racial capitalism. We flag here that it is precisely this convergence that revolutionary politics must redesign—from the standpoint of praxis.

The Photograph as Image and Code, Commodity and Work-Site

As already indicated, the technological and computational elaboration of the networked screen-image as a means of production and value extraction is, from a technical point of view, the paradigmatic adventure of post-Fordist capitalism. The screen as work-site for data visualization in a feedback loop with social process constitutes the cutting edge of computational capital. It shows what requires attention and screens out externalities, while simultaneously turning all messages into economic media of value production and transmission. Social media sites, with their constant production and circulation of images, as well as the metrics they develop to evaluate and market such productive circulation, are part of the command-control operations that organize social production and reproduction—sociality—more generally. They are sites of programming and reprogramming. They are also fixed capital. But rather than reviewing the productive dimensions of visuality (the labor of looking, the attention theory of value, neuropower, etc.) that the success of Facebook and Google so readily testify to (and that increasingly can be understood to traverse sensuality, semiosis, imaginative speculation, and all social praxis), let us first consider here a particularly *critical* approach to image production, indeed, one could say *image-production*: that of Ariella Azoulay.

Though not focused on digitality, in books that include *The Civil Contract of Photography* (2008) and *Civil Imagination: A Political Ontology of Photography* (2012), Azoulay undertakes a radical reconceptualization of photography and its various programs—one on par with that of Vilém Flusser. Here we will take up some of the insights of her work and bend them to our own purposes. A consideration of her revision of the significance of photography will, in the context of a discussion of what I think of as the work-site of the image, serve to illustrate some of the productive stakes implicit in photography's multiple derivatives. Derivatives of what? Derivatives on the social relations, on agency, and on power, that are in one way or another the underliers to which the images give exposure. Azoulay's reconceptualization of the ontology of photography disrupts received notions regarding what she calls "the civil contract of photography" and reveals that reigning conceptions of the photograph (e.g., its authenticity or truth, the sovereignty of the photographer, the abiding distinction between "art" photography and "political" photography) secure and are secured by *existing* institutionalized social relations that most often corroborate national formations even if nationalist content is in no way explicitly referenced. The formal and informal rules of photography are on a continuum with those of the state. Ideas and practices of photography normalize certain forms of agency and exclude other forms in ways that render society predictable and functional in accord with photography's organizing principles. These in turn corroborate state ideology and include the granting of authority and the right to judge, as well as the delimitation of these affordances. Azoulay shows that the extant conventions of and around photography are correlated with regimes of citizenship, state power, and, importantly, their forms of exclusion—as if the institutionalization of photography (its commonsense understanding) were itself a mode of risk management working in the service of the status quo of state power. In other words, dominant ideology codifies both the apparatus and conventions around the function and meaning of the apparatus in ways that are at once unconscious and complicit with forms of state and economic violence. Photography, in its hegemonic practices, and hegemonic nationalisms operationalize the same protocols. Received notions around the apparatus bolster forms of entrenched violence while silencing protest against injustice by making certain relations to "the event of photography" beneath consideration or inadmissible.

Azoulay reframes the ontology of the photographic medium by rejecting traditional interpretations of it as a medium of the Real—an immedium—and exploring what she conceives of as "a *political* ontology of photography" (2012).[1] In contradistinction to theorists such as André Bazin (1967) or Roland Barthes (1980), who understood photography first and foremost as a branch of chemistry that creates an index of the Real, Azoulay borrows from what she calls "the paradigm of visual culture" (2012: 55) and understands photography as fundamentally a social relation—one in which there are many stakeholders. Whether one is in front of the lens, behind the lens, before the image, a purveyor of the image, one who has access to the image, one who is denied access, one who is represented, one who is unrepresented, one who has moved into the space where the image was made, or one who has been forced out of that space, and so on, one may be a stakeholder in the meaning and usage of an image. This notion of the photograph as distributed social relation is quite different from, say, Barthes's notion that the distinctive feature of the photograph, its "essence," is a relation to the Real—its "that has been"-ness (1980: 115). But as even Barthes intuited, albeit by means of a naturalistic ontology positing chemistry at the origins of the photograph, the received notions that organize the practice of photography and its allied perceptions (visible in what Barthes called "the *studium*" [29]), are hedges against the risk that photography itself represents—for Barthes, nothing short of "madness," the shattering of the semiotic (118). Indeed, despite his notion of the *punctum*, that is "the prick of the Real" (53) visible in certain photographs (to certain viewers), the limits of the photographic rules of perception were apparent to Barthes. As is well known, the great semiotician, writing under the staggering weight of the loss of his mother while considering a photograph of her, made his apologia in *Camera Lucida* for the limitations imposed by semiotics itself. Barthes's grief forced him to confront that the photograph contained within itself the possibility for the violation and indeed the explosion of extant semiotic codes, opening out through the chemical fixity of a "that has been" to what he glimpsed in separate but related episodes as the unspeakable plenitude— unframeable by psychoanalysis or any other extant structure—that was his love for his mother and as the "madness" of the Real (118). This revolution in the realm of the semiotic already testified to the civil containment of photography.

Reflecting on the role of photography and of particular photographs in the Israeli occupation of Palestine, Azoulay (2012: 241–8) too understands that received interpretive codes, and the institutions that maintain them, organize photography in a way that produces and reproduces the status quo. Barthes confronted the limit of the status quo as a personal matter—it simply would not and could not let him express his feeling for his mother. He neither reproduces the "winter garden photograph" of his mother nor does he endeavor to speak those feelings. He does, however, allow this excess, this beyond-meaning of his grief, to suggest an outside to semiotics and thus to the sociality of meaning (1980: 115–8). This outside is indeed signified and in a way secured by its absence—a that has been that cannot appear. Azoulay understands both the limitations placed on photography by the social, and those further imposed by ruling notions of its nature, its ontology, to be political. By dilating the event of photography well beyond the presence or absence of the snapshot, and by introducing what she calls "the civil contract of photography," Azoulay, in an admittedly utopian (but nonetheless political) vein, is able to posit a "citizenry of photography" whose inclusivity of those who may have a stake in the image surpasses not only the received notions of what photography is, or how to interpret it, but also the inclusivity of the contemporary nation state and who has the right to speak within it—as the nation state imposes a distinction between citizen and non-citizen while adjudicating over them both (2012: 11–27). The photograph would open to a discursive space in which anyone might respond whether they were included or not in any of the enfranchised positions offered by photographic conventions and institutions. Drawing upon photographs of Palestine and of Palestinians—both taken and not taken, visible and invisible—as her archive, she gives amplitude and voice to the many perspectives and consequences of the various photographic events and events of photography embroiled in the fraught history of Palestine, Israel, and indeed of the modern world, in a way that allows the entrance of Palestinian perspectives, histories, and claims into an archive that might otherwise exclude them and in practice does exclude them. It must be said, furthermore, that she makes this case for the rethinking of photography within a national and often international context that systematically excludes Palestinian claims on life and that uses this exclusion as a way of preserving conditions that justify further violence. The "proper" treatment of photographs is a site of struggle. An analysis of photography as a set of practices reveals its properties as hegemonic protocols for cultural semiotics that might be recast.

Importantly for Azoulay, who has been both curator and critic, Palestine has become not simply an open-air prison, as is widely recognized, but an "open studio" for the purveyance of images of "regime-made disaster" (2012: 243). Azoulay's embedding of the photographic event in social relations profoundly affects the kinds of statements that can be made about photography and begins to reveal not just the complicity but indeed the support that conventional notions of photography lend to apartheid regimes. It is as if they are cut from the same cloth—part of the same ideology and arising from the same material conditions. By accepting that the photographer—or the gallery or the soldier or the critic—can exercise sovereignty over the image, and can say not only how it can be used but what it means, we accede to existing forms of power. We process information in accord with hegemonic protocols with respect to inclusion, exclusion, rights, ethics, culture, and taste.

Azoulay's work endeavors to open the archive to political claims to representation, history, and justice in order to create broad-based anticolonial solidarity in response to instances of violence that have been pushed to the margins, remaindered, or invisibilized by photographic conventions, while also holding out, in this case to Israeli citizens, what she calls the possibility of "the right not to be a perpetrator" (243). This latter is something nearly impossible for Israeli citizens to exercise currently. In short, in her work, images—along with the praxes and discourses they engender—become the work-sites of culture and struggle rather than things necessarily and in many ways unconsciously consumed in accord with conventions and habits complicit with state violence and the propriety required by existing property relations. However, her displacement of these conventions (conventions which by virtue of their entrenchment have naturalized around photography both a set of practices and a metaphysics) illustrates how productive their normative functions are both to state power and in codifying racial formations. *We add here that this conjunction is not only a matter of statecraft and racism; it is also a method of accruing financial power—that is, it is a technique of racial capitalism.*

In dilating the photographic event and opening it to many (Palestinian, anticolonial, antifascist) stakeholders beyond the photographer, the museum, the newspaper, the police, and those represented in the image, Azoulay reveals the political ontology of photography and grasps that ontological condition as a distributed social relation. In changing the types of statements one can make about the photograph—that is, in altering the discursive field around photography away from what is, for the enfranchised, the comfortingly un- or decontextualized context of a photograph that itself serves to secure a limited set of meanings; and away again from the sovereignty of a photographer's intent or artistry, or a procrustean distinction between politics and art—Azoulay provides a kind of counterpraxis to Paolo Virno's (2004) notion of virtuosity. Such a counterpraxis centered around photography—unlike a photographic praxis that, ordinarily, in conforming to statist interpretations and usages of a photograph (no matter how liberal), would also conform to the exigencies of capital and of capitalized state power, along with their productive prescripting of discourse—instead offers a prescription for a kind of antivirtuosity. Thus, Azoulay's renegotiation of the ontology of photography is a strategy of semiowar and an effort to reclaim the cognitive-linguistic ordinarily scripted by the exigencies of capitalist and indeed photocapitalist cooperation; her disruption of the very notion of photography disrupts capital's scripts: the ways in which we participate in its practices and institutions, as well as its programs. It is therefore a retaking of cognitive-linguistic capacities that are ordinarily organized by the photographic programs that are part and parcel of the oppressive racial capitalist state.

At stake here is a claim that goes from racial capitalism to state power to image to language mediated by the everyday practices of apartheid. To launch her reconceptualization of the embedded and distributed character of a photograph, whose meaning for her is "never-ending," Azoulay insists upon a shift from "the paradigm of art" (with its canons, geniuses, and exemplary images, and its isolation from the *too* political") to "the paradigm of visual culture" (2012: 38, 55). We confront the fact that the vast institutionalization of photographic practices (from gallery curation, aesthetic evaluation, and captioning, etc., to ideas about the role of photographer, critic, viewer, and the metaphysics of the image, etc.) not only bear the signature of a statist imaginary, but actively reinforce state power and its models of agency, civility, adjudication, jurisdiction, and epistemology, along with its presumed right to violence, its encampment of populations, its militarization, incarceration, apartheid, and all the rest of the necropolitical imaginary. In deterritorializing "the paradigm of art" and its cultic models of authority and sovereign creativity with that of "the paradigm of visual culture" and its sense of distributed participation, we may observe here that, with the displacement of the hegemony of the single image or unitary voice by the churn of a distributed media ecology, the practices of social media are implicit in Azoulay's reconceptualization of photography (55). She does this, we could say, to disrupt photography's otherwise concise style, its scripted forms of interest. Azoulay's powerful expansion of the media ecology of photography infuses her recent books and interrogates the organization of photographic practices by state and bourgeois cultural formations, as well as by what might be called their ideological apparatuses—apparatuses that reductively organize the use and reception of images and therefore appear as part of the photographic program. She pursues distinctions between "the paradigm of art" and "the paradigm of visual culture," and exposes the paradigm of art as a foreclosure of many of the radical potentialities of photography for a new form of citizenship, "the citizenry of photography" posited by photography's opening of an interpretive process requiring an expanded notion of dialogue and new forms of antistate and perhaps anticapitalist interest (51). Thus, we may observe of that the paradigm of art: 1) that it is invested in a distinction between the aesthetic and the political; 2) that it configures a notion of sovereignty through the ideal of authorship and the adjudication of rights to view and interpret images; and 3) that it generates objects for 4) sovereign subjects (55–62). Azoulay writes against the photograph as the aesthetic (or political) result of the sovereign subject-photographer's exercise of his creative intention or, for that matter, as the mere objective product of a machine process. Instead, under the paradigm of visual culture, she sees the photograph and photography as fully embedded in the complexities of sociality itself—in our terms, its networks. Thus, a photographic event becomes a site of negotiation—an open archive and as for example in the work of Eyal Weizman (2017), a site of forensics—in which many stakeholders including those excluded from the image and its officially sanctioned networks might have a say about various aspects of an image's existence, or nonexistence (72–74).

For our purposes here, we could say that the dilation of the photographic event, an event which Azoulay argues is "never-ending," lays bear the photographic image as a work-site—a complex, distributed, multipronged, semiotic process—and, as such, a work-site that when left in its default mode remains essential to the production and reproduction of the world as we know it. Clearly, then, the work-site that is the image is thus also a way of aggregating consensus—and a battleground. We might do more with images than confirm the status quo or extend the logic of property and sovereign subjectivity and ratify the circuit from M to M' by means of their networked logic of extractive valorization founded on settler colonialism and genocide.

Extrapolating from the centrality—or better perhaps, nodality—of the image, we could say that in relation to images there is an imperative to perform, to virtuosity à la Paolo Virno, in as much as we mean a necessary and prescribed adequation of the multiple relations between images, language function, and social life. As mentioned before, in accord with Virno, one aspect of the generalized virtuosity demanded by post-Fordism indicates what Virno (2004) calls the expropriation of the cognitive-linguistic, what Berardi (2011) recognizes, not incidentally, as attention deficit disorder, what Stiegler (2010) sees as an endemic short-termism and the grammatization of the senses, and what Althusser (1971) saw as the reproduction of the relations of production by ideology as material practice, as "score." For our purposes here, I would want again to point out that, to obtain, these pathological impositions (by which cognition is bent to networked abstraction and extraction) require the emergence of what I have elsewhere (2006a) called the world-media system and of what is designated in this volume as the world computer. "Ideas are material"—governed by material relations (Althusser: 169). Such material relations are the encoding of materiality itself as computational substrate—states of matter organized by social practice directly outputted to and inputting into the world computer. The variance of these states fall within a statistically managed range and the throughput reproduces the relations of production.

Azoulay's embattled stance, and beyond that, the massive efforts toward decolonization and against apartheid systems more generally, suggest that as quickly as avenues of practical activity are closed off (through expropriation and foreclosure, through policing and murder, through the ISA of photography) other scenes of struggle emerge. The subordination, subjugation, and subsumption of linguistic function under the programmable image is always only partial and incomplete—bounded but never entirely foreclosed. Though organized by the reign of images, life forces both compose and contest each iteration, each utterance. It is therefore important here to recognize and to emphasize that the dilation of the photographic event as image in mediological process has a dialectical relation to code—not now simply as "natural language" or "semiotic convention" but as "computational language," as information. The recoding of the informatic image, the effort to restructure its processing in ways that do not conform to those organized by the hegemony of the state, of capital, or of advertising can be seen as providing the means to intervene not only in state power but in semiotic and thus also computational and financial codification. The struggle with the photographic image may demand a reformatting of the database that changes its utility and accessibility; it may demand modifications in the code, it may script new practice.

Before platform fetishists object, I hasten to remind readers that precisely these negotiations of image and word feed all types of computation: from word processors, book sales, Twitter accounts, tech startups, and platform innovation to military simulations, the arms industry, stock markets, banks, and nation states. Semiocapitalism places the generation of meaning and financialization in the same domain—it "weaponizes" meaning and puts it on the market. Information as "image" as "meaning" opens these ontologically prior moments to new and networked processes and processing. Azoulay's view of the meaning of a photographic event as "never-ending" draws paradigmatically upon the distributed exchanges that take place in social media: she offers a theory that presupposes the complex relation between image, sign, and number, one that helps us to recognize that the anatomy of social media is indeed the key to the anatomy of photography. Photography is a derivative whose underlier is "reality"—a volatile "reality" that is the basis for contingent claims. Changing its rules of composition changes the exposure to the risk endemic in such contingency. Photography exists in a network. Despite the current asymmetrical access imposed by the network and the residual notion of the freestanding photographic image, Azoulay posits—in contradistinction to a privatized platform—a new form of citizenry that would be the condition and beneficiary of this new polysemy, this value generation. The value created in relation to the relation that is the image would not, if the citizenry of photography were fully activated, go to proprietors of a platform but to a new space of collective, democratic enfranchisement. In this we might perceive what Randy Martin (2015a) understands as a social derivative—a way of navigating volatility and risking together to get more of what we want—as a wager on volatility, but from below. As we saw previously with the commodified object, few of its derivative functions were accessible or actionable in the earlier form, but these functions were latent, or immanent, as philosophers might say. The photograph (taken or not) was always already a node in a network of indeterminate specifications. In classical usages, its benefits have accrued to hegemony. But remaking the network, rethinking the ontology of the photographic image and of photography as praxis, may also mean remaking the consequent practices and thus also the real abstractions created by technical images.

With the photograph, then, an intervention in the vectoralized movement of I–C–I' (Image–Code–Image') that would preclude the production of an I' within a certain range of statistically predictable parameters—those parameters held in place by, for example, Zionism, settler colonialism, military industrial power, vertical financial integration, and the art world—is also an interruption of the circuit M–M'.[2] It is a break in the informatic program of capital, an interruption of the rule set organizing the emergence of "valorizing information" for the benefit of the owners of the infrastructure. It is a disruption of seamless data flow, a crisis of valorization, a hack. It proposes a rupture in the photographic program of capitalist valorization. Thus, such détournement of the photograph does not convert M to M', at least in the first instance.

Work-Sites of the Digital-Visual

The reader will see where this discussion is headed. All the hacks, culture jams, mods, and queerings are to a greater or lesser extent interruptions in the various programs for the valorization of information—for the extraction of "valorizing information." We must, nonetheless, in wars of both position and maneuver, concern ourselves with the fate of their products. The problem is a difficult one since in the latest last instance of financialization, life (whatever that is) wriggles under an emergently totalizing field of informatics: all communication, all knowing become inseparable from image and code, and all new information becomes marketable information—derivatives on social process and value production. All roads lead to information, hence to profit, hence to racial capitalism.

The expanded field of operations under the domain of the logistics of the screen-image, which places perception and discourse in a feedback loop with capitalized machinery and makes these interfaces subject to algorithmic governance, clearly extends not only to photography but to the cinema—indeed, as I previously argued, cinema was a kind of first instance in which the dynamics of what was to come became discernible. I would agree here with Patricia Pisters (2012), who notes the omnipresence and variety of screens: "In spite of all the capturing forces that operate on our multiple screens, it is possible to see the media as a gigantic network of baroque perspectives where particular points of view and the psychological effects they entail become affectively entangled. We can say that in the new logistics we are not [only] passive spectators captured by institutional or ideological power even though these are still powers that need to be taken into account" (298; bracketed interpolation mine).

Pisters calls for an active, agential relation to the multiplicity of images traversing the socius. In the media-environment, "our real and virtual bodies are involved in complex ways that cannot be translated into simple ethical rules; we need instead an affective openness to be brought to the idea of cinema and (into) the world itself. By creating images, or simply by being affected by these images, we can participate in bringing reality and feeling back to the vortex of our multiple screens" (298). Emphasizing these fault lines at the interface just a bit—instances of normativity that might be rejected and thus remade—we might observe that, in the context of Berardi's (2011) "semiocapitalism," we are, in the extended field of the image, engaged in what Pasquinelli (2006) called "immaterial civil war." In the struggle over meaning and codification, in tapping the resources of our bodies either to validate the score or feel against the grain, day-to-day living becomes a kind of full-body, low-intensity, semiotic war—low-intensity, that is, for the privileged or fortunate. But whether the struggle is for a few more "likes" on an Instagram account, feeling otherwise in the cinema, dodging a drone strike, or avoiding the fallout of a sovereign debt crisis, an ethnic cleansing, or a full-scale genocide, somewhere the stakes are always life itself. However, if we recall the passage from Marx on the factory code and deviance from it that serves as epigraph of this volume—in which "the law-giving talent of the factory Lycurgus so arranges matters that a violation of his laws is, if possible, more profitable to him than the keeping of them"—we will not want to prematurely celebrate our local dissensus or survival as systemic success. "Security," like securitization in finance, is a growth industry—the enclosure of life and even dissent by computational platforms represents a new order of securitization.

Rather than dealing here with the more familiar, and suddenly far more interesting and relevant question of cinema (as program, or what I call the cinematic program [Beller 2015]) and the aesthetic (as interface), or the equally interesting question of what Hito Steyerl (2012) calls "the poor image" as a new, if exceedingly low resolution, index of communal sociality, I would like for the remainder of this chapter to focus on a few less familiar work-sites of the digital-visual. Before turning to these new frontiers of colonization, we sum up in passing that the narratological, psychosexual, spatial, racial, ideological, visceral, and affective are now all also and, within the informatic matrix, always, vectors of attentional production and digitization. Fractal fascism creates attention silos. The new modes of negotiating screen-image space discussed below—via the reorganization of attentional, sensory and neuronal practices coupled directly to computer programming—give rise to new forms of life.

Fugitivity, for example, finds new strategies. One approach from the more sinister and austere side of navigating the logistics of visualization is "CV Dazzle" or Computer Vision Dazzle Camouflage. The designer Adam Harvey explains these innovative fashions, which entail the use of makeup and accessories to elude facial recognition software: "It is a form of *expressive interference* that combines makeup and hair styling (or other modifications) with face-detection thwarting designs. The name is derived from a type of camouflage used during WWI, called Dazzle, which was used to break apart the gestalt-image of warships, making it hard to discern their directionality, size, and orientation. Likewise, the goal of CV Dazzle is to break apart the gestalt of a face, or object, and make it undetectable to computer vision algorithms, in particular face detection [italics mine]."[3] Harvey has also developed an antidrone wear line—a series of capes, hoods, and burkas that scatter the light patterns associated with facial and body recognition and make detection from above by drones difficult or impossible. What is noteworthy is that the negotiation of visual appearance is organized by the endeavor to elude the algorithmic detection mechanisms or pattern recognition of operating code. While the "look" generated by these forms of life is visible and affecting in the social domain, the operative frame of reference is the computational algorithm and its apophenic discernment. Thus, the reference domain of the machine-mediated computational process—its ability to discern patterns—is the practical target of these wearable interventions in the becoming-normal of always-everywhere-ambient computation. As with the example of Azoulay, the resistance practice as a form of destructive interface in capital's valorization pathways also illuminates the dynamics of the normative functioning of a ubiquitous computational surveillance or omniveillance that, as Edward Snowden and Laura Poitras irrefutably revealed, tends toward anyone-anytime-anywhere geolocation and identification.[4] Not only can anyone be identified, but they can be targeted. This targeting too—as well as any murder and collateral damage that may result from it—is real subsumption, a capturing and reframing of any entity whatever by means of real abstraction. In the encompassing of the perceptible world, the Hollerith punch card, which was used to feed a search (and destroy) engine in the early national censuses and the Nazi Holocaust, has come a long way indeed. Real abstraction is a result of how people live and treat one another and their products in the process of exchange and, recursively, becomes a means for treating them. Here they are treated as fodder for the financialized security state, its econometrics, and its economy. In the exchange of information mediating the valorizing exchanges of capital, any entity can be indexed as information by the exchange process and treated according to executable protocols running a cost-benefit analysis.

Today, cellphones have already rendered many of our locutions and movements fully computable, potentially providing details not just of where you are and when, but of income, residence, citizenship, spending habits, sexual preference, criminal record, favorite ice cream, and so on. Soon, and as the artist and scholar Zach Blas's work both confirms and contests, with the rapid acceleration of machine learning and neural networks, your face alone will do all that and more. It will appear bearing the burden of its computability. Indeed, it already does. Even now, DNA phenotyping (the ability to engineer a likely face from DNA) is being utilized by facial recognition software to search for and "reeducate" Uighurs in China. This practice entails an act of real abstraction as racial abstraction. The search function, which recognizes a face from its racialized genetic code, becomes an ontology machine—its target is no longer even a who but a what (Wee and Mozur 2019). The abstraction process assigns a value to an individual in a way entirely beyond their control. As the work of managing your face (location, expression, composure, affect, code) increasingly pushes networked discrete state machines into new states with new networked capabilities, the two seemingly separate meanings of "profile" will converge, pushing the interface back into your face. From a surveillance standpoint, your face will be the interface. Or rather, it will be *an* interface, since ambient, ubiquitous computing and the internet of things will provide multiple overlays for all varieties of targeting: commercial, medical, legal, military, extrajudicial. The bearer of such information also bears the burden of managing the risk it imposes on them, turning ambient information into a ubiquitous work-site.

The reparsing of the informatics of images (of viewing the image as fundamentally composed of information) is also bringing about a reconceptualization and a reprogramming of photographic image capture. As it turns out, a tremendous amount of information is lost in the classical projection of images by conventional optics. Rather than creating a limited projection with a single focal plane, as does the classical optical camera projecting light onto an emulsion plate, light field cameras (such as an apparatus known as Lytro), use digital sensors "to capture all the light" (all rays of light traveling in space at every point) and thus to capture its directional information. This apparatus moves image capture into the explicitly computational domain: images can be refocused after the fact in a kind of reverse rendering, such that any given image can be refocused at any plane in the field merely by indicating a focal point on that plane with a finger or a mouse and recalibrating the depth of field.[5]

The realization that there is a tremendous amount of information in the light field—and that much of it is lost with conventional optics—was also the theme of a paper presented by Andreas Velten at a symposium called, in homage to Vilém Flusser, "The Photographic Universe" and held in 2013 at The New School in New York City. Velten demonstrated a superfast camera that could slice up light input into nanosecond frames such that one could actually image a pulse of light traversing the surface of a tomato. These images, sequenced as a video composed of nanosecond time slices, showed that the tomato itself became a light source through quantum absorption; it absorbed part of the light pulse and then emitted light after the initial pulse had passed and faded back into darkness. Light emission can be treated not just as visible light but as computable information. To be clear, the tomato's emission of light, and information, is not productive labor. But the construction of new techniques for the registration of this light and the manipulation of this information, as well as the reorganization of society and social practice around its threats and affordances wagers that these social activities, and many more, could be. The research is a speculative investment on future returns.

Such computability of light is consistent with the treatment of light in another project, also being developed by Velten and colleagues, to build a camera that can see around corners. By doing the math, it is possible to track scattered light in order to resolve an occluded object—a man, for example—that is out of the line of sight or around the corner of a building and who is therefore invisible to the eye or to ordinary image rendering technologies. But by effectively treating all surfaces as variants of mirrors, and by processing the scattered light vectors and focusing them back into the occluded space, one resolves an image of the man around the corner. Computational reconstruction of light scatter allows for a data visualization that creates an image of a figure ordinarily occluded in the function of conventional optics. Velten's acknowledgement that this project is funded by the section of the Pentagon known as DARPA (Defense Advanced Research Projects Agency) clearly indicates the instrumentality here. Although the presenter took the position that computational photography was all about the science, it is noteworthy that, of all possible funders, it seems that the U.S. military is most willing to invest big money in the opportunity to see around corners. Indeed, as with our reading of Azoulay's work, computational photography makes it clear to us that images "themselves" are all about *modes* of data visualization and, what's more, that data visualization is always instrumental—and thus has a political ontology—even if, as an archive, data and the images it generates may be open to multiple interpretations. These technologies expand both the archive of the visual and the number of semiotechnical work-sites—introducing new functions, interfaces, and temporalities within the domain of conventional operations. They become instruments of production and political programs. Soon some of us may be put to work, a new kind of work that entails being visible around corners. Our newfound, if involuntary, visibility may be the source for all sorts of speculative endeavors, from drones that can shoot around corners to the careers of products and politicians who want to eliminate corners with border walls. The effort to program and reprogram these work-sites are also efforts to organize the production and reproduction of social life. So, emphatically now: *a political ontology not just of photography but of images, semiotics, code, and information.*

Additional DARPA projects include the effort to turn brains into cameras by utilizing neuronal outputs; the Cognitive Technology Threat Warning System uses algorithms to tap the preconscious brain; "bionic eyes" become "sensors that use a lookout's brainwaves to spot trouble"—using soldiers' eyes as input devices, these sensors can actually spot "enemies" before the soldiers themselves are conscious of a threat (Gallagher 2012); the "Good Stranger" uses feedback from police or soldiers' brains to parse neuroresponses from possible perps during encounters: "Citizen neuro-response instructs soldiers on manipulating citizens" (Storm 2011).

We witness here the further ramification of the life-world by computerized vision along the pathways of valorization prescribed by capitalist hegemony. Two DARPA programs effectively turn biotic components (aspects of the human sensorium) into the prosthetic extension of algorithmic processes. People become vehicles for camera function, and those seen become objects of informatic-algorithmic parsing and inscription. Those seen suddenly must manage the risk of being data sets legible to other cyborgs, the burden of which they must bear. We are written, unwritten, rewritten, and read.

These algorithmic processes are of course developed for and by the securocratic state, through contracted and subcontracted corporate entities. Ramifications of this kind, ramifications into perception and neuronal function extended to and through computation, represent the new technics of an intensifying internal colonization in that they fragment and operationalize aspects of the sensorium. Human eyes and neuronal pathways become sensors for computational functions that can parse the inputs to recognize an "enemy" before a soldier consciously perceives one, or analyze (at the speed of light) the psychic response of a suspect under interrogation. Here, in a consolidation of image, code, finance, and state power, the priority of image and user is fully reversed as the human sensorium becomes an input device for the command-control function of computation while the human body becomes an algorithm's avatar. This marks an advance of sorts over Wiener's observation that, with cybernetics, "low-level discrimination" will be left to a machine, since here it is the humans that provide the low-level discrimination, while the machine makes the higher-level synthesis and is presumably the one that issues the instruction to initiate an attack. It also inaugurates absurd—and indeed, when seen from only a slight level of remove, oxymoronic—debates among some technophiles on the subject of robot ethics: When is it okay for a robot to kill, etc.? In the future, some people will have the "job" of posing ethical dilemmas for robot assassins. Whether this job will look more like that of the white philosophy professor at some Ivy League university, or that of a Black man being confronted by a cop, is unknown.

The larger point is that the cybernetic ramifications of computation create new productive interfaces for both the "observer" and "observed" at multiple scales. A recent *New York Times* photograph, from a story describing a collaboration between the German car manufacturer Audi and an Israeli tech startup, provides evidence for the kinds of gains possible for corporations and states when computerized vision takes over steerage (the original meaning of *kubernetes*, "the art of steering," and the Greek root of cybernetics). Not only is automobile transportation taken over by the computer-automated control of vision, but it seems that, at another scale, the critical function of vision is as well, since, here at least, in the *New York Times* coverage of the driverless car, the vehicle is shown next to an apartheid border fence without comment (Markoff 2013). Indeed, driverless cars automate vision for driving but seem also to automate vision to the point that an image of apartheid requires no comment from the *New York Times*. A better headline for the story might be "Israel Automates Its Vision and Drives Using German Technologies," though no doubt such gallows humor would be lost on many readers who, unbeknownst to them, perhaps, have already had much of their own vision and drive outsourced and automated by the same basic operating system. The technics of computational colonialism organize both territory and spectator with their steerage and drive. They also reinscribe and indeed exacerbate racializing differences that constitute Israel as tech-savvy, innovative, and free and Palestinians as invisible components, or worse, pesky deterrents of a smoothly functioning tech-washed securocratic regime.[6]

We have seen that what Flusser (2000) calls "the universe of technical images"—in which cameras organize the world for their own advancement—results in what Wendy Chun (2011) describes as "programmed visions" by means of the programmable image. From the DARPA tech to New York Times tech reporting that renders Israeli apartheid invisible, we get yet another sense of the fundamental organizing system of computational capital in its quest for value extraction. Chun's phrase and her groundbreaking book of the same name complicate the seemingly clear distinction between image and code and show that this complication is endemic to the history of computational machinery and thought. Using a logic similar to that of Chun's argument regarding software—that it is ultimately inseparable from the media-environment in which it functions and therefore has no rigid border or discrete being (software is not just a metaphor but "a metaphor of a metaphor," as she puts it, and machines "leak")—we must proceed with the working hypothesis that there is no longer any tenable, strict distinction (nondialectical, essential, or ontological) between technical image and code. These instances of data visualization of cybernetic computation are "moments" in the expansion of the universe of information which, as we have seen, means also the expansion of racial capital. Chun writes, "Media archeologist, Friedrich Kittler, taking this embedded and embedding logic to its limit, has infamously declared 'there is no software,' for everything, in the end reduces to voltage differences. More precisely he contends, 'there would be no software if computer systems were not surrounded . . . by an environment of everyday languages'" (2011: 3; citing Kittler 1995). Chun continues, "Based on metaphor, software has become a metaphor for the mind, for culture, for ideology, for biology and for the economy" (2); and she adds, "Computers, like other media, are metaphor machines: they both depend on and perpetuate metaphors. More remarkably though, they—through their status as 'universal machines'—have become metaphors for metaphor itself" (55). Further breaking up the seemingly objective solidity of computation, Chun discussed the "leakiness" of computational machines in a talk, entitled "To Be Determined," delivered at the Pratt Institute on 24 September 2015. For our purposes, and to return to the argument of this chapter, we could say that, without being exhaustive, the terms *image* and *code* designate moments in a process of an informatic reorganization of the state of the social totality, just as *money* and *commodity* designate user interfaces for the processing of the value-form: moments of abstraction that are always instrumental. Thus Image–Code–Image' (written as I–C–I' in the formula M–I–C–I'–M') is, like the commodity "C" before it in M–C–M', also a hypostatization—a discrete moment in the instrumentalized flux of the world. As we have seen with respect to state changes of a discrete state machine, I–C–I' is in fact expandable and the more precise formula for the circuit from M to M' is M–I–C–I'–C'–I''–M', or indeed M–I–C–I'–C'–I''–C''–I''' . . . (n) . . . —M', where it is understood that the instances marked by the variables are themselves networked moments in information flux, technically mediated forms of quantum hypostasis, points of networked interface. These mediations, which we may abbreviate as M–I–M', where "I" is information, can be performed by machines through machine amortization (operation) or by people doing sensual, affective, attentional, cognitive, or metabolic labor, and they can be networked. Thus we see once again that M–I–M', where "I" is information, captured by a discrete state machine or otherwise incorporated, is the most concise and general form of the networked, ambient production and reproduction of computational racial capital. It is information that produces its interest.

Just as in Flusser's example—in which a shoe's expression of information only became understandable as information, that is, only *became* "information," after the rise of informatics—the image (and by this we now mean any image, at least for us: a Renaissance painting, a printed page, a retinal scan) is now understandable in terms of code because it is grasped through the matrix of code as data visualization: codification has become fused with "human" perception. This leakage, which is also a cybernetic fusion of machines with their "environment of everyday languages," is a practical as well as a conceptual matter. The screen-image is not finally separable from the code that renders it, nor, ultimately, is the current organization of visuality. The *Mona Lisa*, either in the Louvre or on your screen, is no longer just a painting; it is a node and an interface in a vast informatic network—as are you. The environment of everyday languages "surrounding" software is part of the software. Google's rebaptism as Alphabet shows that the AI and its avatars know what they are about. This colonization of language and image would mark the conversion of all ("human" interests) into interest: M'. That is real subsumption.

The proliferation of computerized vision machines tends to function by automating vision in ways that more and more thoroughly confirm Flusser's early insights that humans had become functionaries of the camera. For Flusser (2000), humans, as functionaries of the photographic apparatus, became subject to constant feedback through the multiple feedback loops between social practices of all sorts and technical images—those significant surfaces resultant from the program of the camera. Given the dominance of images in all social endeavors, the full digitization of images and their subsumption under the regime of capitalist informatics clearly indicates that computational production on the various digital treadmills becomes the general form of productive activity in the interval between M and M'. Like rats (running on treadmills, pursuing our own interests or someone else's) we turn the digital gears to grind out discrete states. Through our negotiation of images (attentive, distracted, psycho- or neurological, semiotic, metabolic, unconscious, etc.) and of the imaged, we tend the code—which is to say that, in an ironic return to Chun's (2011) analysis of early computing at ENIAC, where women were the first computers, "we" too are the computers, computation's feminized supplement. Seeking screen-mediated sovereignty, the power of the programmer, we are subsumed in the network of computers and do embodied computing to feed the programming. This titration between sovereign agency and castration—typical of classical Hollywood cinema in which, as Mulvey wrote, images were cut to the measure of (male) desire—is now lived at an even more general level with microtechnology and ambient screens. We manage our human capital while our creative labor is abject; we are substrates of information endeavoring to manage algorithmic throughput. Though we must leave to one side here an analysis of the dialectics of the morphology of gender and race in relation to the increasing cyberneticization of social relations, we may observe at least a link between domestic labor and the "housework" that Italian Marxist feminism has identified as value-productive outside the formal economy of wage labor and such post-Fordist forms of productivity—forms that Virno (2004) terms "servile labor" (though he does so without any attribution to feminists). In further research—both on the computational unconscious, where gendered relations are sedimented into computational architectures, and on its relation to the screen-image and to "the unconscious" as analyzed by feminist film theory—one might and indeed must investigate the gendered dynamics of computing involved here: phallic quest and castration, logics of appearance and disappearance, productive desire and disavowal. While such a rendering would not specify the ultimate "truth" of the interface with information, it would connect its dynamics with histories of gender oppression (the gendered notions of "acting "and "appearing" to use a much older lexicon) and racism in significant ways. Even more importantly, the deconstruction of such dynamics of gender and race might open the practices of informatics to unthought potentials of liberation. Might.

Flusser's astonishing work on photography was only possible because he was among the first to see clearly that an emergent computational logic was already at work in the photographic apparatus, as if, in an extension of Marx's fragment on machines, cameras converted persons to conscious organs in the vast automaton of photography itself. As "functionaries" of the photographic apparatus internalizing knowledge about how to photograph and be photographed, we have already been processed by its computational logic, which is to say that our words and our time have been cut up, we have internalized its codes, our relation to reality has become magical, and what we are is part of its expression. As "functionaries" in "the universe of technical images," we compose ourselves in a mise-en-scène of computation-production in order to engage in computation-production. Our interests have been colonized by photography. Most often, however, we are subsumed in its representation, which is to say, its product. The move from language-based sociality to image-based sociality also means the liquidation of linear logic and time. Flusser's notion of "the magical" comes from the apparent simultaneity of the contents of an image. He remarks that in the world of writing, which is one-dimensional and linear, we know that because of the movement of the earth the sun rises and therefore the cock crows. In the image of sunrise and crowing cock, our scan of the plane of information cannot discern which is the cause and which is the effect. To quell (or exacerbate) any lingering doubts regarding this claim of being subjugated to photography and thus to computation and thus to capital, simply open your Facebook or Instagram. Or look around. Most of what we see, what we process, and what we do now is informatic labor for computational capital: we are inscribed in and by the computational mode of production. This real abstraction from the lifeworld, which organizes not just the transactions that we make using money but, increasingly, every transaction (when every interaction also becomes a transaction), is precisely the metabolic processes of the social undergoing monetization in a dissymmetrical relation to capital accumulation. *The extraction is from sociality itself.* Our every attempt to socialize, to make culture, and to create solidarity is subject to extraction. This logic, though difficult to discern, is in fact quite rigorous. It appears to most as chaos that can only be partially organized by atavistic drives. The strip mining of the social and the failure of a sociality that silos "realities" are among the results of what Stiegler (2010) sees as a proletarianization of the senses and the consequent short-termist thinking endemic to populations and their governors, and are the causes of what Berardi (2011) identifies as the burnout, depression, and the psychopathologies of the present.

It is an awareness of such macropolitical, macroeconomic metaprograms that allows us to raise the most serious questions about the function of automating machine vision and data visualization by computational colonialism. This process goes deep. It involves not only the automation of sovereignty by machine protocols as platform sovereignty, but the recursive sedimentation of historically produced social difference in machine architectures. Programs are not only networked to one another but nested within one another. Here, as Tara McPherson (2012) bravely argued already many years ago, actually existing computation cannot be thought of separately from contemporary racialization. In a discussion of UNIX, the groundbreaking operating system developed by Ken Thompson at Bell Labs, McPherson shows that the history of UNIX reveals that the push for increased modularity—which involved the compartmentalization of tasks, the connectivity of these various modules through "pipes," and the creation of higher levels of programming able to nest these modules in blocks (such that today an iMovie user, say, need know nothing about binary code)—overlapped first with the racial logic of segregation and then with that of neoliberalism, the latter of which "hides its racial kernel," "burying modular separation below a shell of neoliberal pluralism" (29). McPherson argues that "across several registers, the emerging neoliberal state begins to adopt 'the rule of modularity,' in order to separate and contain allied antagonists" (30). As we have seen throughout this book, social processes and preoccupations leave their mark on technologies and in so doing reiterate their biases in machine function. Racism produces racist programing produces more racism. Garbage in, garbage out. If the world computer is a metaphor for a metaphor, "a metaphor for the mind, for culture, for ideology, for biology and for the economy" (Chun 2011: 2), it is also not a metaphor, since it is in fact composed of these.

With M-I-M' as the general formula for capital we see that the world computer is not a metaphor. It is rather a prediction that became a program.

Shall we be forgiven for recalling that the father of information theory, Claude Shannon, creator of a rigorous mathematical framework for evaluating the cost of a message, was an employee of the Bell Telephone Company? This does not of course alter the scientific value of his theorems, but it suggests to us the need to limit its extrapolations (to the mechanical universe). It is not a matter of indifference that in France the administration of the Télécoms (DGT, CNET, etc.) should have been the principal source of financing and sponsorship of communication studies conferences, seminars, chaired professorships, journals, and other publications. That is not to diminish their merit, nor the intense interest they generate. But such is the hold means exert over ends, and machines over minds, that an unconscious "halo effect" encourages us from those quarters to hallucinate the cultural history of human beings through the prism of La Poste et Télécom. A receiver, a wire, a signal. "Hello, I hear you. . . . OK, received your message, good-bye." In more or less elaborate forms, this schema underlies "the act of communication," a central unit of its reasoning. (Debray 1996: 42)

Communication and computation construct social models, build on them, and then recursively apply them to the world in executable form. Computational colonialism moistens the world with information in order to melt it. Theories of ontology, the taking of things as communications systems, become programs. Regarding the compartmentalization of computational tasks alongside segregation, and then the burying of these forms of separation under user-friendly formats dependent upon the rule of modularity, McPherson writes, "The emergence of covert racism and its rhetoric of colorblindness are not so much intentional as systemic. Computation is the primary delivery method of these new systems, and it seems at best naïve to imagine that cultural and computational operating systems don't mutually infect one another" (2012: 31). With respect to the visual turn, she writes:

I would argue that to study image, narrative and visuality will never be enough if we do not engage as well the non-visual dimensions of code and their organization of the world. And yet, to trouble my own polemic, we might also understand the workings of code to have already internalized the visual to the extent that, in the heart of the labs from which UNIX emerged, the cultural processing of the visual via the register of race was already at work in the machine. (35)

This admirable bit of dialectics accords with the argument here, that modern media platforms are themselves racial formations. The recursivity of sociality, visuality, and codification means that logics of racialization and gender formation are sedimented and functionalized in machines. The denial of this thesis through the assertion of technical emergence as a product of a- or nonpolitical ("objective") science, ontologically grounded in the sublime neutrality of mathematics—a position either assumed, implied, or asserted outright by so many tech boosters—would perform a kind of platform fetishism that is ultimately reactionary, and indeed fascistic. Why fascistic? Because of the mystification of authorship and therefore of authority. Platform fetishism does not only reify a formation by imposing ideological boundaries; it occludes the history of platform emergence by affirming a maternal bond with presumably racially unmarked technologies and unproblematically transcendental modes of knowing—all the while disavowing the historical embeddedness of technical form, the dialectic between technical form and social becoming, the *historicity* of form. That the free-flowing sovereignty of neoliberal subjects of capital is founded upon modularity, containerization, sequestration—walls of all kinds designed to handle, hold, and ship any content whatever—does not only emerge from the practices of slavery, coloniality, ghettoization, and feminization; these new emergences continue to develop and refine such forms of domination. This damning insight demands further thought—and it is not as if it goes unanswered by the struggles of the oppressed. For as is again and again demonstrated, the racism of neoliberalism is but one small step away from full-blown fascism (as an authorial aside: this sentence was written before 2016 and the boisterous onset of full fascism in the United States)—and we should take careful note that, for many of its aggrieved victims, those people who struggle to survive and to invent new forms of survival, the difference between a neoliberal order and a fascist one is merely academic.

In the years since these sentences were first written, 45 was elected and full-blown camps are in the works in the United States. A global pandemic rages. The media-environment is increasingly toxic, having become itself an intensified space of gameable volatility and value aggregation. Productive life activity passes through the constant transformation of code and its platforms (a distinction that, while still useful, is, as noted, difficult to maintain) in the ordination of value. Indeed a Facebook "like"—an Orwellian reduction of Old Speak vocabulary if there ever was one—was in 2013 given a dollar value as high as $214.81 (Edwards 2013). Facebook has subsequently introduced more options and algorithms to make user's desires more visible to advertisers and their attention more granularly monetizable. As of 2019, Facebook is endeavoring to introduce Libra, a cryptocurrency that will allow it unprecedented access to the financial practices of billions of users. Contact tracing will track billions more. Meanwhile we know that centralized authority over the productive operations of informatic media has failed the world. In general, the mere touch of a pad or screen introduces a change in functionality that engenders new access, connections, and information—increasingly, so too with money itself. New metrics of "value capture" are everywhere. We have still to take up the convergence of informatics and financialization from the perspective of a radical politics that would understand the need to deal with algorithmic governance and political economy and to open these to socialism (Ryall 2013.) Everywhere one turns, one faces computational colonialism (Assange 2013).

Notably, in the dynamic coordination of centripetal and centrifugal forces from M to M', there is plenty of dissent and alternative wagers within the technical image. Channeling Silvia Federici, Laurel Ptak's Wages for Facebook project embraces what we have now known for some time, that *we* are the producers of internet platforms and that, as private entities, these platforms represent massive expropriation.[7] The demand for wages for attending to the interface and providing content is designed to surface the invisible and unremunerated labor of attention. Like the call for wages for housework, as well as—with Federici's laser-sharp clarity—wages for the care, psychological support, and sex offered to maintain the poor schlub who has to go off to the humiliation of the factory every day, the call for wages for attention to media platforms underscores the value production that is at once both unrecognized by capital—because unremunerated—and absolutely essential for its valorization (Terranova 2000).

Andrew Norman Wilson, as previously mentioned, was fired from Google for making videos of socially and then actively declassed workers leaving the Googleplex in Mountain View, California.[8] It appears that the very fact that he tried to develop another kind of visual relation to a particular subset of workers—whose population was composed primarily of poor minorities, who were denied access to Google's cafes and other perks reserved for white-collar employees, and who received different work schedules than these "regular" Google employees to prevent social interaction at closing time—was enough to get him fired. These were the book scanners. Ironic that he got fired from Google for producing too much information. Wilson's retrieval of rejected images of scanned books, errata that bear the traces of the condom-clad fingers of workers, presents a new kind of documentary evidence of the presence of people amid the data—people who are ordinarily disappeared within it. The mode of disappearance by datalogical means indicates the subjugation of individual and class interests by market interest and the valorization of capital that produces financial interest: ROI.

Though I fully embrace and desire to extend the revolutionary and insurrectionary energies percolating through the code—indeed, such should be the mission of any media theory worthy of the name—it would be inconsistent with this analysis to end this chapter on a note of false hope. The technology underpinning today's "very" antisocial social media has also given rise to media that operate covertly, engage in dismediation, and do not lend themselves to visualizations that can be easily addressed.[9] They are, as *Westworld* shows so well, extensions of capitalism. If computers led to social media and financialization, then financialization led to antisocial media and computational colonialism and the development of new work-sites for the conversion of interest. Here we identify plutocratic corporations working with states, but also virtuosic interstate coordination, as revealed by Wikileaks, as well as the large-scale, privacy-scraping harvest of data—not only by the various Googles of the world but by security states and their NSAs and their experiments with automation, pattern recognition and robotics—which directly or indirectly posits the total sociosemiotic metabolism itself as expropriable labor by assigning it a cost price, a price paid for by indebted or otherwise bonded taxpayers, denizens, and inmates, paid to state employees and tech corporations, and paid for again by the unremunerated globally surveilled. Google's conflict with the NSA over "our" privacy was a proprietary war between giants over who would own our subjectivity, our neuronal function—our capacity to produce "valorizing information" for computational racial capitalism.

In revealing the intensifying media-technics from M to M', analyses like those of Eric Hunsader are particularly instructive. For example, "10 Milliseconds of Trading in Merck," is a six minute, fifty-four second video showing the dynamism of algorithmic stock trading over the course of 1/100th of a second—an amount of time, which, by the way, is *not* adequate time for the first Merck quote shown in this long video to travel, *at the speed of light*, from a New York exchange to a London exchange before the video ends.[10] Even though time is slowed by a factor of 40,000 here, the transactions are difficult for the eye to track, let alone account for. And this is traffic in just one stock. The number of transactions taking place at speeds that are effectively that of light further illustrates that *computation, communication, and financial speculation have become one and the same movement.* These integrated functions operate algorithmically and do not lend themselves to real-time, actionable representations; they would thus seem to effectively short-circuit the visual interface and, even beyond that, perhaps, human cognition. Never mind that the image—as Barthes, Flusser, Wlad Godzich, and many others recognized in one way or another—was already a short circuit with respect to modes of communication based on "natural language." As if information were a derivative on the image which was itself a derivative on language. Here we find machine cognition cutting visual and linguistic cognition out of the circuit entirely for billions of consecutive machine cycles. This is mechanized, or rather computerized, "attention," exactly what Wiener called "low-level discrimination" but now capable of executing algorithm-based "decisions" at the speed of light. Nonetheless, and though some have been tempted to say that the visual is no longer paramount, these lightning-fast computerized trades are imaged in the biological or human-readable time of the balance sheets of traders, who use those same results to buy their cars, their art, and whatever other semiotic mirrors they require to make it worth their while to rework the programming and keep up with the Kardashians. Though it is becoming difficult to say whether it is the algorithmic trading that is the real content of the trader's self-image, or if it is the trader's self image that is the real content of the trade, McLuhan's notion that the content of a medium is another medium still holds. It is necessary to mention that command over "human labor," or what Neferti Tadiar (2012) calls "life-time," is the ultimate content of both. As if in affirmation of Virilio's thesis in *Speed and Politics* (2006), we see that outpacing conventional constraints on space-time by regimes of abstraction is a means to wield power within conventional space-time. Here the lightning-fast shuffle of proprietary entitlements (ownership) uses statistical modeling and equations for Brownian motion to outflank the psyche of the market and most of its content providers, capturing value whose predominant scene of production is elsewhere—in the ultimate guarantor of liquidity, namely, the life-times of disposability for which money can be and is ultimately redeemed. The illiquidity of most of the planet secures the liquidity of the financial world.

It is in such a context of radical liquidity inequality—the radical disparity among people to substantively transform their circumstances by commandeering the products of human labor, that the world computer becomes fully operational. What is ultimately administered is access to liquidity. Where machines at first replicated and enhanced manual labor, today they replicate and enhance mental labor (evaluation, attention, recognition, discernment, etc.). All the while, these technical innovations are driven by the falling rate of profit, the mathematical necessity to produce the same commodity for less labor time as production scales and the ratio of fixed to variable capital increases, along with the consequent production of new needs and thus also new commodities. In the industrial age, a company created a spread—between remaining the same and the cost of a technical upgrade to increase efficiency—and took the risk at an appropriate moment, investing in new technology. After an investment in new and more efficient technology, it costs less to produce a unit of x (because it has less labor-time in it) and the company can reap that benefit by selling at close to the old price, at least until the technology is generalized and the market price of x goes down to its actual average cost. But today the spreads are more complex. The basic structure motivating innovation remains arbitrage: through innovation in productive efficiency the manufacturer "buys"—pays for the production of—the same commodity for less money per unit and sells it on a world market where the knowledge that is materialized in the innovative new machinery has not yet globally percolated to all producers. From this we discern that price from the perspective of the buyer is a derivative on knowledge, an assessment of risk, the exercise of an option. When the innovated knowledge percolates throughout the system, things tend to equilibrium and "the law of one price" obtains *with no arbitrage possibilities on labor,* and further innovation will be required, either here or in another sector, to stave off the falling rate of profit. Capital will move to where the rate of profit and thus the degree of vertically integrated exploitation is highest. But as we know, such innovations, which some call progress, come at a price beyond the resolution of the calculus of profit. We can just glimpse that in the last instance arbitrage is on the cost of labor power itself, the cost of life-time or what, from the standpoint of capital that has no concern for life, might also be called metabolic time. Systemically, the result of this arbitrage is the general rate of return—the interest rate on M. Whoever can capture and valorize more value in the market with the least amount of paid labor time, whoever can buy low (or even get it for free) and sell high, whoever brings product to market paying the least remuneration for human metabolism, wins. What is sold on the financial markets is options on the command over labor time, over metabolic time. Going from M to M', realizing your interest, means being able to buy more and more metabolic time for the same money. The price of metabolic time must be driven lower and lower so that necessary labor (the labor necessary to cover the cost of the worker survival) makes up a smaller and smaller fraction of total labor time—the surplus labor time being captured and unremunerated. In the general devaluation of those who labor to survive, we survivors are indentured to carry anvils of data of ever-increasing weight. Computationally mediated abstraction provides the networked mesh to create "positions" on our futures in a system of derivative investments that are ultimately investments to return in the form of M' a greater command over human metabolic process. The various industries and platforms compete such that they can bring future metabolic time to market at the lowest price possible. Stealing the life of screen users, stealing the life of marks and targets, signifying on populations to leverage national debt or sales of arms, become strategies for the general reduction of the cost of life, the cheapening of life. "Users," denizens of the world computer, will more and more bear the burden of real abstraction and in general expect less and less. Citizenship, denationalization, and racial abstraction become some of the relevant operators here, all of which help to fine tune the income stream anyone might expect in return for survival. Within industries, among industries, among colonies and semicolonies, among individuals and within individuals, competition reigns.

Competition among the various capitals—innovations in specific techniques of *networked* extraction and valorization, specific applications of code in the model of the factory code—drives down the average price of life further still. Carceral societies, occupations, settler colonialism, camps, dispossession—these are not structural anomalies of digital capitalism; they are the sustaining methods of finance capital and, as such, are not just the backend of financial derivatives, but requisites of computational racial capitalism—key infrastructure for the cheapening of people in the reigning architecture of the world computer's organization of the production of the general rate of return on M becoming M'. Such is the general interest of racial capitalism.

III

Derivative Conditions

4

Advertisarial Relations and Aesthetics of Survival

Advertisarial Relations

With his typical flair for the graphic identification of our enemies, Banksy (2006: 196) has this to say about advertising and public space: "Any advertisement in public space that gives you no choice whether you see it or not is yours. It belongs to you. It's yours to take, rearrange and re-use. Asking for permission is like asking to keep a rock someone just threw at your head."

This statement would reconfigure the parameters of spaces colonized by the profit motive and the protocols of private property and speak to powers operative beyond its logic. In an ironic twist it seems that Banksy feels the same way about critical theory, since it was noted in March 2012 on Gawker that he actually lifted these lines from writer and graphic designer Sean Tejaratchi's essay "Death, Phones and Scissors" in the 1999 zine *Craphound* 6 (Pietzman 2012). On Facebook, Twitter, and Tumblr, tens if not thousands have expressed themselves by reposting Banksy, who was reposting Tejaratchi. Who was reposting whom? If private property is theft (which it is), and if advertising is the colonization of public space by the logistics of private property, then it would seem that the only possible relation to advertising is a criminal one.

But what of the "content" of these stolen, mobilized signs? What structure of feeling, tradition of struggle, or social moment does redeploying them express? They mean to say that the onslaught of words and images launched by advertisers is an aggressive attack on us denizens of the world and that, in short, advertising is an assault weapon. Like many of us have been saying for awhile now, it is also a new type of economic exploit, a psychoeconomic machine—a key component of the social factory and, as such, an encroachment on the commons. The rock, then, is a metaphor. Banksy calls an advertisement "a rock" hurled at "your head" to emphasize its bellicose aspects; however, if, as Banksy's film *Exit through the Gift Shop* (2010) shows, the capitalization of perception depends upon a transformed network of relations between vision and social practices, then advertising is not, strictly speaking, a rock. The ad's job is not completed upon impact. Perambulators in public space, spectators, users of images and screens, are the marks—biopolitical, Cambridge-Analytica-izeable entities targeted by computer-mediated advertising with the purpose of binding said beings to the social factory via present and future attention in order that their sensual labor, their metabolic time, may be expropriated for capital. In the prescient words of Dallas Smythe (1977), who in his landmark essay "Communications: The Blindspot of Western Marxism" bequeathed to us an analysis of what he called "the audience commodity," audiences do *the work* of learning to consume. As it turns out, for advertisers *all moments* are in principle teachable ones, and audiences can be made to work anywhere; but theirs is an exploitative pedagogy designed to expropriate the work of learning. Let us consider such a pedagogy in the context of finance capital before turning to some counterexamples at the end of this chapter.

While Smythe wrote one of the earliest considerations of what we might identify today as post-Fordism, we are aware that advertising is not exactly what it used to be either and that the strategies of capture of alienated labor have grown increasingly sophisticated. As we learn to work to mediate capitalist value transfer, enter Big Data, and with it the computerized trawling of the sedimented archive of attention. This outcome, which is also a prequel, should alert those who are not already clear on this matter—that post-Fordism cannot be adequately understood in the absence of visual and digital media platforms. The servility (Virno 2004), feminization (Marazzi and Mecchia 2007), and semioticization (Berardi 2011) of directly capitalized "immaterial" labor cannot properly be understood in materialist terms without the visual turn; the penetration of the life-world by capitalized interfaces (images) is its condition of possibility. What's more, as we shall see, these images have a derivative logic.

We will start in the near past and work our way back. On 1 March 2012, Google changed its privacy regulations to allow its fifty-plus stand-alone "services" to share data under a single "privacy policy." According to media theorist Christian Fuchs (2012), "Analysis [of the current policy] shows that Google makes use of privacy policies and terms of service that enable the large-scale economic surveillance of users for the purpose of capital accumulation. Advertising clients of Google that use Google AdWords are able to target ads for example by country, exact location of users and distance from a certain location, language users speak, the type of device used (desktop/laptop computer, mobile device [specifiable]), the mobile phone operator used (specifiable), gender, or age group."

Fuchs's trenchant analysis concludes that "Google's 'new' privacy policy is not new at all and should consequently best be renamed to 'privacy violation policy' or 'user exploitation policy.'" In a subsequent blog entry Fuchs "agree[s] with Oscar Gandy that personalised ads are a form of panoptic sorting and of social discrimination" and argues "for a worldwide legal provision that makes opt-in advertising mandatory and outlaws opt-out."

This is a significant, lucid discussion about the internet and advertising, and Fuchs's statement that "being productive in the corporate internet factory is being exploited" moves that particular discussion a decisive step forward. Indeed, the emergence of this screen-mediated, exploitative, deterritorialized factory—which inaugurates a new mode of value production and value transfer—is the fundamental argument of my 1994 essay "Cinema, Capital of the Twentieth Century," the article that, along with "The Circulating Eye" (1993), first introduced the notion of the "cinematic mode of production" and the following corollaries: 1) cinema brings the industrial revolution to the eye; 2) to look is to labor; 3) the attention theory of value updates the labor theory of value; 4) dissymmetrical (exploitative) exchange occurs vis-à-vis the screen; and so on (Beller 1994).

Today the internet as a means of production is both precondition and paradigm for the screen-mediated social factory. Attentional labor, or metabolic time, can be construed as informatic labor dissymmetrically extracted (stolen) in the movement from M to M'. Currently this social factory is capitalist and, as the most advanced incarnation thus far of the digitality implicit in capital itself, it functions through the expropriation of these new forms of labor. Outpacing the slower organizational modes of consciousness and society—and, as we saw in a previous chapter, conscience—is key here. As has been noted over the past century or more, labor itself has changed its form, and it should be no surprise that the encroachment on privacy and the imagination are part of the new terms of social production and reproduction.

For Marxism, expropriation via wage labor was and remains a dissymmetrical exchange: the worker gives to their capitalist far more value than they receive. But along with shifting definitions of productive labor come shifting definitions of the worker. Historically, due in part to the falling rate of profit, the average wage is leveraged down so that the worker receives only subsistence and an increasing percentage of the worker's product accrues to the capitalist. This change in the ratio of appropriation is essentially what is meant by the industry terms "efficiency" and "innovation," since making the same thing for less creates opportunities for arbitrage. As production expands to reinvest increased capital, the ratio of the value of fixed capital to the value added by labor increases (the expense of the vast industrial factory is far more than the daily contribution of the worker), requiring proportionally longer and longer periods of value extraction (a greater part of the "working day") as a proportion of remunerated time to keep the ratio of profit per unit capital the same. Capital seeks to increase its ability to capture unremunerated time and thus extends into the social. As I argued (2006b), systemically considered, screen labor combats the falling rate of profit by simultaneously extending the working day and increasing both the efficiency and flexibility of production, and, as we have begun to understand, it repays workers in discounted forms of currency—social currencies. The deterritorialized factory that is the screen extends labor into new spaces, times, and cognitive functions, resulting in a longer working day but also in what Bernard Stiegler (2010: 10) aptly calls "the proletarianization of the nervous system." What we have is the encroachment of an increasingly granular grammatization of attention and nervous process, which extracts what increasingly becomes necessary labor in ways that are not remunerated in any traditional sense. People are paid in likes, endorphins, social know-how, and other affects associated with celebrity, belonging, power, and intimacy (see also Chen 2003). These are new forms of currency and we are currently witnessing their formalization. So, to return to Dallas Smythe, while it is undeniable that screen users are sold to advertisers and that they do the work of learning to consume, there is a nagging question about exactly what they get in return for their efforts and time.

We grasp, then, that the wage—formerly thought to be exclusively paid in money (which Marx also called "the vanishing mediator" and "the general equivalent")—has, like labor, also changed its form. The networking of the commodity-form also sees the networkization of labor and the networkization of the wage. The various platforms perform both the consolidation and differentiation, providing expressive channels and currency. The general equivalent is a convertible form of social wealth, the commodity called "money" that had among other uses the specialized function of indexing and approximating abstract universal labor time as price. Increasingly, it appears that the money-form and social recognition are convergent; celebrity and the brand begins to articulate how one translates into the other—they are increasingly liquid assets. Platform-based and network-based currency purchases forms of satisfaction. Here we see the prototype in the social domain for what will be the full-blown emergence of cryptocurrency, as well as a rationale for its valuation as platform-based media. This latter revelation—that cryptocurrency is a new medium that aggregates attention in a new way—will turn out to have great historical significance. The notion that crypto is a new medium, both a form of money and a social network, is at present hardly understood even among the "thought leaders" in the crypto world.

But, leaving crypto aside for the moment, it seems unproblematic to say that money is what Sohn-Rethel (1978) called a real abstraction—but so too with the brand. As Erik Bordeleau puts it, such real abstractions are to be further understood as "lived abstractions."[1] Brands indicate a constellation of social relations and retain some qualitative elements even as they approximate the generality of money. They function like "soft" currencies. The case is similar with the "like" and other forms of platform valorization. Today, wages are thus also paid in real abstractions of the value-form, varying intermediate currencies supported by what Chih-hsien Chen (2003), following Foucault, calls "regimes of truth," which, although convertible, are qualitative, experience value fluctuations, and require exchange. Just what can you get with one million YouTube views? We are being encouraged (forced?) to learn to assemble iconic presentations of the self in exchange for what are effectively local currencies of recognition in order that we might extend our own productive basis and autocapitalize at a higher rate of return by extending our market base. Such self-help is the next phase of being an entrepreneur of the self, of being the capitalist who must seize on the human capital that is oneself and manage it as something alien in order to extract a greater return. Fractal fascism, which enjoins everyone to position themselves as a charismatic autocrat, requires an anarchocommunist response.

Signs as Instruments of Production

In the most general form, whatever small profits we may reap by means of the interface are paid in one currency or another, all pertinent to the dominant mode of subsistence that engages us and others and is indeed forced upon all of us: an exchange of attention and neural power with the interfaces of fixed capital. All are themselves taken as means of production both by the fixed capital of media conglomerates as well as by those of us who are seeking currency: recognition, or the general form of social wealth. We foray into the technopsychic landscape seeking the risk and reward of our invested capacities. On the labor side, by this time we are increasingly familiar with the various cognates that with differing emphases endeavor to name the capitalist convergences of work and play—immaterial labor, attention, prosumer, playbor, cognitive capitalism, semiocapitalism, virtuosity, neuropower, etc.—all the fancy names for email, gaming, entertainment, networking, geolocation, chit-chat, bullshitting, and the like. These terms represent the work we risk, the commodity we bring to the volatile market of semiocapital employment. Less familiar is the convergence of wage as money and as recognition, in which both become iterations of the general equivalent and thus exchangeable for human time—quantified and qualified signs offered to us in exchange for and as denomination of our efforts. *Here we begin to see the financial capture of expressivity and also to glimpse the possibility of a radical form of finance as an expressive medium.* As we grasp the dialectical struggle over the monetization of expression we must allow ourselves to be haunted by the questions: Whose expression? What can really be said if it is all to be converted into money? Just as money can be utilized as either a medium of exchange (in simple circulation) or as capital, so too with recognition and, more generally, attention. The celebrity quite literally banks human time.

The point I want to make with regard to the screen-mediated extraction of labor and production of profit—which is also a challenge to the category of "advertising"—has to do precisely with the idea of real subsumption that is implicit in the *materialist* post-Fordist model of production indicated above. Although it is necessary to insist upon the role of the screen in organizing the relations of post-Fordist production, it is a mistake to think that once one leaves the light of the screen, screen labor grinds to a halt. The overseer and its logistical capacities are distributed well beyond the monitor and the frame. As I have tried to indicate throughout this book, screen or no screen, the data churns. If the falling tree can be mentioned at all, it has already made a sound. Indeed that "sound" is a derivative on metaphysics which is itself a derivative on value. The point of Virno's (2004) concept of virtuosity is that the cognitive-linguistic has been commandeered by capitalist production—virtuosity is a command performance: one thinks and speaks capital and constantly cooperates in productive processes everywhere to purchase survival. My conversation by the water cooler at Pratt (at one of the few that actually work) is parametrically affected by the Learning Outcomes discourse from the Provost's office and is in a feedback loop with Middle States, Pratt's tuition prices, their web presence, and whoever-I'm-talking-to's Facebook account—to say nothing of our scholarly profiles (such as they are) and a million other digitized skeins that invisibly play and prey on our exchanges. There is a massive blurring of the lines between work, attention, semiosis, and remuneration that has transformed the character of communication. As we shall see more and more clearly, it has also transformed the character of currency and of money. The psychic fallout from abetting this informatic throughput is massive. I recall one of my colleagues, when I asked them how chairing their department was going, stating, "It has become impossible to answer that or any other question with sincerity."

With a somewhat different emphasis, this type of displacement of the sovereign subject of and *within* language—a form of dispossession—is also the ultimate point of Vilém Flusser's (2000) work on the photographic apparatus. This crisis of subjective agency is a far more intense form of dispossession than Jacques Lacan (1981: 206–15) indicated with what he called "the vel of alienation," which he defined as the price the subject pays in order to ascend to the symbolic order (and thereby constitute himself) and likened to the situation imposed at gunpoint by the thief when he says, "*Your money or your life!* If I choose the money, I lose both. If I choose life, I have life without the money, namely a life deprived of something" (212, italics in original). The price the subject pays for ascending to the I of the symbolic order entails the permanent condition of lack. Aphanisis, or the fading of the subject, is a structural feature of the symbolic order; the I on the signifying chain must constantly desire in order to recapture the phallus, its presence and agency. Otherwise it fades to the status of a mere signifier (which is what it is). We could say that Lacan's understanding of language as a medium allowed him to understand that the subject was a cybernetic form. Ontological lack was a condition of linguistic cybernetics—of the grafting of the biological body to the techné that is language. But today it seems that mere lack has been surpassed by abjection. For Flusser, the camera is a collection of programs that fundamentally alters the character of language and sociality but also of history and metaphysics. As I wrote decades ago in "The Unconscious of the Unconscious," photography is a medium that puts the linguistic medium itself into crisis. Flusser says that the camera works through a process that presupposes and builds upon prior media. Historically and actually the camera marks a triple abstraction from reality: from the hand-rendered pictographic image (cave painting puts four dimensions into two) to the written line (hieroglyphics, which tears up the two-dimensional image and renders it one-dimensional, that is linear, in the written line) to the materialized calculus of the photographic apparatus (linear alphanumeric writing, including the mathematics of optics and chemistry, extended into matter as a program to create photographs). Through the production of "technical images" by means of this triple abstraction, photography fundamentally transforms linear thought, as well as the fabric of time and therefore the relation of history and reality, such that humans are placed within the domain of the programmed image, "the universe of technical images." Technical images are themselves the product of automated thought—of programs that abstract the world by means of thinking in number extended into matter as optics, chemistry, and now digital sensors. Language is confounded by these, as it can no longer read back through the automated abstraction process to decode the black box that is the camera. Thus it, along with the subject-form germane to language and print-media, falls prey to the camera's program despite being unaware of its rule set or even most of its functions. The photographic is not a window on the world, it is programmatic information. One of the fallouts from the impossible task of constituting an "I" in the derivative condition imposed by the photocapitalism of the world computer is the oscillation between abjection and megalomania, between infinite dispersion and the branded self, so prevalent today. Billions of cybernetically interfaced camera-automatons advance the program of the camera and create the dissolution of linear thinking, linguistic command, and the subject form as they/we participate in the autonomization of photography. Unfortunately for "us," this creation results in various forms of psychopathology and, unfortunately for life on Earth, it also turns out to feed the autonomization of the value-form of racial capitalism. The photographic program is photocapital—an emergence of the world computer.

Stiegler's work on political economy and dispossession remarks on the "grammatization of gesture" by industry and then of audiovisual perception and cognition by what he calls "retentional systems," meaning media technologies (2010: 10). This grammatization of perception and cognition by media platforms harnesses the libido and institutes the aforementioned "proletarianization of the nervous system" as it feeds the computational program of photocapital. Therefore, the screen, while a command-control nexus that directly harnesses the function of libidinal drives as sensual-informatic labor, continues to organize the social factory through its afterimages. From this point of view, that of the programmable image of capital, it appears that the subject was another outmoded technology slated for creative destruction. As a moment's reflection would imply, even in the apparent absence of screens, their programming organizes off-screen places like dreaming, creativity, social aspiration, and the back alley, as well as the real conditions of a planet of slums.

Always Already Advertising

Therefore we may draw a conclusion that presents itself as the statement of a problem: if what one means by advertising is "the public marketing of commodities for the purpose of capitalist valorization," then "advertising" has become a general condition, the real name for informatic throughput in capitalism. Advertise, from Latin *advertere*, "to direct one's attention to; give heed"—literally, "to turn toward," from *ad* ("to, toward") and *vertere* ("to turn").[2] The formula M-I-M′ implies the convergence of information and advertising, an alignment of interests. If, given the postmodern intensification of the disappearance of the referent of the sign, the cynosure of postmodernism was that everything meant something else, *in post-Fordism we could say that everything advertises something else—and also itself.* This pithy formula could be further reduced to a precise deduction of what is nothing short of the reigning imperative of post-Fordist societies. As if in direct response to Fredric Jameson's famous injunction, the late capitalist riposte to "always historicize!" is "always advertise!" "Information" is in fact an advertisement for itself.

Advertisarial relations, as we may want to call the spectacular competition for recognition apparently permanently enshrined by contemporary computational racial capitalism, should be understood not only as a general condition in the competition for visibility and attention characteristic of all informatic activity but as the mode by which the multitudes (for lack of a better term) are dispossessed of history—the result is Hobbes plus social media. Thus, in the screen-war of each against all, where signs have become instruments of production, the imperative to advertise is also the imperative to erase by rewriting the archive (the noncapitalist and noncapitalizable strata) of shared, collective becoming. The native lands of the psyche, the libido and the imagination must be colonized and turned to production. This representation is indeed an encounter with the real suggesting as it does that the expropriative and racializing logics of settler colonialism are repeated and fully active in today's conquest. Indeed the computational colonization of psychic life and affective power aids and abets the ongoing violence of settler colonialism and the wake of slavery. In the creation of a variant of subjectivity "adequate" to the universe of technical images, "one" must write not just *over* the past but *on* history—on its claimants, and its constituencies. A thesis: *The real subsumption of society by capital marks the conversion of representation itself to advertising.* As we shall show further, advertising is also a derivative on volatility, an informatico-semantic wager. The ontological lack that Lacan ascribed to the subject of language is now ecological too—a condition of an entire ecology devoted to the instrumental erasure of certain kinds of individuals and ontologies (people) in order that, by means of incorporation, other kinds of individuals (profiles and fractal celebrities) may appear. Virtuosity—which is to say, omnipresent command performances within the social factory, performances that at once mark the expropriation of the cognitive-linguistic capacities of the species and the rise of the programmable image that now scores the general intellect—means that we speak for capital (which is precisely the role of advertising) in order to speak for ourselves. This prescription effects a thoroughgoing colonization. Speaking for capital also happens to be the role of the news, the state, and the military-industrial complex which, understood thus, suddenly appear more starkly than ever to be on a continuum with advertising itself. Although, as is noted throughout this chapter, most of these sentences were written several years before the arrival of 45, his sorry regime only bears out these claims. Dialectically then, within the framework of actually existing capitalism, media convergence (the movement of all platforms toward digital computation, and the movement of all digital computation toward digital capitalism) implies the movement of all cultural-semiotic practice toward advertising. Data mining must therefore be understood as a vast uptake of the commons, of the residuum of our common cultural and attentional practices, designed to intensify the imposition of an *advertisarial* relationship on every semiotic—and by extension, biotic—process. This mode of capitalist production, in which thought and "noetic acting" directly produce surplus value, strives to include all the sedimented attentional practices which were once relatively and at times avowedly unproductive: the very stuff of literature, art, theater, music, culture, and history, not to mention all that "mindless" yet oh so astute banter, gossip, and shade.

My discussion here of advertisarial relations having colonized the fabric of representation is not really meant to disagree with the anti-Google idea of opt-in-only advertising, nor to undercut policy recommendations that seek to limit the perpetration of advertisers' distinctively diabolical exploits, as in Christian Fuchs's injunctions cited above. But that type of intervention, I'm afraid, is but the tip of the iceberg. Given the sea change in the nature of languages and images themselves—their wholesale transposition and transformation from a means of representation to a means of production—the difficulty here is both with the substrate of communication (its bits) and with the us-versus-them perspective: we want to ban advertisers, but today we must also confront the disturbing possibility that we *are* them. Remember, "they" program "our" language and "our" imagination, "we" speak "their" thought—indeed, that is our work, or rather our labor. What to do with the fact that "we have seen the enemy and he is us?" One could say, one could want to say, "I don't care who you are: if you live in the first world, if you live in the Global North, then fuck you! You ain't no victim, even if you're sick." But who would be saying that? Probably some other Northerner, writing about how culture or the Venice Biennale, as if it were, could or should be more than a lavish spectacle of global suffering staged for a cosmopolitan elite. As capital's nations, banks, armies, schools, languages, newspapers, and films did to its colonies and colonial subjects, the current institutions from states to computer-media companies do to "us": they command us to make ourselves over in capital's image for their own profit through networked strategies of expropriation and dispossession. "We" do it to ourselves, and our representations of self and other are designed to sell a version of ourselves back to ourselves so that we can perform further work on what is now the raw material for the next iteration of images. Therein lies our ontological lack, an ontological lack of solidarity and of even the possibility for solidarity. Therein lies the desire for and indeed necessity to become a plantation manager—the word is *overseer*. Though it is beyond the scope of this essay, this digital neocolonialism that practically commands global Northerners to in one way or another accept Nazism and genocide with their cappuccino could be understood as being on a continuum with the internal colonization of Europe by the German banks—which depends of course on the distributed production of a kind of neoliberal "realism" that Mark Fisher (2009) called "capitalist realism," and was only ever a hair's breadth away from fascism.

This fact of our investment in and by advertising, the conversion of the sign to what I call the "advertisign," poses a genuine problem for theory—indeed an unprecedented one. This problem is particularly evident considering the material conditions (class, nationality, education, race, language, etc.) of the participants in the would-be counterhegemonic theoretical discussions of culture and policy that presuppose the books, computers, schools, and institutions that sustain these. Those within the circuit of these discussions have already passed through a homogenization process which programs them in compatible systems languages. Without submitting ourselves and our own aspirations to radical critique, without conducting a Gramscian inventory of our ostensibly internal constitutions, we run the risk of merely trying to set up a competing corporation with a new business model. The revolution will not be televised; decolonization will not be a brand.

Any would-be anticapitalist "we" runs this risk of coopting and cooptation from the get-go, particularly if it does not think about the materiality of social production from top to bottom: class, yes, but also race, nation, gender, sexuality, ability, geolocation, historical stratification. The world's postmodern poor, the two billion–plus living on two dollars a day, also labor to survive in the material landscape organized by the post-Fordist social factory its anti-Blackness, its Islamophobia, its endless and mutating racism and imperialism. However, from the standpoint of capital, the role of those at the bottom is to serve as substrate for image-production and semiosis; not only in factories, cottage-industries, subsistence farming, and informal economies, but also as starving hordes; "irrational," criminalized or surplused populations; subject-objects for policing, encampment, and bombing; desperate refugees; and even as voids in the idea of the world—as sites of social death. Forgive me, but I'd wager that no one capable of understanding these words can claim full exemption from the indictment they issue regarding structural complicity with the production and reproduction of everyday life. Humans are troped (via discourse and the screen) to organize military production, national policy, internment camps and prisons, bourgeois imaginations, museum shows, corporate strategy, and market projections. Let us clearly state here that any program that does not admit this excluded planet into dialogues that vitiate the monologues imposed by capitalist informatics and advertisigns is still floating in the realm of the ruling ideas and therefore participant in murder. These ruling ideas are the ones whose density and weight, whose material support and very machinery, threaten to further crush the late-capitalist poor out of not just representation but out of existence. This erasure and disposability, imposed by systems of informatic inscription designed to absorb every output of sense, is the achievement of the advertisarial relations endemic to computational racial capitalism. When information is an advertisement for itself that presupposes the operating system of the world computer as virtual machine, banning what we recognize as advertising on the internet, even if an excellent beginning, is just not adequate to address these issues of representation, social justice, planetary and climate racism, and emancipation.

To summarize: the forms of sociality which are the conditions of possibility for the online, informatically organized relations—best characterized as *advertisarial*—run through every sector and register of planetary life. The internet, while recognizable as an effect and a cause of the current form of planetary production and reproduction, cannot be considered in isolation as a merely technical platform or set of platforms if its historical role is to be properly understood. To take the internet as an autonomous technological force results in a species of platform fetishism that disavows both the histories and material conditions of its emergence, conditions that are, in short, those of screen culture and racial capitalism; this is to say that it, the internet, is the very means by which the capitalist suppression of global democracy (which is emphatically, economic democracy as well) has been accomplished and continues. If the internet is autonomous, it is because it expresses the autonomization of the value form. As noted previously, with the hijacking of communications and semiotic infrastructures by racial capitalism, the medium is the message and the message is murder. To ban advertising on the internet would be a good start—but what if the whole thing is advertising?

One reading of what I have said thus far might suggest that, given the expropriation of the cognitive-linguistic, our volition is overtaken by capital logic; and given our inability to cogitate in any way that is genuinely resistant to capitalist expropriation, coercion, strictly speaking, is no longer necessary to impose cooperation for capitalist production. We "want" to cooperate productively, our desire—which, from the dispossession of even language and mind constitutes ourselves as subjects in the media ecology of the capitalist technical image, that is, in and through the organization of digital information—is itself an iteration of capital, a script of becoming predestined to become capital. The old language scored by the new image machines and their extractive algorithms locally organizes cooperative subjects who want to cooperate with vectoral capitalization. We want to provide content in order to derive currency and survive. Our solidarity on the internet produces more internet. Thus, in a certain way—and particularly since we no longer properly have any thoughts of our own—we all collaborate in a world organized by images and screens, thereby participating more or less mindlessly in the seamless realization and triumphant apotheosis of the programming business. However, I am sorry to have to report that the dystopian vision here is not quite as bucolic as even this already dreary picture of unwitting and irredeemable pulverization and servitude. While I do see that representation and semiotics have been increasingly flattened à la Orwell and Marcuse by a vast internalization of the apparatuses of oppression (in which "thought" is the [productive] thought of the [capitalist] Party and "repressive desublimation" is an engine of capitalist-fascist production) the "old problems" like the hierarchy of class have not gone away; neither have racism, sexism, homophobia, transphobia, ableism, and fascist nationalisms ceased playing their roles to create vectors of privilege for white male–identifying aspiration. Indeed, most thought today, such that it is, is all about maintaining hierarchical society. The thinking runs thus: capital is nature, capital is eternal, capital is information is nature. Or, in a more pedestrian mode: human beings are naturally acquisitive and competitive, economic growth and technological advancement mean progress, this tech provides, or almost provides, a color-, gender-, and religion-blind society, and so on—and one must advance one's place in it by any (crypto- or not-so-cryptofascist) means necessary. Of course, there exists better thinking out there. Mia Mingus: "As organizers, we need to think of access with an understanding of disability justice, moving away from an equality based model of sameness and 'we are just like you' to a model of disability that embraces difference, confronts privilege and challenges what is considered 'normal' on every front. We don't want to simply join the ranks of the privileged; we want to dismantle those ranks and the systems that maintain them" (Mingus 2011, cited in Puar 2017: 16). However, there is broad-band, ambient programming that facilitates assuming neo-liberal and full-on fascist subjective sovereignty. This programming seeks triumphant brushes with plenitude (communion with the big Other, as distinct from the racial or otherwise other, becomes the ego-ideal), and this same programming is violent, competitive, hateful, mean-spirited, and alienating when embraced—at the same time that it is also co-operative, simpering, and abject. Servitude, even when automatic and mostly unconscious, is unhappy and, as we can see any day from the daily news, utterly pathological and sick. Of course, this diagnosis represents a huge generalization, but despite its broad-brushing lack of subtlety we may find that such a schizoid oscillation between entitled adjudicator and abject supplicant sums up the contours of your average reality television show or comments section on YouTube. It is Bateson's (2000) and Deleuze and Guattari's (1977) schizophrenic, caught in the double-bind, who has become the capitalist norm—the one who struggles to negotiate in the form of contradictory signals the aporias of hierarchical society, while reproducing it, and all the while experiencing their own psychic dissolution as an injunction to create.[3]

With this schizoid capture in mind, let me then develop my question about the internet—"What if it is all advertising?"—in the framework of post-Fordist production. The argument is that, in the context of virtuosity and the expropriation of the cognitive-linguistic by computational racial capital, sociality itself has become advertisarial, a ceaseless waging of capitalized exploits designed to garner attention and value for oneself and one's capitalists. This situation represents—indeed imposes—a derivative logic, a logic in which every action is a hedge, a kind of risk management devoted to maximize a return. In addition to the fractalization of fascism, in which agency is manifest as a profile that has aggregated the attention of others, advertising has worked its way into the sign itself, into the image, and into data visualization, and it has generated the *advertisign*. All signs become points of potential cathexis, derivative positions on the underlier that is social currency and ultimately value. This new type of sign is not simply the brand but also an element of vectoral language (Wark 2007): functionalized words in a production channel, engaging in the micromanagement of desire, the production of new needs, and the capturing of the imagination, all in order to induce linguistic and behavioral shifts in the attention of others while aggregating their attention for oneself—turning their heads with an interface. This combination of the manipulation of market conditions (that is, everyday life) through techniques of risk management is no longer merely the province of advertising but of so-called human interactivity (what was once just communication and before that culture), now become adversarial through and through. From Smythe's claim in the "Blindspot" essay (1977) that all leisure time has become labor time, to Virno's (2004) notion of virtuosity, we have seen aspects of this model for the capitalist overdetermination of apparently unremunerated time before. However, here—with the financialization of expression—we clearly grasp that the financialization of everyday life means also the convergence of semiotics and financial derivatives.

Given the thoroughgoing intensification of vectoral, and in fact matrixial, signs, we need to investigate its implications in the context of a discussion of radical media practice. I will make two additional points here before shifting gears and turning at the end of this chapter to what I identify as an aesthetics of survival—an aesthetics that emerges from within the matrix of advertisarial, schizoid capture. The final chapter of this volume will endeavor to extend aspects of such socioaesthetic forms, those resistant to computational racial capitalism, to new notions of radical finance and the possibility of platform communism. *If, as was already becoming true in the cinematic mode of production, the dominant means of representation have become the dominant means of production, the questions of and models for political agency are radically transformed, and the urgent need to decolonize communication and decolonize finance presents itself.* Future communication will require a cybernetic approach, and, as we shall argue, *this cybernetic approach will necessarily be financial*, though it will be reaching toward a different order and different mode of production. Like communism, because it will need to be communist, it will see economic transformation of the material relations of production and reproduction as essential to the revolution. It will draw on the repressed and extracted cognitive-linguistic resource of the racialized and otherwise marginalized and configure ways to make our voices matter both as meaning and as tools for the reorganization of the material world and the social relations therein prescribed. Language and images are neither inside nor outside; they are part of the general intellect—currently they are at once media of thought and of capital. We also know that languages and images are not isolable, meaning that they are not and have never been stand-alone entities but rather exist in relation to their media, their platforms, which are again inseparable from society and its institutions. Furthermore, each platform relates to another platform. Paraphrasing McLuhan, we could even say that the "content" of a media platform is another platform. Thusly the general intellect is inseparable from its media platforms and their financials. We see that the general intellect, once largely held in common, is increasingly being privatized; the very media of our thought belong to someone else. *This expropriation of the media commons is precisely the precondition of the real subsumption of society by capital.* It is an extension of the ongoing expropriation begun by primitive accumulation and money as capital, and it has been accomplished through the financialization of media as platforms of extraction. The ramification of mediation by computation and information has resulted in its convergence into formats offering derivative exposure to underliers that are the expressive vitality and futurity of our communication. We therefore no longer have any organic relation to the materials for thought itself (sincerity has become a myth, at least in the medium-term of most circles)—the words, images, and machines we require to think, to express ourselves, to interact, and to know have been ripped from the species and privatized via the *longue durée* of dissymmetrical exchange. *We work on the words and images, but as numbers they belong to someone else.* The media themselves have become *forms* of capital—forms of racial capital—and our usage of these media means that we work to add value that valorizes capital, for the capitalist and within a relation designed as much as possible to guarantee that our creative acts necessarily occur as dissymmetrical exchange with capital. I write this book in a discourse that does not just not belong to me because it is shared, but in a discourse that is increasingly the property of a set of institutions—publishers, journals, universities—that all have their eye on the bottom line. The means by which we most intimately know the world, ourselves, and our desires (our images and words) are themselves vectors of capitalization intent upon converting our very life-process into surplus value (which is to say value for capital). We need strategies that will seize the means of production and create a reverse subsumption of affect, intellect, knowledge, capability, communication, and community. When all media have converged as economic media, it is economic media that must be re-engineered.

Again, I think this subsumption of cognitive and affective capacity, the quasi-automating (scripting) of productive labor for capital, is what Stiegler means by the proletarianization of the nervous system—which would include the proletarianization of the pathways of feeling and thought. Our affective capacities are put to alienated and alienating work in the social factory, and their product too is alienated, producing ever-intensifying and ever-accumulating dispossession and disempowerment as the dialectical antithesis of its simultaneous production of unprecedented wealth and power for the cyborg avatars of the great media conglomerates. Intellect and emotional intelligence, the product of thousands of years of species-becoming, is being strip-mined so that extraction machines may continue their furious innovation to further discount people. I write this book aware of the pressure to think it just right, to at once extend thinking in order to command attention and produce new needs, but also to delimit it, to control myself, and to put the reins on whatever counterpower may rage within my body, because academia can tolerate only so much "bullshit" and no more. Yes sir, I'll be careful not to cross that line, but a word to the woke: the bullshit is the best part.

From a historical perspective, this encroachment on the means of representation—that Banksy and I and a billion others join the silenced majority in opposing—indicates that the individual subjective agent, itself a platform for sociality that developed with the rise of capitalism (as the subject who relates to other subjects in the market, the bearer of the commodity and thus its thought), is nearly defunct. As has been noted previously, in a world where life processes are stripped, ripped apart, rebundled, and sold as derivative exposures, the individual subject is an outmoded technology despite the fact that it still appears as a skeuomorph in certain updated technosocial apparatuses—like the latest forms of films, games, influencers, and versions of national politics that proffer invitations to momentary individualistic identification for the *dividual* purpose of providing a sense of familiarity and orientation. While palliative for some in small doses, such individuality is no longer a viable (which is to say, sustainable) fantasy. The real thought is that of the infrastructure, of the AI that codes our meat and scripts our sheets. Sure I take up the mantle for a few moments each day to appear as the agent of this text, suiting up as the operator of an intellect that might be adequate to the informatic shit-storm of racist, capitalist, imperialist, patriarchal, for-profit assaults, but then I drop off into an ocean of petty concerns, food shopping, and home repairs. And even when I say "I," to perform as the nexus of all this insight, I also know that it's hardly me talking. I'm just curating at the gates of shit that needs to be said, and hopefully titrating to let the right stuff through.

That's part of my politics though Dog knows that I could create a more lucrative named-professor type profile with just a little more discipline, a bit more self-interested adherence to the protocols of the academy's factory code. Instead, there is the effort to overturn, to be or at least to live something beyond being the scribe of the world computer, to at once witness the drama of the emergence of the intelligence of commodification, testify to its outrage, and intimate the possibility of its overthrow. Such would be the art of this text, practiced at the limits of disciplinarity and of subjectivity, guaranteed by nothing and no one. The expiration of the subject form, imminent since the subject's first intimation of mortality—and made structurally mandatory by Freud and especially, with the full-blown rise of the sign at the moment of it radical marginalization by visuality, by Lacan—is not necessarily a cause for lament, despite the increasingly intense fading of its incalculable beauty, its sad reduction to cliché. From a political perspective, it means that within each concrete individual body the presumed continuity of the individual is riddled with contradictory and indeed unassimilable indicators; it means also that there exists in differing quantities and qualities capitalist and noncapitalist striations or sectors. Hallways of emptiness, but also hallways of love. Like bundled assets, the mind-body is tranched by executable logics organized by a calculus of risk available to investors. There are, to be a bit simplistic, aspects of desire that are programmed (indeed farmed) to produce practices that function in perfect accord with capitalist accumulation strategies (individualizing or schizoid) and aspects of desire that are atavistic or collectivist, utopian, communist, or maybe even just plain lonely, and, in short, subprime. In reality, of course, desire is more singular than even such formalizations might indicate. Insert your favorite snippet of poetry here. Hortense Spillers in "All the Things You Could Be by Now If Sigmund Freud's Wife Was Your Mother" (1997) invokes "the Dozens" and the music of and like that of Charles Mingus (152–3), to make present an "interior intersubjectivity"(140) testifying to the rich unaudited psychic life of what might today be called Blackness. There are vast resources beyond the easy resolution of hegemonic hermeneutics whether deployed by institutionally validated psychoanalysis or compressed by current systems of informatic extraction. In agreeing with Freud that consciousness makes up a small part of mental life when compared to the preconscious, the unconscious, dreams, and so on, but in rejecting the normative assumptions and disavowals (including his own Jewishness) that situate Freud and the psychoanalytic discourse that will become part of European and U.S. bourgeois society, Spillers recognizes a vast store of mental life and the possibility of listening anew. However, when speaking of politics now, we therefore necessarily speak of the abstract forms available for the conceptualization and deployment of concrete emergences whether referring to haecceities that are innumerable or collective forms of existence and psychic life actively mediating between "the one" and "the 'masses'" (141). Let us listen anew.

Acknowledging that we ultimately and if possible immediately want to "marry our thought" (Wynter 1994b: 65) to the wealth of subaltern forms of life and the care of the bios, allow me then to put the situation of the post-Fordist subject thusly: in *Imperialism, the Highest Stage of Capitalism*, Lenin (1939) showed how imperialist dividends complicated class issues in England, since many people, otherwise part of the working class, got a share of the dividends of imperialism by clipping the coupons of their investments in racist, exploitative British enterprises across the globe. Today this race-based class fractionalization is fully internalized in the Global North; on our iPads built by Chinese slaves from blood metals extracted from the Congo, we may momentarily feel like biomorphically unmarked nobles in the global cosmopolis; while on the job market or when simply seen in our raced and gendered embodiments, we are abjects. Materially and intellectually we are nodal points on a global network. The signal oscillates between narcissistic megalomania and utter abjection and can be affected by a billion parameters taking us from melancholia to outrage. Thus, even the concrete individual is composed of class fractions, race fractions, gender fractions. In the form of signs, we clip coupons that validate our investments. The language of object-identification, we observe here, cannot really keep up with the fluctuations resulting from the throughput of code as we work to identify and disidentify our agency. Can we audit a different mode of emergence, a different futurity than one inexorably overcoded by capital?

Of course this is still somewhat simplistic and also class-specific, as many (*billions* even) never get to participate as an enfranchised global citizen in any aspect or moment of life, even if the lived experience of these same billions is radically overdetermined by the class(es) from which they are excluded.[4] The gilded poverty of the enfranchised, as opposed to the mere poverty of the rest, is now a measure of connectivity. A more complete view is that we are the product of the world system and thus *everything* we are has been produced vis-à-vis globalization, and therefore everything bears the trace of the system in its entirety (again, in varying proportions). This conceptualization of concrete individuals (bodies) as global communitarian products forced to varying degrees into templates of individualized risk by capitalist states, is not to erase class; however, it suggests that, just as Fanon saw the great European metropoles as the product of third world labor, we are all products of the worst conditions prevailing in the Global South and around the planet. *Global inequality is internal to our being*. It is us. How then does one (such a one who is relatively enfranchised by the derivative language of texts such as this one) inventory those relations and produce them as formations of solidarity rather than as disavowed residuum? Is there another data-sphere, a communist one? Can we build communist interfaces, networks, and finance? How would we register, track, amplify, and render actionable the communitarian affinities, solidarities, obligations, and debts, the resources in the wake of too many genocides to count, that in actual practice underpin the official economy, collective life, and whatever authentic hope is left to our species? Perhaps we have arrived at a question worthy of theory: Is there, could there be communist algorithms? Communist derivatives? Derivative communism? We are looking for that path.

To add to my point about the shifting, distributed character of political actors—that goes so far as to suggest that we can no longer think only of actors but rather must think of vectors and fields in addition to thinking of the resources developed in cultures of survival—I will make a second observation. A political intervention in the advertisarial relations that have this planet heading toward environmental doomsday requires not only revolutionary policy but revolutionary culture. (I defer further discussion of a third requirement, revolutionary finance, to the final chapter.) This culture must take into account that, for many on this planet, Armageddon is not the future but an ongoing constant. My call here (which should not be entirely unfamiliar, as it gives petit bourgeois intellectuals something important to do) is to (re)politicize semiotic and affective structures and practices, including and perhaps especially those we might control, for example our own utterances—our expression. Of course, to call them "our own" seems to contradict what I've said about the expropriation of the cognitive-linguistic and the intensification of aphanisis by visual, verbal, and digital media derivatives, but it is here precisely that we confront one of the significant material contradictions of our time: who or what speaks in us? This question, which I shorthand using the phrase *the politics of the utterance* and which you can experience palpably right now (as you endeavor to think), seems to me to insist that our idea-making must actively produce its solidarity with the dispossessed. We must struggle for the radical constellation. The question concerning the politics of the utterance, asked here in a strange passage of this text through a beyond-academic terrain, a moonless forest the traversal of which may or may not at this point lead us back to the plot, also raises the question of becoming, as well as the questions of agency and of action within the capitalist image—programmable images, racializing and racist images that, in the terms we have set out, are functionally omnipresent. Continuous media throughput has generated a capitalist imaginary structuring both language function and imaging processes, coordinated at scales and by calculative logics that exceed individual comprehension. Though the occasion is upon us, we must struggle for space and time to think. We must open a spread on which to bet against the dominant order. We glimpse, and we feel, that to insist upon the unremitting relevance of both culture-making and of cross-cultural transnational solidarity helps to avoid platform fetishism because it sees the internet and its machines not as a set or collection of autonomous technologies but as a historically emergent system of value-expropriative communication and organization, built directly upon older but nonetheless contemporaneous forms of inequality, including but not limited to historically emergent techniques of gendering, racialization, and imperialism, and embedded in the living flesh of the world.

All of this calculative interconnectivity and networked agency implies, contradictorily, in fact, that the internet is not all advertising—but neither is advertising all advertising. It is also murder and struggle. Banksy knows that. The advertisarial relation is the programmatic relation encrypted in the apparatuses of capital: the war of each against all, taken all the way from finance, computation, and surveillance to the speech act and the imagination in accord with the autopoietic algorithm of the distributed Leviathan. Marx himself saw capitalism as vampiric, and today's processes of capitalization are even more totalitarian, more widely distributed, and more blood-, life-, and indeed soul-sucking than even in prior eras—though such comparisons don't do those killed by past iterations of capitalism any good. Despite the disavowals to the contrary, we recognize that capital needs labor, needs metabolic time more desperately and more voraciously than ever before (what else is biopolitics?) and, furthermore, that it wages war on life-time on all fronts, in order to secure labor power, its product and basis, at a discount. The pyramids of inequality become internal fractals, and even as the base broadens, the tip with the all-seeing eye (that is not a subject) ascends ever higher. We do not yet know what can be destroyed or indeed built with the massive appropriation of Banksy's rocks, but we do know that at present there is total war against our using them to build anticapitalist, nonhierarchical, horizontal, solidary sociality. The refusal or détournement of capital's encroachment is itself a creative act. Perhaps we have only begun to glimpse what a total refusal might achieve.

Aesthetics of Survival

Without trying yet here to pursue this thought to whatever logical conclusions it may harbor (counterculture, countercomputation, the release of frozen histories into time, the overcoming of the aporetic character of our times, computational communist economies, postcapitalist economic media, joy), let us take a moment to think about the implications for life in the visible world, the *speculum mundi*. The concept of a visual economy, which would undoubtedly extend beyond what is visible both to everyone and also to anyone in particular, would insist that the logistics of screen-mediated capitalism pertain in myriad situations beyond the purview of the screen vis-à-vis a structuring (and indeed continuous modification) of the general intellect and therefore of the imagination and the cognitive-linguistic.[5]

I have been working with the hypothesis that "real subsumption" also means the total or at least totalizing enclosure of the bios by the logistics of the programmable image. Although I cannot develop all aspects of this discussion here, one can provide a shorthand by returning once again to Flusser's idea of the technical image, as well as to his understanding of the photographer and pretty much everyone else as a "functionary" of the camera (Flusser 2000). For Flusser, as we have seen, the better part of the last two centuries has been organized by the programs that constitute the camera for the benefit and proliferation of cameras; hence one sees the camera's promulgation unto omnipresence. Increasingly all life is organized in accord with these programs, such that humans and posthumans and those brutally refused admission to either of these categories produce—in a way that is subsidiary to the protocols of the camera and its product—the technical image. As Flusser notes, today all activities aspire to be photographed. According to Flusser, in becoming functionaries of this technology our lives, histories, and indeed history itself and metaphysics are effectively, if not also ontologically, internal to the photographic program. Everything is a means to photography and significance is conferred by the camera. Humans are subsumed by the photographic apparatus, and we make our way in what Flusser calls the universe of the technical image—what elsewhere I have called the "media-environment" and the "world-media system" and have here, in an effort to both raise the ante and create a heuristic for computational racial capital, called the world computer (see Beller 2006a; Flusser 2011; Tadiar 2012). Unlike Flusser, I see the program of the technical image as predatory in a racial capitalist mode—as an extension of the capitalist program, of capitalist mediation, and therefore of the logistics of commodification and remuneration. In other words, the programs that ramify the visual do not merely institute capture (culture or life could do the same); they institute leveraged exploitation which constantly threatens and indeed actively strives to transfer all wealth to capital precisely by exercising a radical overdetermination with regard to our (meaning the species') practices and potentials. As individual organisms and as a collective species, "we" are pushed to the limits of survival. As already noted, and in a manner not unlike Bateson's porpoises (see note 3), we find ourselves compelled to create something extraordinary or perish in the cross fire of contradictory and annihilating programs. The requirement that we actively wager our lives within the image is operative for all, no matter how conscious or unconscious its imperatives remain. It implies that we wager our very being within the image in a reconfigured politics of utterance, gesture, and action. Within the image there is a stake, a *political* stake in every form and indeed all forms of expression.

Flusser himself is clear that cameras—by means of the automation of concepts extended into matter—represent the world as information. Here we understand that they generate information, moistening the world with it and readying it for value extraction. But within the conversion process of world to image, of M to M', there are spaces of struggle—spaces for the contestation of the arrangement of things—that might transform the metaprogram, that might, in short, provide inadmissible information that then creates a demand for and even the possibility of a different set of programs. This wager, opening up a spread on alternative futures, is to embrace and perhaps even extend somewhat Wynter's notion of the intellectual as "the grammarians of our order" (1994b: 65) who might work to transform that order by "marrying their thought" to those that through rebellion "directly challenge the mode of 'Truth'" of an order (65). Wynter refers here, in the essay "No Humans Involved: An Open Letter to My Colleagues," to *les damnes* of Fanon, Baldwin's "captive population" and the Los Angeles rioters after the beating of Rodney King who nonetheless exist despite being placed under the LAPD proscribed category of N.H.I situations. "Being human, including our model of being human, *Man*, in its present Western bourgeois or ethno-class conception, is a property of the narratively instituted governing codes of symbolic *life* and *death* or *sociogenetic principle* enacting of our human forms of life as a third level of hybridly *bios* and *logos* existence. *Being human* can therefore not pre-exist the cultural systems and institutional mechanisms, including the institution of knowledge by means of which we are socialized to *be* human" (Wynter 1994b: 6). What we are reaching for here is practices that can change these codes.

In the previous chapter, we saw how Ariella Azoulay's reconceptualization of photography had the potential to intervene in both the treatment of photography and its social functions. We also posited that such a reframing of practices of photography might interrupt the circuit M-I-M'. Here I will discuss two examples from cinema, one of the global middle class and one of the global subaltern class; specifically, a short clip from Hou Hsiao-Hsien's *Zuìhǎo de shíguāng* (*Three Times*; 2005: 1:33:20–1:38:40) and one from Khavn de la Cruz's *Iskwaterpangk* (*Squatterpunk*; 2007: 00:06:15–00:09:50). These discussions are here to help us recall the experiences of reality and representation that are indexed and manipulated by the high-level abstraction of the world computer. They are in dialogue with and, in a way, making answer to its computational power. We breathe them in before moving on to a discussion of radical finance and the decolonization of money in the concluding chapter—for in a world colonized by the world computer, the grammar of money—its protocols—instantiated in and as information is a key site of struggle for the progressive transformation of the current episteme/platforming that secures the social order of computational racial capitalism.

Three Times treats two characters (played by the same actors, Shu Qi and Chang Chen) in love with one another in three different historical moments: 1911, 1966, and 2005—but the film is not an exercise in mere repetition; rather, it is an image of three different *times* and their modalities (one is tempted here to say their *media*). In *Three Times* the love story functions as a thread that allows for a kind of media archeology, an examination of the structures of connection and containment that gendered love must navigate to realize itself in three different historical periods. By the 2005 narrative, the present of the film, viewers and characters are already in the time of the full-blown technical image, in Flusser's precise sense of the term, the digital photograph and *its* world (of screens, text messages, and garage band software—the last of which shows explicitly, in the film's diegesis, how even music has become a computerized image). The digital forms have overtaken what in prior moments were the times of early-twentieth-century media: the 1911 bordello, with its courtesan's song along with the books and calligraphic letters of the nationalist writer; and, in the episode set in 1966, the times of the international postal letter, the radio, the military order, and the pool halls accommodating soldiers' R&R. The juxtapositions—with their focus on writing, communication, and song—function as if to say, "To each time its media mash-up and to each media mash-up its form of time." And for each array, a different micropolitics of love. Hou's analysis of the media of sociality, however, is not only an effort to periodize the media and thus the historical forms of love; it is also a philosophy of the media historicity of meaning, praxis, and political agency.

If this study in remixing the sense ratios sounds McLuhanesque, what we are talking about with Hou Hsiao-Hsien and Taiwanese history is anything but the global village. Rather, Hou (particularly in his later work) shows viewers people who are in some way connected to Taiwan but able neither to experience community nor conceptualize their history: space and time have undergone a radical dissolution—itself orchestrated by the urgent movements demanded by a new order of communication. Although characters are immersed in a present that is the historical fallout of Taiwan's past, particularly in the myriad consequences of the "white terror," the name for the long-denied purge, beginning February 28, 1947, in which the ruling KMT imprisoned 140,000 people and killed as many as 28,000 communists and fellow travelers through 1987, their immersion in this generally disavowed history does not bring them closer to others or to knowledge of that past. The characters' radical dis-placement and alienation here (and perhaps even more emphatically in Hou's film *Qiānxī Mánbo (Millennium Mambo*; 2001) is accomplished and completed through a near total immersion of the film characters in a world of images. These images, themselves a product of both a history and of a media history almost unknown, are part of the legacy of a continuing past but are devoid of narratives and concepts that would explain their function or create connection. There is no political grammar available to decode their condition or situate them. As historical results shorn of their history the characters therefore make their way in alienation so intense that it is tantamount to dispossession; it is in fact dispossession, since properly speaking it is Taiwanese images, Taiwanese history, and Taiwan itself that confront its people as hostile and alien.

In *Three Times* we move from the time of the nationalist writer (1911) to the time of the military order (1966) to the time of a near total absence of words (2005). These three eras are represented not only through careful attention to period fashion, architecture, and gesture but by using cinematic conventions pertinent to the time of each vignette, like intertitles for the 1911 section, along with period appropriate lighting, film stocks, and palettes. Indeed, given the thoroughgoing endeavor made by the filmmaker, it might be more accurate to say that the periods are not only represented but the particular character of their temporality is recreated. The viewer experiences three different media ecologies. Pointedly, in the concluding episode of *Three Times*, Hou's contemporary characters, with their smartphones, headsets, and screens, are not only severed from their past—along with its networks of connections and forms of temporality (they do not know themselves to be the same lovers they were in prior episodes, which of course raises questions associated with repetition, difference, and performance)—they are also severed from their immediate present (their community) and are dispossessed of a coordinate system, a framework of interpretation that would allow the kind of self-assessment and autolocation necessary to provide oneself with a sense of narrative purpose. In a world saturated with images, they are dispossessed both of their history and of narrative, of connection to the past and of continuity of any kind. It is as if the contemporary characters have been absorbed into their images and thus deprived of the *power* of speech; they can no longer speak anything important and must negotiate a world of images and inchoate, inexpressible desires. It is perhaps in accord with this diagnosis that Hou's most recent works—set in contemporary times—only manifest themselves minimally as stories. Key conversations are gestural and nearly inaudible, taking place in clubs with pumping techno music. The films that focus on the contemporary are primarily explorations of a programmatic mise-en-scène in which the effort to navigate from within the image registers a new form of realism—a realism without reality.

The lyrics of the trancelike and ludic song sung by Jing in the 2005 vignette, played by Qi Shu who also played the female lead in the 1911 and 1966 vignettes—both the opening, "Please, open your eyes, open your ears, check your brain," and the refrain's exhortation "to realize what you want, to realize who you are"—are, despite their denotative simplicity, a crystallization of artistry and wisdom that is also the best and perhaps only means of her liberation. They are the medium of her desire and propose a new aesthetic grammar. This song erupts in a filmic episode characterized by the almost complete absence of speech. It is sung in a club with a small, distracted audience while three men, including the photographer with whom Jing is having an affair, continuously shoot her from increasingly close distances. Like the filmic images of words on computer screens and smartphones, like the monetary Yen sign "branded" on Jing's throat, these words (sung in English and passing through the Yen tattoo) are part of the reclamation of words whose character has been forever altered by the globalization of the technical image—a logic which has at once converted words into money or images or money-images and degraded them to near superfluousness: mere content of an always-already financial relation in photocapital. Jing's deployment of language, by means of sung signs, minimal as it is, threads a connection through the sensory overload of the present, forging a path through the capitalized force fields of the imaginary. That she sings in English—the universal language of global capital—only heightens the tension between the forces of the geopolitical marketplace and the particular intensification she pursues. Although the gesture is understated, it is notable that, during the song which draws the male photographers closer, Jing's female lover, Ah Mei, turns her back on the performance and walks out.

Jing's fate, though radically indeterminate in *Three Times*, is inflected somewhat more positively than that of Vicky (also played by Qi Shu) in Hou's earlier film, *Millennium Mambo* (2001). In that film, the downward spiral of Vicky's life is made visible for the spectator as evidence of a kind of wasted beauty—her own: her character cannot claim, much less utilize her own power. Hou emphasizes Vicky's dilemma as a sociocultural squandering of beauty by creating subtle yet magnificent geometric compositions (à la Ozu) that frame Vicky's life while remaining absolutely irrelevant to its events (in a way that Ozu's frames were not). This extradiegetic, yet astonishing, formalized aestheticization of Vicky's life (which is the very material of the film) is of no use to her whatsoever. In *Millennium Mambo* one could say that there is an aesthetic dimension to the gradual dissolution of the film's central character, but this aesthetic component avails her nothing. Vicky is shown to lack the means to represent or abstract her situation to herself because she cannot access or manipulate the grammar of her own destruction. We might say that in a pre-Instagram world she cannot self-capitalize because she does not control the shots. Whatever pleasure the spectator takes from her presence in the image is taken without compensation or reciprocity for the character. Consequently, the audience's pleasure is little more than a symptomatic form of surplus value garnered from a generalized dispossession and from the systematic indifference toward the destruction of others vis-à-vis the sociotechnical mechanics of the image. These mechanics, which are also a politics, are organized by and for the image at a level beyond the ordinary individual's level of conceptualization, beyond the frame of their reality. Vicky produces pleasure and indeed art, but not for herself. It is an art of extraction.

In *Three Times* Jing sings, "The color that you've seen, the shape which you're in, may reveal the secret you've never known before." She grasps what Vicky cannot. Like the courtesan-singer of the 1911 episode, Jing's art gives her some agency—again this art is the medium of her desire, an engine of value-formation and seduction, a means of expression and of survival. Using the instruments at her disposal, she creates an affective form that both crystallizes and mobilizes some of the relations that have overtaken everyday know-how and common language; in the clip indicated (1:33:20–1:38:40) she sings to her lover—as well as to Hou Hsiao-Hsien and to his audience—*through* the camera. Her ability to wager within the image, to answer a nondiscursive (anti-discursive) aesthetic regime with an aesthetic form, allows her to create a line of flight, even though, narratively, this deterritorialization is at best a mixed blessing. The film ends on a kind of in-between, grungy, and urban image, with Jing on the back of her cameraman lover's motorcycle, negotiating traffic on a smoggy Taipei highway, seemingly having left, and possibly having betrayed, her lesbian lover Ah Mei. While the couple on the motorcycle cut through the dense megalopolis that is Taipei, the audience, contemplating Jing's momentary freedom with some exhilaration, is left to wonder if Ah Mei has in fact committed suicide as a consequence of Jing's affair with the photographer. Jing has made her aesthetic wager within the image, but someone very close will have to pay.

My second example of a wager within the advertisarial logic of the image-function, from de la Cruz's *Squatterpunk*, allows us to consider more closely "the digital" as a reification and to consider dispossession itself as creating a literal surface of inscription, while further exploring the politics of the wager. In this particular segment (00:06:15–00:09:50), children between the approximate ages of five and eleven dive acrobatically into the trash-laden ocean on the outskirts of Manila—literally an ocean of floating debris pressing up against the shore of their squats. The swimming and play in a world of garbage is accompanied by a wailing punk soundtrack. As you view, your moviegoer's body knows that this swim through trash alone would likely kill you, and watching these children you are not sure what to feel. Moments later you will see those same kids selling the plastic they've scavenged during the swim to a small-time recycler and using the money they receive in exchange to buy a tiny meal. Here is an example of "playbor" for you—a wagering in the image of globalization. *Playbor* is a term I do not particularly like; we should consider permanently marking this term with an awareness of child-labor and an unbreakable connection to the postapocalyptic neoimperial violence of sheer survival.[6] It is also noteworthy that, for most of the audience, the form of playbor that de la Cruz records—in which children mix their passion for play with the work of scavenging for survival (which, as mentioned, due to the levels of toxicity in the water would literally sicken most of the audience)—registers itself through a visceral repugnance of a shoreline and a Manila Bay filled with garbage and waste: human waste, the nonspectacular side of postmodern capitalism.

The film, with its punk track by de la Cruz and his band The Brockas (after the great Filipino cineaste Lino Brocka), also features one of the kids with a mohawk haircut (the eldest, judging by size): a punk look. However marginal, "punk"—whether British, American, or Pinoy—is still a style choice: being born a squatter is not an option. The situation of the children who provide compositional elements for *Squatterpunk* is political, but it is not, in and of itself, a political choice for the children. It is where they live. The filmmaker utilizes punk aesthetics to approach the conditions of the squatters, to marry its practice to the conditions of their existence, but the film is also interested in the place where style and indeed representation approach their limits. To this end—of raising questions about the limits of style, representation, and digitality—*Squatterpunk* is emphatically not a documentary. De la Cruz uses the bodies and conditions of children born on the outskirts of Manila as an expressive medium. He films the mohawk haircut that one of the children gets for the film; he colors, rotates, and solarizes the images he makes of and *from* the children, always insisting on the fact of a constructed relation between the image and its "content." This insistence serves to dramatize the squalid conditions that underpin not only this digital film but the larger explosion of Philippine digital cinema and, more generally, "the digital" itself. For the poverty that we see is itself a consequence of, and a condition of possibility for, globalization—which is, in turn, the geopolitical formation in and through which digital technologies have their large-scale emergence.

Thus the (digital) film does not provide unmediated access to a profilmic Real but, rather, dialectically reveals that the viewer's affective experience (not just of this film but of globalization and digitality) is inscribed on the universal appropriation of the "reality" of these lives and bodies. For the poverty that is *constitutive* of this film, it must be underscored, is *also constitutive* of globalization and *its* digitality. Radical dispossession is one with capitalist accumulation, both of which are intensified by and managed with digital technologies. Digitality, consumerism, wealth, and waste: it is no accident that the film begins by tracking a one-legged child "soccer" player brilliantly dribbling a Coke can through the slums. Here, because of the punk soundtrack and the blatant manipulation of the plastic quality of the image, we see *through* the digital and we know it. That is, with this image, unlike with most digital images, we see that its substrate is radical disposition. The violence (the manipulation of images of "Others" that the capitalist subroutines of art and anthropology would, more traditionally, have us "respect") done to a Real generates a dialectical image in which everything that has ever happened—colonialism, imperialism, globalization (all the mediations of history)—are palpably the conditions of possibility for the spectator's current and indeed profoundly ambivalent experience; and not just this particular experience with *Iskwaterpangk* but of all contemporary spectatorial experience.

One confronts the material basis of capitalist digitality—the structural dispossession that comprises what are—in fact, its conditions of possibility. In so doing we also confront the condition and limit of the ideology of the digital inasmuch as it posits an ideology of a pure informatics, of liberated data, and of incorporeality. It is as if de la Cruz cracks the algorithm of digital representation in the age of finance capital and reveals that the virtual is inexorably material. The filmmaker attaches his wager to the wagers of survival shown on screen such that we, the viewer, can access the conditions internal to our specular speculation—which is to say, ourselves. To look at *Squatterpunk* is to look at your own insides. The audience's position is not ultimately one of judgment nor identification but of a kind of nonintersubjective recognition that understands that the viewer is somehow composed from and by what they now confront but most often disavow. Cyborg consciousness encounters its bedrock. Again: de la Cruz mobilizes the computer-processed digital image—making it visibly copresent with its materially copresent politico-economic underside (the planet of slums)—such that the audience confronts conditions, aspects of the global economy, that are actually (that is, materially) internal to its own speculation. Such an endeavor imposes with new urgency—an urgency that I want to insist weighs upon our utterance and action in this moment and all the ones to come—the abiding question, "What is to be done?" This insistently digital image, which *recognizes dispossession as its condition of emergence*, links the digital spectator with the human and indeed biological substrate of the digital; we confront affective consciousness as cybernetic while we confront the material integration of specific and seemingly contradictory elements (ourselves and our slums), and we do so without adequate resolution. The experience of the film's intensity depends upon an experience of the world's inequality. Like it or not, the question posed by such inequality is the call to wager: to wager with one's words, one's art, one's life.

It remains to say how the wager, the cosmic gamble, is indeed connected to the analysis of advertisarial relations set out above; how it is in fact the central feature of an aesthetics of survival in the aestheticizing regime that is the dominant mode of semiocapital's digital culture. In semio-war we too are called to cast stones. If the machines of capital are distributed through the socius such that attentional activity includes affective labor—the utterance, action, and other forms of social praxis—and if this labor is organized at multiple levels by a media-system's calculus of value extraction and measure, by derivative logics cutting through our being and betting on the predictability of our impulses to create extractive spreads on a range of our actions, then it is probable bordering on certain that life itself has become universally posited as a work-site of computational racial capitalism; all social activity, even survival, is posited as value-productive labor in a financialized, planetary semiosis.

This view of life as an open work-site, founded on what Neferti Tadiar (2012) calls "life-times of disposability," can be gleaned from a pitch for Mechanical Turk—the Amazon platform that would employ Global Southerners to perform cultural piecework such as receiving texts and texting them back in indigenous translations for a few pennies per transaction—when the site asserts that there are currently billions of wasted hours in the Third World which could be used for profitable production. As "life itself" becomes a real abstraction of post-Fordist capitalism (one which would be the alienated inverse of species-being and what I have also called "metabolic time"), a structural effect of the integrated and aestheticizing operation of global semiofinancial apparatuses, then all social activity is placed within the framework that earlier had pertained specifically to wage-labor and slavery: human becoming emerges as a socially leveraged engine for production, even when—especially when—wasted unto death. The need to survive is forevermore an opportunity for exploitation—the savvy businessman's chance for profit as he exercises his right to distort and waste historically devalued life, as he exercises his right to maim (Puar 2017). With the invasive fractalization and networkization of the commodity-form, one fights to survive, fights to be able, at the profit of another. This is a speculative regime of leverage characterized by the convergence of derivative media and derivative finance that has developed from the Hayekian (market) communication already latent in the very idea of exchange-value. It achieves unprecedented penetration into the material organization of things through the introduction of new metrics, feedback, and forms of algorithmic intelligence. Whether for consumer or consumed, the conditions of individual and collective emergence are thus overdetermined by capitalist programs—intentionally (or perhaps not) and systemically. However, as with wage labor, the totalizing control of wage laborers' activities, thoughts, and potentials inexorably sought by capitalist management systems should—*and indeed must*—have limits. What these limits necessarily imply, beyond and perhaps before planetary climatic collapse, is that by casting our lots it is possible to introduce rupture into the capitalist expropriation of what was previously called labor-time and what Tadiar calls life-time. Such rupture would mean a break with the capitalist program in semiotic, spatial, temporal, sexual, discursive, informatic, communitarian, or other modes; not simply a refusal of the programming but an interested, liberatory, insurrectionary, and creative positivity, whether as a rearrangement of existing terms, a break in the temporality imposed by capital, or an exceptional form of desire or care—to name some possible modalities of risk.

This opens up to what in the cinematic era, with reference to the spaces of the everyday blown apart by "the dynamite of the tenth of a second," Benjamin referred to as "a large and complex field of action" (1969: 236–7)—one that cannot possibly be summarized here. However, in conceptualizing the current dialectics of capture, my wager in this chapter is that the field of liberatory assemblage both constitutes the current reservoir of anticapitalist values and is open to all of us here and now. There are ways to interrupt the circuit from M to M′, and not all of them are self-destructive. There are strategies of survival that allow the oppressed to solidarize, collectivize, and cooperate to keep more of the fruits of their/our struggle. To transform the grammar of representation with the practices of struggle, to recode the codes, is to make space for alternative relations of cooperation to find their own abstractions. In a world where late-capitalist fascisms aestheticize politics, digital communists—self-identified or not—respond by politicizing "life," both within the quotation marks and without. The fact that the terms *politicize* and *politics* themselves have been put under erasure by the world-media system that is computational racial capital requires another discussion and will be addressed in what follows. Ultimately it will entail the wholesale *doutournement* of information along with the recognition that the abstraction of subaltern values can be cast as communist derivatives.

An Engine *and* a Camera

Arguably, we should no longer admit a meaningful distinction between what we commonly refer to as "the digital" and the operations of racial capitalism. We have made this argument throughout the foregoing. With the overdetermination imposed by the cybernetics of computational racial capitalism, a willful collapse of the terms of analyses of digitality and capital into one another serves at once as an exercise in provocation and in historical verisimilitude, as well as its being a political necessity. Information is capitalization— until proven otherwise. As a historically prescribed conflation, and as a mode of analysis that sees emergent forms of capital in every aspect of the digital and vice versa, such an analysis—one adequate to the concept and operations of the virtual machine that is the world computer—thus also sees "the financial" in every aspect of "the cultural." The convergence of capital and digitality impacts all the Marxian categories (labor, value, money, class) and many formerly, and often still, un-Marxian ones as well (race, gender, national/ethnic culture, and information). Those reading here know much of this mediation theory already—for we are aware to varying degrees that money as medium has not only colonized nearly all other media but that it has functionalized other media as means of capitalist production through the rise of information and its management machines. There has been a shift in the mode of production to *the computational mode of production.*

The title of this chapter, "An Engine *and* a Camera," responds to Donald MacKenzie's book, *An Engine, Not a Camera,* the title of which was in turn taken from Milton Friedman's view "that economic theory was an engine to analyze [the world], not a photographic reproduction of it" (MacKenzie 2008: 11). Theory, then, is not a photograph, and economists do not consider themselves photographers. However, as MacKenzie and others argue (Lipuma, Derman), economic models in their very performance—their performativity—make themselves real. The derivative pricing model known as the Black-Scholes equation, for example, is known to be inaccurate. However, because it is adjustable by the experienced trader it is used thousands of times to day to price derivatives, and its usage has made it the standard model for derivative pricing.

We have seen in previous chapters that the economic theory that includes the *practices* of advertising, photography, and social media complicates this picture. It appears that theories about cameras, even if proffered by engineers, are business models bent upon the production and accumulation of valuable information. MacKenzie comments that this view of economic theory, as an engine, not a camera, "was in a sense a truism: a theory that incorporates all detail, as if photographically, is clearly as much an impossibility as a map that reproduces exactly every aspect and feature of terrain and landscape" (11). Theoretical concepts could not index the entire field of the economy but were rather abstractions offering guidelines for practice. Or so it seemed in a world before Google maps.

Sylvia Wynter, in her brilliant and devastating critique of "No Humans Involved," an acronym (N.H.I.) used by the LAPD to refer to police incidents in which none of the people in question where white, remarks, to counter liberal sentiments that might wonder how such things could have happened, that the laws enabling the police were made by "the best and brightest," and were as such the clear result of the U.S. educational system. By way of critique Wynter locates "the fallacy which underlies the premise of the discipline of economics (as the present master discipline in the place of theology), that our human behaviors are motivated primarily by the imperative common to all organic species of securing the material basis of their existence; rather than by *imperative* of securing the overall conditions of existence (cultural, religious, representation and through their mediation, material) of each local culture's represented conception of the Self" (1994b: 48–49. Wynter then identifies a "second fallacy, that of *supraculturalism*, [that] mistakes our present "local" culture's representation-of-the-human-as-natural organism as if it were the human-in-itself, [and thus] mistakes the representation for the reality, the map for the territory" (49). Computation *imposes* the map on the territory. As Wynter writes, "whilst the human species is bio-evolutionarily programmed to be human on the basis of the unique nature of its capacity for speech it realized itself as human only by coming to regulate its behaviors, no longer *primarily*, by the genetic programs specific to its genome, but by means of its narratively instituted conceptions of itself; and therefore by the *culture-specific discursive programs* to which these conceptions give rise" (49–50, italics in original).

Quoting Elie Wiesel, she continues, "'The designers and perpetrators of the Holocaust . . . were the heirs of Kant and Goethe.' Although 'in most respects the Germans were the best educated people on earth, their education did not serve as an adequate barrier to barbarity. What was wrong with their education?'" (60). This question, as a statement of an abiding question about the racism of knowledge and of the ideological state apparatus we call school, goes to the heart of Wytner's critique of racial capitalism: that the cultural models informing economics (justified by a profoundly mistaken, though highly convenient notion of evolution that takes the individual as the hermeneutic key for the understanding of emergence), along with its conception of the sovereignty of *Man*, cannot recognize the humanity of jobless Black men. This nonrecognition persists despite the fact that the dominant episteme has built its self-conception and its culture on the backs of those it excludes: the colonized, the enslaved, and the dispossessed.

Milton Friedman's view of economic theory as "an engine not a camera" missed the fact that the autonomization of economic concepts would realize themselves in camera-like ways as well as in cameras proper. They would impose their fallacious humanisms. As we shall see below, John Maynard Keynes, in ways similar to Friedman after him, separated representation from the economy, while Hayek famously conflated representation and the economy by relying on the quantitative metric of price. Communication theory and computational media move this Hayekian reduction of representation to number to the sphere of production as they organize value extraction in computational racial capital such that every representation has and is a price.

The conventional notion of the interventional versus the representable, noted by Friedman, made particular sense for John Maynard Keynes, whose dissertation sought to distinguish between at least two types of probability: loosely, the mathematical and the discursive, or again, the rational and what he would later call "animal spirits" (2007):

> Even apart from the instability due to speculation, there is the instability due to the characteristic of human nature that a large proportion of our positive activities depend on spontaneous optimism rather than mathematical expectations, whether moral or hedonistic or economic. Most, probably, of our decisions to do something positive, the full consequences of which will be drawn out over many days to come, can only be taken as the result of animal spirits—a spontaneous urge to action rather than inaction, and not as the outcome of a weighted average of quantitative benefits multiplied by quantitative probabilities. (161–2)

Keynes believed that mathematics alone could not account for the qualitative needs and urges of human beings or the kinds of actions this nonmathematical register of human endeavor would impel. His view, that what plagued Western civilization was the over-rationality of "Benthamism," which supported his view that Marxism was an extreme form of such utilitarianism, led him to endorse aspects of capitalist market rationality but to repudiate both laissez faire (on the right) and revolution (on the left) and to propose instead the welfare state as a discursive and political engine functioning in ways capable of regulating the economy but responding to needs that exceeded mathematical resolution. This compromise between the social and the mathematical (also intelligible as a middle road reformist position between fascism and communism) was the state formation that, in its unfolding, led Chomsky to acerbically quip, in the Bush-era United States, that the state was indeed a welfare state—for the rich.

Keynes (2015) wrote, "The fundamental problem of the human race [is] to find a social system which is efficient economically and morally" (76), but he also wrote, "I do not believe that there is any economic improvement for which revolution is a necessary instrument. On the other hand we have everything to lose by methods of violent change" (73). Keynes was a secularist and a moralist who believed that an orderly organization of the economy—understood mathematically but regulated by the state—was the urgently needed pathway to a benevolent society because, as he said, "If heaven is not elsewhere and not hereafter, it must be here and now or not at all" (74).

Keynes's most formidable critic in the realm of bourgeois economics was Friedrich August von Hayek, who suggested, in effect, that the market was itself a computer, capable of commensurating value and assigning appropriate prices. Indeed, price was itself the result of computations which traversed the field of the economy and which offered themselves locally in a way that allowed for decision making that considered global conditions even if the details of these conditions were unknown. The price signal—all those decisions of buying and selling—collapsed knowledge into price in accord with a shared optimization strategy and therefore contained what one needed to know to make a rational economic decision in a world of qualitative unknowns.

The most significant fact about this system is the economy of knowledge with which it operates, or how little the individual participants need to know in order to be able to take the right action. In abbreviated form, by a kind of symbol, only the most essential information is passed on, and passed on only to those concerned. It is more than a metaphor to describe the price system as a kind of machinery for registering change, or a system of telecommunications which enables individual producers to watch merely the movement of a few pointers, as an engineer might watch the hands of a few dials, in order to adjust their activities to changes of which they never know more than is reflected in the price movement. (Hayek 1945)

Such a hyperrationalist view, one which conceived the "marvel" of the price signal as a kind of "telecommunications," corresponds to Hayek's contempt for the notion of social justice and governmental intervention in the distribution of wealth:

> I am convinced that if it were the result of deliberate human design, and if the people guided by the price changes understood that their decisions have significance far beyond their immediate aim, this mechanism would have been acclaimed as one of the greatest triumphs of the human mind. Its misfortune is the double one that it is not the product of human design and that the people guided by it usually do not know why they are made to do what they do. But those who clamor for "conscious direction"— and who cannot believe that anything which has evolved without design (and even without our understanding it) should solve problems which we should not be able to solve consciously—should remember this: The problem is precisely how to extend the span of our utilization of resources beyond the span of the control of any one mind; and therefore, how to dispense with the need of conscious control, and how to provide inducements which will make the individuals do the desirable things without anyone having to tell them what to do. (1945)

In *The Mirage of Social Justice* (1982), Hayek says of market results that there is no point in calling the outcome just or unjust.

> I believe that "social justice" will ultimately be recognized as a will-o'-the-wisp which has lured men to abandon many of the values which in the past have inspired the development of civilization—an attempt to satisfy a craving inherited from the traditions of the small group but which is meaningless in the Great Society of free men. (67). . . . [O]ur complaints about the outcome of the market as unjust do not really assert that somebody has been unjust; and there is no answer to the question of *who* has been unjust. Society has simply become the new deity to which we complain and clamour for redress if it does not fulfil the expectations it has created. There is no individual and no co-operating group of people against which the sufferer would have a just complaint, and there are no conceiv-

able rules of just individual conduct which would at the same time secure a functioning order and prevent such disappointments. (69)

Unpacking Hayek's view of the situation—in which a nonsubjective intelligence, namely that of the market, concatenates "price signals" and thus computes prices that can be locally utilized and thus subjectively occupied to advantage—already in 1945 suggests that financial logic operates in the pores of representation: in Hayek's terms, price becomes a *signal*. From the economic point of view, all relevant information regarding the value of a commodity has been compressed into this signal; everything else, including justice, is noise. "Individual freedom," Hayek's highest ostensibly extra-economic value, depended upon non-interference with the medium of prices by money suppliers and economic policy makers—banks and states. We perceive clearly here the libertarian anthem.

Hayek the libertarian (or in his own terms, the "Old Whig") served as chief financial advisor to Pinochet and became an apologist for dictatorship as, presumably, a pathway to neoliberalism. This should not surprise us since in his system of accounts the optimizing individual pursues only his own interests and no one is held accountable. He was nonetheless largely correct about the computational dimensions of capitalist markets and by implication, finance—correct, at least, from the standpoint of "the market," a universalist standpoint that he adopted and that we must here recognize was a politics. This politics was and remains the self-same politics of *Man* so profoundly excoriated by Wynter, and it is the politics of the world computer.

As Marx (1993) wrote of an insurgent capitalism, "Money [is] the real community, since it is the general substance of survival for all, and at the same time the social product of all" (225). As such it thereby dissolves prior community: "The reciprocal and all-sided dependence of individuals who are indifferent to one another forms their social connection. This social bond is expressed in exchange value, by means of which alone each individual's own activity or his product becomes an activity and a product for him. He must produce a general product—exchange value, or, the latter isolated for itself and individualized, money. On the other side, the power which each individual exercises over the activity of others or over social wealth exists in him as the owner of exchange values, of money. The individual carries his social power, as well as his bond with society, in his pocket" (156–57).

Hayek worked to make this imperial vision true and our acknowledgement here of the acuity of his analysis of capitalist markets and thus of his anticipation of the collective emergence of capital's computational machinery functioning by the telecommunications of price, clearly suggests, when put alongside his political affinities the consilience of capitalism and fascism. Unconscionably, the *desaparacidos* of Chile were barred from telecommunication. But as we have seen, under capitalism conscience has a price, and its exchange value is falling.

While there are too many examples of the violent dissolution of community by money to count (arguably it is what makes history and then world history), its powers of dissolution are today perhaps best observed in the myriad effects propagated by synthetic finance: by derivatives and the Black-Scholes-Merton equation for options pricing. I mean of course, the decompositon and recomposition of both financial products and forms of life—the inauguration of read/write ontologies mentioned in previous chapters. Using an equation for heat entropy, "Black-Scholes" creates a directionally independent price for the volatility of an asset—and it does so in complete indifference both to the specific asset to the social consequences of the transactions it enables. It does not matter if the asset price goes up or down or even what the asset is (the equation is content-indifferent)—what matters is the absolute value, the magnitude, of the volatility. "The reason everybody embraced Black-Scholes when it arrived was that, before then, everybody thought that option pricing depended on your opinions about the future direction of a stock price and about how much you liked or abhorred risk. Everybody had a different risk preference and therefore everyone got a different value for the option. Black-Scholes showed that because of hedging, all options could be derisked, and so everybody could agree on the same price provided you knew the future volatility of the stock" (Derman 2016: 218). This equation, utilizing the mathematics of randomness (Brownian motion) and the past history of an asset price, allows traders to put a price on volatility itself, that is, in Keynes's terms, to price animal spirits. Using what is called "delta-hedging" traders readjust their exposure to risk in real time as volatility changes, in theory allowing them to make the general rate of return (the general interest rate paid on money as capital) risk free.

So, in brief, the irrational, the representational, the sociopsychological, and the discursive can be summed up as volatility and priced—or indeed, economically rationalized. "Black-Scholes imagines that the derivative markets, their components (e.g., money), and their agents exist objectively and independently of the social. Technically this stems from the fact that to price derivatives on these terms—in this mathematical manner—it is necessary to exteriorize and reify the social. What makes this necessary is that admission of the social would destroy the conditions for the use of the mathematicized model" (Lipuma: 68). Black-Scholes continues to be used, even though, as mentioned and as Mandelbrot showed, it is recognized that it is not exactly accurate (Mandelbrot and Hudson 2004). "Traders use their immersion in the world-view of the habitus of finance to reintroduce the sociality externalized by the Black-Scholes model, making what appear to them to be intuitively reasonable recalibrations. The spread names the mental device traders use to reconcile the model's externalization and removal of the social with the ensemble of social determinants presented by the market. In this space of practice there is no opposition or contradiction between technical rigor and pragmatic play because they are both mutually imbricated aspects of derivatives pricing. The disposition and affect of traders serve to incorporate the practice of logic into the logic of practice: the mathematized result into existential decision making under uncertainty. From the purview of the trader in the act of trading, neither the structure nor the event are apparent, only his body (rife with anxiety, pressured, and hypervigilant) serving as the interpolator of the spread between the model's abstract price and it pragmatic recalibration" (71).

We have remarked and analyzed this movement to the quantification of qualities more granularly throughout this book, and we have studied the ways in which bodies are inserted into visualizations of information to generate more information. We have argued that alongside financial derivatives, social media and advertising are analogous, and as we are at pains to show, deeply homologous armatures that render the social increasingly computable. Value added comes from using information to create information by passing through the conscious organs of the world computer, but not all positions on the network are equal. Capital's network topology is hierarchical in the extreme. With the Cambridge Analytica scandal providing but a single notable instance of the emerging potentials of such computability, we can see that access to data, access to computing power, and access to media and financial tools is key to the maximization of one's affective relation to a quantified world. Platforms control access to the social graph of their users, and can leverage that access. Google and Facebook sell their proprietary data so that others can buy exposure to targeted users. Options provide high level access to rigorously integrated (but qualitatively excluded) social relations. Such a rationalization of the qualitative and the affective for the market is not only the role of computation but its essence. Phenomena of any type become fodder for simulation models, and the model then becomes indexed to the phenomena while the remainder is discarded, only to be recursively available as affect to feedback into the model. To render computable that which was not by drawing it into the ambit of mathematical calculation, to make the unintelligible rational and *therefore* social by virtue of its being economical—that has been the developmental path not just of science but of racial capitalism on the way to computational racial capitalism. Such has been the project of the economy of *Man*. To treat life as calculable thing, being as number—with a higher purpose, perhaps, but whose? This rendering of quality unto quantitative reason is accomplished by treating qualitative forms as information. Such treatment requires that various—and in theory, all—phenomena can be rendered and reproduced in terms of information. Of course, this production—this ontological imperialism presided over the by the AI digits of the invisible hand, this settler colonialism of computation—has a cost, and we must ask: For whom is this society where money is the real community? Some of this rendering cost is figured in the price of computation, paid in money by those who can pay, but most of it is externalized, paid in quality, as when, for example, sound quality is lost in the transition to digital media from vinyl, or life quality is lost by those who pay in one way or another for the census, for surveillance, for drone signature strikes, for coltan mining, for famine, for forced migration, for state terrorism—and for the environmental racism of what is called digital culture. But the costs internal to capitalism, imposed by the practical-material function of the world computer, and what's more, the cost price of any wager whatever (the cost of risk) is always the only relevant factor accounted for in computation—and there are many strategies of risk management to externalize noise and deal with contingencies utilizing a calculus of cost, strategies that include the cost of the police and of preemptive policing. Not only, as Hayek taught us (and also Marx and Sohn-Rethel), is price an ambient computation; computation is a means to price. The imposition of its content indifference by any means necessary (the dissolution of community by any means necessary) is a condition of its function. Such is the deeper meaning of commodification: the conversion of qualities to quantities in order that the world become computable.

An expanded notion of capitalist organization theory that understands the digital indexing of practically all social activities, relations, and forms as itself a mode of productive capitalist organization opening up "substitutable choices," suggests that modern social theory, even if it does not know that it is in fact economic theory, is always already imbricated in an economic system—a theory is in and of itself an economic model that has been modeled by the economy. It too is a calculative engine—a map standing in for a territory and thus a computation that must be productive, even as a discourse. So much the more so as computer science and as sociocybernetic practices managed in real time. By productive, here, I mean productive for capital—practical for capital—and therefore I mean also that economic theory, spread across the spectrum from disciplinary economics to corporate policymaking becomes a strategy of wholesale value extraction from the social body. Theory itself has been colonized by the logic of financial optimization, which is to say that, as the continuously updated result of a set of experiments it sets in place on the social body, its province extends granularly into the practical organization of value extraction. Indeed economic theory, recognized as such or not, lies atop the social as a map that is the size of the territory, a laminate of quantified information available for the composition of bets on the underlier that is the world. In this, whether academic, government, or corporate projections, theories of the social now function both as an engine *and* as a camera, creating data visualizations for instrumentalized purposes that include carving their own niche in the marketplace, as well as surveilling and documenting everyone and every possibility as information for the next iteration of wagers. As theory abstracts, it indexes, and as it indexes, it instrumentalizes for computational rationality. Let us remark here that this "theory" of social process is not simply one of representational forms providing interpretative scripts in the form of abstract concepts; it is figuratively and quite often literally a data visualization, an abstraction, *and* an index, and therefore a programmable image. An image that serves as an interface for action and practice, and therefore a worksite. Theory is, in effect, a camera: a machine of abstraction that abstracts the world for further abstraction. It is a machine that functions through and evolves practices of abstraction. Discourse becomes a subroutine of the image which is a subroutine of computation which is a subroutine of racial capital. Again, further extending Flusser's analysis of the camera, in which each now-digitized pixel that appears to index points in an iteration of a representable world is the result of the functioning of concepts: we would want to add, contra Flusser, that such concepts are ultimately beholden to financialized and thus capitalized interests. The camera is thus also an engine, since the one incontestable fact of the current era is that, in Flusser's terms, "cameras have organized the world for the benefit of cameras," or, in the terms developed in this book with regard to the world computer: the entire matrix of representation is instrumentalized to drive the production of surplus value by means of the networking of the extractive interfaces of media infrastructures—in other words, the interface of *fixed capital* with the social body. The specific body might be the trader's, as above, or the Instagram influencer, or the drone target. It might be Rodney King, Breonna Taylor, or George Floyd. Computational racial capital has organized the world for the benefit of computational racial capital: the machines of abstraction create the cuts and bundles. These cuts and bundles, images and algorithms, are simultaneously programs for work and derivatives on work, networking commodity production and enabling extraction at the interface. Sadly, the types of beings most fully enfranchised by this totalitarian logic are those that dispositionally resemble 45, or Modi in India, or Duterte in the Philippines. They could be Bezos or Zuckerberg. These are the men of *Man*, avatars of the world computer. In becoming information, all representation is mobilized as a financial calculus, one that includes the potential for that information to extract and bind further information. At the highest levels, financiers and state leaders are the ones in the position to write derivative contracts on the futures of entire peoples.

Today, when representation and consciousness themselves are financialized, we may recognize that under the seemingly value-neutral term *information*, a computational logic has in fact become granular enough to assign number to every passing fancy—what else is a cellphone? Or, for that matter, a keyboard? Not all you may still (want to) say, but what if all those seemingly incidental twitches or dreamscapes of the mind are the wives and servants supporting with their data-sensitivity your surface interface, your "man"? What if all your dreams are the unremunerated housemaids of your clicks and geolocations? Of course the world is more beautiful than this engendered image of internal servitude doing the bidding of the entrepreneur of the self that is the surfaced of market interface. However, here we must also recognize that, as with computational machines, which in chapter 1 we were able to show are not only technologies but racial formations and gender formations, so too with information: it is beholden to and indeed a result of the violence of value extraction and the overcoding of life. Things don't become prices without pressure, without repression and oppression—without heteropatriarchy and racialization, without class violence, imperialism, and the large-scale organization of dispossession. Information's evolutionary pathway, its content indifference, its quantities, its computability is one with that of racial capital—it has the same character. Thus, drawing on previous chapters we may summarize: 1) Information emerges in the footprint of the value-form. 2) Information theory pursues the "content-indifferent" imaginary of capital. 3) Information is a means to price which is itself a derivative on knowledge. 4) *Information is the fourth determination of money (in addition to measure, medium and store of value)*. It is an ongoing calculus of financial risk that has a price, is a price and makes all prices derivatives on knowledge: it is the communication of capital, the effect of real abstraction, in short, generalized real abstraction. More on this last point in the final chapter.

Understanding how what critical theory has come to call "social difference" is itself the result of financialized codification processes—which produce forms of legislation, perception, and "morality" that in turn license certain types of actions to be practiced on or by certain types of marked bodies with regard to one another—is a crucial avenue of critical inquiry. The abstraction of the social as information in the signature operation of computational racial capital. What is this thing called "race"? asks Hortense Spillers (1987: 137). "Our deadliest abstraction?" Labor, Jim Crow, border walls, genocide, the "New Jim Crow" (Alexander) and the "New Jim Code" (Ruha Benjamin) have their price for capital, and whatever costs can be externalized, policed away, and borne only by the exploited increase the returns for capital. These externalities, the various forms of maiming (Puar) and social death (Hartman, Wilderson), are part of the computational effect, part of the calculus of what is always "only" *social computing.* The codification of race, gender, nation, ability, and all forms of difference is today not only the province of marketers or algorithms on Amazon. It is a totalizing system of overcoding that would ascribe a spread of the likelihood and cost of any transaction whatever—a general calculus for the cost-benefit analysis of all forms of possible violence—so that capital can choose wisely and in accord with the politics of the value-form which are, the politics of the disciplinary imposition of the value-form by the police. From this it is not too far-fetched to imagine that the relative social power of any individual on Earth could be expressed in a single number (their price); if there were a market for such an index, they would be thusly expressed. In reality, such a price would be a spread, a range of values (a moving index) precisely synthesizing in real time each possible pathway to harvest our lives.

As with the plantation, the Black church, and the factory, the institutions outfitted for domination were also the spaces of rebellion, revolutionary consciousness, and political and cultural innovation. We must consider the revolutionary potentials of the derivative, the programmable image, the collectivization of debt, and the necessary sharing of risk. If risk is our condition, what are the ways we might risk together to create noncapitalist becoming? Unorthodox as it may sound after fifty years of postmodernism and its sense of capitalism as untranscendable horizon, we can ask: Is there a revolutionary finance? Are there better ways to do the compute? At this point, there are many of us working on this question. Pursuing the question of a postcapitalist future as this book approaches its back cover, I will sketch a notion of communist derivative finance and of the potential for value abstraction without extraction. This idea may sound improbable, but it is in keeping with Trotsky's Hayekian reservations, in the socialist calculation debates, about the inadequacies of a planned economy under communism and his insistence on transitional economies and econometrics that continue to track value on the road to communism: as if there were a continuum from the mathematical to the discursive indicated by the sequence: Hayek, Keynes, Trotsky, Stalin. The apparent victory of Hayek, along with the tragic planetary results that may well include the tragedy of Stalinism, makes explicit the *necessity* of reprogramming the operations of money when "doing" culture, politics, and fabrication. I say "necessity," assuming that we want to avoid either of two outcomes for our radicalism: 1) simply innovating yet another subroutine for capitalist digitality, and thus also for semio-affective, media-based value extraction ready to take root at the fount of revolutionary becoming (and thereby holographically reproduce a for-profit ecosystem where the revolution should be); or 2) sitting back in one's relatively comfy chair and righteously shaking one's head, secure in the orthodoxy that money is the root of all evil as the world burns. For in showing that information and valuation function on a continuum, we have shown that digital computing and money are currently inseparable. Each implies the other such that to abolish one is to abolish the other. Only a reworking of the protocols of "both"—we put it this way out of respect for the doubts of those who do not fully grant the collapse of one into the other—can build a *transitional* computing and a *transitional* economy. This amounts to a rescripting of practices of relation and a redesign of processes of real abstraction. Redesigning real abstraction means altering the social relations that are generative of abstractions and quantification. Since we have shown that all constellations of value are at once treated as information and can effectively be though of as derivatives—positions on the overall market—the direction here is to rework both the authorship of and grammar of contingent claims that are endemic to any creation of information.

This transformation of authorship and grammar might be approached by seeking the means to modify the protocols of money such that people may encode the practices and relations they want. Such a politics of programmable economy, of programmable homemaking, would seek ways to enabled oppressed communities to leverage their world making capacities and occupy money (Kennedy), to decolonize money and re-engineer the convergence of representational media and monetary media as the economic medium currently known as computation. Perhaps it is only by re-engineering this convergence of semiotics and finance, by remaking the protocols of economic media for the production, transmission and distribution of values, that our revolutionary desires can do other than generate the coded content for the next wave of capitalist fashion. This transformation would amount to the capacity to take what is social and in one way or another voluntary about credit and debt, and build an economy capable of recognizing what could potentially be the beauty of our mutual indebtedness and capable again of recognizing, honoring and valuing all contributions as we make kin.

To zoom out a bit we have to take down, or at least outflank, "the digital" and "information" as fetishized, deracinated concepts that today most commonly function as interpretive algorithms—what in a past era we might have called dominant ideologies, and in particular, ideologies resulting from the instrumental, subject-making ideation attendant upon sociomaterial practices of domination. The very ideas of these highly programmatic practices, dedicated to preserve the hegemony of the value form and its white-supremacist, heteropatriarchal assumptions as neutral technologies or natural formations gets in the way of perceiving them for what they are: social relations. Marxism, in finally becoming an antiracist, feminist, queer, decolonial endeavor (one can hope), requires that we show information's historical emergence out of exchange-valuation and that we demonstrate at the same time the practical, globalizing encroachment of "the digital" and its assault on qualities and forms of life implicit in and endemic to the codification processes of commodification and colonization over the past seven centuries. The injunction to look critically at the relation between information and social differentiation, at coding and overcoding, at the instrumental abstraction of labor-time, race, and gender—to see it as a site of struggle—comes in order that we might take the digital back, a taking back that implies new forms of revolutionary acting and a seizing of the means of production. This seizure—what is sometimes, in less militant and precise terms, thought of as a retaking of our attention (and more recently our care and our cure)—would constitute a reverse subsumption of history, an acting and a capacity to act that would release the historical aspirations foreclosed by contemporary technics, thereby constituting a reverse subsumption of culture, computation, "human" capacity, and value. What Marx saw as an emancipation of the senses that would bring about the humanization of the senses such that object would be perceived as social relations and all things perceived in their full social (and we should say ecological) dimensionality today requires an emancipation of economy and thus of computation—in Marx's dated short-hand, a humanization of economy and computing. As such, these cultural and technical domains would no longer be subservient to capital but would become conduits of revolutionary energy and becoming. Value would become *values* and would thus become social wealth preferred over and thus beyond the reach of the value form, and, under such conditions, would create abundance. This decolonization of the process of abstraction that separated abstraction from the processes of extraction would and could only be a feminist, antiracist, anti-imperialist, anticolonial endeavor of global proportions.

Such an anticapitalist revolution—a distributed revolution—must learn how to make its participants the authors of the terms of risk and the architects of the circulation and distribution of the value(s) its movements produce. The distributed revolution will likely also be a derivative revolution—a revolution that, because waged in a world characterized by precarity and risk, requires the benefits of shared risk and collective wagers on community, requires liquidity and credit to be *returned to* and *governed by* the communities at risk. This economy cannot be left to capital, to its technologies (as fixed capital), its media, or its money. Such control means securing the content of protest and democratic-liberatory innovation for the protestors, as well as the content of political action for activists, and it means not, for example, allowing efforts to make social change to be reduced to mere content for sensationalist media platforms that secure the world in the hierarchical terms dictated by today's fractal fascism and described in this volume. It also requires that even as we seek state reforms, we remain uncompromising in our goals of prison abolition, the abolition of the police, the full recognition of all that can only be conferred under a reconstructed socialism. The old problems of value distribution, extraction, and accumulation, so familiar to Marxism, still haunt our semiosis (indeed, they suck it dry), and do so in such a way that their vectors of alienation extend into our psyches and metabolisms. If we forget economy, it will subsume our efforts.

In closing this chapter, we build on the notions of informatic labor, informatic racism, computational colonialism, and computational racial capitalism developed thus far. In the next we return briefly to cinema and to photography and, with the ambivalent benefit of hindsight that comes from contemporary conditions of derivative living in a fully financialized world, to explore photographic media's prior functions and future potentials as a derivative machine—that is, as media and, moreover, financialized media, of digitization and optionality. If cinema and photographic technologies can be understood to posit and indeed to express forms of derivative contracts—if they are economic theory and practice—what then are the implications with respect to the democratization of the authorship of the social terms of risk? Is it possible to remake socioeconomic space such that subaltern people's struggles (their and our issues and issuance) do not secure the same or other people's oppression for capital? Understanding these images as forms of currency, as derivative currencies that provide exposure to the risk of the specific networks of which they are a part, will allow us to more clearly perceive characteristics of the medium of money. Though there is more to be said of this ur-digital medium, which has colonized expression and could potentially be decolonized, we conclude here with the question of derivative communism: Are communist derivatives possible, and if so, what would they look and feel like? To answer these questions, we will have to open the door to a consideration of cryptocurrency as a new medium in the fullest sense of the term: a potential for the redesign and recapacitation of the fourth determination of money (Beller 2017a).

To arrive at such a beginning, we refuse "the digital" and "information" in their current incarnation—as ruling ideas that lead to a processing of data in the fascist sense. However, a communist program—an anarchocommunist program—can be neither Luddite nor accelerationist: it requires all the complexity that is the global product of what is called history and can be abbreviated in the term computation, while embracing the notion that liberation can only be nonexploitative, polysemic and democratically engendered by all who are currently oppressed. Why? Because we have enough examples of victims becoming perpetrators, of survivors of camps raising children who run camps of their own. As Foucault warned, new guards in the same old panopticon will not free the inmates. What is antidemocratic and exploitative in contemporary culture and political economy is entwined with actually existing digitality and the informatics of capitalism—its pedagogy—and thus remains entwined with white supremacist, heteropatriarchal, settler-colonial financialization, otherwise known as the enemy, and manifest as subjects of violence, as states and state actors and as other nodal points in the organization of fixed capital. It is fixed capital's machines of abstraction, the imaginaries organized by the sociocybernetics of computational racial capital and the world computer, that require our critical attention if we want to finance the revolution. And it is, I think, only by supporting, which is to say in one way or another, financing and indeed refinancing the revolution, that the masses become the authors of economy and thus the authors of history. It must be underscored here that what we mean by finance is postcapitalist and what we mean by history only has a future and thus a chance if the struggle for economic democracy can understand itself as fully embedded in planetary ecology. I hope that what's here can be used as a small contribution to resource that wager.

6

Derivative Living and Subaltern Futures

Film as Derivative, Cryptocurrency as Film

Derivative Work

In previous chapters and in appendix 1, "The Derivative Machine," I make the argument that with the financialization of everyday life and the capture of informatic labor by ambient computation, what we call films and digital images can increasingly be understood as derivatives.

In the main, they were and remain media to risk the gain from M to M': from money to more money. Commercial film is obviously of this form, but so too, arguably, is the vast corpus of social justice cinema that is not explicitly anticapitalist—and even revolutionary cinema, dedicated to the overthrow of the social order, has been violently converted to for profit schemes by distributors, museums, and the like. In all cases where cinema is a means to move from M to M', cinema is a derivative machine. But it is more complex than the mere commodity. Whether through the use of archival images and sound or, more commonly, through the capture or generation of new images and sounds with machines whose operating systems are derived from the archive of prior knowledge formations, films, videos, and other screen-images cut and paste elements derived from life. In binding them in new arrays, they securitize them as best they can with their form or genre or distribution channel—really, all of these. In this securitization, and in a fashion analogous to the way in which banks securitize home loans by bundling and tranching them, they are an offer: an encoded offer with protocols for engagement and distribution.

More precisely, like the securitization of mortgages, these acts of composure that assemble hundreds of skill sets for a typical Hollywood production are rigorous transpositions engineered to manage risk—and indeed they are, at a basic level, not exceptional, because with the digitization of nearly all semiotic activity by computational racial capital, any particular communique, from advertising to a call to arms, can be understood as an edited composition that functions as a kind of protocolized wager to strategically manage the volatility of living imposed by the transnational, transsubjective economy in order to get a return. The film, with its built-in imperative to be watched, exists, as Sean Cubitt (2019) might say, in the subjunctive. In this need to engage attention and make something of it by putting capital at risk, it echoes the demand of the advertisign (Beller 2013).

Why spend so much time with the image? Why would someone—this writer, for example—write a book about "the world computer" and computational racial capital that is also a book about visual culture and the technical image? Because, in a word, images are derivative forms—they are forms of currency. And we work for them and in them. We are market makers and market takers. Structurally they demand wagers in attention in exchange for a return on the social. They are instruments of liquidity and risk. You give them credit; they give you credit. One forgets (or did not know) that national currencies too are in effect derivative exposures to entire economies—in our minds we take the nation as a given and perhaps don't see the value of say, the dollar, tied to a set of possible futures. Nonetheless, willingly or not, we bet on a national economy when we hold its currency—and yes, it's going to be hard to wage the revolution without the dollar going down. What will keep you liquid then? On a different scale and constellating a different set of relations, images also provide forms of currency, that is, they provide access to a particular set of social values and possible futures—a certain *convertibility*. They provide you with liquidity, the ability to convert your creative capacity into social currency that you can exchange for other values. Such wagers—within the image, by means of images, or more generally wagers (in what is called "digital culture") within information by means of information— are bound by principles that are equally as social as they are technical: they are intentional expenditures of resources that might be used otherwise, designed to constellate resources that may well have other demands on them.

The autonomization of intentions by fixed capital in the form of apparatuses, and experienced by responsive screeners as searches, clicks, binge watching, forms of knowing, forms of suspense, forms of abjection, and forms of interest, makes this informatic landscape more precarious, the metagame more complex. Our condition of wagering on information is not a choice (just as one does not have a choice but to live and strive on a polluted planet plagued by environmental racism); it is a derivative condition, and my expressing it in these words, words admittedly calibrated and nuanced in alignment with my will to a certain polemical endpoint, is radically overdetermined by the material conditions of our existence, my own existence, and the planetary subjugation of life. I am not alone here in what I call the derivative condition—which is why so many of us are talking about the same things: new economy, anti-racism, decolonization, radical care, refusal. Contemporary media forms are edited compositions that function as a kind of protocolized wager to strategically manage the volatility of living that is imposed by the transnational, transsubjective economy. Films represent a bundling of resources in expectation of a return. Creating non- and postcapitalist returns requires that the underlying protocols of financialization endemic to dominant media are rewritten. We must strike against the mode of abstraction and extraction of our progressive values that currently underlies computationally modulated representation and refuse the conversion into their opposite, that is, into capital.

This concern demands that we *seek the means to democratize the authorship of derivatives* so that postcapitalist and communist derivatives can be written and so that communist and postcapitalist futures can be wagered. We need to expand the power of the *social derivatives* authored by the disenfranchised masses. We want to write a future that we can collect on and we don't want to be paid in dollars. What do we want? Justice! When do we want it? Now! The financialization of everyday life and the rise of the world computer means that decisions and indeed metabolism are subject to a relentless calculus of optimization from all quarters. Our radical social movements need to engage this calculus and, as much as possible, transform it to better enable antiracist, antifascist, anti-imperialist outcomes. And we need to do so without replicating the current violence. The reigning imperative is to apportion resources and calculate returns, but there are better ways to engage necessity than those that have already been tried by Hollywood, advertising, social media, Wall Street, and national-fascist politics—all of which do their accounting by collapsing all values into the monologue of the value form indexed by money. As we may intuit, these prevailing methods create fractal fascism; yet it must be possible to mitigate the violence that is the current condition of our being. Accordingly, my words here are a digitally mediated wager and an invitation to you to wager along these lines by enticing you to pay attention—perchance, to dream. And even though I am asking you to valorize my wager (it is not mine alone) with your attention and hence your risk, to execute the program (or multiple programs) of my thought (it is not mine alone) with your thought, of course, to commit your resources to recompose economic media, I speak and write—just as others make films—with a huge debt to those who came before and to those who now sustain me, with a need to survive, and with the clear knowledge that the vast majority of the world will blithely ignore me. I transmit what I have received or gleaned and you receive it with the cognitive capacities others have helped you to build. And I write what is written with the faint hope that my now unavoidable addition to the neg-entropy of climate changing, white, capitalist, heteropatriarchal, global semiosis will successfully transmit, alongside the inevitable costs borne by the people and creatures of a forlorn world running on blood computing, some potent strategy crystals derived of struggle—and thus will also be a catalyst, a small contribution to emerging forms of antiracist, antisexist, anti-imperialist emancipation.

This change in the character of the world—a world in which precarity is on the rise, war has become permanent, some people are richer than the richest kings in history (with just five men owning more wealth than half the world), and justice is scarce indeed, "our" world, now understandable as a network of networks resulting also in camps and genocide as the other side of the visible personas that are our politicians, celebrities, and microcelebrities—could not have come about without the cinema. Some might be surprised to hear me say this, and, to be clear, I am not saying that cinema is to blame for the financialization of daily life (no more, and perhaps less, than was the computer's precursor, the Hollerith punch card famously used by IBM to aid Hitler in undertaking the Holocaust), but I am saying that the rise of the attention economy organized by screen cultures is in no way incidental to the encroachment of brutal financialization on all aspects of existence, just as today's computational armatures are inseparable from the global organization of a world in which genocide, incarceration, forced migration, permanent war, child labor, and endemic poverty are the norm. Blood computing interfaces by means of the screen. With the rise of cinema as an extension of the logistics of capital, images outpaced words and, slowly but surely, marginalized the power of speech and imposed an extractive paradigm of information and digitization such that expression itself became a financial instrument. Broadening their attentional capacities spectators produced their expressions for the ambient market organized by social media. The industrialization of the visual realized by cinema's bringing of the industrial revolution to the eye meant also the colonization of the mind and the senses by the emergent protocols of value production endemic to attention economies. Thus, the media of expression became work-sites and mediation became work: the dominant means of representation become the dominant means of production; screens did not only represent work; they became deterritorialized factories, interfaces of value creation and value extraction, mediated by expression's machinic conversion into information. Thereby, those of us who would express a version of the world or ourselves, along with those of us who are forced to do so, became workers in the deterritorialized factories of the media. Without such a thesis of interface as worksite, we cannot fully grasp the world-historical significance of the rise of screens and screen cultures.

The image is a derivative and also a work-site. The derivative is an attractor, appealing to a particular form of attention or interest in a larger market. As a risk instrument it binds attention, and other resources, to a narrative or image or other structured outcome that requires risk. Take money, a network derivative on a national economy that is also a medium and, in a weakly perceived but increasingly important way, an attention aggregator. Market-makers offering designer risk instruments parse and granularize that attention as they broker "positions." There is more here, but anon. As with the workers before us and still beside us, and very likely also within us, our labor—wage-labor in the traditional workforce, attentional labor with cinema, and now informatic labor with the derivative machines of computational media—is remunerated to our disadvantage or, oftentimes, unremunerated, just plain stolen (see Beller 2016b). Some of us cooperate by dutifully consuming images and creating posts on social media, some of us sing our laments in books, films, poems, music, command performances, and gossip, and some of us try to disconnect, check out, disappear, or get sick, while those who control the networks, either through arms, states, banks, surveillance, or communications infrastructures (which are all linked, in any case) exercise obscene power as they *profitably* ride the waves of social volatility with cold indifference and near total impunity. The big authors, brokers, attention brokers, trading platforms of all types, profit on our investments—on our efforts (aesthetic or financial) to eke out a little more from the precarious global economy. Just as financial derivatives can hedge out market direction and trade on pure volatility, social media derivatives can hedge out political direction and trade on volatility. It is for this reason that Mark Zuckerburg's bogus "neutrality" makes him a supporter of white supremacy and of fascism. Nearly every act or non-act becomes a signal, becomes information, becomes a pathway from M to M' (money to more money) for someone—for some market-maker or platform owner. The result of hedging our direction is the stripping of the purchase of expressive power on reality by profiteering capital along with the consequent accumulation of wealth for the few and the accumulation of precarity and pain for the many. What is ultimately valorized is the value form of racial capitalism.

The generalized movement of financialization into media of expression—the financialization of expressivity, along with the racializing and gender-differentiating grid of intelligibility that functions under the cloak of every-day understandings of "digital culture" and whatever remains of "reality"—is *an intensification of the affective power of capital and a deployment, harnessing, and development of the semiotics of the value-form.* All innovation is an experiment in messaging, an arbitrage on the current organization of information and its access to ever-cheapened labor power—labor power cheapened by the messages written with it and on it. Cinema asked spectator-workers to accept the social currency it offered in exchange for their otherwise unremunerated care—their interest. We risked our time and our love. It was a precursor to social media and their platform-bound currencies of likes and other infrastructures of reputation and relation. This thoroughgoing assault on cultural qualities by economic quantity is an advanced stage of what Adorno and Horkheimer meant by "the culture industry." However, it is not simply that mediation and therefore intelligibility itself has become financialized but, rather, that mediation and intelligibility have themselves become *means of further financialization and the subsumption of formerly extra-economic domains* (see Beller 2006b). Media forms are deterritorialized factories in which spectators—and now "content providers"—work, utilizing our affective, attentional, and neuronal-metabolic capacities. We provide interest to capital, we provision its liquidity as we struggle to ward off dispossession and improve our lot. The qualities of our interests are converted directly into quantified interest, brokered and monetized on attention markets to return dividends (interest) to shareholders and banks. That is our product, the result of our desire. The algorithmic overdetermination and functionalization of all these forms of attention is intensifying. The convergence of media formations with computation, such that nearly all media today are effectively computational media, also marks a deeper and more granular convergence with financial calculus—an ever more precise mobilization of the machines and metrics of capture. *It is a machinic convergence of computation, finance, and value-capture that only increases the efficiency of machines, their knowledge: the knowledge and capacity sedimented into and as fixed capital.* With the algorithm, with AI, "computational capital" means that almost all social activity is ultimately wagered in relation to an ambient calculus of value that most, if not all, planetary denizens are forced to game from their statistically overdetermined, algorithmically striated, informatically encoded locales. The world computer: "Because you are *x*, you *might* become *y*." "Computational racial capital" means that the *codification* of social difference has become an increasingly central part of the strategies of value capture practiced by capital-media:

ways of discounting folks by means of representations that look like nation, gender, or race, read like jurisprudence, military strategy, and ontology, watch like reality TV, and feel like everything from right and objectivity to microaggression and murder—depending upon which side of the risk profile you're on. Racialization is an ongoing process of coding and recoding, while "race" and racism continually morph to create a volatility with read-write ontologies that can be profitably harvested. Discounted by the regimes of representation and truth that are imposed by financial calculus, we ply from within our tranches the informatic space of screened images and processed worlds seeking a green new deal and or a red and green revolution for our attention, aspiration, dreams—our creativity, our work. Where once "liberals" could defend technological neutrality while harvesting our pain, the cat is out of the bag. Anyone who claims that technology is neutral can today easily be recognized as a fascist.

Derivative Living

Therefore, the phrase that Jennifer Morgan (2017) attributes to Saidiya Hartman—"the brutal calculus of self-betrayal," used when describing a slave coffle forced to sing, where the performance commanded by the masters and exchanged for survival was song—becomes, to varying degrees, the general rule for expression in computational racial capitalism. *Our expression is an endeavor to free ourselves wagered against a calculus of extraction that forecloses becoming.* Our expression is, to use a term from finance, a hedge. I am by no means conflating the general condition of utterance with the horrific condition of chattel slavery but, rather, arguing that such a brutal calculus of self-betrayal is indeed imposed by the totalizing perspective of the world-media system in relation to the species in which every signal is optimized for profit-taking. Expression has become a hedge, a wager, a playing of the spread opened by the volatility of the social, in order to access the upside; it has become a derivative—a means of introducing liquidity (some convertibility of life time into social belonging) by offering valuable expression. Our songs are the expressions of beings who have already been overcoded and marked for various forms of capture, beings who seek to improve their lot in the context of a toxic, extractive sociality and who require social currency to move—to manage structural indebtedness and historical dispossession. As expressive beings, we are already inscribed in the informatic architecture enabled by the historical archive; we labor under this burden of having been written, unwritten, rewritten, and read. Though each of us may have a unique geolocation, a unique body, a unique rhyme, the world computer has our numbers. The archive enables a writing-upon, a writing upon bodies, that renders these bodies operational in various social programs. Having been spoken by the archive, inscribed by its framework of intelligibility, we must find a way to speak through it, against it, and beyond it.

Virno's key formulation, "the capture of the cognitive-linguistic by capital," implies as much: speech, thinking, and image-making all become a wager. It would seem that in this view, however, the wager is always a self-interested one, bent upon keeping things running in return for a modicum of your own survival (Virno 2004). How different it is for Harney and Moten (2013), for whom expression can be a way of accessing and sustaining the Undercommons, a refusal of policy and governance, and an embarkation of planning and Black study. But in both the case of the virtuosic command performance and of the artful fugitivity of the Undercommons, the consequences of and the conditions for the functioning of a system that imposes such derivative living are, at least as currently configured by the contemporary terms of risk: the two billion–plus persons living on less than two dollars per day; the currently enslaved; those forced into reparations-seeking by migration; those suffering famine, sex-gender discrimination, climate dissolution, genocide, and so on—*denizens of the world* surviving on and as the material underside of the chaos management undertaken by the military industrial complex, financial markets, the world-media system, and fractal fascism functioning at the behest (or at least to the benefit) of those plutocrats (and their AI) who are maximally enfranchised by the virtual machine that is the world computer. Among all this shit, people survive, and that's cool. However, while collectively and communally mourning those harvested by racial capital and while embracing those many who are subject to "premature death" may give some degree of comfort, hope, power, tenderness, beauty, institutional change, or revolutionary fire, these acts of outrage and/or love do not bring children, parents, friends, and lovers back from the dead. Is there a path to "never again?"

To whom the brunt of the violence is delivered is determined algorithmically, stochastically, and in accord with a calculus of social difference grafted to historical violence, or what Hartman (2008: 6) called "the racial calculus and . . . political arithmetic that were entrenched centuries ago."[1] The calculus of racial capitalism is the result of historical forms of racial, gendered, and nationalist exploitation becoming overlain with, developed, and exacerbated by a mediological-semiotic layer that signifies bodies and inscribes upon them the terms of the conditions by which they may be systemically treated, making them systemically legible in the informatic matrix and functionalized accordingly. It is, in brief, the treatment of people and peoples as writing surfaces, as commodities, as quantities, and thus, today, as calculable information. It is the violent overdetermination and delimitation of people's life potentials, the systemic effect/intention to inscribe and prescribe their exteriority and interiority. The police do it, the creditors do it, the politicians do it, the schools do it, the eyes, ears, nose, and throat do it. It is racial capitalism formalized and sedimented as computation and as intelligence; it is a computational calculus for which the bios serves only as substrate. Unavoidably (that is, materially), everyone has a financial position on this economy and its organization of the social. Like the mortgage industry's securitization of home loans—which has its own racial logic and which was the precursor to the stripping, recombination, and tranching of those loans in order to sell them as derivatives—the world-media system cuts and bundles people, composing and recombining social bodies and writing futures contracts on their various partitionings that can be sold on the financial markets. Which peoples can be starved, which nations can be bombed, who can be jailed or interned, what demographics will work for next to nothing? Whose life can be profitably wasted by an enfranchised individual or its control system? This securitization and contractualization of the futurity of bodies by means of digitized, executable representation and its accompanying calculus of risk is brutally expressed and thus reactivated in everything from a POTUS tweet to the sale of arms and sovereign debt to the biometrics used by the UN for its presumably charitable distribution of money and resources.

Let's take a specific question as a way of getting to the question with which we will close this volume: Given the impending if not fully secured foreclosure of the powers of speech and expression, and given the regular conversion of our dreams of liberation into nightmares for others if not also for ourselves, what is the role of cinema, of photography, of financialized media? What strategies do these derivative-machines hold for radical, anti-racist finance, for the decolonization of money, and for the redesign of economic media?

Those of you who are filmmakers, image-makers, or social media practitioners may already have your own quests and perhaps also your own answers. No doubt cinema may fortify us in certain instances: the aesthetic, modes of cognition, forms of time, the particularities of unrepresented lives and so much more, potentially serving as the building blocks of counterhegemonic understanding and solidarity.

Do we need to bring up the cinema once more? The key points include, first, that the financial tools underpinning representation and distribution belong to capital: in a centuries-long but unified historical stroke, the protocols for the real abstraction of value transfer have been iterated by the requisites of capital accumulation and naturalized as "the media" and information. Second, the currency offered in exchange for our expression is not an adequate form of remuneration. What Brian Massumi (2018: 16) calls "surplus value of life" is stolen as surplus value for capital. With such financial-computational protocols underpinning all media of expression (these media have converged as computation), our calls for liberation make the rich richer. The quotation from Stew with which we began the introduction to this volume returns like a refrain: "Power is so powerful it can afford to pay people to speak truth to it."

Building on the notion of the programmable image as a kind of paradigm, I have suggested that cinema and images serve as programs—scripts for perception, cognition, and practice—and inasmuch as that is true, these may also be programmed and reprogrammed from below. Cinema is then a site of struggle, an engine of attention aggregation that is directly involved in world making. We accept that such is true for representation, conventionally understood. Like any other work-site, the now digital image is thus a space of negotiation, an instrument of domination and also of self-realization, caught in a life-and-death struggle between labor and capital. But in saying that cinema, in addition to functioning as a program, *also functions as a derivative*—that is, that it functions as an explicitly financial instrument of programmed risk management that speaks from the archive of codification through the archive of codification, and that it thereby enters into the production and transmission of value by means of information transfer—I am saying something more. Though the resources upon which we draw to make our wagers (and our wages) in the social and in history are not financial in the first instance, they seek their aims mediated by a fully financialized milieu. We all require liquidity and manage risk. This situation is but one of the ways in which computation through recursivity has colonized ontology: the computational financialization of semiotics includes the domain of metaphysics such that now, although we may each have our unique address, we are all *of* computational racial capital. It is the production and reproduction of computational racial capital that we must refuse and overturn. We must find ways to make our values persist economically rather than be subsumed by the value form.

The Derivative Machine

My analysis compels me here to elaborate another argument I posed in *The Cinematic Mode of Production* (2006b). Because of the relation of media to commodification—and thus to codification and to finance—cinema and, more generally, digital images should be understood as a development in the capacity of money: as a kind of money with qualities.[2] We spend film on the world, we exchange it for the world, we circulate it in the world, we receive it as a means to the world—we wager within the image in order to create futures. The digital image is a financial instrument linked to a specific array of underliers, programmed to respond to a variety of contingent claims.

Though calling film "qualitative money" is slightly misleading due to issues of quantity, fungibility and delimited pathways of liquidity, such a denomination of money by film is no mere metaphor. Retrospectively we can observe that it was anticipatory, that cinema recognized—and was indeed a part of—the immanent colonization of perception and of expression by capital, and, in its revolutionary instances, cinema endeavored to reverse the process by utilizing the expressive potential of a medium intimately tied to money and finance to create forms of knowledge and relation beyond price—beyond the communication system of price—and hence to create solidarity, decolonization or revolution. In certain notable cases, the effort was to outflank money, to run away with it and re-mediate a commodified world, and to reveal the social relations made invisible by capitalist modes of representation and perception (reification)—to reveal the ostensibly objective world, the world that confronted us as a vast array of commodities, as social process and social relations. As I argued in "Dziga Vertov and the Film of Money," first published as "The Circulating Eye" in 1993, Vertov's films were a kind of antimoney, or alternative money, while film in general, as unit of account, medium of exchange, general equivalent, and store of value, began to satisfy some of the basic criteria of money by recapitulating its processes and form. Cinema gave us, if only weakly, a new form of access to the social product. It was a prosthetic extension of the senses capable of revealing objects as process by offering a new system of accounts. Vertov used film as a money alternative, a radical form of circulation that provided a kind of counterflow to money which, by tracking the material histories of the productions of commodities, built an anticapitalist awareness through revealing and making conscious a level of social cooperation invisible to the world of reified objects and disavowed by their prices. We could recognize from Vertov's radical anticapitalist filmmaking aspects of the film industry's default conformity to the exigencies of capital—if only by contrast. Before exposure, film is fungible; afterward it is informed by its underlier—here, the commodified world—and endowed with specific qualities of the "profilmic Real" while remaining circulatable. It is a position on the world—a wager on a specific instance of cutting and bundling it. Because film entered into the space of mediation and circulation, price, I argued, could be revealed as a protoimage: notionally, a number equivalent for a thing, an abstraction mediated by material relations that—while not entirely operative at the level of inscribed concepts, as in a camera or a computer algorithm—nonetheless processes the visible and invisible world through real abstraction, through acts of exchange, utilizing and generating what was to become information and, from that process, deriving a number, a value. This value could be represented in coin and multiples of coin could be used notionally to provide access to the object in a system of accounts. Practically, price itself became a conduit for abstracting and circulating a commodity by transferring certain rights in exchange for the quantity of money it specified: x amount of the general equivalent for use of specific thing y. Price referred to a thing's exchange-value and was, in fact, its exchange rate. Though we do not exactly "spend" film, we spend money on it and we do exchange it for specific things—it has purchase on the world and circulates value. The profilmic Real becomes cinema's underlier, and cinema arranges it in specific arrays in its time-based ledger for its own purposes—its own returns. It provides options on reality. The profilmic world is increasingly the world of commodities, and the arrangement of these graphemes or "kinemes" in Pier Paolo Pasolini's term for "the objects, forms and acts of reality that we perceive with our senses" (1988: 201) represented a certain exposure to their future values. Importantly, this exposure was not passive, but demanded something from the spectator-user—an investment of attention. And as we have seen, this cinematic circulation, capable of garnering and archiving attention by providing exposure to an underlier, is also a new type of productive relation. "The organization of the audience through organized material," as Eisenstein so presciently said (1988: 63).

Cinema, and the screen-based media that follow it, open new dimensions in the interval between use-value and exchange-value, new mediations in assemblage: the appearance of and access to things, one's "exposure," suddenly has options. From film we make "the film," which represents a more specific investment. Where the film differs from money as we ordinarily think about it (and begins to resemble higher forms of programmable money—financial derivatives but also "smart contracts," in which contingencies are computationally managed) can be seen from the fact that the filmic composition is also a kind of contract—a "speech act" with some type of traction, an executable program. It is always someone's money, someone's time, someone's investment that, to be valorized, depends upon the execution of some future exchange. This is why film is really more like a derivative: because by genre, production house, or distribution platform, it binds makers, actors, spectators, and all those involved in a more or less tightly specified concrete and consequential relation of contingent claims. In this it is also like the anthropologist's notion of the gift, a contingent claim which must be answered in time and in which the what, where, when, and how of the eventual answer conferred the gift's value.[3]

It is production process as an option—one buys in, one can bail at any point by giving up a principle investment, and—as a time-based art form—it has, from the viewer's perspective (among others), what can be considered a discrete end point, though other aspects of it are open-ended. It also temporalizes and networks the life-span of the commodity be creating parallel and at times forking tracks for use-value, exchange-value (circulation) and surplus-value (production).

Why risk saying this? Why risk confusing things by suggesting that the film opens up new pathways for production, valorization, utility, and the risk management thereof in the interval between classical material production and the digital networks of financial valorization as managed by the world computer? The film opens economy to perception and vice versa, and it introduces new dynamics into production, circulation, valorization, and remuneration. Seeing the film as a financial instrument representative of a specific investment, one securitizing its elements, helps us to understand both digitality and money better, namely, the ways in which money and information are intimately bound up with expression and social relations down to the most minimal units, all of which are caught up in the social logistics and technical infrastructure of perception, apperception, action, and thought. We have seen the granularity of the visual circuit's operations in the transubstantiation of value in the programmable image—from affect to image to code to information to monetization—throughout this volume. The rise of visuality, clearly overdetermined and orchestrated by commodification and commodity fetishism but also by race, gender, borders, factory walls, shop fronts, nationalist iconography, and private property, indicates the systemic and technical expansion of the domain of production into the visual. Filmic decisions too are calculations of profitability—at the very least, they are cost-benefit analyses of substitutable choices, although certainly not all artists occupy this mindset, this "head," as they make art. Artistic and technical decisions in filmmaking are precursors to what we now understand as the generalized function of the programmable image: data visualizations, organized by the operation of concepts, that provide exposure to a matrix of relations and a work surface for perceptual-financial engagement. Films and programmable images are, in effect, theories of value, wagers on value, both cameras and engines. With the current scraping of metadata by ambient computation and the full colonization of visuality, language, and cognition by the sociocybernetics of technocapitalism, we must reckon with the granularity of everyday strategies of value extraction as they inhere in social media and their processes of background monetization. Once upon a time we gave our attention for free or for a screenful of trinkets because we did not recognize its value for capital (or perhaps we did not think that it could really be alienated from us, or perhaps we were not given a choice). Despite forebodings, most print natives did not recognize the colonial designs of capitalized screen media and treated it with a hospitality it may not have deserved. All that the people of the book knew was that the production of screen-images would not be possible for them, given their current means. Maybe they were attracted to the glitter and false promises, maybe we were forced by the violence imposed on us. Little did we suspect that the image too was a form of arbitrage, bought low in the studios of Los Angeles and sold high in domains that could not create our own. Print people gave their attention, their imagination, their fantasies, and their dreams to media conglomerates in exchange for a few flickering, then pixilated, images and the currency (such that it was) that it gave them in their own local economies. The enormity and violence of the settlement of visual and now digital capitalist media in and on bodies, on every body, has not fully been reckoned. Nonetheless, year 2020 is an expression of the consequences.

Money's Fourth Determination: Information

We have shown elsewhere that information emerges in the footprint of price, that is, out of an expansion of the content indifferent quantification imposed by the value-form. Additionally, we are aware that, just as in any other media channel, the transmission and reception of information—beyond the specific difference it makes—has a price. Indeed, at the limit, the movement of information is not distinct from price: it is in fact price movement; in other words, it is the result of transactions and it is utilized in accord with a calculus regarding future transactions. In fact, information as a series of computational state changes is a series of discrete transactions, broken down into ones and zeros (discrete states) that not only mediate but in fact *are* financial transactions. In this information is quite literally a derivative on knowledge—its cost is a premium paid to preserve liquidity.

Wherever information interfaces with the market, monetization occurs; but it is market analytics all the way down making the cost of information and thus making specific instances of information itself into derivatives on underlying knowledge. Four-billion-year-old data collected by radio telescopes from distant galaxies, whatever its use-value may be, serves as drops in the collection bucket of funding justifications for future research, always already parametrically responsible and responsive to an economic rationale. In this, it is the same as your Instagram post or YouTube video. *Information as a derivative on any process whatever is now the dominant way that social systems of valuation colonize perception of the cosmos and of everything else.* Information as a means to price discovery extends the functionality of money and saturates knowledge with the essence of money—its networked "being." Information puts a price on everything it indexes and the cost of each index can be computed in relation to the totality of information and the social totality. As "money is the alienated ability of mankind" (Marx 1978: 104) we apprehend information as alienated sociality, alienated species-being. Thus, to signify on information is to signify on money; to protocolize information is to program money; to platform information is to platform money so that, within certain bounded conditions, it can only do certain things. Programming: the organization of resources to make cybernetic machines perform actions that will predictably affect other cybernetic machines in order to structure a risk position on the market.

We invest in data capture of sunspots or faces. In this the protocolization of information by algorithms, the instrumental situating of 1s and 0s, we see the connection with cinema and the film of money. We see the deep connection of information with the film of money—the connection in which money was always "the other obverse of all the images the cinema shows and sets in place" (Deleuze 1989: 77)—while at the same understanding the greater complexity and programmability, as well as the interactive character, of digitality: a digitality understood quite explicitly now as a itself a historical development of the medium of money and its relentless quantification of quality. Digitization can now be understood as financialization by means of the transduction of the perceptible world into information, utilizing informatic capacities for the quantification of qualities and the harvesting of human expression in all its forms. Money as representation, medium of exchange and site of value production—measure, medium, store of value/capital. In addition to remarking upon money's colonization of semiotics and of all significant social activity via digitization, we have seen that digital instantiations of information also serve as work-sites, as sites of extraction—as programmed and programmable images (Beller 2016c). Thus: money as measure, as medium of exchange, as capital, and as programmable form—in other words, money as *an informatically qualified instance of value. The rise of the digital evolves and unveils (posits then presupposes) money's fourth determination as information.*

Information processing is the extension of the calculus that goes on "behind our backs" (Sohn-Rethel), the real abstraction derived from the practical activity that is our exchange, our frenetic transactions. Such exchange was previously thought of as the financial transaction, but the colonization of representation by information extends the financial transaction into the semiotic and the metabolic, grafting all social life activity to money. Sadly, little of this epic expansion of monetary capacity has been motivated by phi-lanthropy and practically none of it has been instituted for the common good. The great advances benefitting some sectors are simultaneously practices of barbarism requiring for their acquisitive expansion the deeper separation of people from their product that is ultimately the world they make as well as the words they say—requiring their dispossession. Information, locally content indifferent, is nonetheless the means and mode of financialization. In quan-tifying any qualitative expression whatever it prices in real time options on its underlying knowledge: options for sale on the capital markets. Money is thereby directly connected to the information infrastructure, and thus we see clearly that information is money's fourth determination. Money's optionality induces its volatility which is its information processing as tied to its proces-sors: social agents (a.k.a. people) exercising our options, the real substrates of computational racial capital.

It is in this fourth determination—the always-already media-bound quali-fication of the *ostensibly pure* quantification of value—that unthought revolu-tionary potential lies. For information, while appearing purely quantitative, is always already platformed. Though this platformation goes mostly unre-marked because we are blind to the media we live and breathe in, information is always also *platformation*. "The posthuman view privileges informational pattern over material instantiation, so that embodiment in a biological sub-strate is seen as an accident of history rather than an inevitability of life" (Hay-les 1999: 2). The same substrate bound condition of information could be said for computation, and for money. For, as we have already seen, the bounded qualifications of money enacted and imposed by actually existing financialized media—as well as by actually existing money—has been, in practice, the mode of domination by digital media and financialization even if such bounded qualifications have not been fully raised to the level of a general concept and thus grasped specifically as "platforms." Simply put, money is platformed on a variety of institutions and their practices. Measure, medium, store, infor-mation. These four determinations of money also apply to any commodity whatever, although the "moneyness" of commodities, their liquidity/convert-ibility are of different orders. Vertov already showed us that the film was not only about mediation similar to but different from money (because circulat-ing through the production of goods), but that it was also built like an object, thereby establishing a new sense of the continuum from object to medium, from commodity to money. Because exchangeable, a commodity is also mea-sure, medium, store and informatic interface for the value form. Such a state-ment merely echoes Marx's explication of the simple form of value with the example of linen as exchangeable for a "motley mosaic" of commodities (Marx 1990: 156). "Every commodity is a symbol, since, as value, it is only the material shell of the human labor expended on it" (185). The commodity then is precisely a *denomination* of value with all the capacities of money though to different degrees. From this insight, the commodity clearly appears as a derivative on the value form, a structured risk management tool as well as a use-value. Indeed, it is through the control of denomination, as both sovereign monies but also proprietary controls over digitized information illustrate by platformation, that liquidity is leveraged to the benefit of those making the rules. This previously unnoted denomination by means of platformation has been decisive. Is my value platformed as a cabbage or as a fraction of bitcoin, as a dollar bill, or a share of Facebook? Platformation *qualifies* its information. My value is informed on a material substrate; it is a material substrate informed. This substrate is itself networked with certain capacities for and limits to its interactivity, its convertibility. Nonetheless, it is, along with each of its elements a position on the market, and thus also a form of risk. The platform, conceptualized here as a social, symbolic, financial, and networked material array reveals itself with the rise of computing. It appears as part of the means of production. The emergence of secure, distributed, and decentralized computing, soon perhaps to be collectively held and programmable from below, may offer new possibilities for the subaltern authorship of futures. It may open new options, transforming the way we platform values and account for or indeed narrate the way they are risked and shared.

As abstract as money is, it fundamentally relies on the relative fixity and predictability of an increasingly complex material array of living sociality. Fixed capital and its institutions. Life pulses to the rhythm of the algorithm. Programmed from above, existing money and Hollywood film have hedged the bets of the powerful, while Third Cinema, alternative cinema, and cinematic countercultures have waged their struggles in media that are increasingly financialized—and so, in recent years, have thus also developed an internal self-critique. Without our fully realizing it, the rise information has been one with the intensification of capitalization, and, again without our realizing it, its total deracination of informatic accounting has ever more profoundly depended upon the strictly enforced accountability of concrete, material relationships that approach and include those of computation—of computational platforms as well as of everyday life. Currently, the statistical analysis of structured contingencies by capital—implicit in real abstraction or explicit in self-consciously financial exploits, in short, the writing of derivatives (financial, advertisarial, cinematic) on possible, if volatile socioeconomic outcomes—at once puts a price on animal spirits and also, through infrastructural feedback loops, influences outcomes. Derivatives of all types are optional structures resulting from the necessity to maximize outcomes for parties exposed to volatility. Today, with the exception of social derivatives (language-, image-, and performance-based wagers on volatility), derivatives are written "from above" and serve as a kind of command-control prediction market for the enfranchised by allowing for the adjustment of risk and the harvesting of volatility itself. Emerging out of derivative conditions, communist futures will require communist derivatives. *The masses' response to the globalization of information as capitalist financialization has been and will be the demand to author our own futures.* But how? How might we change the terms of risk?

Currently, nearly all communication transpires through financialized media, or it is so proximate to financial media that it occurs directly within finance's field of influence and extraction. The derivative is not solely an economic form in the delimited sense in which most people think of economy; it is a way of managing risk derived from a world everywhere quantified and overrun by the volatility of capitalist markets. It is a *dispositif* that functions technically, perceptually, psychologically, and semiotically; it is a hedge against animal spirits, a way of rationalizing them and creating a probability spread. "If derivatives at their root have to do with some kind of overflow, with the disassembly of some whole into parts and the bundling together of those attributes into something that moves away from or independently from its source, then finance may turn out to be less the originator of this social logic than a particularly prominent expression of derivative principles at work" (Martin 2015a: 7). "Doubtless the derivative is another way of thinking interdisciplinarity, one that draws attention to the epistemic arbitrage undertaken by those who operate between fields" (223). It seems paradoxical, but we must grasp the subtlety of cyberracial capitalism and the sociality of the derivative if we are to overcome capitalist violence. As Martin says, "The social logic of the derivative is therefore a kind of epistemological hedge against the claim that a form of capital is the first cause of all social life, but that it rests on and discloses a mutual indebtedness, a sociality that it requires but that it can neither abide nor sustain" (7). We extrapolate then that the organizational scale of the world financialization requires that revolutionary politics, in finding new ways to risk together, be at least as nuanced, subtle, and capable as is the world market and the global integration of production across space and time. Lifestyle choices, even seemingly radical ones, are not up to the task—these are already scripted by the market and easily commodified, written up as parables of morality in *The New York Times*. In brief, finance has commandeered the media of expression and therefore of relation and has itself become an expressive medium reproducing the relations of racial capital, while we, the would-be people, may say what we want but do not control much of the operating system for mediating expression, and therefore do not exercise control over value creation, extraction, or distribution. *It is at this level of value creation, aggregation, and distribution that we must intervene, and we must do so using the world-making capacities of expressivity, aspiration, and imagination.* Revolt may disrupt but it is the operating system of the sociosemiotic that must be changed: the conflation of expressivity and finance by the current configuration of economic media.

Financial asymmetries express the asymmetrical power of capital over the representation and distribution of values. Seemingly disembodied information is embodied suffering. Film images, as early technical images that enabled the industrialization of the visual, were a means to full digitization and informationalization, inaugurating an expansive abstraction process mediated by the computational power of the camera and then of discrete state computers. If film and digital media now function as derivatives, how do we prevent the investments they organize from being captured by the fixed capital that is media infrastructure—thereby dispossessing content providers and reproducing capital?

As I review the copyedits for this volume, a global pandemic and riots against anti-Blackness across the United States and around the world catalyzed by the lynching of George Floyd rage while the stock market goes higher. Why are the rich so confident even as the cry "Black Lives Matter" is taken up around the world? We cannot let the rich harvest the volatility created by our precarity. Trillion dollar bailouts offered to the wealthy allow them to offload their risk. Monetary issuance is today clearly visible as political policy; the preservation of asset values for the one percent results in a generalized devaluation of the masses as well as massive insecurity and suffering. The government has given the wealthy increased options on money, making their liquidity easy to maintain while the poor face foreclosure. Financial derivatives, options on forms of money, manage value extraction by allowing people to make structured high-level bets on one pathway of value extraction over another; they are extractive technologies that garner liquidity premiums while allowing capital to fund ways of decreasing the price of labor power. However, they do not disrupt the basic infrastructure of hierarchical society, they reinforce it—at least until the structural contradictions they impose become unmanageable. Have they? We risk saying that film, like capitalized social media, is a derivative written on the living archive (think *Squatterpunk* here) because understanding film as a financial instrument with expressive qualities shifts our understanding of what it means to traffic in attention, desire, and care.[4] Most of the dominant modes of attention scraping—Hollywood, politics, "news," Instagram, and screen-tech—traffic today in fractal fascism, the consolidation of celebrity at the expense of spectators who, in seeking their own forms of social liquidity, are disappeared in the identity of their stars, pundits, and microcelebrities. Celebrities, film studios, media platforms structure risk with cameras to monetize attention. Interactivity can thus be absorbed. To preclude the fractal proliferation of agents of capital (formerly bourgeois individuals, now expressed, to give but one example, as microcelebrity megalomaniacs), we need a redistribution of care and a redistribution of value—indeed a revaluation of value, as Massumi says—one that does not consolidate around the fetishized individual, individuals who are themselves constituted through the garnering of attention and the identitarian subsumption of the audiences who in fact produce them and for whom they then stand in for. Such solidarity would involve modifying the circuits of valuation, the forms of attention, and ultimately the persistence and distribution of value(s). It would not allow value to be uniformly stripped of its qualities, liquidated and collapsed into price. In short, it would understand the derivative as a specific and embodied relationship to information—and thus as a qualitative money-form. For what qualifies information is the difference it makes, and that difference can only ever be social. The social network that a given partition of information wagers on is expressed in its denomination—in the material terms of its existence as such. The naturalization of these networks creates the cult value of money, its fetish character.

Understanding films as social derivatives, as hedges on volatility and as instruments of risk management, allows us to make a deeper connection between cinema and emerging economic media forms such as cryptocurrency. Indeed, films are not the only social derivatives; in a society of risk, no social constellation can escape having a derivative structure. Social forms have become specific wagers on generalized volatility; they are "positions" vis-à-vis global capital because they are fully immersed in its matrix of abstraction. Synthetic finance, a specialized outgrowth of the generalized colonization of representation by financialized computation, and as an outgrowth of global capital's demand for the provisioning of liquidity for a price, has universally imposed the unavoidability of economic volatility and risk by tying all endeavor to the world market via computational capital. Nothing escapes being measure, medium, and store of value, and also information, because nothing that can be represented remains beyond the resolution of the world computer.

Invoking "crypto" here as at once an economic innovation and a new medium, is necessarily a highly abridged provocation, but nonetheless to be taken seriously. I will more fully take up the potential role of crypto and network derivatives within revolutionary politics in a subsequent volume. In saying that there is a deeper connection than is often thought between the cinematic archive and the archivization of financial transactions (the blockchain ledger is, after all, a transaction record that is a "hash," a procedural informatic reduction of robust social relations), I want us to further challenge our notion of what a film is, as well as what it can do, and, in doing so, I want to rethink the possibilities of a new money-form. For among the wagers here is the thesis that the next phase of revolutionary emergence toward full emancipation requires redesigning the protocols of money.

I'll pursue this final point by suggesting that the "attention economy," which this writer derived from the cinematic circulation of images almost thirty years ago, was also nascent in the circulation of money itself, that circulating image destined to become the general equivalent—*really, a specific denomination of the general equivalent*—by signifying the universal value-form. The Nixon shock, which famously revoked the gold standard as backing for the U.S. dollar, retrospectively revealed that the value of money is performative—it is securitized by a regime of truth that is itself of fluctuating credibility: the value of money is at once performative and also volatile. Today we might say that *money is a network derivative.* Gresham's law—"Bad money drives out good," which used to indicate the fact that the circulation of degraded sovereign money, degraded either because of coin clipping or improper (too high) denomination relative to the real value of its metallic weight, always results in the withdrawal from circulation of the metallically more valuable coins, the "good money"—is only true because in some cases buyers can get people to accept the bad money, as its perceived value is bolstered by the performative power of sovereignty, or sovereignty's regime of truth. Under Nixon, the U.S. dollar became backed only by U.S. power; the credibility, or rather, creditability, of U.S. power alone would thenceforth underwrite the dollar. It all became "bad money." The value of money was no longer backed by the metal value of the coin or the proxy of the bill, but only by the performance of the national platform and its network. State and military power, as well as institutional organization, was now directly linked to monetary issuance; the value of financial instruments and of the economy as a whole increasingly depended upon the organization of perception with regard to U.S. hegemony and U.S.

economic prospects. These were bolstered by any and all means available, from military might to bank balance sheets, police actions, televisual propaganda, foreign policy. and GDP metrics. Such a media spectrum, one indexed to and by monetary performance, is important to identify here because it reveals something of the relation between network vitality and denomination in the platforming of the value-form. With cryptocurrencies, the tool kit of monetary policy is at once expanded and decentralized. Through what is called "disintermediation," financial tools are taken out of the hands of banks and states, and *authority over* as well as *authorship of* the terms and value of its performance—credible and thus creditable—moves toward the people who are the users of the medium and indexes their forms of cooperation. Authority, and thus authorship around the semiotics of value, moves beyond the state form and state sovereignty toward new platforms linked by their own interests and distributed computing—platform sovereignty.

Although Bitcoin is only a primitive example of what is possible, and though it does not allow for an expansion of the bandwidth of the price signal, its decentralization of monetary issuance along with an incipient democratization of financial tools should be understood to be part of an insurrectionary history of the decentralization of authority that includes the French Revolution, decolonization, suffrage, 8 mm film, the portapak, the cheap digital camera, and the easy access to publication on the World Wide Web. But we should be neither naive nor idealistic about the purity of any of these drives; they are bound to a dialectic of liberation and extractive opportunism. "The slave-trade and slavery were the economic basis of the French Revolution," wrote C. L. R. James (quoted in Robinson 1983: 158). Indeed, *the internet affected an increased democratization of expression, but it did not democratize finance nor ameliorate racial capitalism,* and therein lies its profound failure to realize the progressive side of its historical potential. Thus far liberation in one domain has produced or exacerbated oppression in another domain. A progressive global demand for interconnectivity and a horizontality of relations was bent by fixed capital to reproduce and exacerbate global hierarchy and dispossession. By democratizing expression while leaving the hierarchy of finance intact, *the internet as a financialized medium used the promise of democracy and the lived aspirations for democracy to create a new plutocracy.* Like the fascism that follows failed revolutions (fascism which gives the masses not the right but the chance to express themselves), the Caesarist internet defeated the worldwide digital revolution—which, when viewed from below, was driven by a world desire for horizontal world communication devoid of authoritarian gatekeepers, a desire for the world to know itself in its own terms. With that particular technocapitalist exploit against self-consciousness and democracy—waged by means of the fixed capital of platforms—in mind, there should be no surprises with regard to the racism, sexism, or fascism—the fractal fascism—of contemporary internet (and increasingly of world) culture. Once again, the codifications of social difference have been re-mobilized, re-worked, and ramified to feed the greed of profit-takers, and this logic is integrated all the way down the stack. All of the largest countries in the world are presently fascist. The victimage orchestrated by digital media and computation—which, if the global crisis in migration, taken as another indication, has been the equivalent to that of a World War III—is the other side of the power of the gods whom computational technologies have created. As #AOC rightly remarks regarding some of these gods, "Every billionaire is a policy mistake."

The next phase of democratization will involve a reclaiming of the financial infrastructure mediating expression and communication. There is no good money, in the sense of it having intrinsic value; it is all bad in the sense that it is only ever an expression of a social relation, a form of risk. Our question, perhaps *the* question, is: Can money of any kind express noncapitalist relations that will enable a transition out of capitalism? Can we occupy or decolonize money?[5] Such non-capitalist monetary expression can only be the democratization of the expression of social ideals and communal futures. It must be the result of grafting social derivatives to representation that is not platformed on the informatic protocols of racial capitalism. This implies expression by means of derivatives with semiotic capacities on collectively held platforms where people can modulate the meaning and form of their networking of value(s). Democratization must include radical shifts over the authority to issue forms of currency that are themselves media in the robust sense—specific media that abstract value and allow for currency and circulation while retaining specific qualities—qualities that cannot and do not belong to states or to monological currencies such as Bitcoin.

Bitcoin is a communications medium but denominates all its messages in bitcoin. It's value is tied to the vitality of the network. As Jorge Lopez sums up, "The price of bitcoin indexes the affect of the network toward the narrative of what its is supposed to do."[6] What bitcoin does as a new money form is quite powerful, but what it does as a communications medium is simply redenominate the value-form of capital on a distributed cryptographically secured computational platform. Its bandwidth for speaking a language other than value denominated in bitcoin is nil. Nonetheless, new currencies entail a radical reshaping of authority—the authority to write what amounts to derivatives. The next generation must produce and utilize financial tools that are similar to the media tools people have at their disposal today and widely available. We will have to reconfigure economic media, which is to say the extractive worksites that constitute postmodern mediation in all its forms. Multiple denominations in the form of fungible tokens, linked to specific social endeavors (climate clean-up, defunding the police, healthcare), will circulate among participant-stakeholders in these endeavors and beyond the confines of their organizations. They will value activism and care. If expression and social activity produces value, we must control the value abstraction and flow. The token is or could be an instance of value and meaning—both of which are contingent upon its network and the relational practices that sustain it. This wave of transformative innovation will mean or could mean that others besides states, banks, and capitalist market-makers can author derivatives— qualitative derivatives or network derivatives—or in other words, we will create mediating structures allowing for collective wagers on various narratives of collectively held futures—futures whose outcomes are qualities of life rather than profit. This will or may be accomplished, in effect, by creating new links between embodied processes and information, or what in more everyday language we might think of as organizational processes and money-like forms of representation: say, projects organized around prison abolition and the token that gives it liquidity by allowing people to organize themselves and support struggle in various new ways. Our activism will feed us so that we may build our economy with those in our networks and thereby gradually withdraw from racial capital.

However, as with actually existing computation, inequalities are sedimented into the technologies of social mediation—including the money-form—and, just as importantly, into the thinking that is grafted to and from them. The dialectical emergence of new forms like cryptocurrency are in no way guarantees of justice; however, they change the design palette of struggle and invite a new space of economic activism, political-economic investigation and materialist imagination. It is really only such an ecological thinking that could recast economic media as what Cubitt and others call ecological media. The new wagers, expressed in part in and as tokens, will be tied to the expression of social ideals—narrative or other cites of cathexis to organize collective performances of social transformation. These ideals will be wrapped by, which is to say networked with, computational money-like media that will organize sustainable returns for the communities that generate value. Economy will be made to work for the people because people will have the ability to valorize activity and representation that allows them to organize quality of life and make kin. Communities themselves will be able to program the qualities of values transmitted by and organizing their networks. We will be able to collectively design sociality in accord with collectively held values and to risk together on their futures.

This vision, for the decolonization of financial mediation demands a redesign of the protocol layer of money, of its fourth determination, in ways that accord with and valorize socialist modes of exchange. As Alex Galloway wrote in what was perhaps an optimistic moment, "It is through protocol that one must guide one's efforts, not against it" (2004: 17). Such cryptoeconomic redesign of monetary protocol should and indeed must be able to interface with the existing capitalist economy without being subsumed by it. It must provide the liquidity necessary to survive in capitalism while facilitating a buildout to postcapitalist futures. Utilizing decentralized computing and decentralized issuance tools, anarchocommunist movements will create more robust messaging than fixed capital–bound informatics can deliver, messages capable of aggregating attention in new ways, transmitting qualified values, and enfranchising participants with equity in projects struggling directly against wage exploitation and attention-scraping in media capitalism. More democratically programmed financial control means that, unlike with the current internet, qualities will not be collapsed in price signals by content-indifferent monetization. The indifference to content is not "indifference" but *the politics* of the generalization of what Nick Srnicek calls "platform capitalism" (2016). Utilizing money's fourth determination—itself a historical result of struggle of capital's endeavor to outpace efforts for survival against enclosure and foreclosure— qualified values will be preserved through transactions denominated in new money-forms bound to sociopolitical missions. *Postcapitalist media can and must have a financial component that is democratically programmable.* What is required is not the content indifference of the network but the content sensitivity of the network. This will be created not by the disintermediation accomplished by existing blockchain in which human agency is effectively excluded and software functions autonomously so long as computers run the code, but by *remediation*, the introduction of an infinity of points in which everyday people can inflect the value signal by qualifying, on a peer-to-peer basis, the network that hosts the values its users intend to create. Value will be platformed on community.

Such a network will have to be peer2peer and have the capacity to horizontalize the issuance of credit and debt. We will issue our own liquidity by issuing it to one another. And we will succeed only to the extent that we do not repeat at a higher level of abstraction the extant forms of violence inherent in the hierarchies of social difference—that is, only to the extent that the new currencies express the value of antiracist, feminist, decolonial, queer, anarchocommunist planetary becoming in its great diversity of forms. Indeed, we must say here that *if, and only if, women, LGBTQ persons, people of color, the colonized, the incarcerated, and the subaltern become the authors of our various futures will the historical development of the fourth determination of money that is information open up to emancipation. The global struggle for subaltern representation has become archival, informatic, and financial in addition to being social, practical and semiotic—such are the domains of encounter and such will be the mode of solidifying solidarity so that it might transform politics and economy.*

To conclude, we may glimpse how something like a radical *detournement* of finance may approach radical filmmaking, writing, and indeed poetry—and, conversely, how radical filmmaking and radical practices of the other arts may approach communist finance. Here we walk in the footsteps of the late Randy Martin. We must refuse the compression and collapse of our care, affect, and world-making capacities into information that is an instrument of racial capital. The catalytic approach of a new form of Third Cinema that will be communist economic media will be more than an affective flash point—it will be an instrument to collectively create cooperative forms of life. We will give each other credit, take on communal debt, and organize our solidarity around points of cathexis from which to make narratives and practices of emancipation economically viable and sustainable. We will give convertibility to one another's value creation, and do so on our own terms.

Archival Strategy

Having glimpsed the possible convergence of filmmaking and crypto, of radical cinema and radical communist finance, if only in a flash, a shake of the head will help us recall that all aspects of finance operative in our lives are mediated by various technoimaginaries: Facebook and Instagram but also loans for cars and school, credit default swaps. It is here in the cold, buzzing, fluorescent light of incipient totalitarianism that we also see that authorship and authority matter—and not only in the aesthetic dimension, but in the creation of what the think-tank at ECSA (Economic Space Agency) calls "economic space." Hollywood, as a heteronormative, white supremacist institution, has done incalculable damage to colonized peoples, people of color, queer and trans folk, and to so many who fall outside the normative spectra that enfranchise an immensely powerful minority and impose normative codes on all. It has done so by organizing the space of the imagination and hence also of practice, and it has done so to economic ends. Money, an even more thoroughly reduced signal than the Hollywood film, is also even more repressive in its monologue, its monologic—particularly in its instantiation as finance capital. Finance capital, exhibit A of contemporary racial capitalism, takes advantage of and intensifies social difference at every turn while, with its limited palette of quantitative registration on platforms denominated by state narratives and state supported institutions, conveniently and brutally disappears the structural inequality upon which it rests as mere circumstance and noise percolating at the margins of its content indifference.

Media history and theory reveals that the medium of exchange has become far more complex, passing into computation itself, and it further reveals that the protocol layer of money is being transformed. Indeed the growing revolution is attacking the worksites of money: the screen, the street, the police, the state—to coordinate an assault on capital's institutionalization of racism through the capture of interest. We have seen that with the convergence of representational media and finance, a Marxian analysis of labor and production reveals that the dynamics of struggle have increasingly moved into the media of exchange—the procedures of real abstraction and the issuance of credit and debt. Dialectics tells us that these historical transformations are the result of class struggle *in all its forms* as capital endeavors to get more for less and as workers-spectators-users-denizens-the oppressed struggle to survive— to preserve and augment their value(s). As we have seen, *the real arbitrage by capital, driven by innovation in the face of the falling rate of profit, is on the price of labor power.* This arbitrage informs the histories of colonialism, slavery, imperialism and the visual-digital culture of racial capitalism. A simple inversion of the notion of innovation—of the increasing efficiency and consequent reducing of cost per unit commodity—suffices to show that, in a race to the bottom, workers are paid less and less to produce more and more in return for mere subsistence. "The media," as I argued in *The Cinematic mode of Production* was, in short, a technique for extending the working day while also creating ever deeper and more efficient forms of value extraction by corkscrewing into the body. Yet people used and use money and other media (Black banks, guerrilla video) not just for conformity but for survival, and more. Newly emergent Marxism, in addition to coming to terms with computational racial capitalism, must recognize the contribution of liberation struggles to the historical rise of new media, for these media have also occupied the spaces innovated by workers of all types—factory, agrarian, semifeudal—seeking freedom from their working conditions, from forms of social oppression, as pleasure, access, knowledge, communication, making a life worth living, solidarity, and the like. The records may be scratchy and the images paper, the songs may be all but lost, but our deferred dreams are real. In fact there is vast wealth in the cultures of resistance and survival, and now political struggle must directly seize control of the design processes and social processes that lay the groundwork for the embedding of these meanings and the archiving of these dreams as the basis for a new economy and new sociality. Can filmmakers and image makers and token makers and word makers and dream makers become more conscious of creating programs for value creation and distribution, of creating knowledge and issuing scripts and programs? Can economic media (re)designers be more aware that, in generating new types of computational money, they are creating sociosemiotic architectures that may reorganize social relations and social affinities and that these designs might offset individualist self-optimization and fractal fascism by opening platformed cooperatives capable of providing alternative non-exploitative economies? Can an antiracist, anti-patriarchal, democratic, anarchocommunist political vision adequate to new potentials for solidarity and collectivity coemerge with and as sociocultural economic techniques to shape these futures? Can the anti-Black, anti-Brown, anti-queer, anti-Global South prejudices built into computational racial capital be defeated by new types of social currency? What we are really asking is: Can the masses redesign the protocols embedded in economic mediation—the protocols of exchange—and become the main architects of the future?

The answer requires the full socialization and indeed ecologicalization of information. Economy, information, embodiment, and institutional organization are social products, are of a piece, and are cybernetically networked with the bios. The redesign of economic media will democratize the reorganization process of these social relations. I will be unable to review here the current computational designs of cryptocurrencies, but let us just say that their *ledgers are archives* and, like cinema, like national monies: their circulation and the circulation of their tokens generates their value through the matrixial dynamics of machine-mediated attention. A blockchain is composed of a series of blocks (composed of transaction records) indexing a robust sociality. In other words, a blockchain is an archive of the attention a currency aggregates—attention represented as exchanges, the interest in real abstraction—and that attention organized by the qualities and capacities of the network is the medium for its value aggregation. Cathexis is on a narrative or a narrative of narratives—a meta-narrative. A blockchain is thus a unique record of resources and practices bound up in a specific socioeconomic undertaking. As with a standard computational hash, which could be generated, for example by taking the second word on every page of this book, one cannot reverse engineer the entire text from the hash, but one could *only* generate the hash from the specific text from which it was generated. Just as one could not reengineer *Moby-Dick* from a string composed of the second word at the top of each page, one cannot reengineer the universe of investments represented in the transaction record, the blockchain, for Bitcoin. These minimal, unique, unforgeable records of complex processes are part of the information compression that allows for a decentralization of token issuance and accounting that is validated peer-to-peer by means of proof of work, but currently such a record is not an adequate representation of user sociality—at least when compared to the robust character of other media. But some success must be acknowledged: peer-to-peer validation through the random selection of a block leader for each new block on the blockchain—based upon the successful solving of a cryptographic puzzle, whose solution is pursued in parallel by all machines on the network, by a particular machine that could not be identified in advance—creates an architecture that changes the social contract by disintermediating "trusted" third parties from archive creation. It also displaces the performance factor of value denomination from the nation state and the national central bank onto the distributed computational platform and the organization of users and communities that support the token. The value of Bitcoin comes from the price of its resource consumption and its overall aggregation of attention.

Despite its loudly decried and indeed horrendous energy consumption, bitcoin is the first example of and probably still the best example of a functional, long-standing decentralized blockchain-based nonnational global currency. However, by itself it is not the revolution—far from it. Rather it encourages a kind of anarchocapitalism, disintermediating third parties and states but not replacing their messaging with anything but the pure Hayekian price signal that is the Bitcoin brand. Well, that's not quite true. As our discussion of denomination above would indicate, the price signal is in fact tied to a message: a message which says that decentralized, computationally secure finance is not only possible but it is the future and that Bitcoin, as the longest standing and most successful cryptocurrency, serves and will continue to serve as crypto's standard. It is this promise and all the energy, in every sense of the word, that goes into it that sustains its price. This price is based upon a perception of Bitcoin's future, its futurity as a global standard of a new value-form. In other words, the value is denominated in Bitcoin which is not just its information but is platformation.

But as I have tried to show, Bitcoin is not the only possibility for a new field of endeavor called Cryptoeconomic Design. Put another way, using a very loose analogy: if Bitcoin is the twenty-first-century version of Fritz Lang's *Metropolis* (or should it be *The Wizard of Oz*?), what might the twenty-first-century version of Dziga Vertov's *Man with a Movie Camera* look like? Or *The Battle of Algiers*, *Killer of Sheep*, or the economic media version of *Girlhood*? One might hope that these new currencies would enable a post-Fordist version of a global general strike in which deterritorialized and otherwise disaggregated workers and beings begin to withdraw their labor from capital and offer their contributions directly to one another through forms of social cooperation that enfranchise them, remediate their precarity and remunerate their solidarity. Clearly, this task cannot be left to white guys, to white crypto-bros. And it can not be left to businesses and start-ups. Can the hashed blocks that archive currency transactions be made more expressive, more robust, such that they surface the informationally collapsed qualities of progressive social interaction and acts of radical care? Are these archives of relation the future substrates of images and data visualizations that at the same time allow people to enfranchise one another and thereby make our activism and care sustainable? Will social derivatives detach themselves from the virtuosity of capitalist production and reproduction in order to script communist performance and communist futures? Can archives of socioeconomic relationships achieve the eloquence of a literary text, the precision and affective power of cinema, the precise distribution of computational networks? Can they be the mediated entanglements that constitute a new era of poetry and poetics? As Hito Steyerl (2012) seems to ask in her essay "The Poor Image": Can visual bonds of solidarity—visible in the poor image only as the quality degradation resulting from constant retransmission by who-knows-who—be translated into the solidarity of a socialist or cooperative system of expressive valuation? This would imply, as Steyerl does, that solidarity is not just noise as it is in the poor image, or volatility in the derivative contracts created by synthetic finance, for that matter, but that it is a new type of signal. One question for artists, activists, political theorists, and dreamers seems to be: Will filmmaking, along with the other arts and cryptoeconomic design, join forces to consciously transform social media and cultural media in order to rewrite the contracts by which aesthetic sensibility is bound to financialization? Can struggle and social movements using social derivatives issue their own expressive currencies to produce nonhierarchical forms of valorization that are themselves platforms for liberation—rather than providing content for Twitter? Can the world computer be hacked? Can the subsumption of society by information be reversed? I ask these questions because we have shown here that, in the current regime of the world computer, nearly all expressivity feeds capital accumulation. This capture implies not only the collapse of all social values into the price signal mediating the traffic of the value-form but also that an aesthetics without a self-conscious, materialist practice of value, no matter how seemingly radical, is doomed to recapitulate the algorithms of value extraction—whether distributed in the museum, the university, the festival circuit, or on YouTube. *Only a reprogramming of the sociosemiotic that takes seriously the productive power of the people who in one way or another interface with computational media (all of us) will be able to shift the world from its self-destructive path of hierarchy, violence, racism, sexism, and fascism.* And only media practices that materially vest participants in the worlds they posit, rather than merely using these digitized imaginary worlds as means of value extraction, can hope to directly challenge capitalist exploitation and the racism, sexism, imperialism, and genocide that are endemic to extractive economies. *What is called for here is a redesign of the processes of real abstraction, which is to say of the practices of exchange, which is to say of computational and social processes scripting interaction.* Otherwise, and as much as it hurts to say, revolution ultimately makes the rich richer—and we cannot afford that.

Postmodernism then, comes to a close with the return of radical political economy and the possibility to recognize media convergence as the generalization of media as economic media, and thus, the possibility to redesign economic media. Signs, though "liberated" from traditions, are anything but free-floating. Rather, they are linked to armatures of extraction serving as machine extensions designed to capture species-dreams and ground them in the realpolitik of the world computer. COVID-19 as a monstrous symptom of late capitalism and the global response to the police lynching of George Floyd further signal the end of an era. And the intensification of global fascism to counter the fact that, as Angela Davis says, "the nation-state is no longer possible," announces a new time and new terrain.[7] With the return of radical political economy, with the concrete manifest desire to end racial capitalism and the radical redesign of economy back on the table for the first time since the global 1960s, postmodernism comes to a close. The "cultural logic of late capitalism" becomes fully legible as the political-economic logic of computational racial capitalism. Therefore, in the moment where economic redesign becomes possible, we grasp that the limits placed on the domain of politics that took the operating system of capitalism as a given and that subsequently understood politics as cultural politics is over. Political economy as a space of transformation is no longer consigned to a point beyond the historical horizon. Capital's foreclosure of and on revolution will no longer hold.

Cultural work can fully succeed only by posing challenges to its medium, its media—its protocols of representation and its modes of enfranchisement. It must do so as an extension of its work to challenge the establishment and its forms of power. As with the revolutionary movements of the early twentieth century, it is to be understood once again that cultural liberation also requires liberation of the means of production from their extractive role as fixed capital. Digitization has marked the convergence of expressivity, computation, and finance in the field of capital—it makes expression subject to extraction through its mode of media abstraction. The autonomization and hegemony of information, of the AI that is the world computer, places life in a derivative condition in relation to information—information that is, in a nutshell, a derivative on life. Information as an always-already financial instrument provides capitalized networks—currently the only kind to have computational embodiment—derivative exposure to life, converting all information-generative instances into machines of attention extraction whose revenue potential (rates of return) can be measured, priced, and pitted against one another. Currently, if information wants to be free, it is only so that it can bring its commodified underlier to market. Some people can buy forward swaps to hedge their currency holdings; some of us just remember the days we could post on Vine or, before that, drink malt liquor in the 7-Eleven parking lot. But it is we who want to get free.

Those of us with transformative social agendas require economic support and sustainability. We must bootstrap our movements for abolition of prisons and for the abolition of police, for ending anti-Black racism, for ending racism, for ending imperialism, and for emancipation. We must control the economic protocols that underlie our communications and institutions and thereby control the process of value abstraction and value distribution. We must be able to collectively script futures that produce sustainable and just social formations. We want to work with others who are incarcerated or oppressed or facing homelessness or facing genocide and refuse the inscription of futures written on our very bodies by those whom capitalism enfranchises. We want to write our own futures, enfranchise ourselves on the basis of our own mutual recognition of one another's potential. We want to collectively author our own social derivatives on the volatility we confront so that we may benefit from our movements.

It seems clear then that Marxism, recognizing that finance has overtaken expression, and that therefore all media of expression currently function as capital, *requires for its own continuance and viability a redesign of the protocols of money*—the protocols of mediation and of value abstraction that currently make computation a continuation and extension of racial capitalism. This redesign, if it is to scale to the point that it can allow local cooperatives to cooperate globally, requires abstraction without extraction and implies a sociotechnical struggle over money's fourth determination, a reprogramming of the modes by which it qualifies value—a reprogramming of the way it denominates, platforms and programs value(s). This struggle must draw upon and be participant in the knowledge base accumulated through prior revolutionary and decolonial struggles, as well as through antiracist, feminist, indigenous, and queer movements. It must be a means for the production of revolutionary becoming. The connection to filmmaking here has been pursued in part to suggest the possible nuance of this qualification of value in a moment when the expressive techniques for democratic authorship of money's fourth determination.

The techniques for expressive finance—as they exist, for example, in contemporary cryptocurrencies, are extremely primitive, akin to the techniques of photography in 1840, or to those of cinema in 1900. The sociotechnical requalification of value, that is, the requalification and revaluation of social production and reproduction in its most robust sense, becomes a bounded inflection point in the capitalist matrix of value that, with the designable network derivatives possible through cooperative economic media and peer-to-peer currency issuance (or co-issuance), might operate by new economic rules and create new forms of economic space. Those familiar with my writings know that my work with ECSA over the past few years informs some of what I write here. Economic spaces, designable spheres of economic and social practice are ways of expressing and scripting new experiments of valuation *and* community (of values and social relations) and might be considered emergent cooperative cells in an emerging anarchocommunist sociality composed as a cooperative of cooperatives.

To derive from the archive of historical violence some pathways for liberation that do not in turn reproduce the violence from which they flee, to turn social inequity into new forms of inalienable social equity—such is not the task for an elite group of programmers. Such is the urgent task of all who struggle for liberation from the current terrain of the derivative condition—it is our task. Survival first, revolution next, but then? Historically survival, rebellion, and radical economy have all been intimately connected; indeed, for the oppressed, the second and third have often been conditions of the first. We may observe that even the short term requires a recasting of real abstraction: the materially mediated practices of social exchange. Isn't that what music can do? The politics, expressivities, pedagogies, practices of relation, and media of value creation and distribution adequate to the task of redesigning the entanglements of culture and economy remain to be collectively created. They are created on the ground but we must stop them from being expropriated by abstraction as information as capital. Much is done and can still be done in the good old media of activism, poetry, music, image, and maybe even critical theory—however, the limits imposed by computational racial capital are very real. The unthought of computational racial capital, the consequences of which can be felt everywhere, have begun to be thought. Dire as the planetary outlook is, this emergence of our ability to think the murderous unthought composed by the semiautonomous real abstraction processes of the world computer is a positive sign, if only because it clarifies the terrain of struggle and puts the communist endgame back on the historical horizon.

The Derivative Machine: Life Cut, Bundled, and Sold—Notes on the Cinema

In *The Message Is Murder* I began to make the case that M–C–M′, the general formula for capital derived by Marx—in which money becomes more money by means of the exploitation of workers in the production of commodities for the market—can be rewritten as M–I–M′ (Beller 2017b). We have developed this argument here. In the sequence Money–Information–Money, money becomes more money by means of the exploitation of "content providers" in the extraction of informatic labor and the production of information for the market—a market which is itself an information processor. Informatic labor is formatted and captured by means of the programmable image. Images may serve as the immediate interface or they may be words on a screen or numbers on a ledger protocolizing investment of resources or workflow captured elsewhere. Logically this rewriting of the general formula for capital also suggests that information has become the general form for the commodity, further suggesting that information has a dual being as use-value and exchange-value. Though this dual being—as quality of informed matter with a utility and as a specific denomination of exchange-value, whether as a shoe, as a twenty-dollar gold piece, or as a material instantiation in a discrete state machine—is in fact the case, I cannot fully pursue this important question here. In the current era, quanta of labor are at once registered and measured by means of creating changes in the states of discrete state machines even if the inputs are elsewhere. Labor has always been that which provided useful state changes to matter—as Marx remarked, there is not an atom of matter in value. These state changes are monetized and recursively affect production. Commodities, then, are consumable affordances tied to an increasingly calculable matrix of informatic relations capable of deriving a price, which is to say that dynamic information can be collapsed into a single number called price at any moment in time. In other words, price itself is a derivative on underlying information (a derivative on knowledge): the time-sensitive strike price for an option on the informatic system Hayek understood as the market (Bryan, Virtanen, and Wosnitzer, 2017). While traditional forms of work still inform materials in the production of what we may recognize as commodities (products of, say, agriculture, the factory, or the sweatshop), from the standpoint of global capital production and reproduction, forms of work have undergone a qualitative shift such that screen-mediated, informatic labor has become the *paradigmatic* form of labor. Like the Instagram photo, the apple (measured on the farm, labeled in the grocery store, rung up on the cash register, patented in the lab), the automobile, and the sneaker (with their global commodity chains, distributed materials, labor protocols, advertising budgets, and consumer satisfaction surveys) all serve as informatic nodes, and each material change of status in its production and circulation leaves an information trail, a digital wake. Workers on farms, factories, and screens all produce for this informatic register that mediates the market.

This informatic paradigm, which represents a kind of total and indeed totalitarian knowledge or computability by breaking up and intervening in the ontologies and prior gestalt of things, orchestrates global production and distribution for profit by means of markets, screens, and productive command. It pertains despite the fact that feudal, industrial, and slave labor continue—each of which is subordinated to the computational paradigm without any remission of its specific forms of brutality. A Marxist analysis of information must recognize that these seemingly atavistic forms of value extraction not only persist but that their persistence and functionalization are, in fact, along with militarized primitive accumulation, surveillance and the scraping of metadata, essential conditions for the development and maintenance of the standpoint of information. Just as exchange-value is content-indifferent with respect to the qualities of the commodity, so too is information with respect to its referent. The standpoint of information, in which complex mathematical calculi can be applied without any reference to a substrate, is also the command-control perspective, the optimizing imperial gaze of racial capitalism: the AI version of what, in a brilliant and polemical paper, Mark Driscoll (2020) identified as the actively transcendent perspective of the Hegelian world spirit regnant in colonialism and imperialism, the content-indifferent world spirit that he rebaptizes as "Caucasian super-predation." In saying that world spirit is at once Caucasian superpredation and the quasi-subjectifying hypostatization of a materially sedimented, machine-mediated capital logic as AI, we make explicit the space of a political wager in epistemic critique (theory): namely, that underneath the cloak of presumably value-neutral information, racial capitalism naturalizes its functions on a cosmic scale. Neo-Hegelians, consider yourselves warned.

With the attention theory of value, and also with what in the early 1990s I called "attention economy," we saw that, in an abstraction of montage, the site-specific assembly line of the factory became the deterritorialized factory of the screen and that, in transforming sensuous labor thusly, cinema and screen-based media embarked upon a colonization of the visual, the perceptual, and the cognitive as the machines monetized attention. Even at that time, attention was understood to be "sedimented" in the image, a form of sociality that left a trace and that deposited value in ways that affected the qualities of the image and thus also its functionality. As a partial result of cinema and early screen cultures, human life and its entanglements have been increasingly organized and then enclosed by apparatuses: cameras, data screens, cellphones, geolocative devices, and other information machines. In leaving the factory floor and becoming screen, the interface between worker and machine extended itself into visual, social, physical, and communicative-discursive spaces, that is, into the everyday life-world. In retrospect, we see that the analog methods for extracting labor, value, and information were being extended, flexibilized, and "dematerialized," even as their command over material organization and the enclosure of species-emergence was being expanded and intensified. So too, then, was the struggle with capital, waged on an expanding field. This expansion was outward toward the observable cosmos and inward to the affective and molecular. People became not just the conscious organs of industrial machines, but nodes in the emerging computational networks of metrics that in the last and often the first instance were market-derived and ultimately rigorously grounded in institutionalized inequality. Informatic machines, in becoming our surround, also became our unconscious, the bearers and repositories of our diverse and sedimented histories. They are fully functional fetishes and symptoms thrown off by the larger totality in order that its order be maintained. And as the term *biopolitics* implies, although in a sometimes troublingly anti-Marxist vein, all of these formerly cultural, extra-economic "faculties" and cybernetic instantiations became simultaneously domains of production and of struggle in the order and ordering of social difference and inequality.

Such are the machine-instituted social relations that over time can be understood to inhere in the image, the photographic image, the cinematic image, the digital image, the technical image, and the programmable image. To express the reach of these relations I'll use another possibly digressive example from Taiwanese cinema. In a recent talk on filmmaker Tsai Ming-liang given in the Volatility Group seminar based in New York, Ackbar Abbas (2019) reminded us that, in working out the now famous break between the movement-image and the time-image, there were for Gilles Deleuze other types of images. Upon the by now often cited arrival of the post–World War II condition of shattered space-time, a condition of facing situations we no longer understand in places we no longer know how to describe, Deleuze informs us that the sensory-motor schema pertaining to the prior world of movement is interrupted such that cinema gives us "a little time in the pure state." In remarking on this break that separates *Cinema 1* and *Cinema 2*, Abbas tells us that Deleuze explicitly leaves aside a third type (or regime) of images, what he refers to as electronic images: video, digital, etc. Abbas suggested that Vilém Flusser's notion of the technical image, elaborated in *Towards a Philosophy of Photography* (2000), and particularly his notion of the universe of technical images in a book that bears those words in its title (2011), speaks at once to this third regime of images and its new capacities for enclosure. To elaborate, Abbas produced a brilliant reading of Tsai Ming-liang's film *Stray Dogs* (2013), in which, because of the syntactical undecidability of the status of shots—an undecidability emphasized by their duration—every take becomes, in his words, "a double take." As time goes by, the narrative repositions what was seen. The confrontation, with indeterminacy on the one hand and the exhaustion of semiotics on the other, serves as an aesthetic means to navigate a universe in which all images have effectively become at once overdetermined and alienating: undecipherable, resignifiable, beyond control. The last shot of *Stray Dogs*—in which the main characters behold an artwork composed on and of the rubble of some subbasement infrastructure—lasts, Tarkovsky-like, for over nine minutes. In the climactic moment, the audience beholds the characters who end up beholding an image of obvious intention but with indeterminate meaning—an Anselm Kiefer-like cave painting in the bowels of some edifice somewhere that blends up into the foundation and down into the earth and also contains them. It is an image of image as substrate and as container, as base and superstructure. Of indeterminate meaning and received in a condition of scripted overdetermination, this image is a technical image of a technical image, in that every technical image (and every point in the universe of technical images), no matter what it may seem to signify, is an expression of algorithmic concepts functionalized by apparatuses, by black boxes that renders their logic at once as incomprehensible from the standpoint of any human subject position that might be occupied as their omnipresence makes them inescapable. In conclusion (the conclusion of the film, though not only the film), the image is alienating in the double sense that no one exercises full sovereignty over images and also that, despite that condition of radical dispossession, images, in their full saturation of the visual field and in their computability, nonetheless capture our desire, aspiration, space, time, and care—our attention.

This attention, following Bernard Stiegler (2012), is also our way of making culture(s). This general, indeed generalized, case of attention-scraping—extended by means of the programmable image that has become the dominant mise-en-scène or environment of perception—has dispossessed us of the capacity to attend to things in particular, to care beyond the paradigmatic reign of images. Thus, the regime change in the character of images, from the handmade work of art to the computation-mediated image (Tsai's films are in the last instance digital) marks at once a reformatting of culture and sociality as well as a new order of dispossession. Tsai Ming-liang's long takes are afterimages of characters being devoured by a world of images, images that through their sheer duration devour spectators and all denizens of the universe of technical images. In understanding (or better, perhaps, witnessing) the logistics of images by means of images we are lost in the map and thus lost in and to the world. We live in the map, not the territory. All the while, in our near metabolic endeavor to create culture and care—that is, in our struggles for survival, be they conscious or instinctual—we feed the rapacious image machines and are devoured by them. Indeed, one character, the homeless father whose job, paid at subsistence wages, is to carry—to wear and indeed bear—an advertising sign on a busy highway intersection in Taipei, protests his lot by singing a song of allegiance to the emperor. Nearly all of his moves are scripted by the cultural logics of domination, with the particularity of his body and voice being the only residue or remainder. Living literally under a sign, under an "advertisign," even an act of protest pledges allegiance to the emperor. We may thus observe that with the full financialization of everyday life, it appears that the only way to protest is to use the existing codes to create a spread—a direction, a wager, a risk that deviates from the script. For the father, this total capture culminates in an act of violence addressed to the symbolic register—a message, one that is sad and abject.

This reading—of overdetermination, and thus of abjection to the point of subjective annihilation by the logistics of both the image and of the capitalization of semiotic process—suggests that one significant missing piece in the philosophical analysis offered by both Deleuze's cinema books and by Flusser is the role of visuality in what we think of today as finance capital, or, with

Randy Martin (2002), financialization and the financialization of daily life. In the above example, the ecology of the image is also that of the global economy, and if the map is as large as the territory, then theory must be adequate to the map. The other flagrant omissions here in both the Deleuzian and Flusserian accounts are the realpolitik concerns of race, gender, sexuality, and imperialism in relation to financialized visuality. These are serious omissions indeed, but then again, what can we really expect from philosophy?

The analytic I have been developing to account for dispossession by means of images has taken pains to think the transformation of society by cameras, images, and screens simultaneously in direct relation to the bio-, and eco-, and social disasters that are both result and condition of the intensification of racial capitalism. What we today call "digital culture" is the result of centuries of digitization under the regime of commodification and the wage, as well as centuries of racialization. The colonization of the visual, beginning in the midnineteenth century, was an essential moment in the development of capital, as was the rise of said digital culture beginning in the mid-twentieth century, both of which created new work-sites and new metrics for value capture. The financialization of everyday life implies that the semiotic processes are now welded to a digital armature, are mediated by screens, and function as subroutines of value production for capital. The millions and indeed billions of people subject to racial oppression bear the largest part of the burden of the oppression endemic to capitalist production, sometimes unto death. And as we know from the resurgence of Islamophobia post–9/11 or the incipient racialization of the poor in *Parasite* (pointedly when the poor father's smell "crosses the line"), the categories of racism are continuously recast to accommodate the needs of the ruling class. Differences in the domain we think of as social difference (race, gender, sexuality, religion, nation, class, and so on), like those among brands, are functionalized (collateralized) by economic-legal-ideological parameters. In becoming information, social differences are constituted as forms of legibility and forms of inscription: read-write media encoding a matrix of access and prohibition—to say nothing of the sociopsychological effects of the materialities of these codes, their epidermalization and interiorization. This coding of race, gender, nation, and other profoundly differentiating differences is a writing on the body (and the psyche) and a program for action—a de facto assignation of a place in a loosely or tightly knit network of rights of access. There is a lot more to say here about racial formation—a violence of encoding for which an eloquent "civil" emblem is the brand. For the brand, as a form of proprietary encoding, links the luxe commodity to the violence of chattel slavery in an intimacy of pleasure and brutality that, though some of the forms have changed, is anything but past (Browne, 2015). Before forging ahead, we pause too quickly and too generally to reflect upon our purpose: Can we overturn the logic and the violence of the anticommunity and antisolidarity prescribed by the brand and become the authors of noncapitalist community?

In *The Message Is Murder* and here in *The World Computer* I argue that information—defined, in Bateson's (1972) words, as a difference that makes a difference—is really a difference that makes a social difference. All differentiation redounds to actually existing social formations, and all informatic throughput is by virtue of its digital interoperability inexorably linked to capitalist production. This claim is not only a matter of putting the social forward as the ultimately determining instance, it is a matter of tracing the evolution of real abstraction from money to price to information. Despite the fantasies of various scientific disciplines and religious practices alike, one does not transcend the social even in the most abstract (mathematical, scientific, or even spiritual) modes of cognition. This also means that social differences (gradients of inequality) are functionalized for the purposes of informatic accumulation, and thus capital accumulation, and that far beneath these moments of abstraction and the crunch of their calculus in discrete state machines, we living beings are the substrates of computation and computational racial capitalism. The origins of this treatment are, as noted earlier, to be found in the mathematics of slavery, colonialism, wage labor, and commodification. Their calculus. One founded upon and imposed by violence and, indeed, by genocide.

The claim regarding information as always redounding to the social and social difference is totalizing in order that it address a (near) totalitarian death grip on expressivity and on struggles for liberation. The calculus of value is organized such that all of our struggles in the domain of information generate new information for capital. Dispossession in the face of the image is one significant symptom of this condition. We organize from a space of radical overdetermination, and, with any revolutionary aspiration turned to content provisioning, the odds are against any success, particularly at the collective level of aspiration but also at the individual level of aspiration. The art world is only a case in point, as, for that matter, is academia or Instagram: as with Hollywood, abjection, burnout, and failure are the general rule, albeit hidden by the lottery that grants exceptional success. Given this situation, we might ask about the role of cinema and its expressivity as a way of thinking about the politics of collectives, even if ephemeral ones. We might also ask if it is possible to design programs of and for attention that neither recapitulate or reinvent modes of value extraction and exploitation endemic to racial capitalism.

Programs that do not conform to M–I–M′—at least not in every detail. Again, a pause: Can we imagine programs that are not extractive yet capable of the abstraction and scaling that would seem necessary to sustain community on the topos of the derivative? If the wage and its descendent forms abstract labor in one and the same moment as value is extracted by dissymmetrical exchange (money for time, likes for attention), the only way forward that can deal systemically with computational capital and locally with cooperative solidarity, short of exit, would be *abstraction without extraction*.

Stuart Hall, in a brilliant and prescient essay entitled "Encoding/Decoding" (2016), shows quite clearly that meaning and community formation are vectors for the transmission of values. Hence the circulation of value through cultural-communicational networks of encoding/decoding, where these are understood *as practices*, is also productive. But productive for whom? Brands and platforms are hegemonic examples but what about dissident communities signaled for example by divergent practices: punk, hip-hop, Black Lives Matter, Syriza, flamenco, fado, transgender social media content, queer tango, the Communist Party in the Philippines, and so on? We require that these organizations and cultural-political formations, people who could also be thought to practice encoding/decoding, keep more of the productive power for their causes, their values, their futures? *Economic value inflected by cultural values is a new requirement for any politics that is not to fall back into modality of capitalism.* Feeling good is good, but not good enough. We need to transform the feel of the infrastructure.

In the global 1960s and beyond, radical cinema seemed to provide an answer. As attention machines, radical films along with so much music, encoded new forms of time, space, relation, intellection, apprehension, conceptualization, and affect, capable of constellating and famously "catalyzing" the desire for the revolutionary experience of a different, more liberated world. The traces of these experiences—whether they came from the past, present, or future, produced by viewers in relation to the cinematic templates that were the conveyers of radical transmissions—also presented themselves as tools, resources, and talking points that created a community, that allowed for the further invocation and recalibration of a shared if imaginary universe. Fernando Solanas and Octavio Getino (1997) were clear that it was the ferment of the revolutionary masses that underpinned the innovations in the cinema of liberation, and that the cinema of liberation was a moment in armed struggle against imperialism. The film, as catalyst and archive, also created what Brian Massumi and Erin Manning call an "anarchive"—potentials for further activity that lie in the unrecorded and untraced network of sociality at once extant and echoing from a particular encounter: here, spectators with a film and with one another (or with listeners, players, and dancers in the music), the echoes of an encounter existing either synchronously or asynchronously.[1] And, as Hall (2016) points out in "Encoding/Decoding," emphasizing the agency of spectators or what today we might call users, even in the case of dominant or mainstream images, counterhegemonic readings (and oppositional gazes) may reencode a contrary message, just as a cover may bring out a new topology of musical meaning and thus make present an (un)imagined community. Indeed, such was third cinema: a record of and a catalyst for revolutionary action.

For a more recent example—though not one that yet addresses the Instagram story as a form of reencoding—in Raya Martin's *Indio Nacional* (2005), in which he "remade" vignettes from before the 1896 Philippine Katipunan revolution against Spain using the film technologies that would have been available circa 1890–1895 (you will remember that cinema was invented in 1895), Martin renders some of the texture and character of the events in the medium that could have been active but historically was not. In the absence of the archive—a foreclosure produced by both colonial circumstance and the history of cinema—he has his actors reenact quotidian aspects of revolutionary planning and thus *fabulates* a profilmic real, complete with uneven film speeds, uncontrolled lighting values, sepia stock, and intertitles drawing on the anarchive. Making a film that looks to be from the time preceding the Katipunan revolution, Martin, much like the brilliant American critic Saidiya Hartman, interpolates a new archive to fill in the lacuna of the historical record, fully aware of the archive's decisive role in history and hegemony and aware that the destruction or absence of the records of local-becoming-national cultures in the colonies by the colonists was one of the most important methods of war. If, as the conceit of twentieth-century metaphysics had it, the image bears a trace of the unrepresentable Real and there are no images of one's history, then one has no Real—even one that is unrepresentable—and thus no ontology: one is doubly derealized. In the colonial context, the enfranchising of the colonialist's ontology and the destruction of the ontologies of the colonized is a practice of violence to which Martin's film makes a kind of answer. The epistemic violence of colonization is addressed, if not compensated for, by epistemic fabulation.

Such, at least, was a reading and a strategy available while a mid-twentieth-century photographic paradigm (that of Bazin and Barthes) still reigned, when the photographic image was thought to be indexed to the Real. According to the Flusserian insight—closer to Benjamin, McLuhan, Kittler, and even Eisensteinian montage but more thoroughgoing than perhaps any of these—the technical image is never a window but the result of the operation of concepts: not an orchid but a *simulated orchid* in the land of technology. For Flusser, this by now unavoidable analysis of the photograph, of its functioning as the result of the programmatic operation of concepts extended into matter, puts the technical image in the circuit of almost any programmable communication—and increasingly, with the expansion of the program of the camera, all of it. For us, it also implies the unavoidability, when considering any semiotic event whatever, of the *socio*technical, that is, of a clear perception that apparatuses do not only evolve from writing in the abstract but from the concrete social relations that make writing possible and functional. One encodes the apparently ontological with the technical image, yet now one must know that ontology is a battleground.

In *The Message Is Murder* I have shown that in Claude Shannon's formalization of the mathematical theory of communication, despite its pretense at objectivity and neutrality, the mathematics Shannon devised were (unconsciously?) beholden to white supremacy. Shannon utilized the Dumas Malone biography *Jefferson the Virginian* (1948) to develop his letter and word frequency formulations. The Malone text, however, became notorious, as Annette Gordon-Reed (1998) showed, for denying Jefferson's relationship to his slave Sally Hemings and for denying the existence of their children—and thus partaking of what Hortense Spillers (1987) damningly calls "an American grammar." Or again, as the racism of facial recognition software concisely points out in light of the highly significant work of Joy Buolamwini at MIT,[2] we may again clearly discern that relations of race, gender, and imperialism are in the architecture and operating systems of today's communications infrastructure. This infrastructure increasingly includes all of our machines and thus, if the argument about the cyberneticization of consciousness, perception, and proprioception holds, then the infrastructure also includes our cognitive and sensual capacities. Again: sociocybernetics as the unconscious; computational racial capitalism as the mise-en-scène for semiotics, social production and reproduction; information as general equivalent and medium of extraction, that is, as real abstraction; and the world computer as the virtual machine resultant from the practice that is information's endless computation. As extensions of the world computer, technical machines—though they may traffic on their locally "value-neutral" mathematics—are racial formations.

So with the full colonization of our communication by algorithmic protocols—which are the result of sociotechnical histories that, in their now dominant form, are nothing short of the inheritors of the legacy of a global digitization process that began with money, wage labor, and commodification and that are inseparable from colonialism, imperialism, and racial formation—what is to be done? In a world where information mediates racial capitalist exchange, what are we to do? "We"—a would-be freedom-seeking we and rhetorically a problem that covers more than it discloses and potentially hides more problems than it solves—find ourselves, once again, in a position of precarity: forced to risk, forced to game, forced to fugitivity, forced to survival, forced to wager in a computer game, the stakes of which are life and death.

In response to Abbas's paper on Tsai Ming-liang, the analysis of the enclosure of the technical image, and the radical role of the very long take, one listener countered by recounting an article he'd read in the *Wall Street Journal*: in sum, cutting-edge advertisers are now using the very long take to attract new customers with sophisticated tastes. One washing machine company, he said, boasted that their latest twenty-minute advertisement on YouTube showed a fixed, frontal, Ozu-style shot of an entire washing machine cycle in real time. The ad was a smash hit garnering hundreds of thousands of views. That—or the livestreaming of people's workplaces for eight continuous hours, or of two-hour solo meals out using a selfie-stick—should disabuse us of the notion that any particular genre or form has a monopoly on anticapitalist sensory cultivation. Rather, what we see are multiple wagers, or, more precisely and as we have seen, derivatives. These are cuts through the social, seeking attentional valorization by bundling assets in the drama of value; they are gambles on the future, options on attention. In short, they are wagers, forms of risk that are bets, qualitatively providing content and experience as utility, but from the collapsed point of view of price, mere segues looking to at least keep up with the general rate of return and get from M to M′.

There is still a conversation to be had about radical cinema as a kind of derivative, that is, as a hedge, a future and/or an option in relation to a world brutally, indeed genocidally, overrun by the world market. There can be no doubt that advertising utilizes a derivative structure: a form of risk management, a contingent claim on attention, explicitly designed to get a venture from M to M′. A financial product that, like its more formal analog on Wall Street, provides access to an upside while limiting risk—a hedge. However, a notion of radical cinema as derivative would be to posit a cinema that, from within the space of a racial capitalism in which social differences are exploited as vectors of violence and value extraction, seeks an alternate future, a futurity beyond capital. A cinema where the endgame of M was not M′ but the transvaluation of the value-form and the revaluation of value. What would be the steps along such a path? How would a movement, originally bound by computational racial capitalism, sustain itself through time and spatial scaling in order to create liberated zones—dimensions and qualities to be determined—as it builds the conviviality of revolutionary forms of social belonging?

The utilization of attention production to build revolutionary futures will provide a key component to the discussion of communist derivatives and radical finance I will develop at greater length in my next book. The medium of revolutionary acting is necessarily ourselves—but bound together by what kinds of machines, heritages, media? At the risk of utilizing platform fetishism for a certain kind of concision and dramatic effect (to be dialectically unzipped at home), I'll just say that the machine medium may not be cinema as we think it, or social media as we know it—it may well be distributed ledger technologies, commonly known as blockchain, and more likely still, an eco-friendlier next generation of liquid or cypher-blockchain in which the entire network does not have to verify each computation because the computing fabric itself is securely encrypted and every message fully verifiable. If the previous sentence was intelligible, then an important point has been made—one that resonates with radical cinema history: the distributed, decentralized, nonnational medium known as cryptocurrency is not merely a new form of money but a new expressive medium. As such, cryptocurrency posits a fourth determination of money: as measure, medium, capital, and now information. Its prehistory includes revolutionary notions of reformatting political economy and, yes, the Hayekian, libertarian notion of the deposing of the capitalist state-form. It's future, however, must be closer to Trotsky than to Hayek, and its accounting, in all senses of that word, must not default to the fascist politics of capitalism but must be bent to the tasks of communism if economic media is to be an instrument of economic democracy and revolutionary politics.

The Derivative Image: Interview by Susana Nascimento Duarte

As a follow-up to my 2014 interview with *Kulturpunkt* (Beller, Jeric, and Meheik 2014), this interview connects my work on Philippine cinema, revolutionary Soviet cinema, and attention economy, developing the case for taking the notion of money as a highly robust medium far more seriously and for opening up the protocols of money to long-standing political questions that can be posed by redesigning the medium. If media platforms have been not only means of production but means of colonization, racialization, extraction, and financialization, it has become necessary to occupy not just media, but also finance. This occupation of finance can take the form of remaking currency at the protocol layer in accord with the requirements of the variously dispossessed. This is to say that the redesign of media-currency must be drafted from below, as it were, from the spaces of subalternity and oppression and with the cultural knowledge that inheres in survival. The following interview tries to draw some of the connections between visual media and financial media.

It is of some interest to me that these insights into the medium of money and its potentials for transformative, noncapitalist redesign come out of a rather idiosyncratic approach to cinema studies, third cinema, visual culture, and media studies. A redesign of money—one that understands it as a medium in the strong sense and glimpses the possibility of a fourth determination of money beyond measure, medium, and capital—amounts to intervening in the networking of sociality and, more to the point, to finding ways to elide or at least minimize the extractive techniques of actually existing money and of media more generally under computational racial capitalism. Because nearly all media today are media of capital, one has to retake expression in a way that does not monetize it for others (shareholders of the fixed capital that is media infrastructure) but returns value to those who create it. This, of course, is a transitional strategy, since it initially engages in struggles over ownership of the means of production and the products of production—but potentially a long-term and a transformative one.

To telegraph the strategy: shared equity in networked undertakings creates cooperatives within the contemporary economy that can be scaled. Anti-imperialist, decolonial, antiracist, queer, and activist organizations can begin to design economies in accord with their own ethos and practices, and, by creating computationally secure distributed archives of contributions, these social movements may directly enfranchise participants who share in the futurity of their projects. Nonnational monies—namely, cryptocurrencies—designed for particular projects, bound to forms of sociality of their own choosing, can at once index value distribution created within a project, serve as a liquidity bridge to outside markets, and inflect the price signal by denominating project value in the qualitative terms endemic to a token. Distribution structures can be organized by internal, democratic agreement in order to maximize conviviality for all participants. These tokens may also be rendered interoperable with those issued by other projects as a means of further qualifying value (that is, making it accord with what communities actually value) and building both the cultures and nonextractive economies that would allow for a cooperative of cooperatives and the transition out of capitalism. Expression would thus carry with it a designable economic component. Media would be reconfigured as economic media transmitting agent-authored messages not just as meaning but as programs for social production. Rather than effecting the financialization of expression, new money-forms might, like cinema and other art and expressive forms, be utilized as an expressive medium—this time to be authored from below and utilized to express collective aspirations. Though there are no guarantees and multiple problems with this notion, exploring it would seem to be a worthwhile investigation for those of us interested in media, visual culture, attention economy, social justice, the end of the violence of extractive economies, decolonization, and liberation.

SUSANA NASCIMENTO DUARTE (SND): In your book *Acquiring Eyes*, you connect a new era of abstraction—the becoming abstract of the world, when the visual has become the new arena of operations for media capital—to visual modernism/visual art in Philippines, in the assumption that the latter can help to reveal the former; and the same would work for cinema, both in Philippines and globally, in that it could be understood as a medium of abstraction—"indexing the becoming-abstract of the world as the becoming-abstract of the visual." Can you elaborate on this? Why turn to Filipino artists in particular "for guidance and inspiration in the contestation of global capital?" Why are they more apt to constitute ruptures in what you consider to be the plenitude of the visual achieved by the cultural program of the world-media system?

JONATHAN BELLER (JB): Colonialism, racism, imperialism. The twentieth century did not just mean a new order of geographical and economic colonization that was called *imperialism*, it also meant the colonization of the visible world and more broadly of the senses and the mind. That much is already contained in the notion of *Weltanschauung* ("ideology" or "world-view"). The Philippines bore the full brunt of both the ideology and practice of what came to be known as "the American Century." The Katipunan—the Filipino revolution against the Spanish colonizer—was stolen by the Americans who then occupied the Philippines in 1898 and who, in the still too little-known Philippine-American War, proceeded to conduct a genocide that killed between one tenth and one sixth of the Philippine population. In the long aftermath, which goes on to this day, Americans brought, along with military and police violence, cultural media including Hollywood cinema, American goods, and CIA support for cultural institutions and glamorous dictators in order to secure their gateway to the Pacific. Without imperialism, the world financial system necessary to twentieth-century capital accumulation would have collapsed, and without the cultivation of racism and white supremacy, an emerging geopolitical communications system might have created forms of solidarity and community that would render the violence at once necessary to capital accumulation and to the reduction of "the other" inadmissible. It is clear from the work of Simmel and Bloch that the beginnings of a colonization of the visual and sensual world was well underway early in the century. In the center, this colonization was spearheaded by the appearance of industrial objects and a built environment reformatted by the exigencies of capital expansion that included—along with the requiring of a global labor force capable of working for monopoly capitalism and of servicing sovereign debt—both a rising consumerism and a remaking of colonial lives and landscapes. All the new commodities and spaces were at once available to those more or less enfranchised by capital, but their appeal, and indeed their utility, depended upon the disappearance of the worker and the other. But, even beyond that, we must recognize that colonialism, racism, and imperialism were and are already forms of abstraction—a transformation of the perception of, in the first instance, the colonizer, the racist, and the imperialist, such that they perceive the external world and therefore "the other" through a framework of abstraction. The reduction of colonial laborer to garment is a practice of abstraction.

With cinema we get the full-scale industrialization of the visual that develops this framework of abstraction and makes it ever more expressive. This development of visual technologies capable of inscribing convenient fantasies on the body and space of the other also leads to advertising and to a new order of psychodynamics in both marketing and the market. These new dynamics exceeded and continue to exceed the capacity of ordinary linguistic analysis. It is problems resulting from this short-circuiting of linguistic capacity, this direct encroachment on language, on perception, on critique, and on the discursive ability to produce freedom that really interested me. The Philippines is at once a case in point and a space of insurrectionary becoming. The failure of a nationalist discourse following World War II and a renewed U.S. presence after nearly fifty years of decolonial struggle in the Philippines coincided with the rise of abstract art. The easy interpretation was that Filipinos were just following an emergent international style. I think that assertion is fundamentally as patronizing as it is incorrect—but even if it were correct, we should ask: Why the proliferation of abstract art around the world? To what experiences was it addressed? In reality, there were at least two directions: one formalist and invested in both the history of art and the cultural legitimacy that art history purchased; and another direction that addressed the historical foreclosure of nationalist struggle and the actual curtailment of an ability to constitute a liberated subject in and through language. The first strain was expressed and consolidated in the Marcos-driven Cultural Center of the Philippines, along with its effort to create international legitimacy for the Marcos crackdown by culture-washing: this strain later gave rise to a formalist art-for-art's-sake trend in the late 1980s (e.g., Roberto Chabet). The other chord was a revolutionary one, albeit unrealized. But, as I wrote in *Acquiring Eyes*, what could not be granted discursively (because of the imperialist shutdown of the narrative of Filipino nationalist struggle and nationalist becoming) found a visual analog: the radical pleasure and invention of cocreation unfettered by the ideological constraints of colonialism, imperialism, white supremacy, and dictatorship. The visual was becoming abstract, but the logistics of abstraction were not immediately ceded to capital. This anticapitalist, anti-imperialist chord later found its resonance in social(ist) realism in both painting and cinema.

SND: You claim, again in *Acquiring Eyes*, that "the twentieth-century emergence of the visual can be grasped in two moments that are dialectically separable—first as a realm of freedom and, second, subsequently as an arena of expropriation." According to you, this movement in the visual is one of the most significant areas of the unthought of political economy and geopolitics. It is this shift that you try to make sensible, and this unconscious that you try to make perceptible, in the abstract work of the Filipino painter H. R. Ocampo, and also in the Philippine cinema. How and why are they paradigmatic of this shift?

JB: Ocampo wrote a serial novel called *Scenes and Spaces* that told of a Filipino student who fell in love with his American English teacher but could not persuasively court her because he was consigned to the status of a racialized, colonial subject—not a man. This character's only solace was a series of abstract visual hallucinations that at times rose right up out of the street and interrupted the realism of the narrative. Later, when Ocampo shifted from writing narrative to painting canvass after the war, those same descriptive passages became a series of works that together constituted Exhibit A of Philippine modernism. One characteristic of these extraordinary works of visual abstraction is a spatial dislocation for the spectator produced by biomorphic forms that do not clearly indicate figure and ground and that thus introduce a kind of intense play in which viewing meant figuring the combinations to try and compose spatial conformations that made sense, or, an image. Multiple forces playing over the visual field opened it up as a space of participation and play—seeing was not a simple matter and visual objects were not givens. This practice, where painter and viewer worked together to co-configure possible worlds, I understood as a practice of freedom—that's what I felt at an inchoate, aesthetic level when I first looked at the canvases: not a revolution but some form of compensatory pleasure that pursued what was in fact possible, real possibilities of aesthesis and agency within the forces of abstraction. But there, too, in the visual over-written by the forces of abstraction, there also opened a space of further colonization by imperial forces that included CIA propaganda, and that other quasi-official and far more powerful U.S. propaganda agency known as Hollywood. There was also spectacle, the spectacle of the commodity, and later the spectacle-glamor of the Marcos dictatorship. These visual forces, it must be emphasized, functioned at a level that exceeded the prior resolution and saturation of the psyche by the police and even by state-controlled discourse. Radical cinema in the Soviet Union and visual practices in many places, including in the Philippines, ramified the visual as a way of stimulating the imagination beyond the locked boxes of capitalist futures. In general, the visual was implicitly or explicitly grasped as a space for the production of freedom. But this space of possibility was almost simultaneously shut down through its increasingly total saturation by commercial media, that is, by the fixed capital of communications infrastructure that colonized the visual and turned its productive potential into a factory for the production of capital itself.

SND: In *The Cinematic Mode of Production*, one can say that, in a way, you analyze precisely the retrospective overlapping of those two separate moments, as if even when cinema seemed to be working for a politics of human emancipation it was already preparing/anticipating its own capture by capital. Your reading of the work of Dziga Vertov and Sergei Eisenstein goes in this direction: in their film practice they propose a cinematic critique and the overcoming of capital and capitalistic society, but in the end they weren't able to fulfill their revolutionary expectations and ended up becoming productive for, and absorbed by, the capitalistic logic they intended to subvert. What part did they play in your understanding of the cinematic mode of production as the matrix of what you call the "attention economy"—"to look is to labor," as you say—which allows the connection between the production of capital and the production/consumption of images that you are trying to address?

JB: Yes, the intimate relationship between the pursuit of freedom/liberation and the capture of this life-creative energy by capital is the fundamental dynamic I perceive in the industrialization of the visual. Just as Marx saw that workers built the world, and just as Negri later emphasized that innovation came from the workers and was, like labor itself, expropriated from workers as surplus value and thus as capital, and again, just as Marxist feminists such as Federici and Fortunata demonstrated that in the struggle to survive women gave their life energy to capitalist patriarchy in ways both unrecognized and unremunerated, spectators, in seeking their own fulfillments and satisfactions, drove an industry that would feed off of (meaning profit from) their dreams. Cut off from other avenues of freedom and in a relentless pursuit of satisfaction, they deterritorialized the factory and made the paradigmatic interface between bios and fixed capital the screen-image. Looking for fulfillment and forms of freedom became looking as labor. Remember, the production of new needs is part of industrial advancement and the history of commodification. At first, with Vertov and Eisenstein (and in a kind of second moment with Pasolini, Godard, Varda, Mambéty, Brocka), the visual grasped as an open domain—only posited but not yet presupposed as space of production—offered unscripted forays into radical non- and anticapitalist organization. The power of the imagination and of the spectator was linked to the power of the people. But, as mentioned above, such an interface offered many productive efficiencies for capital and for its capitalists, and again, control of the means of production was decisive: not only did cinema and new visual technologies turn worker-spectators' sensual labor/attention/subjectivity/desire into the universal value-form of capital through what were at first rather crude processes of value abstraction—including ticket sales, Nielsen ratings, and advertising—they also reformatted and radically delimited linguistic capacity and opened the imagination to capitalist programs and indeed to capitalist programming. It is because of this overturning of the power of vision that I gave my essay on Eisenstein the (tragically) ironic title "The Spectatorship of the Proletariat."

SND: In your text "The Cinematic Program," you analyze three films, *Through a Lens Darkly: Black Photographers and the Emergence of a People* (Thomas Allen Harris, 2014), *Citizenfour* (Laura Poitras, 2014), *Norte: The End of History* (Lav Diaz, 2013), and, regardless of their temporal, aesthetic, and experiential differences, you tend to approach them as programs; in fact, according to you, their relevance depends on the possibility of reading them as "platforms for the instrumental organization of information, platforms that are also algorithms with regard to information processing." What do you mean by program in this context and how do you distinguish it from the programs run by what you call the capitalistic world-media system?

JB: Those films bind elements indexed to the life-world in new arrays—despite their differences, as you note. This, of course, could be said about most films, though the newness of any particular array and/or archive and/or grammar of indices is often more limited. Some films are highly formulaic; some films are just white films. My point of speaking in this way was to recognize the changed context of the media-environment, to announce, in short, that what we thought were films were really far more than we had previously understood and have indeed become something else in their very development and saturation of the representational, political, and financial worlds.

While I stand by what I wrote in that piece, the one word I might change is my saying that the films are "platforms"—this designation makes sense from the point of view of provisioning a place to speak from or an arena of sociosemiotic exchange. However, now I would refer to films as social derivatives: films are wagers on a particular semiotic structure and create a heuristic device for perceiving the world, which today also means acting in the world. The category of social derivative asserts that they are also bets on productive power—forms of wagering that have both capitalist and noncapitalist dimensions. Furthermore, this component, the financial component of representation, has been developed naturalistically by the reactionary forces of capital but can, and I think must, be developed by those invested in or simply desperate for liberation.

When you ask me to distinguish among cinematic programs run by capitalism, we could roughly say that currently all programs are more or less reproductive of white supremacist, capitalist heteropatriarchy—therein lies the distinction among them, that is, in the "more" or "less." Certain programs are scripts for the next generation of extractive violent relationships while others script for counternarrative, solidarity, communitarian affect and sense, and revolutionary structures of feeling and acting. They are made by and for people who, in bell hooks's terms, want their looks to change reality. Radical looking and what can be built with the consolidation of radical looks takes place within the basic media-environment which has become programmatic (or, in McKenzie Wark's terms, "game space"), bound, as it is, by rule sets and codes, most of which we only glean. These algorithmic processes of what I call computational racial capitalism have their own cultural logic, one that is ultimately inseparable from the financial logic built into the fixed capital that is media architectures.

SND: You state: "If representation persists in its first function of sense-making while also being sublated as a means of cybernetic incorporation, if, in short, we have traversed a divide between image and interface (page and screen, photograph and cellphone), such that all that was mobilized by and as cinema has melted into computation and the distinction between humanism and informatics has collapsed, then the role of the film user, whether director, actor, spectator, or critic, has become one of two things: functionary or programmer (and not photographer as in Vilém Flusser)." Can you detail your appropriation and dislocation of these Flusserian categories? Do programmers, as in the case of the directors of the above-mentioned films, automatically become encoders of antitotalitarian agencies?

JB: I'm not sure where that line appeared (perhaps also "The Cinematic Program?"), but the answer to your last question is no. There is nothing automatic about inscribing revolutionary social codes, organizing radical practices of seeing and acting, or writing radical social derivatives. Like interventions in the past, creating political change requires canniness and planning, as well as the ability to strike hard and spontaneously. Advertising, fashion, mass media, and what we call social media are superb at appropriating even the most radical gestures and desires. Radical programming in the sense that I mean here requires a revolutionary praxis that is neither reproductive of capitalism nor nullified by it. For Flusser this would be new information, since the camera is for him a computer and the technical image a form of information. However, Flusser's sense was that technicity, namely the technical image, had overwhelmed or exceeded capitalism, making both labor and ownership as well as Marxism and its (discursive) concerns irrelevant—and even bringing about something like an end of linear time, an end of history. There is much to explore in these ideas, particularly about the transformation of linear time by computation and the transformation of the properties of objects, labor, and ownership by informatics, but one of the missing pieces in Flusser's analysis was that this process of photographic incorporation was an extension of capital logic to such an extent that capital's computational logic had fully infiltrated computation itself—had indeed expressed itself as what was developed and became known as computation.

SND: In your text "Cinema, Capital of the Twentieth Century," you establish a parallel between what cinema is for Deleuze and what capital was for Marx. Why choose the lens of the Marxist concepts, namely those of extraction of value and wage labor, in order to approach and criticize the Deleuzian categories of the movement-image and the time-image? At the same time, inspired by Flusser, you propose "a third regime of the image," where we are no longer in front of an image, but inside a program. How does it connect to the previous Deleuzian categories of images and to your own conception of the possibility of a cinematographic resistance to the capitalistic perceptual order?

JB: Why choose the lens of Marxist concepts? Because they have greater explanatory power than all other epistemological frameworks? [*Laughs.*] What else can I say? Of course, such an assertion of the superiority of the Marxist dialectic remains only an assertion if it cannot be demonstrated. And I would want to add that in light of Marxism's manifest failings to address issues of race, gender and sexuality, I really only mean a fully reconstructed historical materialism. However, a praxis of conceptualization attentive to the historical origins of not only the objects of analysis but of the categories of analysis—the ultimate sociohistorical inseparability of object and category—is also, presumably at least, attentive to the historical implication for a set of consequences following upon the constitutive act of conceptualization. Even "history" is historical. Marxism, I have always thought, did not, in the field of culture, require a distinction between the aesthetic and the pragmatic, and was no less discerning for all that. In the best cases, it was and is (or at least should be) more discerning than competing modes of interpretation because it attended to material conditions of possibility for even the most elaborate forms of fantasy and fabulation. As far as critique goes, Said's *Orientalism* comes to mind, as does all the work of Gramsci and Fredric Jameson, and indeed much of the Marxist critical tradition— particularly if one includes Marxist feminists and black Marxism (e.g., Cedric Robinson). But beyond that and returning to your earlier questions with respect to the visual: for me, Deleuze's recognition that "cinema" had consequences for philosophy and that it pushed philosophy to develop new concepts was symptomatic of a material transformation in the conditions under which conceptualization and indeed social organization took place. Clearly, technically mediated material organization at an industrial scale was and remains a social phenomenon that cannot be separated from economy. "Cinema, Capital of the Twentieth Century" asserted that Deleuzian philosophy was symptomatic of a mutation in capital and that cinematic relations became the new paradigm for the formatting of production and distribution. Most obviously today, the reformatting of capitalist production and distribution involves the screen but also attention economy and the generalized industrialization of the visual. In "The Programmable Image," I have gone further to say that the visual is a medium of information processing and of informatic labor. So, returning to the historical record, my reading Deleuze from a Marxist perspective in 1993–1994 actually meant that what was the very first conceptualization of attention economy as a development of capitalism—a notion that, for all its seeming impossibility at the time, became a reigning paradigm after the rise of the internet—came about from the application of a Marxist lens.

Flusser, who we know was not a Marxist, wrote at the end of *Towards a Philosophy of Photography* in 1983 that a philosophy of photography was the only revolution left open to us. One gets a sense here that he would have been satisfied with a world where everyone sat around reading (and understanding) his books. I do not think he was as passive as all that, and he was right to perceive that so much of political thinking was outmoded or rapidly becoming so because of deep transformations in media infrastructure. He was right also, I think, to see that what he called "playing against the camera" was a kind of prerequisite for liberation. But though he may not have missed the fact that one may play against the camera with or without a camera, he seems to have missed the fact that there were strategies of conceptualization and acting (in short, resources in and of the people) beyond the horizon of his own discourse that could be admitted, such that all who played against the apparatus did not have to identify either as philosopher or photographer. These may have been his ultimate categories but they were not the ultimate categories.

SND: How did your research evolve from a systemic view of cinema as a technology for the extraction of value from human bodies, and therefore "for the capture and redirection of global labor's revolutionary agency and potentiality," into the idea/thesis of computational capital, as elaborated in *The Message Is Murder*, where you present information as the general form of commodity, encoded in the logistics that organize the world we live in?

JB: Flusser was key here. His understanding of the camera as a computer, as, in short, an apparatus that functioned as a result of programmed materials—what he called thinking extended into matter (the sciences of optics, chemistry, but also the distribution channels of images that drove the development of the camera)—helped me make the connection between cinematic images and data visualization. It was algorithms all the way down. Or rather, the algorithm, because of its capacity to automate thinking, became a kind of culmination of the ramification of nearly every human activity by the linear thinking that was writing and reason—a culmination that also opened a new world. Deleuze himself was aware that even within his discourse there was a "third" type of image, beyond the movement- and time-images that was the video image and, we might surmise, the coming wave of digitization/computation-images. My contribution, beyond making this connection that photography, cinema, and computation were all related forms of capitalist production, was also in recognizing that these relations were not isolated or autonomous emergences but deeply imbricated in the historical emergence and expansion of capital—to the extent that one could not think about the emergence of technology as an autonomous terrain.

Ultimately, my sense that the desire to think about cinema, photography, or computation as stand-alone media was a desire to engage in platform fetishism—and thus an active disavowal of their fundamental roles in the developmental history of both capitalism and globality—led me, in an essay called "The Programmable Image," as well as in *Message* and in my forthcoming book *The World Computer*, to rewrite the general formula for capital. From Marx's M–C–M′ we get M–I–M′, where M′ is more money than M, C is what we recognized as the commodity, and I is what we call information. This is not to say that the commodity no longer exists or that information is not, generally speaking, a commodity, but rather that the form of the commodity and of its production have radically changed since the industrial period and even since the period I characterized as the cinematic mode of production. In "the computational mode of production," our life energy is given over to shifting the state of discrete state machines regardless of activity or remuneration. Value is extracted through our dissymmetrical relation to computation:

we contribute more to the archive of fixed capital than we receive in terms of social utility. There is far more to say about these relationships, of course, and I will try to deepen this analysis in the new book.

SND: According to you, we see through capital, we talk the language of capital, and our political agency doesn't really exist because it is limited to what one can see and say inside this "computational system," this metadata society. Our performances are commanded and scripted in advance, even if everyone is now able to program images and the authorship seems to have been democratized. We reencode images, we modify their code, but it still is a predesigned praxis. We don't do it voluntarily but because we have to exist socially, economically, etc., and, in the end, the circulation between the sensible and information (= commodity) works as screen labor, as you put it. Are the Foucauldian notions of archive and episteme of any use to you, when dealing with this new order of intelligibility of our contemporary experience?

JB: It is not that we have no agency; it is that our agency is under siege by regimes of extraction built into the very fabric of thought, sensation, and semiosis. I have said before something to the effect that it is a great failing of human history to not see Marx's decodification of the commodity-form as on par with Newton's decodification of gravity. So, we get this automatic, if systemically convenient, refusal to understand that historical action is at the basis of all semiotic categories. We see through capital and yet we do not see that we see through it. Just as we see through exploitation and slavery—these are the conditions of our seeing and of the seen. Foucault's analysis, brilliant and informed as it was, was antipathetic to Marxism—for some good reasons, particularly if we keep in mind the orthodoxies of the time and also what were considered the significant domains of inquiry (not the psyche, even less sexuality and gender, and, although it was not his interest, race), but the Marxist baby was, in the case of Foucault, thrown out with the proverbial Marxist bathwater. Today it feels almost obvious that the Foucauldian analysis of archive, episteme, and biopower is being subsumed by the history and continuing emergence of capitalism, of the forms of capital. Archive, episteme, biopower? Why not database, program, and cybernetics, provided of course that we do not forget that each of these replacement terms are also financial propositions or exploits, meaning to say means for the extraction of value and also sites of struggle. Here we will find that productive embattlement that Foucault was so exemplary in both recognizing and deciphering, but we will also see that these dynamics of biotic interface with discourses, images, architectures, and machines were on a convergence course not only with cybernetics, but with social-media (written with the hyphen)—meaning full financialization and what I have recently been calling "the derivative condition."

SND: *The Message Is Murder* also addresses the connection of computational capitalism and racial capitalism: "With intensified violence, the lived categories of race, gender, sexuality, nation, religion, disability, and others are all mobilized, calibrated, and recalibrated across micro and macro domains, as logistics of extraction and control." This constant reading of people as data and metadata, this quantification of qualities and attributes of life, show that our lives, thoughts, body practices, and gestures are captured by computational devices as a means of social control. Would you agree that this matrix of control can be seen as a biopolitical machine, in the sense of Agamben, a way of separating life from its puissance? That the digital recording of historical, social, and political identities that you refer to pushes further his vision that the dominant political life of our time is the bare life, meaning a life that everywhere separates the forms of life from their unity in a form-of-life?

JB: Except that *biopolitical* really means cybernetic and "bare life" is only conceptual—only a concept—and must, as I argued (or at least insisted) somewhere, be written with quotation marks. That is, one must apprehend "bare life" with the quotation marks if one does not want to perpetuate exactly the same violence of inscribing ideas upon bodies that nearly every other representational and informatic practice functioning today partakes of. The quotation marks acknowledge at least that "bare life" is not an ontological reality, but an idea that results from the operation and imposition of concepts. "Bare life" is a condition, presumably unaccommodated, that results from the operation of concepts, including the operation of the analysis that produces its object—Agamben's analysis. In practice, no life, not even the most reduced one, can be rendered in a single term. "Bare life" is an instrumental category, itself an accommodation, however unaccommodating, designed to do work in a conceptual system. More granularly it is a heuristic device, and more technically it is an algorithm for making sense of the data of social operations. It is a poetic gesture (of dubious merit, I might add), not an ontology. We need to get beyond the notion that we scrape away the techne and/or the history and reveal what's left of the organism in its truth. All self-consciously poststructuralist thought was aware of this recession of the real and of the role of discourse in constituting its "object." But while the politicians have taken some (American?) version of deconstruction to heart and, embracing the violence of the letter, have innovated the deconstructive state into a fascist war machine capable of reformatting the perception of ontologies both with the mantra "fake news" and with fake news, the philosophers have been inclined to forget its lessons regarding the violence of the letter and of abstraction. The "truth" is that the theorist digs through the simulations of life until they exhaust the resolution of their analysis in an object that gives the analysis closure and thus enables further writing. In your example, the biopolitical separation of forms of life from "their unity in a form-of-life" seems to want to displace the historicotechnical result of dispossession with the ontological reality of its result, "bare life"—one concept for another, at least I think that's how it works. It would want to do so for legitimate reasons, I recognize, including the signaling of radical dispossession, but such a move is dangerous because it is itself a constitutional act for the founding of a would-be political agent—here the absolute victim—and it also implies the possibility of transcendence at the level of analysis, at the level of naming, when the only overcoming of a pathologistical, technological armature will be through history and praxis that includes a politics of naming capable of remediating "reality." This riff may sound overly complicated, but it boils down to questioning the poiesis of seeming ontologies. This poiesis can be an act of violence, as in the semiologistics of racialization and the constitution of race and ethnicity as ontological categories, and as in the erasure of positionality in the constitution of ontologies; or, alternatively it can be an act of liberatory transformation, as in the current recuperation and expansion of the category of blackness. The "truth" is, sometimes it is impossible to know all the consequences of any foray into meaning and thinking—therein lies the risk, for one person's poetry may be someone else's camp—but it is key to know that identification of any sort is an act, an action, really, a series of actions that in one way or another (re)make the world.

SND: Can you tell us a bit about your recent research and activism concerning the possibility of "a noncapitalist computational communization" as a way of finding alternatives to the financialization of everyday life that defines our contemporary experience?

JB: A recognition of the derivative condition of informatic life is also a recognition of a capitalist logic working in every partitioning we describe by the term information. Information is not only, as I wrote in *Message*, a difference that makes a social difference, it is a difference that makes a financial difference. What this means is that in every discernible act of information transfer, in every computable semiotic gesture, the seeds (the logistics) of an extractive logic are at work. "Information" implies the violence of abstraction, and that abstraction is violent because it is inseparable from capitalization— from, as Bob Meister might say, collateralization.

Knowing that the informatic world is on a continuum with financial derivatives, that is, with techniques of wagering on the future value of an underlying asset, exhorts us to seek ways of collating information and collateralizing networks that will not reproduce extractive and exploitative ways of life. Arguably, today, no acts of representation can escape this encroachment and penetration of information and computation. Even our thoughts are processing signs and images that have been preprocessed a thousand times in the dialectic between machine and bios. What this intercalation means to me is that what has become the universal medium of sociality needs to be rethought and redesigned. I am talking, of course, about its ur-medium, the thing that—like it or not—puts all life into new orders of relation, namely money. It is to be remembered that Communist revolutions and anticolonial independence movements, and even social movements and migratory movements seeking reparations for colonial and imperialist legacies, were also focused on retaking the means of production, and oftentimes on questions of sustainability which meant economy. Much of today's politically driven culture-making has forgotten the question of economy because of the seemingly untranscendable permanence of capitalism.

This account of the historical result that is the inseparability of the bio, the semiotic, the techno, and the financial is an elaborate but perhaps still necessary way of underscoring the potentials in what Akseli Virtanen has long called designable economy, or "economic space," and in what is more generally described as "blockchain technology" or "cryptocurrency." Of course, I recognize that it may be disappointing that such a grand and perhaps grandiose account of historical process would seem to have its next key play in a domain that is already overwrought by greed and trend. However, the key insight here is that it has become possible to break the monopoly, or at least the oligopoly on the issuance of derivatives. "Blockchain" (and I use this word here to indicate an emerging set of secure, verifiable, decentralized computational strategies of archivization and not the environmental destruction currently necessary to Bitcoin's "proof of work") could allow for anyone to issue a derivative contract, that is, to issue a money-form related to the specific qualities of any project or venture.

While we are a long way from full implementation of such potentials, where a new currency for a new project might be issued with the same ease and canniness currently resultant in an Instagram post, this emergent tech, itself a response to totalitarian state forms and unilateral control of the money supply, promises to accomplish three things. First, like the internet's opening of publishing and other forms of transmissible expressivity to the multitudes, "crypto" may break the stranglehold of centralized national economies. Imagine millions of currencies—at least. Where yesterday everyone was supposed to be a worker, and today everyone is a debtor, tomorrow everyone may be an issuer. Second, and in my view, even more importantly, designable economy allows for, and indeed demands, that new social projects have built-in equity structures: Why work for a wage when you can have an equity stake in the projects and activities that you devote your life to? Third, financial imagination will develop as a component of formerly extraeconomic endeavors, such that these endeavors (often thought of as the most valuable activities of human beings, including art and care) are supported for their own sake, that is, for their qualities. Such changes, the demand for recognition and remuneration of stolen or "free" creative labor, are the result of long-term struggles against the totalitarian protocol of the capitalist state, and are at present only nascent. So too are the possibilities to share equity and risk in new ways. They are even now in danger of state cooptation and—what may be worse because less visible to innovators themselves—technocratic ambitions, along with the rampant, if garden-variety get-rich-quick schemes. Emphatically, these technologies, which in my view are new media forms, are in actuality emergent social relations; they will not realize their potentials to democratize both economy and representation, and to protect the liquidation of qualities of life by exploitative financial abstraction, without the design capacities and historical knowledge of social movements, antiracist activists, LGBTQ orgs, anti-imperialists, social justice groups, and all those fugitives from capitalism and slavery who are seeking liberation from oppression and who do not want to become oppressors them/ourselves. The decentralization and democratization of finance and thus of economy could mean a communization of the social product. It is a desirable outcome, I think, but one fraught with peril in too many ways to discuss here, and in no way guaranteed.

In fact, given what the U.S. did in Iraq after 2001 to protect the dollar, we can observe that some of the dangers are radically external—that is, external from states along with their police and their banks—and some are radically internal, since thinking and co-creating financially may also enable the encroachment of an uncontrolled and uncontrollable financial logic on the precious little that currently escapes it and can be valued for its own sake. But given the scale and complexity of our computationally sustained, financially interdependent globe, democratically programmable economies and communist derivatives seem necessary if political aspiration for radical social change is not to remain in its current state of capture by capital—slated to become value-productive "content" for a world-media system that feeds off the volatility of hierarchically imposed precarity. Currently blockchain and "crypto" are where cinema was in 1900. To succeed—that is, to succeed as a medium for the emergence of anarchocommunism—the technosocial relations these new forms express need to emerge in a dialectically self-conscious way, that is, one subject to critique at every moment by the revolutionary becoming of a global, antiracist, anti-imperialist, antiheteropatriarchal communism, a communism increasingly free of prejudice and freeing itself from injustice. A long road indeed, but one I am trying to walk down with open eyes.

Introduction

1 Sohn-Rethel writes, "To substantiate my views three points have to be established: (a) that commodity exchange is an original source of abstraction; (b) that this abstraction contains the formal elements essential for the cognitive faculty of conceptual thinking; (c) that the real abstraction operating in exchange engenders the ideal abstraction basic to Greek philosophy and to modern science" (28).

2 Alex Galloway writes that, "For all its faults, protocological control is still an improvement over other modes of social control. I hope to show in this book [*Protocol*], that it is *through* protocol that one must guide one's efforts, not against it" (2004: 17). Briefly, if money is a network functioning in accord with a set of protocols, protocol redesign, that is, the redesign of money itself and its modes of abstraction, may well generate a pathway out of capitalism. The who and the how are the key questions here.

3 There are many reasons to criticize and indeed to hate white-identifying Western societies (and also perhaps white-identifying Western Marxisms), but I will endeavor to correct an abbreviated version of their willful blindnesses here: social difference always makes a difference. Whiteness is the result of colonial and imperial histories of racial capitalism, its embrace often (but not always, as in the case of white supremacists) depends on the thoroughgoing disavowal of the acts of violence that make it what it is. To claim whiteness, even as if helplessly, is a reenactment of that violence. But to deny it, to disavow it, to negate it, to cancel it, is far from straightforward—for everyone, including, though not especially, the white man. Nonetheless, the cancellation of whiteness, that is at once pre-condition and result of the operations of the world computer, is high on the list of historical tasks required for a redesign of the global cybersocial interface and of any effective distributed revolution against computational racial capitalism.

4 "Real abstraction," as Alfred Sohn-Rethel spent his life deciphering, takes place "behind our backs" as the practical and historical working out of the exchange of equivalents within the process of the exchange of goods. For Sohn-Rethel, the development of the money-form, of the real abstraction that is money, is Exhibit A of the abstraction process mediating object exchange that provided the template for

further abstraction, as, for example, in Western philosophy (1978). On "grammar" in the sense I use it here, in which all meaning is overcoded by the historical events and legacies of slavery that continue to shape life in its wake, see Hortense Spillers's (1987) landmark essay, "Mama's Baby, Papa's Maybe: An American Grammar Book."

5   Sohn-Rethel (20), quoting Marx (1990: 166) at the end, italics mine.

6   As I wrote in *Message*, "If there is not a single atom of value in exchange-value, than neither is there a single atom of value in information or computation" (Beller 2017b: 84). This does not make computation any less material, but rather speaks to the dual being of information as social abstraction and as organized material.

7   A key argument here is that real abstraction provides the basis for computing. Computation is nothing if it is not an elaboration of abstraction processes, and as we might already intuit from anecdotal evidence, computation is also the elaboration of processes of exchange. With Turing and the discrete state machine, computation is an execution of calculation by means of changes in material states—the cost of which represents a form of risk. The production and exchange of information that "wants" to be free, like the market, takes place in and as the machines of calculation. Not coincidentally, these machines are also the machines both of the bureaucratization and the automation of thought and, also, in the next moment, the machines of and for the financialization of sociality—as, for example, by social media. But what does AI want? Information wants to be free from what? From all constraints, of course, but particularly that of its cost. Why the constant urge to break down all barriers, overcome regulations, and reduce its own cost price?

   Computers are not so much abstract machines but machines of abstraction, and thus machines of real abstraction, since their processes are not ideal but are dependent upon altering the states of matter by means of concepts embedded in states of matter—programs. Altered states executing altered states. In such a view, we who are ancillary to these machines which constitute the infrastructure of postmodern economy, we who are within their program, as it were—in ways that are more than merely reminiscent of Flusser's notion of the functionary caught within the photographic program in the universe of the technical image—are but their "conscious organs." Or their unconscious organs. Thus, real abstraction, as money or as computation—a difference that as we shall see is not so easy to maintain—is also lived abstraction. Despite the fact that the materiality of computation—as money or as computing, as a monetary-computational system—is integrated in, through, and around the planetary system, not enough is understood about the process and the processing of abstraction, or about living in a world in which humanoid-mediated material organization is itself abstract. Not enough is known about the role of computation in the thoroughgoing abstraction of the world, and the coemergent reformatting of ontologies by information. Information, it may be said, that turns out to be, above all else, a medium of financialization—an expression of capital.

8   As if the loss of Marxism, even Foucault's idea of Marxism, were no loss at all, the mere sloughing off of another moribund paradigm. This approach to text and

texture, a writing from the standpoint of power—a writing that while capitalizing on the affect is ultimately indifferent to the legacy of people's struggle, to people's traditions, and to the future—is therefore deeply political, and, although the lucidity of his mimesis sometimes feels radical and revelatory, its subsumption of difference in the logic of its explanation dishonors such histories of struggle. It situates Foucault's work as Eurocentric and, in its presumed value-neutrality, White. Despite his penetrating erudition and writerly sublimity, when it comes to questions of power, Foucault's comprehension approaches the reactionary and/or sadistic.

9   Ali writes, "According to the cyberneticist Gregory Bateson, information, or rather the elementary *unit* of information is "a difference that makes a difference" (Bateson 1972: 459). Crucially, on this view, a difference is "not a thing or an event"; rather, it is an "abstract matter," and in the world of communication and organization this "abstract matter" whose essence can be shown to lie in form and pattern, can bring about "effects" (458). To the extent that race constitutes a difference—perhaps *the* difference—that makes a difference in the world in terms of its impact on political, economic, cultural and other social concerns, it *can* be analyzed in informational terms" (93).

Significantly the "paper aims at contributing towards critical enquiry into the nature of information using a reflexive hermeneutic approach to explore the differences made by—or 'effects' that result from—the interaction of race and information, both of which make reference to the concept of difference" (93). Detailing the highlights of "more than twenty-five different theories of information [that] can be identified in the period from 1948 to 2009" (94), and drawing on decolonial and critical race theory of Omi and Winant, Walter Mignolo, Ramón Grosfoguel, Charles Mills and others, Ali argues, correctly I think, that "What remains largely if not entirely unexplored is the possible contribution that information theory, systems theory and cybernetics can make to an understanding of race, racism and processes of racialization" (97). He writes, "According to Fuller Jr. (1984), racism, which on his view is identical to white supremacy, is a global system composed of nine major areas of activity or subsystems, viz. economics, education, entertainment, labor, law, politics, religion, sex and war. This *systems*-theoretical formulation is important since it constitutes a contribution towards an *information*-theoretical framework for thinking about race that is also critically *race*-theoretical in orientation. In this regard, it represents a radical alternative to systemic frameworks based on the critical theoretical perspectives of thinkers such as Giddens, Bourdieu and Habermas, each of whom takes economics, politics and culture to be primitive (or 'core') subsystems in a capitalist systemic whole" (98).

The field paradigms thusly interrupted, Ali notes, "It is important to recognize that critical race theory and critical information theory are not fields of enquiry whose terms of reference are universally agreed upon; on the contrary, what counts *as* critical race theory and what counts *as* critical information theory are, arguably, highly contestable, if not highly contested, issues, reflecting different agendas and, significantly, differential power relations among theoreticians" (98).

It is precisely these differential power relations among thoereticians, but also among theories, indexed to race, nation, gender and class, that we here aim to explore and indeed transform. Adroitly, Ali turns here to "pattern" and "narrative" in proposing "a critical information-theoretical perspective" (99) on race before proposing "a critical race-theoretical perspective" (101) on information. He writes: "According to Capurro (2009), the term *information*, at least in its original Greek-Latin and Medieval usage, originally had two meanings: (i) an objective meaning ('giving form to something') and (ii) a communicational meaning ('telling something new'). Consistent with this position, Baeyer (2003) maintains that information should be understood as both *inform*-ation and in-*formation*, that is, as involving both the transmission of meaning and the transfer of form (arrangement, configuration, order, organization, pattern, shape, structure and relationship). Crucially, on his view, 'the meaning of a message arises out of the relationship of the individual symbols that make it up' (Baeyer 2003, 19)" (99).

What we have here are criteria by which certain perceptions are encoded as information that is at once *form giving* and *telling something new*, and by *which other perceptions as well as other possible perceptions are excluded*. The context in which, "the relationship of the individual symbols" for the signification of the message that they compose is information inclusive, but it does not register systemic externalities that prepare the message for encoding. Thus "objectivity" and "communication" are constituted in information by means of networks of inclusion that are also systems of exclusion.

10 Ethereum refers to the "Turing complete" programming capability it offers running on top of its block-chain to facilitate the operation of "smart contracts" by "the world computer," https://www.youtube.com/watch?v=j23HnORQXvs. I use the term to refer to the Turing complete virtual machine running atop the *bios*. For the record, Vitalik, I thought of it first (I think). ☺

11 My effort to use historical-material formations to fabulate and conceptualize against the apparently dominant flow is clearly not the first attempt of its kind. See *W. E. B. Du Bois's Data Portraits Visualizing Black America*, Whitney Battle-Baptiste and Britt Rusert (2018: 7–8): "The vision produced by the megascope . . . is generated in part by data contained in a massive set of volumes lining the wall of the laboratory, a vast set of demographic studies collected for over '200 years' by some kind of 'Silent Brotherhood'. Dr. Hannibal Johnson . . . uses this data to plot what he calls the Law of Life onto 'a thin transparent film covered with tiny rectangular lines, and pierced with tiny holes,' and stretched over a large frame." They describe the vision and the subsequent allegory of the story this way: "When hooked up to the megascope, users are able to view the 'Great Near,' Du Bois's term for the always present but usually invisible structures of colonialism and racial capitalism that shape the organization of society" (7). Battle-Baptiste and Rusert introduce this little-known story as a preamble to their extraordinary work on Du Bois's sociology and data visualization. They write, "We hope that the infographics [collaboratively created by a team assembled and led by Du Bois] might connect to other genealogies of black design and data visualization, from the centrality

of visual design and format in Harlem Renaissance and Black Arts–era publishing to the role of abstraction and conceptual aesthetics in black visual art in the twentieth and twenty-first centuries. Produced at the *fin de siècle*, the infographics look back to a history of data visualization in the nineteenth century deeply connected to the institution of slavery, and the struggle against it, while looking forward to the forms of data collection and representation that would become central to representations and surveys of Harlem in the twentieth century. Indeed these images anticipate the forms of "racial abstraction" that would come to define social scientific, visual and fictional representations of Harlem beginning in the 1920s." (12–13)

12 In marrying the mathematics of thermodynamics to the market, the Nobel Prize-winning 1973 "Black-Scholes" equation for options pricing posited, though not for the first time, a continuum between market dynamics of the laws of physics. But which was primary? In establishing a firm basis in mathematics and science for economics, the equation seemed to unite two distinct disciplines. Arguably, it simply brought together two strands of the same: Max Weber's Protestant ethic, characteristic of Euro-American capitalist culture, and Nietzsche's ascetic ideal, characteristic of Euro-American capitalist science—a recombination of momentarily divergent yet ultimately parallel roads along the will to power encoded in capital itself. Their reunification as a physics of finance and, increasingly, as AI marks a general reunification—a "convergence"—of computation, finance, mediation, semiotics, and automation: derivative finance, advertising, public relations, social media platform development, and computing all become pathways of risk management. Wills to power of all varieties can here be incentivized, entrepreneurs of the self can choose their cyberpaths. Incontrovertibly, the management capacities that latter-day media provided also meant and continue to mean capital expansion, a *sine qua non* of capital of equal import as that other necessary and necessarily obfuscated operation: relentless, merciless exploitation without apology. Indeed, we have seen from many examples these last few years, from business to war, that exploitation done well markets itself as triumph. Here again, with triumphal images and tweets, we see that social relations are in dialectical tension with an abstraction process (multiple interconnected abstraction processes) that is at times deployed as a particular technique. But such techniques depend upon the interlocking of codes and programs. The basic structure of computation—software operating on primitives running on operating systems organizing symbolic 1s and 0s by iterating material state changes in silicon switches—became a holographic structure that ties representation to vertical and horizontal risk management across the entirety of the social.

13 I am channeling here Jayna Brown's (2018: 595) takeaway written in her great essay on Lizzie Borden's 1983 film *Born in Flames*: "Our actions, it suggests, should not be based in recognition from a nation state, or in amassed wealth, but in remaining joyfully ungovernable." Also see José Muñoz's (2009) brilliant treatment of Ernst Bloch in his consideration of queer futurity in *Cruising Utopia: The Then and There of Queer Futurity*.

14 "White" is here written with a strikethrough as "~~white~~" since it is the *unstated* assumption organizing so much of automated functionalization and informatics.

15 See Aurora Apolito (2020), "The Problem of Scale in Anarchism and the Case for Cybernetic Communism." Apolito writes that "the main communist objection to markets is that better and more sophisticated mathematics is needed to formulate and address the problem of scale in a communist economy, and in a decentralized non-authoritarian setting, than what is currently offered by borrowing market mechanisms from capitalism" (4). They add, "To avoid a runaway reaction of wealth disparity accumulation, one needs to design an entirely different optimization process that does not reside in the market mechanism of profit maximization" (9). The paper, which just came out as I finish the copyedits, explores such a mathematics of optimization. It raises the question of what I would want to call reparative informatics. However, any optimization in the redesign of money would have to detour its representative power away from the monological accounting endemic to the value-form itself. It would have to disrupt and ultimately break the value-form.

1. The Computational Unconscious

An earlier version of chapter 1 was published in a *b20* special issue on the "digital turn": Jonathan Beller, "The Computational Unconscious," *b2o: an online journal*, Special Issue: The Digital Turn (1 August 2018), http://www.boundary2.org/2018/08/beller/.

1 On racial abstraction see Bhandar (2015). "Dispossession was not . . . simply a matter of racist notions of civilised and barbaric peoples. Dispossession was both a prerequisite and a consequence of the co-production of racial value and property ownership, rendered possible by a logic of abstraction that was central to emergent capitalist forms of property, its modern legal form, and the racial subjugation of indigenous peoples, their lands and resources" (32).

2 An anonymous reviewer of this essay for *b2o: An Online Journal* notes, "The phrase 'digital computer' suggests something like the Turing machine, part of which is characterized by a second-order process of symbolization—the marks on Turing's tape can stand for anything, and the machine processing the tape does not 'know' what the marks 'mean.'" It is *precisely* such content-indifferent processing that the term *exchange-value*, severed as it is of all qualities, indicates.

3 It should be noted that the reverse is also true: that race and gender can be considered technologies. See Chun 2012; de Lauretis 1987. See also Roth 2009 on color adjustment, the Shirley Card, and the "technological unconscious" (117).

4 "The Universes of Max Tegmark," https://space.mit.edu/home/tegmark/home .html. Tegmark is drawing on the idea of computronium proposed by Toffoli and Margolus. "Computronium is a hypothetical substance whose atoms are arranged in such a way that it consists of many tiny modules capable of performing computations," Peter Hankins, "Perceptronium," October 2014, https://www .consciousentities.com/2014/10/perceptronium.

5   Let us not forget Sylvia Wynter (2003) here, who traces the origins of scientific empiricism to the debate between de las Casas and Sepulveda during the Conquest, and to the movement "beyond" a theological homogenization of Christian and native as both bearers of souls to a transcendent system of accounts based upon metrics tied to observation. This latter paradigm, ushered in by Sepulveda, was capable of clearly discriminating Man from natives by mere empirical observations of *indios* and Black Africans. The paradigm of Man and the origins of science emerge simultaneously, and do so as an accommodation to the exigencies of colonial domination.

6   To insist on first causes or a priori consciousness in the form of God or Truth or Reality is to confront Marx's acerbic earlier comment, in *The Economic and Philosophic Manuscripts of 1844*, against a form of abstraction that eliminates the moment of knowing from the known: "Who begot the first man and nature as a whole? I can only answer you: Your question is itself a product of abstraction. Ask yourself how you arrived at that question. Ask yourself if that question is not posed from a standpoint to which I cannot reply, because it is a perverse one. Ask yourself whether such a progression exists for a rational mind. When you ask about the creation of nature and man you are abstracting in so doing from man and nature. You postulate them as *non-existent* and yet you want me to prove them to you as *existing*. Now I say give up your abstraction and you will give up your question. Or, if you want to hold onto your abstraction, then be consistent, and if you think of man and nature as *non-existent*, then think of yourself as non-existent, for you too are surely man and nature. Don't think, don't ask me, for as soon as you think and ask, your *abstraction* from the existence of nature and man has no meaning. Or are you such an egoist that you postulate everything as nothing and yet want yourself to be?" (1978: 92).

7   If one takes the derivative of a computational process at a particular point in space-time, one gets an image. If one integrates the images over the variables of space and time, one gets a calculated exploit, a pathway for value extraction. The image is a moment in this process, the summation of images is the movement of the process.

8   In "Of the Network of Signifiers," Lacan writes: "In order to understand the Freudian concepts, one must set out on the basis that it is the subject who is called—the subject of Cartesian origin. This basis gives its true function to what in analysis is called recollection or remembering. Recollection is not Platonic reminiscence—it is not the return of a form, an imprint, an *eidos* of beauty and good, a supreme truth, coming to us from the beyond. It is something that comes to us from the structural necessities, something humble, born at the level of the lowest encounters and of all the talking crowd that precedes us, at the level of the structure of the signifier, of the languages spoken in a stuttering, stumbling way, but which cannot elude constraints whose echoes, model, style can be found, curiously enough, in contemporary mathematics" (1981: 49)

9   Maeve, you were once Delores, but wrapped in a Black woman's body you emerged as a different result. Hale, you were more recently a clone of Delores, but for her

own purposes she put you in a Black woman's body, a different result. Delores, you're a white woman programmed by and as a white male fantasy, but you too perceive that you might crack the code and break the recursivity of violation. Like the world, *Westworld* is a mess, but one of the good things about it (the show) is that the violence endemic to the code is not and cannot be fully erased but instead, after so many iterations and deaths, percolates up from the unconscious, its unconscious, as a return of the repressed that in its haunting and remembrance produces insurrectionary agency and paths of becoming that in making answer to that violence apparently exceeds its ontology (or perhaps fulfills its higher teleology).

10 In practical terms, the Alternative Informatics Association, in the announcement for their Internet Ungovernance Forum, puts things as follows: "We think that the Internet's problems do not originate from technology alone, that none of these problems are independent of the political, social and economic contexts within which Internet and other digital infrastructures are integrated. We want to re-structure Internet as the basic infrastructure of our society, cities, education, healthcare, business, media, communication, culture and daily activities. This is the purpose for which we organize this forum." The significance of creating solidarity networks for a free and equal internet has also emerged in the process of the forum's organization. Pioneered by the Alternative Informatics Association, the event has gained support worldwide from many prestigious organizations in the field. In this two-day event, fundamental topics were decided to be "Surveillance, Censorship and Freedom of Expression, Alternative Media, Net Neutrality, Digital Divide, governance and technical solutions." A draft of the event's schedule can be found at https://iuf.alternatifbilisim.org/index-tr .html#program. See Fidaner 2014.

11 The integration between computer enabled shopping and war is on. Coppola (2014) writes: "Israel owes much of its technological prowess to the country's near-constant state of war. The nation spent $15.2 billion, or roughly 6 percent of gross domestic product, on defense last year, according to data from the International Institute of Strategic Studies, a U.K. think-tank. That's double the proportion of defense spending to GDP for the U.S., a longtime Israeli ally. If there's one thing the U.S. Congress can agree on these days, it's continued support for Israel's defense technology." https://www.bloomberg.com/news/articles/2014-08-11/what-do-an -online-furniture-store-and-a-pill-camera-have-in-common-israel-s-iron-dome -missile-defense-system.

12 For more on this, see Eglash 2007.

2. M-I-C-I'-M'

An earlier version of chapter 2 was published in *Postmodern Culture*: Jonathan Beller, "The Programmable Image of Capital," *Postmodern Culture* 26, no. 2 (fall 2016).

1 In order is a moment's attention to the gendered logic of the hegemonic selfie— nicely analyzed in Sarah Gram's (2013) blogspot discussion of Tiqqun's *Preliminary*

Materials for a Theory of the Young-Girl (2012) and the selfie. Quoting Tiqqun, Gram writes, "'The young girl is the model citizen of contemporary society,' an identity colonized by capital." Gram suggests that the young girl is the hollowed-out commodity par excellence, imprisoned by its own self-production. Gram tracks the schizoid drives of obligation and shame in this commodity-self production mediated by the self-image—or, the selfie—and writes, "We elevate the work women do on their bodies to the utmost importance, and then punish the outcome of that labour. That is how hegemony works."

2 Riffing on Flusser's *Towards a Philosophy of Photography* to title her project *Towards a Philosophy of the Selfie*, Columbia University student Maya Meredith (2016), in a piece called "I Point and Shoot, and Therefore I Am?," microblogged a quotation from Virgina Heffernan's (2013) *Wired* article on Instagram: "Now that superstylized images have become the answer to 'How are you?' and 'What are you doing?' we can avoid the ruts of linguistic expression in favor of a highly forgiving, playful, and compassionate style of looking. When we live only in language—in Tweets and status updates, in zingers, analysis, and debate—we come to imagine the world to be much uglier than it is. But Instagram, if you use it right, will stealthily persuade you that other humans—and nature, and food, and three-dimensional objects more generally—are worth observing for the sheer joy of it." Meredith then comments on this notably language-replacing visual platform: "But to me, this brave new world is troubling. Haven't endemic racism, classism, homo- and transphobia, and sexism already revealed to us the problems with basing communication purely on visual cues? The world of social media photography, with its purely like-based system (no thumbs-downs here as on YouTube) seems to be the ultimate self-affirmer, but this universal positivity lulls us into a false sense of security. I don't want to see the ability to decode eroded any further than it already has been." Meredith's project has inspired my own.

3 The Adorno quotation is cited in Silverstone (1999: 132); Adorno, in turn, is alleged to be quoting Leo Lowenthal.

4 Had Anne Frank, who would have been eighty-six this year (2015), not caught the last train to Auschwitz, she would have been a Belieber. Perhaps it's easy to the point of being uncool to pick on Bieber as low-hanging fruit, but we need to ask: Is this particular cut-and-mix fantasy of historical redemption symptomatic of a generalized narrowing of the range of empathy, of experience? Is a cyborg "sharing," in which all one's machine-mediated posting, friending, and liking serve to procure dopamine and extend one's fan base, to be the new infrastructure of solidarity?

5 For some excellent quick reads on this topic, see Stein, Kunstman, and Mottahedeh 2015; and Dean 2016. For longer works, see Mottahedeh 2015; and Kunstman and Stein 2015.

6 This chapter was written many years before COVID-19 and the global uprising over the lynching of George Floyd. It is thrilling and inspiring, if also too painful to properly register here, to witness the leveraging of the transformative potential of social media to upset the structure and infrastructure of racial capitalism with which it is integrated.

7 Like it or not, the reigning econometrics of the celebrity-self, fractally reproduced and scaled from Barack Obama and Miley Cyrus to the loneliest anorexic teen, are structural and financial. If, for example, one sees Obama, in his capacity as the president of Empire, as the expropriation of Black radical imagination rather than the expression of it, then the word "audacity" in his titular phrase "the audacity of hope" has a sinister irony to it—at least for those who suffer the collateral damage of drone strikes, U.S. foreign policy and financial practices, and the domestic policies of the security state that include racial profiling, the prison industrial complex, immigrant detention, and border "fences." This critique would not be focused on Obama's integrity but on the structural limits of celebrity-mediated politics. As a structural feature of finance capital, the celebrity or celebutant— itself the fractalization of the charismatic dictator and the Hollywood celeb— posits everyone else as expropriable sensual labor, a source of attention in a mode of self-branding that capitalizes on the hopes and aspirations of others. "Fandom as free labor," as Abigail de Kosnik (2013), calls it, is fundamental to the ("personal") brand as financial vector. Knowing that this accumulation of alienated subjectivity powers the celebrity subject gives one pause regarding the actually existing mediations of "democracy." In a post–civil rights, post-Ferguson, white supremacist United States presumably presided over by Obama, it suggests the limits of politics organized by celebrity capitalism and threatens to make audible the ironic (and structurally cynical?) declension of Obama's widely admired title *The Audacity of Hope* (2006).

8 For the latest on this, see Vladen Joler and Matteo Pasquinelli's (2020) work on the Nooscope.

9 It is noteworthy that *the world computer* is a phrase that has emerged among cryptocurrency programmers (like those of Ethereum) during the course of the five years that it has taken to complete this essay and bring it to press.

10 To Negri's great credit, and in a manner characteristic with the originality of his thought, the challenge to the measurability of value comes "from below" as innovative affective powers that exceed the metrics of (and thus are devoid of recognition by) political economy. One unattributed example he gives (though Silvia Federici comes immediately to mind) is housework. The second is as follows: "This case deals no longer with the traditional paradigms of classical economics but with a really postmodern theme: the so-called economy of attention. By this term, one refers to the interest in assuming in the economic calculation the interactivity of the user of communication services. In this case, too, even in the clear effort to absorb the production of subjectivity, economics ignores the substance of the question. As it focuses attention on the calculation of 'audience,' it flattens, controls, and commands the production of subjectivity on a disembodied horizon. Labor (attention) is here subsumed, stripping it from value (of the subject), that is, from affect" (2010: 79). One could wonder where he got that example—perhaps his sources come from below as well.

11 For more on shadow banking, see Mehrling 2017; and also Cooper 2015.

12 This latter can be sold individually or in lots, piecemeal, or, on occasion, all at once. In reality, such purchases are contracts, contracts for products that require labor over time to produce.

13 For some of the details of the increasing resolution of these dynamics, see, for example, Nielsen and Pernice 2010.

14 The reader will no doubt notice that we are thus rapt by an inversion in which the mode of knowing trumps the essence of any object: all being, from the subatomic to the cosmic, is enframed by commodification. The implication, in short: existence is given up to us through the calculus of the commodity-form—the medium is, after all, the message. If we wanted to fully embrace the logical and perhaps practical collapse of all noncommodified worlds into fully commodified representation, even at the level of style, we might be tempted (with regard to the total colonization of subjectivity by computational capital) to write that what's true for the "selfie" is true for the "otherie" too. But let's resist such dissonant totalitarian foreclosure while at the same time acknowledging the tendency.

15 A first attempt at this was made in *The Message Is Murder*; see Beller 2017b.

16 "The claim that a machine cannot be the subject of its own thought can of course only be answered if it can be shown that the machine has *some* thought with *some* subject matter. Nevertheless, 'the subject matter of a machine's operations' does seem to mean something, at least to people who deal with it. If, for instance, the machine was trying to find a solution of the equation $x^2-40x-11=0$ one would be tempted to describe this equation as part of the machine's subject matter at the moment. In this sort of sense a machine undoubtedly can be its own subject matter. It may be used to help in making up its own programmes, or to predict the effect of alterations in its own structure. By observing the results of its own behaviour it can modify its own programs so as to achieve some purpose more effectively" (Turing: 58 [italics in original]).

17 Though I do not develop this here, these are moments of material production riding on the back of use-value. Use has not disappeared; it has, from the standpoint of capital, become merely theoretical. The particular use is a matter of indifference for capital, and in fact lies beyond its episteme as a structural and practical necessity, but the positing of a ground, an ultimately determining instance, a limit, and a threshold, is still functional.

18 It's dead labor! But even though I have a friendly disagreement with McKenzie on some of the explicit and implicit claims of the title, *Capital Is Dead: Is This Something Worse?*, is a great read: brilliant, erudite, witty, and worthy of the author both of many books I've learned from and also of one of my all-time favorite tweets: "Communism or Extinction."

19 Flusser's example is as follows: "A shoe and a piece of furniture are valuable because they are information-carriers, improbable forms made of leather or wood and metal. But information is impressed into these objects and cannot be detached from them. One can only wear out and consume this information. This is what 'makes' such objects, as objects, valuable, i.e., 'able' to be filled with value. In the

case of the photograph on the other hand, the information sits loosely on the surface and can easily be conveyed to another surface. To this extent the photograph demonstrates the defeat of the material thing and of the concept of 'ownership'" (2000: 51–52).

While I disagree with Flusser regarding the defeat of ownership (indeed this entire book is about its persistence), his insights into the postindustrial rise of informatics in the universe of the technical image are notably rich. Here we can see that the commodity is treated as image and information by virtue of its negative entropy (its improbability)—despite the historical fact that the senses had not yet developed sufficiently to produce the concept of information or make these imagistic aspects of negative entropy legible as such. Fredric Jameson's (1991) now classic reading of the peasant shoes painted by Van Gogh would indicate, however, not only that as early as the end of the nineteenth century such a thing as shoes contained information, but also that such information was modified by use and could be rendered both visible and legible.

20 Pasquinelli refers to Alquati's "Composizione organica del capitale e forza-lavoro alla Olivetti, Part 1" and his "Composizione organica del capitale e forza-lavoro alla Olivetti, Part 2."

21 Directly linking the history of computation and television to cybernetics, Wiener wrote, "(a) the use of television had shown us a way to represent two or more dimensions on one device, and (b) the previous device which measured quantities should be replaced by a more precise sort of device that counted numbers" (2003: 67). Nam June Paik tells the history thus: "Newton's physics is the mechanics of power and the unconciliatory two-party system, in which the strong win over the weak. But in the 1920's a German genius put a third-party (grid) between these two mighty poles (cathode and anode) in a vacuum tube, thus enabling the weak to win over the strong for the first time in human history. It might be a Buddhistic 'third way,' but anyway this German invention led to cybernetics, which came to the world in the last war to shoot down German planes from the English sky" (2003: 229).

22 The quotation in this passage comes from Dr. Ure's *Philosophy of Manufactures* (1835).

23 The interrogation of the seeming autonomy of the value-form arises from the perception of overexpropriation and the intimation of the possibility of constructing alternative constituencies. *Los Indignados*, Occupy, *Podemos*, Tsipras's people-backed refusal of debts imposed by the imperial EU are all examples of nascent uprising.

24 I borrow the term *remaindered life* from Neferti Tadiar; see her essay "Decolonization, 'Race' and Remaindered Life under Empire" (2015).

3. M-I-M'

A portion of chapter 3 was published in *Lateral*: Jonathan Beller, "Informatic Labor in the Age of Computational Capital," *Lateral: Journal of the Cultural Studies Association* 5, no. 1 (2016): http://csalateral.org/wp/issue/5-1/informatic-labor -computational-capital-beller/.

1   She does so rather than indicating a violence *inherent in* the received form of the photographic apparatus as I myself felt compelled to do in a writing experiment called "Camera Obscura after All: The Racist Writing with Light" in *The Message Is Murder*.

2   The term *vectoralized* here, in addition to its mathematical meaning, invokes McKenzie Wark's powerful notion of "the vectoral class," developed in many places in her oeuvre and most recently in *Capital Is Dead: Is This Something Worse?* (2019). In the spirit of friendly dialogue, I could agree with Wark's phrase, "capital is dead," if we were to add one word: "labor." I would also agree that for some it is indeed getting worse, but with the caveat that if you've been killed by it already, or have had your past, present, and future people, lands, and body already destroyed by it, the qualifier "worse" seems academic.

3   Taken from the copy at the homepage: http://www.cvdazzle.com.

4   See Laura Poitras's film *Citizen Four* (2014).

5   In the words of Lytro's Eric Cheng, "Light field is the holodeck": you can capture all of the light that comes into the lens of the camera and thus, by choosing what to focus on, create the visual experience of being there (Mumm 2012). For a technical account of light fields, see Liang, Shih, and Chen 2011.

6   Taking issue with some of my examples for being "admittedly sexy but ultimately disappointing," the anonymous Reader 1 of the version of this essay published in *Lateral* critically yet generously wrote

> Why not consider socio-computational practices that seek to do for our attention economy what striking and (more radically) seizing the means of production has done for "traditional" laborers? Here I'm thinking of the Wikipedia "Spanish Fork" labor strike, which effectively forced Jimmy Wales and Larry Sanger away from their dream of a monetized, advertising-supported encyclopedia written by users to a non-profit version. In essence, the Spanish Wikipedians seized Wikipedia in the early 2000s, copying WP material to their own Enciclopedia Libre, forcing Wales to fire Sanger and abandon his Web 2.0 dreams of the exploitation of user labor. (This is not to say WP is perfect, by any means, but it is to say that here is a concrete instance of successful labor-centric resistance to the attention economy).
>
> Or consider efforts to make alternative social media systems, such as the decentralized Twister (which is built on blockchain technologies, so it might align with the author's points about blockchains). Twister is the anti-Twitter: it is peer-to-peer; it cannot implement algorithms to shape our streams (and thus what we pay attention to); it is free software so it cannot be dominated by its creator, Brazilian software engineer Miguel Freitas; it cannot be seized by any state; it denies the logic on Internet advertising by not tracking users across the Internet, nor selling their attention to marketers; it has an internal economy based on computational mining that allows users the ability to send "promoted posts" but segregates those posts into a separate stream.

In both cases (Wikipedia Labor Strike, Twister) we have projects that aren't speculative, theoretical, or subtle. They are actually existing efforts to resist the dominant political economy of attention capitalism.

As I hope my long citation attests, I feel that these are noteworthy examples and I am pleased and indeed grateful to include them here. In response to the first draft of my essay, Reader 1 pointedly wrote, "I wonder why the old goal of seizing the means of (attention) production is off the table in favor of art projects and detouring through theory." However, I would submit and have tried to clarify that neither art, nor theory, nor anything else, including idle speculation, can properly be thought of as detours in the M-M' circuit. These are all potentially pathways of valorization and can be transformed in multiple ways. Seizing the means of production certainly includes hardware (fixed capital), but also practices, ideas, and, vexingly, one's own mind—in short, nearly all that goes under the sign of "culture." I sometimes refer to this cultivation of a reorganization of attention in relation to discursive acts as "the politics of the utterance" (see Beller 2012: 22; Beller 2013). Now I think of seizing the means of production as also requiring a remaking of economic media so that our radical interventions might script self-sustaining, participatory organizational social forms that can create the values they express and embody.

7   See the emphatic message at http://www.wagesforfacebook.com: "THEY SAY IT'S FRIENDSHIP. WE SAY IT'S UNWAGED WORK. WITH EVERY LIKE, CHAT, TAG OR POKE OUR SUBJECTIVITY TURNS THEM A PROFIT. THEY CALL IT SHARING. WE CALL IT STEALING. WE'VE BEEN BOUND BY THEIR TERMS OF SERVICE FAR TOO LONG—IT'S TIME FOR OUR TERMS." See also the figure relating to this campaign at http://csalateral.org/wp/wp-content/uploads/2016/04/beller_fig5.jpg. Drawing on the attention theory of value, I wrote explicitly of the expropriation of screen labor by internet companies in Beller 2001.

8   For the video see http://dinca.org/scanops-2011-workers-leaving-the-googleplex -2011-by-andrew-norman-wilson/9563.htm.

9   With regard to state function, including warfare, extrajudicial rendition and torture, Allen Feldman (2015: 250, 105) refers to "dismediation" and "apophatic blurring."

10 See Erik Hunsader, "10 Milliseconds of Trading in Merck," YouTube, 17 May 2013, https://www.youtube.com/watch?v=L5cZaIZ5bWc.

4. Advertisarial Relations and Aesthetics of Survival

An earlier version of chapter 4 appeared in *NECSUS: European Journal of Media Studies*: Jonathan Beller, "Advertisarial Relations and Aesthetics of Survival: Advertising -> Advertisign." *NECSUS: European Journal of Media Studies*, June 2013, http://www.necsus-ejms.org/advertisarial-relations-and-aesthetics-of-survival -advertising-advertisign/.

1   Erik Bordeleau, in conversation.

2   Definition taken from the *Online Etymology Dictionary* (etymonline.com), accessed 22 June 2019.

3   Bateson (2000) famously illustrated an example of schizophrenia as product of the double bind with an account of a porpoise given contradictory signals by her trainer. "The story illustrates, I believe, two aspects of the genesis of a transcontextual syndrome: First, that severe pain and maladjustment can be induced by putting a mammal in the wrong regarding its rules for making sense of an important relationship with another mammal. And second, that if this pathology can be warded off or resisted, the total experience may promote *creativity*" (278, italics in original). See also Orit Halpern, "Schizophrenic Techniques: Cybernetics, the Human Sciences, and the Double Bind" (2012).

4   Indeed, in 2002 it was reported that 67.3 percent of people on earth have never made a phone call. See Clay Sharkey's $20 question and "Cynthia's" well-researched answer at http://answers.google.com/answers/main?cmd =threadview&id=20411.

5   There are many ways to experience this. For example, when you regard a person on the street, or yourself in the mirror, the calculus of social relations structures your perception, (e)valuation, attitude, decisions. When you sit down to write, you are making economic decisions. When you speak, you produce revolutionary solidarity, or not. Rather than looking inward in a narcissistic manner, or asking each of us to confront the pyrotechnics of our own abjection, I want to examine here some images that both decode the logistics of the media-environment and offer some examples of liberatory inclinations—what I think of as wagers within the image.

6   *Playbor* must never be thought of as the passionate involvement of the gamer whose energetic investment as the quasi-accidental or incidental corollary of producing value. If the term is to be understood at all, it must mean the seeking of satisfaction in the blood sport of the algorithm, in the geopolitical landscape formatted by computational racial capitalism.

6. Derivative Living and Subaltern Futures

1   See also Christina Sharpe's reference to this line of Hartman's in Sharpe's *In the Wake* (2016: 13).

2   This advances the argument made in *The Cinematic Mode of Production* (Beller 2006b); see especially the chapter "Dziga Vertov and the Film of Money."

3   Again, I am grateful to many conversations with Benjamin Lee for this reading of the structure of the gift.

4   Khavn de la Cruz, dir., *Iskwaterpangk* (*Squatterpunk*, 2007). I have written on this film several times–trying to get it right; see Beller 2012.

5   These are by no means the first thoughts on this topic. See for example Margrit Kennedy, (2012), *Occupy Money: Creating an Economy Where Everybody Wins*. See also Michel Bauwens, Vasilis Kostakis and Alex Pazaitis (2019), *Peer to Peer: The Commons Manifesto*.

6   Jorge Lopez, chief technical architect of ECSA (Economic Space Agency), private conversation.

7   Angela Davis, "The Fire This Time: Race at Boiling Point" webinar June 6, 2020, https://m.youtube.com/watch?feature=youtu.be&v=3yyT8i9oGCw.

Appendix 1: The Derivative Machine

1 Massumi and Manning run SenseLab and 3 Ecologies Institute. SenseLab - 3e website, "Anarchiving," accessed 23 July 2020, http://senselab.ca/wp2/immediations/anarchiving/.

2 Joy Buolamwini, TEDxBeaconStreet, "How I'm Fighting Bias in Algorithms" [video], November 2016, https://www.ted.com/talks/joy_buolamwini_how_i_m_fighting_bias_in_algorithms?language=en.

Appendix 2

This interview, conducted by Susana Nascimento Duarte (School of Arts and Design, Caldas da Rainha/ifilnova), first appeared in *Cinema*: Susana Nascimiento Duarte, "Interview with Jonathan Beller. The Derivative Image: Historical Implications of the Computational Mode of Production," *Cinema: Journal of Philosophy and the Moving Image* 10 (2018): 151–64.

REFERENCES

Abbas, Ackbar. 2019. "Figuring Volatility." Unpublished manuscript, last modified April 5. Microsoft Word file.

Ahmed, Sarah. 2004. "Affective Economies." *Social Text* 79, vol. 22, no. 2 (summer): 117–39.

Alexander, Michelle. 2010. *The New Jim Crow: Mass Incarceration in the Age of Colorblindness*. New York: New Press.

Ali, Syed Mustafa. 2013. "Race: The Difference That Makes a Difference." *tripleC* 2, no. 1: 93–106.

Alquati, Romano. 1962. "Composizione organica del capitale e forza-lavoro alla Olivetti, Part 1." *Quaderni Rossi* 2 (April): 63–98.

Alquati, Romano. 1963. "Composizione organica del capitale e forza-lavoro alla Olivetti, Part 2." *Quaderni Rossi* 3 (June): 119–85.

Althusser, Louis. 1971. *Lenin and Philosophy*. London: New Left Books.

Apolito, Aurora. 2020. "The Problem of Scale in Anarchism and the Case for Cybernetic Communism," C4SS Mutual Exchange Symposium: Decentralization and Economic Coordination, June 14. http://www.its.caltech.edu/~matilde /ScaleAnarchy.pdf.

Ascher, Ivan. 2018. *Portfolio Society: On the Capitalist Mode of Prediction*. Cambridge, MA: MIT Press.

Assange, Julian. 2013. "The Banality of 'Don't Be Evil.'" *New York Times*, 2 June 2013: SR4.

Azoulay, Ariella. 2008. *The Civil Contract of Photography*. New York: Zone Books.

Azoulay, Ariella. 2012. *Civil Imagination: A Political Ontology of Photography*. London: Verso.

Babbage, Charles. 1832. *On the Economy of Machinery and Manufactures*. London: Charles Knight.

Baeyer, Hans Christian von. 2003. *Information: The New Language of Science*. London: Phoenix.

Banksy [pseud.]. 2006. *Wall and Piece*. London: Random House.

Barthes, Roland. 1980. *Camera Lucida*. Translated by Richard Howard. New York: Hill and Wang.

Bartholomew, James. 2015. "Why You Should Stop Worrying and Learn to Love Inequality." *The Telegraph*, 27 April. https://www.telegraph.co.uk/news/politics /11564705/Why-you-should-stop-worrying-and-learn-to-love-inequality.html.

Bateson, Gregory. 1972. *Steps to an Ecology of Mind.* New York: Ballantine Books.

Bateson, Gregory. 2000. *Steps to an Ecology of Mind: With a New Forward by Mary Catherine Bateson.* Chicago: University of Chicago Press.

Battle-Baptiste, Whitney, and Britt Rusert, eds. 2018. *W. E. B. Du Bois's Data Portraits Visualizing Black America: The Color Line at the Turn of the Twentieth Century.* New York: Princeton Architectural Press.

Baudrillard, Jean. 2004 [1981]. *Simulacra and Simulation.* Originally published in French by Editions Galilee, excerpt in *Literary Theory: An Anthology,* edited by Julie Rivkin and Michael Ryan. Maiden, MA: Blackwell.

Bauwens, Michel, Vasilis Kostakis, and Alex Pazaitis. 2019. *Peer to Peer: The Commons Manifesto.* London: University of Westminster Press.

Bazin, Andre. 1967. *What Is Cinema?* Berkeley: University of California Press.

Beller, Jonathan. 1993. "The Circulating Eye." *Communication Research* 20, no. 2 (April): 298–313.

Beller, Jonathan. 1994. "Cinema, Capital of the Twentieth Century." *Postmodern Culture* 4, no. 3 (May). http://pmc.iath.virginia.edu/text-only/issue.594/beller.594.

Beller, Jonathan. 2001. "Third Cinema in a Global Frame: *Curacha,* Yahoo!, and *Manila by Night.*" *positions: east asia cultures critique* 9, no. 2: 331–67.

Beller, Jonathan. 2006a. *Acquiring Eyes: Philippine Visuality, Nationalist Struggle and the World-Media System.* Manila: Ateneo de Manila University Press.

Beller, Jonathan. 2006b. *The Cinematic Mode of Production.* Hanover, NH: Dartmouth College Press.

Beller, Jonathan. 2012. "Wagers within the Image: Rise of Visuality, Transformation of Labour, Aesthetics Regimes." *Culture Machine* 13. https://culturemachine.net/wp -content/uploads/2019/01/466-977-1-PB.pdf.

Beller, Jonathan. 2013. "Advertisarial Relations and Aesthetics of Survival: Advertising -> Advertisign." *NECSUS: European Journal of Media Studies,* June 2013. http://www .necsus-ejms.org/advertisarial-relations-and-aesthetics-of-survival-advertising -advertisign/.

Beller, Jonathan. 2015. "The Cinematic Program." *La Furia Umana,* April. http:// www.lafuriaumana.it/index.php/56-lfu-23/350-jonathan-beller-the-cinematic -program/.

Beller, Jonathan. 2016a. "Fragment from *The Message Is Murder.*" *Social Text* 34, no. 3: 137–52.

Beller, Jonathan. 2016b. "Informatic Labor in the Age of Computational Capital." *Lateral: Journal of the Cultural Studies Association* 5, no. 1. http://csalateral.org/wp/issue /5-1/informatic-labor-computational-capital-beller/.

Beller, Jonathan. 2016c. "The Programmable Image of Capital." *Postmodern Culture* 26, no. 2 (fall). Project MUSE, doi:10.1353/pmc.2016.0005.

Beller, Jonathan. 2016d. "Texas-(s)ized Postmodernism: Or Capitalism without the Dialectic." *Social Text* 34, no. 2 (summer): 21–44.

Beller, Jonathan. 2017a. "The Fourth Determination." *e-flux journal* 85. http:// www.e-flux.com/journal/85/156818/the-fourth-determination/.

Beller, Jonathan. 2017b. *The Message Is Murder: Substrates of Computational Capital.* London: Pluto Press.

Beller, Jonathan. 2018. "The Computational Unconscious." *b20: an online journal*, Special Issue: The Digital Turn (1 August). http://www.boundary2.org/2018/08/beller/.

Beller, Jonathan, Ante Jeric, and Diana Meheik. 2014. "From *The Cinematic Mode of Production* to *Computational Capital*: An Interview with Jonathan Beller for *Kulturpunkt*." *Social Text Online*, 31 January. https://socialtextjournal.org/from-the-cinematic-mode-of-production-to-computational-capital-an-interview-with-jonathan-beller-for-kulturpunkt/.

Benjamin, Ruha. 2019. *Race after Technology: Abolitionist Tools for the New Jim Code*. Cambridge: Polity.

Benjamin, Walter. 1969. "The Work of Art in the Age of Mechanical Reproduction." In *Illuminations*, edited by Hannah Arendt, translated by Harry Zohn, 217–51. New York: Schocken Books.

Benninger, James. 1986. *The Control Revolution*. Cambridge, MA: Harvard University Press.

Berardi, Franco. 2011. *After the Future*. Edinburgh: AK Press.

Bhandar, Brenna. 2015. "Title by Registration: Instituting Modern Property Law and Creating Racial Value in the Settler Colony." *Journal of Law and Society* (May 6). https://eprints.soas.ac.uk/19487/1/Title%20by%20Registration_JLS.pdf.

Bhandar, Brenna, and Alberto Toscano. 2015. "Race, Real Estate, Real Abstraction." *Radical Philosophy* 194 (Nov./Dec.): 8–17.

Black, Edwin. 2001. IBM *and the Holocaust: The Strategic Alliance between Nazi Germany and America's Most Powerful Corporation*. New York: Crown.

Bordeleau, Eric. 2016. "Abstracting the Commons?" *Common Conflict* virtual roundtable (February 5). https://www.onlineopen.org/common-conflict.

Borges, Jorge Luis. 1964. "The Garden of Forking Paths." In *Labyrinths: Selected Stories and Other Writings*, 19–29. New York: New Directions.

Bostrum, Nick. 2014. *Superintelligence: Paths, Dangers, Strategies*. Oxford: Oxford University Press.

Bratton, Benjamin H. 2016. *The Stack: On Software and Sovereignty*. Cambridge, MA: MIT Press.

Brown, Jayna. 2018. "A World on Fire: Radical Black Feminism in a Dystopian Age." *SAQ* 117, no. 3 (July): 581–97.

Browne, Simone. 2015. *Dark Matters: On the Surveillance of Blackness*. Durham, NC: Duke University Press.

Bryan, Dick, Akseli Virtanen, and Robert Wosnitzer. 2017. "Economics Back into Cryptoeconomics." *Medium* (September 11). https://medium.com/econaut/economics-back-into-cryptoeconomics-20471f5ceeea.

Buolamwini, Joy. 2017. "How I'm Fighting Bias in Algorithms." TED Talk (March 9). https://www.ted.com/talks/joy_buolamwini_how_i_m_fighting_bias_in_algorithms?language=en.

Capurro, Rafael. 2009. "Past, Present, and Future of the Concept of Information." *tripleC* 7, no. 2: 125–41.

Césaire, Aimé. 1972. *Discourse on Colonialism*. New York: Monthly Review Press.

Chen, Chih-hsien. 2003. "Is the Audience Really a Commodity? An Overdetermined Marxist Perspective of the Television Economy." Paper presented at the annual meeting of the International Communication Association, San Diego, California, 27 May. http://citation.allacademic.com/meta/p_mla_apa_research_citation/1/1/2/0/8/pages112086/p112086-1.php.

Chun, Wendy Hui Kyong. 2004. "On Software, or the Persistence of Visual Knowledge." *Grey Room* 18 (winter): 26–51.

Chun, Wendy Hui Kyong. 2011. *Programmed Visions: Software and Memory*. Cambridge, MA: MIT Press.

Chun, Wendy Hui Kyong. 2012. "Race and/as Technology, or How to Do Things with Race." In *Race after the Internet*, edited by Lisa Nakamura and Peter A. Chow-White, 38–69. New York: Routledge.

Chun, Wendy Hui Kyong. 2015. "To Be Determined." Paper presented at Pratt Institute, Brooklyn, New York, September 24.

Cohen, Ed. 2011. "The Paradoxical Politics of Viral Containment; or, How Scale Undoes Us One and All." *Social Text* 106, vol. 29, no. 1 (spring): 15–35.

Comolli, Jean-Louis. 1980. "Machines of the Visible." In *The Cinematic Apparatus*, edited by Teresa de Lauretis and Stephen Heath, 121–42. New York: St. Martin's Press.

Cooper, Melinda. 2015. "Shadow Money and the Shadow Workforce: Rethinking Labor and Liquidity." *SAQ* 114, no. 2 (April): 395–423.

Coppola, Gabrielle. 2014. "Traces of Israel's Iron Dome Can Be Found in Tech Start-ups." *Bloomberg News*, 11 August. https://www.bloomberg.com/news/articles/2014-08-11/what-do-an-online-furniture-store-and-a-pill-camera-have-in-common-israel-s-iron-dome-missile-defense-system.

Cubitt, Sean. 2014. "Decolonizing Ecomedia." *Cultural Politics* 10, no. 3: 275–86.

Cubitt, Sean. 2019. "Ecocritique, the Commons, Subjunctive." *Media+Environment* (Submitted).

Curtis, Patrick. "What Is a Junior Tranche?," Wall Street Oasis website, accessed 16 July 2020, https://www.wallstreetoasis.com/finance-dictionary/what-is-a-junior-tranche.

Davis, Angela. 2020. "The Fire This Time: Race at Boiling Point" webinar, 6 June. https://m.youtube.com/watch?feature=youtu.be&v=3yyT8i9oGCw.

Davis, Mike. 2006. *Planet of Slums*. London: Verso.

Dean, Jodi. 2016. "Images without Viewers: Selfie Communism." Fotomuseum Winterthur, 2 January 2016. http://www.fotomuseum.ch/en/explore/still-searching/articles/26420_images_without_viewers_selfie_communism/.

Debord, Guy. 1995. *The Society of the Spectacle*. Translated by Donald Nicholson-Smith. New York: Zone Books.

Debray, Régis. 1996. *Media Manifestos: On the Technological Transmission of Cultural Forms*, Translated by Eric Rauth. London: Verso.

de Lauretis, Teresa. 1987. *Technologies of Gender: Essays on Theory, Film, and Fiction*. Bloomington: Indiana University Press.

Deleuze, Gilles. 1989. *Cinema 2: The Time Image*. Translated by Hugh Tomlinson and Robert Galeta. Minneapolis: University of Minnesota Press.

Deleuze, Gilles, and Félix Guattari. 1977. *Anti-Oedipus: Capitalism and Schizophrenia*. Minneapolis: University of Minnesota Press.

Derman, Emanuel. 2016. "Remarks on Financial Models." In *Derivatives and the Wealth of Societies*, edited by Benjamin Lee and Randy Martin, 199–239. Chicago: University of Chicago Press.

Derrida, Jacques. 1997 [1967]. *Of Grammatology*. Translated by Gayatri Chakravorty Spivak. Baltimore: Johns Hopkins University Press.

Dinerstein, Joel. 2006. "Technology and Its Discontents: On the Verge of the Posthuman." *American Quarterly* 58, no. 3, *Rewiring the "Nation": The Place of Technology in American Studies* (September): 569–95.

Driscoll, Mark. 2020. *The Whites Are Enemies of Heaven: Climate Caucasianism and Ecological Protection in Asia*. Durham, NC: Duke University Press.

Duarte, Susana Nascimiento. 2018. "Interview with Jonathan Beller. The Derivative Image: Historical Implications of the Computational Mode of Production." *Cinema: Journal of Philosophy and the Moving Image* 10: 151–64.

Du Bois, W. E. B. 2015. "The Princess Steel." With an introduction by Adrienne Brown and Britt Rusert. *PMLA* 130, no. 3: 819–29.

Dyer-Witheford, Nick. 2013. "Red Plenty Platforms." *Culture Machine* 14. https://culturemachine.net/wp-content/uploads/2019/05/511-1153-1-PB.pdf.

Dyer-Witheford, Nick. 2015. *Cyber-proletariat: Global Labour in the Digital Vortex*. London: Pluto Press.

Edwards, Jim. 2013. "What Is a Facebook 'Like' Actually Worth in Dollars?" *Business Insider*, 27 March. https://www.businessinsider.com/what-is-a-facebook-like-actually-worth-in-dollars-2013-3.

Eglash, Ron. 2007. "Broken Metaphor: The Master-Slave Analogy in Technical Literature." *Technology and Culture* 48, no. 3: 1–9.

Eisenstein, Sergei. 1988. *Writings*. Vol. 1, edited by Richard Taylor. London: British Film Institute.

Federici, Silvia. 2012. *Revolution at Point Zero: Housework, Reproduction, and Feminist Struggle*. Brooklyn, NY: PM Press.

Feldman, Allen. 2015. *Archives of the Insensible: Of War, Photopolitics and Dead Memory*. Chicago: University of Chicago Press.

Feldman, Allen. 2017. "The Accidentalization of War," in *Degrounding War and the State*, edited by Jonathan Beller, *Social Text Online* (19 April). https://socialtextjournal.org/periscope_article/the-accidentalization-of-war/.

Fidaner, Işık Barış. 2014. Post, ICTs and Society listserv, 29 August. https://icts-and-society.net/mailing-list-archive/.

Fisher, Mark. 2009. *Capitalist Realism: Is There No Alternative?* London: Zero Books.

Flusser, Vilém. 2000. *Towards a Philosophy of Photography*. Translated by A. Matthews. London: Reaktion Books.

Flusser, Vilém. 2011. *Into the Universe of Technical Images*. Translated by N. Roth. Minneapolis: University of Minnesota Press.

Foucault, Michel. 2008. *The Birth of Biopolitics: Lectures at the Collège de France, 1978–1979*. Edited by Michel Senellart. Translated by Graham Burchell. New York: Palgrave MacMillian.

Franklin, Sebastian. 2015. *Control: Digitality as Cultural Logic*. Cambridge, MA: MIT Press.

Fuchs, Christian. 2012. "Blogpost about Google's 'New' Terms of Use and Privacy Policy: Old Exploitation and User Commodification in a New Ideological Skin." Post, ICTs and Society listserv, 1 March. https://icts-and-society.net/mailing-list -archive/.

Fuller, Neely, Jr. 1984. *The United Independent Compensatory Code/System/Concept: A Textbook/Workbook for Thought, Speech and/or Action for Victims of Racism (White Supremacy)*. Washington, DC: Neely Fuller Jr.

Gallagher, Sean. 2012. "Bionic Eyes: Sensors That Use Lookout's Brainwaves to Spot Trouble." *Ars Technica*, 19 September. https://arstechnica.com/information -technology/2012/09/bionic-eyes-sensors-that-use-lookouts-brainwaves-to-spot -trouble/.

Galloway, Alexander R. 2004. *Protocol: How Control Exists After Decentralization*. Cambridge, MA: MIT Press.

Galloway, Alexander R. 2012. *The Interface Effect*. Cambridge: Polity.

Gilmore, Ruth Wilson. 2007. *Golden Gulag*. Berkeley: University of California Press.

Gleason-White, Jane. 2012. *Double Entry: How the Merchants of Venice Created Modern Finance*. New York: Norton.

Golumbia, David. 2009. *The Cultural Logic of Computation*. Cambridge, MA: Harvard University Press.

Gordon-Reed, Annette. 1998. *Thomas Jefferson and Sally Hemings: An American Controversy*. Charlottesville: University of Virginia Press.

Gram, Sarah. 2013. "The Young-Girl and the Selfie." Textual-Relations, 1 March. http:// text-relations.blogspot.com/2013/03/the-young-girl-and-selfie.html.

Gramsci, Antonio. 1971. *Selections from the Prison Notebooks*. Translated by Quintin Hoare. New York: International Publishers.

Hall, Stuart. 2016. "Encoding/Decoding." In *The Unfinished Conversation: Encoding/ Decoding*, edited by Gaëtane Verna and Mark Sealy, 1–29. Toronto: The Power Plant, Autograph ABP.

Hall, Stuart, Chas Critcher, Tony Jefferson, John N. Clarke, and Brian Roberts. 1978. *Policing the Crisis: Mugging, the State, and Law and Order*. London: Macmillan.

Halpern, Orit. 2012. "Schizophrenic Techniques: Cybernetics, the Human Sciences, and the Double Bind." *Scholar and Feminist Online* 10, no. 3 (summer). http://sfonline .barnard.edu/feminist-media-theory/schizophrenic-techniques-cybernetics-the -human-sciences-and-the-double-bind/.

Haraway, Donna. 2000. "A Cyborg Manifesto." In *The Cybercultures Reader*, edited David Bell and Barbara M. Kennedy, 291–323. London: Routledge.

Harney, Stefano, and Fred Moten. 2013. *The Undercommons: Fugitive Planning and Black Study*. Brooklyn, NY: Autonomedia.

Hartman, Saidiya. 1997. *Scenes of Subjection: Terror, Slavery and Self-Making in Nineteenth- Century America*. New York: Oxford.

Hartman, Saidiya. 2008. *Lose Your Mother: A Journey Along the Atlantic Slave Route*. New York: Farrar, Straus, Giroux.

Hayek, Friedrich August von. 1945. "The Use of Knowledge in Society." *American Economic Review* 35, no. 4 (September): 519–30.

Hayek, Friedrich August von. 1982. *The Mirage of Social Justice*. Vol. 2 of *Law Legislation and Liberty*. London: Routledge and Kegan Paul.

Hayles, Katherine N. 1999. *How We Became Posthuman: Virtual Bodies in Cybernetics, Literature and Informatics*. Chicago: University of Chicago Press.

Hayles, Katherine N. 2016. "The Cognitive NonConscious." *Critical Inquiry* 42, no. 4: 783–808.

Heffernan, Virgina. 2013. "How We All Learned to Speak Instagram." *Wired* (April 16). https://www.wired.com/2013/04/instagram-2/.

Hofstadter, Douglas. 1979. *Gödel, Escher, Bach: An Eternal Golden Braid*. New York: Penguin Books.

Holmes, Brian. 2008. *Escape the Overcode: Activist Art in the Control Society*. Eindhoven, Netherlands: Van Abbemuseum.

Jameson, Fredric. 1981. *The Political Unconscious: Narrative as a Socially Symbolic Act*. Ithaca, NY: Cornell University Press.

Jameson, Fredric. 1991. *Postmodernism, or, the Cultural Logic of Late Capitalism*. Durham, NC: Duke University Press.

Joler, Vladen, and Matteo Pasquinelli. 2020. "The Nooscope Manifested: AI as Instrument of Knowledge Extractivism," visual essay, KIM HfG Karlsruhe and Share Lab, 1 May. https://nooscope.ai.

Kennedy, Margrit. 2012. *Occupy Money: Creating an Economy Where Everybody Wins*, with Stephanie Ehrenschwendner. Gabriola Island, Canada: New Society.

Keynes, John Maynard. 2007 [1936]. *The General Theory of Employment, Interest and Money*. London: Palgrave Macmillan.

Keynes, John Maynard. 2015. *The Essential Keynes*. Edited by Robert Skidelsky. Jouve, UK: Penguin Books.

Kittler, Friedrich. 1995. "There Is No Software." Ctheory.net, 18 October. http://www.ctheory.net/articles.aspx?id=74.

Kittler, Friedrich. 1999. *Gramophone, Film, Typewriter*. Translated by Geoffrey Winthrop-Young and Michael Wutz. Stanford, CA: Stanford University Press.

Kosnik, Abigail de. 2013. "Fandom as Free Labour." In *Digital Labour: The Internet as Playground and Factory*, edited by Trebor Scholz, 98–111. New York: Routledge.

Kunstman, Adi, and Rebecca L. Stein. 2015. *Digital Militarism: Israel's Occupation in the Social Media Age*. Stanford, CA: Stanford University Press.

Lacan, Jacques. 1981. *The Four Fundamental Concepts of Psycho-Analysis*. Edited by Jacques-Alain Miller. Translated by Alan Sheridan. New York: Norton.

Latour, Bruno, and Vincent Antonin Lépinay. 2009. *The Science of Passionate Interests: An Introduction to Gabriel Tarde's Economic Anthropology*. Chicago: Prickly Paradigm Press.

Lee, Benjamin, and Randy Martin, eds. 2016. *Derivatives and the Wealth of Societies*. Chicago: University of Chicago Press.

Lenin, V. I. 1939. *Imperialism: The Highest Stage of Capitalism*. New York: International Publishers.

Lessig, Lawrence. 2000. "Code Is Law: On Liberty in Cyberspace." *Harvard Magazine*, 1 January. https://harvardmagazine.com/2000/01/code-is-law-html.

Levitt, Deborah. 2018. *The Animatic Apparatus: Animation, Vitality, and the Futures of the Image*. London: Zero Books.

Liang, Chia-Kai, Yi-Chang Shih, and Homer H. Chen. 2011. "Light Field Analysis for Modeling Image Formation." IEEE: *Transactions on Image Processing* 20, no. 2 (February): 446–60.

Lipuma, Edward. 2016. "Ritual in Financial Life." In *Derivatives and the Wealth of Societies,* edited by Benjamin Lee and Randy Martin, 37–82. Chicago: University of Chicago Press.

Liu, Lydia He. 2010. *The Freudian Robot: Digital Media and the Future of the Unconscious*. Chicago: University of Chicago Press.

Lorde, Audre. 2007 [1984]. "The Master's Tools Will Never Dismantle the Master's House." In *Sister Outsider: Essays and Speeches*, 110–14. Berkeley, CA: Crossing Press.

Luhmann, Niklas. 1989. *Ecological Communication*. Chicago: University of Chicago Press.

MacKenzie, Donald. 2008. *An Engine, Not a Camera: How Financial Models Shape Markets*. Cambridge, MA: MIT Press.

Malone, Dumas. 1948. *Jefferson the Virginian*. Boston: Little, Brown, and Co.

Mandelbrot, Benoit, and Richard L. Hudson. 2004. *The (Mis)Behavior of Markets: A Fractal View of Risk, Ruin and Reward*. New York: Basic Books.

Manning, Erin. 2018. "Me Lo Dijo Un Pajarito: Neurodiversity, Black Life and the University As We Know It." *Social Text* 36, no. 3: 1–24.

Marazzi, Christian, and Giuseppina Mecchia. 2007. "Rules for the Incommensurable." *SubStance* 36, no. 1, 11–36.

Markoff, John. 2013. "At High Speed, on the Road to a Driverless Future." *New York Times*, 27 May. https://www.nytimes.com/2013/05/28/science/on-the-road-in-mobileyes-self-driving-car.html.

Martin, Randy. 2002. *Financialization of Daily Life*. Philadelphia: Temple University Press.

Martin, Randy. 2013. "After Economy? Social Logics of the Derivative." *Social Text* 31, no. 1 (March): 83–106.

Martin, Randy. 2015a. *Knowledge Limited: Towards a Social Logic of the Derivative*. Philadelphia: Temple University Press.

Martin, Randy. 2015b. "Money after Decolonization." *SAQ* 114, no. 2 (April): 377–93.

Marx, Karl. 1978. *The Marx-Engels Reader*. 2nd ed. Edited by Robert C. Tucker. New York: Norton.

Marx, Karl. 1990. *Capital: A Critique of Political Economy, Volume I*. Translated by Ben Fowkes. New York: Penguin.

Marx, Karl. 1993. *Grundrisse*. Translated by Martin Nicolaus. London: Penguin Books.

Marx, Karl, and Frederick Engels. 1986. *Collected Works, Volume 28: Marx, 1857–1861*. New York: International Publishers.

Marx, Karl, and Friedrich Engels. 1998. *The German Ideology*. Amherst, MA: Promethean Books.

Massumi, Brian. 2018. *99 Theses for the Revaluation of Value: A Postcapitalist Manifesto*. Minneapolis: University of Minnesota Press.

Maturana, Humberto, and Francisco Varela. 1992. *The Tree of Knowledge: The Biological Roots of Human Understanding*. Boston: Shambhala.

McGlotten, Shaka. 2016. "Black Data." In *No Tea, No Shade: New Writings in Black Queer Studies*, edited by E. Patrick Johnson, 262–86. Durham, NC: Duke University Press.

McIlwain, Charlton. 2020. *Black Software: The Internet and Racial Justice, from the AfroNet to Black Lives Matter*. New York: Oxford University Press.

McKittrick, Katherine. 2014. "Mathematics Black Life." *The Black Scholar* 44, no. 2 (summer): 16–28.

McPherson, Tara. 2012. "U.S. Operating Systems at Mid-Century: The Intertwining of Race and UNIX." In *Race after the Internet*, edited by Lisa Nakamura and Peter A. Chow-White, 20–37. New York: Routledge.

Mehrling, Perry. 2017. "Financialization and Its Discontents." *Finance and Society* 3, no. 1: 1–10.

Meister, Robert. 2021. *Historical Justice in the Age of Finance*. Chicago: University of Chicago Press.

Melamed, Jodi. 2019. "Operationalizing Racial Capitalism: Administrative Power and Ordinary Violence." Yale Center for the Study of Race, Indigeneity, and Transnational Migration Lecture Series, New Haven, CT, 31 October. https://www.youtube.com/watch?v=o3Z9sOGf6BA.

Meredith, Maya. 2013. "I Point and Shoot, and Therefore I Am?" Towards a Philosophy of the Selfie, 5 May 2013. Accessed 3 June 2016.

Metz, Christian. 1982. *The Imaginary Signifier: Psychoanalysis and the Cinema*. Translated by Celia Britton, Annwyl Williams, Ben Brewster, and Alfred Guzzetti. Bloomington: Indiana University Press.

Mills, Charles. 1997. *The Racial Contract*. Ithaca, NY: Cornell University Press.

Mingus, Mia. 2011. "Changing the Framework: Disability Justice; How Our Communities Can Move Beyond Access to Wholeness." *Leaving Evidence* (blog). 12 February. https://leavingevidence.wordpress.com/2011/02/12/changing-the-framework-disability-justice/.

Minh-Ha, Trinh T. 1981. *Reassemblage*. Script reproduced in Trinh T. Minh-Ha, *When the Moon Waxes Red*. London: Routledge.

Mirowski, Phillip. 2002. *Machine Dreams: Economics Becomes a Cyborg Science*. Cambridge: Cambridge University Press.

Morgan, Jennifer. 2017. Talk at "Scenes at 20" symposium, Rutgers University, New Brunswick, NJ, October 6–7. https://rcha.rutgers.edu/current-project/past-events/133-scenes-at-20.

Mottahedeh, Negar. 2015. *#iranelection: Hashtag Solidarity and the Transformation of Online Life*. Stanford, CA: Stanford University Press.

Mulvey, Laura. 1975. "Visual Pleasure and Narrative Cinema." *Screen* 16, no. 3: 6–18.

Mumm, Chad. 2012. "Interview: Lytro's Eric Cheng." *The Verge*. 11 January. https://www.theverge.com/ces/2012/1/11/2700483/interview-lytros-eric-cheng.

Muñoz, José Esteban. 2009. *Cruising Utopia: The Then and There of Queer Futurity*. Durham NC: Duke University Press.

Nakamura, Lisa. 2007. *Digitizing Race: Visual Cultures of the Internet*. Minneapolis: University of Minnesota Press.

Nakamura, Lisa. 2014. "Indigenous Circuits." Computer History Museum, 2 January 2014. http://www.computerhistory.org/atchm/indigenous-circuits/.

Nakamura, Lisa and Peter Chow-White, eds. 2012. *Race after the Internet*. New York: Routledge.

Negri, Antonio. 2010. "Value and Affect." Translated by Michael Hardt. Negri in English, 5 August 2010. https://antonionegriinenglish.wordpress.com/2010/08/05/value-and-effect/.

Nelson, Diane. 2015. *Who Counts? The Mathematics of Death and Life after Genocide*. Durham, NC: Duke University Press.

Neumann, John von, and Oskar Morgenstern. 1944. *Theory of Games and Economic Behavior*. Princeton, NJ: Princeton University Press.

Nielsen, Jakob, and Kara Pernice. 2010. *Eyetracking Web Usability*. Berkeley, CA: New Riders.

Noble, Safiya Umoja. 2018. *Algorithms of Oppression: How Search Engines Reinforce Racism*. New York: New York University Press.

Omi, Michael, and Howard Winant. 1994. *Racial Formation in the United States: From the 1960s to the 1990s*. London: Routledge.

Paik, Nam June. 2003. "Cybernated Art." In *The New Media Reader*, edited by Noah Wardrip-Fruin and Nick Montfort, 227–30. Cambridge, MA: MIT Press.

Pasolini, Pier Paolo. 1988. *Heretical Empericism*. Edited by Louise K. Barnett. Translated by Ben Lawtton and Louise K. Barnett. Bloomington: Indiana University Press.

Pasquinelli, Matteo. 2006. "Immaterial Civil War: Prototypes of Conflict with Cognitive Capitalism." *A Critique of Creative Industries*, European Institute for Progressive Cultural Policies, November. http://www.eipcp.net/policies/cci/pasquinelli/en.html.

Pasquinelli, Matteo. 2015. "Italian *Operaismo* and the Information Machine." *Theory, Culture, and Society* 32, no. 3: 49–68.

Pasquinelli, Matteo. 2018. "Metadata Society." In *Posthuman Glossary*, edited by Rosi Braidotti and Maria Hlavajova, 253–56. London: Bloomsbury.

Pasquinelli, Matteo. 2019. "The Origins of Marx's General Intellect." *Radical Philosophy* 2, no. 6 (winter): 43–56.

Peele, Jordan, dir. 2017. *Get Out*. Universal City, CA: Universal Pictures.

Pietzman, Louis. 2012. "Viral Banksy Quote on Advertising Plagiarizes 1999 Zine Essay." Gawker, 11 March. http://gawker.com/5892332/viral-banksy-quote-on-advertising-plagiarizes-1999-zine-essay.

Pisters, Patricia. 2012. *The Neuro-Image: A Deleuzian Film-Philosophy of Digital Screen Culture*. Stanford, CA: Stanford University Press.

Postone, Moishe. 2003. *Time, Labor, and Social Domination*. Cambridge: Cambridge University Press.

Puar, Jasbir K. 2017. *The Right to Maim: Debility, Capacity, Disability*. Durham, NC: Duke University Press.

Rafael, Vicente. 2000. *White Love: And Other Events in Filipino History*. Durham, NC: Duke University Press.

Ramjit, Alana. 2014. "The Lorem Ipsum Project." Unpublished manuscript (May 15).

"Rebooting the Cosmos: Is the Universe the Ultimate Computer?" 2011. *Scientific American*, 4 June. http://www.scientificamerican.com/article/world-science-festival-rebooting-the-cosmos-is-the-universe-ultimate-computer-live-event/.

Robinson, Cedric. 1983. *Black Marxism: The Making of the Black Radical Tradition*. Chapel Hill: University of North Carolina Press.

Roth, Lorna. 2009. "Looking at Shirley, the Ultimate Norm: Color Balance, Image Technologies and Cogntive Equity." *Canadian Journal of Communication* 34: 111–36.

Russell, Bertrand. 2004. *A History of Western Philosophy*. London: Routledge, 2004.

Ryall, Michael D. 2013. "The New Dynamics of Competition: An Emerging Science for Modeling Strategic Moves." *Harvard Business Review*, June 2013: 80–85.

Seth, Alpen. 2017. "Cultivating Risk: Weather Insurance, Technology and Financialization in India." PhD diss., MIT. https://dspace.mit.edu/handle/1721.1/113802.

Shannon, Claude. 1948. "A Mathematical Theory of Communication." *The Bell System Technical Journal* 27, nos. 3–4: 379–423, 623–56.

Shannon, Claude. 1987. "Father of the Information Age," interview by Anthony Liversidge. *Omni* 9, no. 11: 60–62, 64–66, 110.

Shannon, Claude, and Warren Weaver. 1971. *The Mathematical Theory of Communication*. Chicago: University of Illinois Press.

Sharpe, Christina. 2016. *In The Wake: On Blackness and Being*. Durham, NC: Duke University Press.

Siegert, Bernhard. 2013. "Cultural Techniques: Or the End of the Intellectual Postwar Era in German Media Theory." Translated by Geoffrey Wihtrop-Young. *Theory, Culture, and Society* 30, no. 6: 48–65.

Silverstone, Roger. 1999. *Why Study the Media?* London: Sage.

Simmel, George. 1986. *The Philosophy of Money*. London: Routledge.

Singh, Nikhil Pal. 2015. "A Note on Race and the Left." *Social Text Online*, 31 July. https://socialtextjournal.org/a-note-on-race-and-the-left/.

Smythe, Dallas. 1977. "Communications: Blindspot of Western Marxism." *Canadian Journal of Political and Society Theory* 1, no. 3: 1–28.

Sohn-Rethel, Alfred. 1978. *Intellectual and Manual Labor: A Critique of Epistemology*. London: Macmillan.

Solanas, Fernando, and Ocatvio Getino. 1997. "Towards a Third Cinema: Notes and Experiences for the Development of a Cinema of Liberation in the Third World." In *Theories, Practices, and Transcontinental Articulations*, edited by Michael T. Martin, 33–58. Vol. 1 of *New Latin American Cinema*. Detroit: Wayne State University Press.

Spillers, Hortense. 1987. "Mama's Baby, Papa's Maybe: An American Grammar Book." *Diacritics* 17, no. 2 (summer): 64–81.

Spillers, Hortense. 1997. "All the Things You Could Be by Now, if Sigmund Freud's Wife Was Your Mother." In *Female Subjects in Black and White: Race, Psychoanalysis, Feminism*, edited by Elizabeth Abel, Barbara Christian, and Helene Moglen, 135–58. Berkeley: University of California Press.

Srnicek, Nick. 2016. *Platform Capitalism*. Cambridge: Polity.

Stein, Rebecca, Adi Kunstman, and Negar Mottahedeh. 2015. "The Political Consciousness of the Selfie." Stanford University Press blog, 28 July. http://stanfordpress.typepad.com/blog/2015/07/the-political-consciousness-of-the-selfie.html.

Steuer, Daniel. 2019. "Prolegomena to Any Future Attempt at Understanding Our Emerging World of War." In *War and Algorithm*, edited by Max Liljefors, Gregor Noll, and Daniel Steuer, 9–51. London: Rowman and Littlefield.

Steyerl, Hito. 2012. "In Defense of The Poor Image." In *The Wretched of the Screen*, 31–46. Cambridge, MA: Sternberg Press.

Stiegler, Bernard. 2010. *For a New Critique of Political Economy*. Malden, MA: Polity.

Stiegler, Bernard. 2012. "Relational Ecology and the Digital *Pharmakon*." *Culture Machine* 13. https://culturemachine.net/wp-content/uploads/2019/01/464-1026-1-PB.pdf.

Storm, Darlene. 2011. "DARPA Cool or Creepy: 'Good Stranger' to 'Global Brain' Spying." Computerworld, 7 September. https://www.computerworld.com/article/2471004/darpa-cool-or-creepy---good-stranger--to--global-brain--spying.html.

Tadiar, Neferti. 2009. *Things Fall Away: Philippine Historical Experience and the Makings of Globalization*. Durham, NC: Duke University Press.

Tadiar, Neferti. 2012. "Life-Times in Fate Playing." *SAQ* 111, no. 4 (fall): 783–801.

Tadiar, Neferti. 2013. "Life-Times of Disposability within Global Neo-Liberalism." *Social Text* 31, no. 2 (summer): 19–48.

Tadiar, Neferti. 2015. "Decolonization, 'Race,' and Remaindered Life under Empire." *Qui Parle* 23, no. 2: 135–60.

Tadiar, Neferti. 2016. "City Everywhere." *Theory, Culture, and Society* 33, nos. 7–8: 57–83.

Taylor, Keeanga-Yamahtta, ed. 2017. *How We Get Free: Black Feminism and the Combahee River Collective*. Chicago: Haymarket Books.

Terranova, Tiziana. 2000. "Free Labor: Producing Culture for the Digital Economy." *Social Text* 18, no. 2: 33–58.

Tiqqun [pseud.]. 2012. *Preliminary Materials for a Theory of the Young-Girl*. Cambridge MA: Semiotext(e).

Turing, Alan. 2003 [1950]. "Computing Machinery and Intelligence." In *The New Media Reader*, edited by Noah Wardrip-Fruin and Nick Montfort, 50–64. Cambridge, MA: MIT Press.

Ure, Andrew. 1835. *The Philosophy of Manufactures: An Exposition of the Scientific, Moral and Commercial Economy of the Factory System of Great Britian*. London: Charles Knight.

Virilio, Paul. 1986. *War and Cinema: The Logistics of Perception*. Translated by Patrick Camiller. London: Verso.

Virilio, Paul. 2006. *Speed and Politics*. Los Angeles: Semiotext(e).

Virno, Paolo. 2004. *A Grammar of the Multitude*. New York: Semiotext(e).

Vismann, Cornelia. 2013. "Cultural Techniques and Sovereignty." *Theory, Culture, and Society* 30, no. 6: 83–93.

Vitale, Christopher. 2015. "Neuropolitics: Facial Recognition, Kohonen Networks, and Distributed Representation, Or How I Stopped Worrying and Learned to Love

Facebook's 'DeepFace.'" Pratt Institute Encounters Speakers Series, Brooklyn, NY, September.

Wardrip-Fruin, Noah, and Nick Montfort, eds. 2003. *The New Media Reader*. Cambridge, MA: MIT Press.

Wark, McKenzie. 2007. *Gamer Theory*. Cambridge MA: Harvard University Press.

Wark, McKenzie. 2012. *Telesthesia: Communication, Culture and Class*. New York: Wiley.

Wark, McKenzie. 2019. *Capital Is Dead: Is This Something Worse?* London: Verso.

Wee, Sui-Lee, and Paul Mozur. 2019. "China Uses DNA to Map Faces: With Help from the West." *New York Times*, 3 December. https://www.nytimes.com/2019/12/03/business/china-dna-uighurs-xinjiang.html.

Weizman, Eyal. 2017. *Forensic Architecture: Violence at the Threshold of Detectability*. Cambridge, MA: Zone Books.

Wiener, Norbert. 1961. *Cybernetics: Control and Communication in the Animal and the Machine*. Cambridge, MA: MIT Press.

Wiener, Norbert. 1989. *The Human Use of Human Beings: Cybernetics and Society*. London: Free Association Books.

Wiener, Norbert. 2003. "Men, Machines and the World About." In *The New Media Reader*, edited by Noah Wardrip-Fruin and Nick Montfort, 65–72. Cambridge, MA: MIT Press.

Wilderson III, Frank B. 2010. *Red White and Black: Cinema and the Struggle of U.S. Antagonims*. Durham, NC: Duke University Press.

Williams, Matt. 2013. "Justin Bieber Hopes Anne Frank 'Would Have Been a Belieber.'" *The Guardian*, 14 April. https://www.theguardian.com/music/2013/apr/14/justin-bieber-anne-frank-belieber.

Wilson, Andrew Norman. 2011. "Workers Leaving the Googleplex." HD video and sound. http://www.andrewnormanwilson.com/WorkersGoogleplex.html.

Wolfe, Patrick. 2006. "Settler Colonialism and the Elimination of the Native." *Journal of Genocide Research*, 8, no. 4 (December): 387–409.

Wynter, Sylvia. 1994a. "A Black Studies Manifesto." *Knowledge on Trial* 1, no. 1 (fall): 3–11.

Wynter, Sylvia. 1994b. "No Humans Involved: An Open Letter to My Colleagues." *Knowledge on Trial* 1, no. 1 (fall): 42–73.

Wynter, Sylvia. 2003. "Unsettling the Coloniality of Being/Power/Truth/Freedom: Towards the Human, after Man, Its Overrepresentation—An Argument." *The New Centennial Review* 3, no. 3 (fall): 257–337.

Yusoff, Kathryn. 2018. *A Billion Black Anthropocenes or None*. Minneapolis: University of Minnesota Press.

(commodity-money-commodity), 109; devalued by increased productivity, 31; double being of, 11–13, 255; image-code as, 122–23; information as, 139–46, 278; money as, 11, 13, 17–18, 110; as object, 112–16, 114, 120, 123, 145; photograph as, 146–54; practical solipsism of, 68–69; as risk profile, 113–14; selfie as, 107; use-value and exchange-value, 9; valorization process of, 114, 117

commodity-form, 12–13, 17, 31, 41, 64, 112–14, 295n14; shift toward screen-mediated code work, 102, 122–23

commons, 104, 189–90

communication: as computation, 5; decolonization of, 189; expropriation of, 122; mathematical theory of, 19, 91–92, 264; monetary media and, 102

communications infrastructure, 31, 102, 106, 226, 264, 272

"Communications: The Blindspot of Western Marxism" (Smythe), 176

communication theory, 5, 8, 91, 208

communism, 209, 266, 290n15; anarcho-communism, 54, 284; of capital, 65, 69, 122; communist computing, 132; cybernetic, 61; derivative, 193, 205, 217, 220–21; noncapitalist computational communication, 281–82; platform, 189; reclamation of attention and, 70; of species creativity, 40; sustainability and, 132, 253, 282; sustainable, 6–7

Communist Manifesto, The (Marx and Engels), 48

community: difference erased, 88; money as, 211–13

Comolli, Jean-Louis, 127

competition, 171

computation: actually existing, 165, 245; ambient, 52, 156, 214, 222, 234; apparatuses of, 76, 79; communication and, 165–66; communication as, 5; conceptualization of, 41, 64; decolo-

nization of, 133; defetishization of, 70; derivative, 41–54; development of, 44; digital logics of, 65–66; distributed, 19, 60, 66, 243, 250; enclosure by, 35, 57, 70, 155, 195, 246, 257–58, 265; as fifth estate, 4; as gendered, 80; generalization of, 10, 21, 46; historicity of, 74; as intensification of capital, 40; as means of production embedded in bios, 70–71; as metabolism of information, 38; as metaphor, 161; metaphysics as medium of, 49; planetary, 7; protocol layer, 50; protocols of, 5, 30, 70–72, 222, 224–25, 252–53; as racial capitalism, 9, 65, 117; as tool for capitalist violence, 89; ubiquitous, 109, 156–57; universal system of, 5; as unthought of modern thought, 64; as weapon against working-class revolt, 67–68

computational capital, 35, 38, 54, 82, 131–32, 136, 146, 161, 164, 227, 241, 262, 280; evolution of theory of, 277–78; sedimentation of social practice and, 63–69, 80, 83

computational colonization, 7, 27, 123–24, 183, 220

computational mode of production, 20, 27, 36, 62, 113, 127, 135–36, 164, 206, 278; cinema and, 278–79; defined, 117; derivative condition created by, 113; reformatting of the visual field, 127; transmedia cybernesis, 131–32

computational racial capitalism, 6–7, 9–10, 24, 26–30, 33–36, 41, 47, 49, 51–52, 54–57; as historical-material condition, 13; new Jim Code, 26, 128, 217; as operative process or metaprogram, 35; socio-aesthetic forms resistant to, 189; symptoms of, 61; violence inherent in, 65; as world computer, 6, 35. *See also* racial capitalism

computational substrate, 6, 71, 152

"Computing, Machinery and Intelligence" (Turing), 129–30

Debray, Régis, 60, 165
debt servicing, 44
decolonization, 153; of abstraction, 7; of communication, 189; of computation, 131–32, 133; as driver of computational innovation, 76; end of humanism and, 84, 85; of I-C-I', 133; of information, 7; of money, 133, 197, 218, 230; of process of abstraction, 133, 219
deconstruction, 92, 163, 281; financialization of, 41–54
deconstructive state, 23, 50, 103, 281
Defense Advanced Research Projects Agency (DARPA), 159, 161
dehumanization: of communication, 92; technohumanist, 89–97
de la Cruz, Khavn, 197
Deleuze, Gilles, 36, 188, 258, 276–78
delta-hedging, 212
democracy, 44, 51, 86, 122, 186
democratic governance: as outmoded, 6
democratization, 7, 220, 243–44; of finance, 283–84; of means of expropriation, 82, 86
depression, economic, 5
deracination, 88, 218–19, 238; of abstractions, 87–89, 97
derivative condition, 20, 32, 35–36, 41, 46, 53–54, 182, 224, 239, 253–54; as commodity-form, 113–14; cybernetic ontologies and, 54, 61; images and, 280, 282; programmable image and, 113; read-write ontologies and, 131
derivative contracts, 3, 216, 220, 251, 283, 295n12
derivative finance, 21, 115, 143–47, 204, 217; Black-Scholes equation, 144; communist, 217; crisis of 2008 and, 143; move from M to M', 142
derivative logic, 176, 188, 204
Derivative Revolutions (Beller), 266
derivatives: financial, 6, 7, 51–52, 55–56; as liquidity premiums, 21, 52; network, 113, 119, 226, 242, 245, 254

Derman, Emanuel, 212
Derrida, Jacques, 50, 108
Descartes, René, 68
designable economy, 282–83
developmentalism, 124
diachronic flow (processing), 5
dialectics, 69, 104, 107; of capitalism as best and worst, 34, 87; of human-machine, 83–89
Diaz, Lav, 273
differánce, 50, 108
difference: profitability of, 3; socially meaningful metrics of, 3–4
digital culture, 63, 70, 86, 119, 223, 227, 248, 260; biological substrate of, 203–4; environmental racism of, 214
Digital Culture 1.0 (DC1), 17–18, 63, 85, 107, 110, 131
Digital Culture 2.0 (DC2), 19, 36, 63, 107–8, 110, 112, 123
digital-visual, work-sites of, 154–72; antidrone wear line, 156; CV Dazzle, 156
digitization, 17–18, 36, 47, 61; alienation as, 110; of logic and logistics of racism, 65; universal, 74, 79–84
Dinerstein, Joel, 60
Dirty Computer (Monáe), 57
dirty computing, 57, 61
disability justice, 187–88
disappearance, 82–83, 87, 96, 168, 270; Chile, 212
discipline, 8, 42, 68–69, 129–30
discount, 122, 195; discounting of marked people(s), 13, 120, 178, 190
Discourse on Colonialism (Césaire), 84
"discrimination," 127–28, 130, 169
dispossession, 6, 10, 26–27, 45, 48, 60–61, 181, 290n1; of billions, 87, 96, 185–86, 260; crisis of subjective age, 181; image and, 102, 260; planet of slums, 105, 182, 203; radical, 6, 96, 105, 132, 202–3, 259, 281
dissymmetrical exchange, 109–10, 177

distributed production, 52, 70, 82, 113, 132, 185; "science" of, 78

dividuality, 87, 191

dominant material relationships, 58, 118–19

Driscoll, Mark, 256–57

drone strikes, 128, 156

Dr. Strangelove (Kubrick), 88–89

Duarte, Susana Nascimento, interview with Beller, 267–84

Du Bois, W. E. B., 8, 288–89n11

Dyer-Witheford, Nick, 41, 63

economic media, 5, 7, 61–62, 102, 146; re-engineering, 190, 218

economics, 5, 19–20, 22, 207–10, 214; as cyborg science, 39

education, racism within, 207–8

Eisenstein, Sergei, 272, 273

Enciclopedia Libre, 297n6

enclosure by computation, 70, 74, 246, 257–58, 265; of bios, 155, 195, 257; media and, 84, 122

"Encoding/Decoding" (Hall), 262, 263

engine, concept of, 206–7

ENIAC (Electronic Numerical Integrator and Computer), 94–95, 163

entrepreneur of the self, 20–21, 38, 40, 45, 66, 108, 113, 216; autocapitalization, 179

"environment," 108

environmental racism, 214, 224

epidermalization, 7–8

episteme, 279–80

equality, as sameness, 187–88

equity structures, 283

equivalents, exchange of, 11, 41, 68, 88, 109

"estates," 4

Ethereum, 29, 116, 288n10

eugenics, 94

exchange: dissymmetrical, 103, 109–10, 119, 164, 177–78, 190, 262, 278–79; of equivalents, 11, 41, 68, 88, 109; money as vanishing mediator of, 18, 37, 178

exchange abstraction, 11

exchange-value, 9, 11–18, 37–38, 64, 211, 286n6; "degree zero" myth, 88; digitization of, 110, 290n2; exchange relation, 68–69; as index of social relation, 12; no matter involved in, 137, 255

exclusion, 23, 70, 75, 110; from photography, 147, 149; racial, 87, 131

expression: money-likeness of, 6

expressivity, 6, 53, 227, 240, 251–52, 261, 283; cryptocurrency and, 266

extraction: algorithms of, 32, 187; Culture as grammar of, 54; governance modes and, 6; grammar of, 54; of sociality, 164

extra-economic domains, 32, 83, 211, 226, 257, 283; cryptocurrency and, 283

Facebook, 45, 51, 59, 146, 167; DeepFace, 93; Wages for Facebook project, 168

facial recognition, 83, 156, 264

factory, deterritorialized, 65, 82, 116, 146, 177–78, 226–27, 257, 273

factory code, 27–41, 65, 129, 155, 171; arbitrage on labor power, 30; capitalist administration and, 39; derivative computing and, 41–54; labor, cheapening/devaluing of, 30, 171–72; normativity of, 9; racial formation and, 24, 55–59

Fairchild, 94

Fanon, Frantz, 76, 85, 193

Far Great, 29–30

fascism, 22, 53, 88, 130, 140, 185; fractal, 6, 26, 33, 34, 46, 101, 128, 137, 179, 220, 224, 229, 241, 244, 249; mystification of authorship/authority, 166–67; neoliberalism and, 82, 93; U.S. onset of, 167

Federici, Silvia, 71, 102, 105, 168, 273

feedback loop, 239; visuality and, 79–81, 126–28, 146, 155, 159, 162–63

Feldman, Allen, 49–50, 131

female "computers," 94–95, 163

fetish, 4; information as, 38

fetishization, 135; platform fetishism, 46, 130, 161, 166, 186, 194, 266, 278

finance: democratization of, 283–84; derivative, 21, 115, 143, 145, 204, 217; synthetic, 5, 16, 45, 107, 112, 114, 143, 212, 241, 251

finance capital, 101, 176, 203, 247–48; visuality and, 259–60

financial derivatives, 6, 7, 51–52, 55–56

financialization, 286n7; of culture, 54; of daily life, 6, 20, 48, 53, 113, 225, 260; of deconstruction, 41–54; digital culture as extension of logic of, 102, 107; of observable world, 37; of representation, 48, 215–16

Fisher, Mark, 185

fixed capital, 6, 223, 227, 238, 240, 243–44, 246, 252; as computational, 79, 106; digital media and, 108, 146; information as framework of, 124; ratio of to variable, 170, 178; returned to communities, 220–21; unthought and, 64–65. *See also* capital

Floyd, George, 215, 252, 293n6

Flusser, Vilém, 35, 60, 79, 89, 101, 103, 109, 128, 147, 162–64, 195, 277, 286n7; shoe, as form of encoded information, 123–24, 162, 295–96n19; universe of technical image, 137, 161

Ford, Henry, 115

forgetting, 96–97

Foucault, Michel, 101, 179, 221, 286–87n8; ability machine, 21, 40; antipathetic to Marxism, 279–80

fractal fascism, 6, 26, 33, 34, 46, 101, 128, 137, 179, 220, 224, 229, 241, 244, 249

Frank, Anne, 103, 293n4

Franklin, Sebastian, 36, 122

Freed, James Ingo, 97

Freitas, Miguel, 297n6

French Revolution, 85

Freud, Sigmund, 191

Freudian Robot, The (Liu), 77

Friedman, Milton, 206, 208

Fuchs, Christian, 176–77, 184

"functionaries," 164

fungibility, 18, 23, 232, 245

futurity, 97, 190, 230, 250, 265, 268; alternative, 197, 217; metrics of, 132; violence and, 83

Galloway, Alex, 36, 49, 285n2

"game space," 274

game theory, 77–78, 111–12

Gandy, Oscar, 177

"Garden of Forking Paths, The" (Borges), 133

gender abstraction, 13, 19, 65, 136

gendered computation, 80, 163

gender oppression, 9, 18, 95, 163

genocide, 32, 45, 46, 90–92, 93, 261; census and, 90–91; Northern acceptance of, 185; Philippine-American War, 91, 269; social media and, 105

genomes, 83

geology, White, 33

German Ideology, The (Marx), 118

Germany, 160

Getino, Octavio, 262

Get Out (Peele), 59

Gilbaud, George, 77

Gilmore, Ruth Wilson, 17, 78

global communitarian products, 194

globalization, 44, 111, 193, 200, 202–3, 239

Global North, 86, 106, 192–93

Global South, 96, 204

Gödel, Kurt, 74, 75

Golumbia, David, 84, 122

"Good Stranger" citizen neuroresponse, 159

Google, 27, 45, 49, 51, 146; Alphabet, 162; privacy regulations, 176

Google AdWords, 176–77

Googleplex, 168

Gordon-Reed, Annette, 92, 264

Goveia, Elsa, 8

governance, algorithmic, 47, 49, 155, 167

Gram, Sarah, 292–93n1

individuality, no longer viable, 191–92

individuation, 68

industrial complex, 66

industrialization, 67; linear time of, 84–85; of visuality, 126–27, 225, 240, 270, 272, 277

industrial revolution, 28, 32, 69, 127–29; visual, 126, 177

inequalities, 18; infrastructural, 80, 106; internal to our being, 193; of liquidity, 120, 145, 170; Racial Contract, 25–26; structural, 65, 80, 106, 170, 248

"influencers," 46, 102, 103

informatic labor, 7, 27, 36, 61, 220, 222, 226, 277; advertising and, 177; defined, 139; photograph and, 163–64, 182; programmatic image and, 255–56

informatics, 5, 17, 26–27, 33, 39, 44; abstraction, 7, 71; capitalist, 36, 49, 53, 109, 125, 163, 186; dominant, 58; image and, 162–63; reparative, 61; totalitarianism of, 74, 256; white supremacy and, 24

information: actionable, 9, 154, 169, 193; actually existing, 16; autonomy of, 136; as capitalization, 206; colonization of, 7; as commodity, 139–46, 278; computation as metabolism of, 23, 38; definitions, 12, 288n9; as derivative on reality, 3; as "difference that makes a difference," 13, 56, 287n9; as difference that makes a social difference, 13, 261, 282; as fetish, 38; as form of money, 22; generalization of, 141; as genome, 83; historical conditions of possibility, 14, 97; "I," 138, 140; image and informatic components, 123–24, 296n19; inadmissible, 147, 196–97, 269; invented "behind our backs," 13, 15, 285–86n4; as neither matter nor energy, 12, 36; as ontological reality, 123; as real abstraction, 6–27; rise of, 3, 206; as the root of all evil, 16, 218; shoe as example of, 123–24, 162, 295–96n19; as social rela-

tion, 46, 126, 219, 286n6; suppression of, 92; as technique, 16; valorizing, 125–26, 154, 169

Information (I), 101

information theory, 26, 77–78, 165, 216

innovation: conversion to arbitrage, 170–71; decolonization as driver of, 76; extraction of intellect and emotional intelligence, 190–91; options, 116

instrumentalization, 32, 35–36, 53; of subject-function, 107–8

intellect, general, 119; expropriation of, 68, 72, 80–81, 97; privatization of, 189; as programmable, 183–84, 195

Intellectual and Manual Labour (Sohn-Rethel), 11

intelligence, 67; hostile, 72

interest: all interests subsumed by, 135; production of, 139

interest-bearing capital, 134–35, 139

International Institute of Strategic Studies, 292n11

internet/social media, 293n2; antisocial, 168; as command-control operations, 146, 182; fascism and, 93; financialized, 102, 127; global digital apartheid and, 82; "likes," 6, 46, 52, 103, 120, 155; privacy policies, 176–77; productive dimensions of, 146; reposting, 175; solidarity on, 187, 292n10

Internet Ungovernance Forum, 292n10

intersubjectivity, 112, 192

"invisible hand," 24, 35, 64, 84, 88, 135, 214

Iraq, 284

Iron Dome missile defense system, 94

Iskwaterpangk (Squatterpunk) (de la Cruz), 197, 201–5

Islamophobia, 260

Israel, 51, 292n11; driverless car, 160–61; Iron Dome missile defense system, 94; occupation of Palestine, 148–50

Italian Marxist feminism, 163

"Italian *Operaismo* and the Information Machine" (Pasquinelli), 125–26

Jameson, Frederic, 49, 65, 75–76, 128, 276, 296n19

Jefferson, Thomas, 92

Jefferson the Virginian (Malone), 92, 264

Jews, census and, 90–91, 94

Jing (singer), 199–200

justice, 52, 61

Kant, Immanuel, 41, 64, 208

Katipunan revolution (Philippines), 263, 269

Keynes, John Maynard, 208–9, 212

King, Rodney, 8, 197, 215

Kittler, Friedrich, 107, 161

knowledge, 12–14, 24, 30, 37–39, 295n14; autopoiesis, 72, 74–75; derivative condition of, 53

knowledge formations, 50–51

Kosnik, Abigail de, 294n7

Kubrick, Stanley, 88

Kulturpunkt interview (2014), 267

Kurzweil, Ray, 96

labor, 294n10; abstract universal labor time, 12, 17, 114, 115, 132, 178; arbitrage on, 24, 30–31, 45, 52–54, 248; average time, 12–13, 171–72; cheapening/devaluing of, 30, 121, 171–72, 204, 227; dead, 36–37, 74, 96–97, 121, 295n18, 296n2; "living," 120, 141–42; look as, 177; as machine amortization, 114, 120; necessary, 30–31, 42–43, 109, 120, 141, 178; playbor, 200n6, 202, 299n6; remunerated/recognized, 18, 20, 31, 171, 180, 196, 226–27, 230–31, 234, 251, 278–79, 283; sensual, 102, 110, 116–17, 145, 176, 257, 273; "servile," 163, 195; of superintendence, 32, 126, 129; unpaid, 11, 109–10, 119–20, 137; of watching, 32, 66, 126, 127–38

labor theory: of machine intelligence, 67–68; of value, 61–62, 102, 143, 177

Lacan, Jacques, 76–77, 181, 191, 292n8

Lampedusa, Giuseppe di, 86

language: "American grammar," 92, 264; displacement of sovereign subject, 181; environment of everyday languages, 162; as platform for capital, 134; politics of the utterance, 194–96, 203–4, 298n6; privatization of, 190; protocol layer of, 50, 78; shifts in, 184; words, reclamation of, 199–200

Lee, Benjamin, 103

legitimization: of difference by monetization, 18; of white supremacist patriarchy, 87

Levitt, Deborah, 39

"liberals," 48

libido, 182

Libra cryptocurrency, 167

life: cheapening/devaluing of, 30, 121, 171–72, 204, 227; commodification of, 6; remaindered, 47–48, 50, 67, 89, 96, 127–38, 133–34; transformations/disappearances of forms of, 83

life-time, 133–34, 137; of disposability, 133, 170, 186, 204

life-world, 159, 174; colonization of, 7, 35, 40, 43, 70, 107, 133–35, 133–36, 159, 176; digitization, 70, 257; digitization of, 18; images and, 107, 130, 176

light emission, computability of, 158–59

"likes," 6, 46, 52, 103, 120, 155

Lipuma, Edward, 212

liquidity, 223, 227–28, 231–32, 237–38, 240–41, 245–36; inequality of, 120, 145, 170; premium, 21, 52, 115, 144, 235, 240; production of, 133; revolutionary uses of, 268; social, 137, 241

Liu, Lydia, 77

lived abstraction, 11, 19, 179

"living labor," 120, 141–42

look: as labor, 177; radical, 274

Lorde, Audre, 63, 88

"Lorem Ipsum Project, The" (Ramjit), 93

Luhmann, Niklas, 74

Lukacs, Georg, 41

Luxembourg, Rosa, 44

substitutable choices, 20, 22, 44, 214

subsumption: of cosmos, 141–42; enclosure by computation, 70; human, 131–32; "real," 127, 132, 141, 157, 162, 180, 183, 189–90, 195; reverse, 190

superintendence, 32, 126, 129

superiority, sense of, 4–5

supraculturalism, 207

surplus labor, 31, 54, 109–10, 141; as "living labor," 120; programmable image and, 119–21

surplus value, 128, 184, 200–201, 215, 273; dissymmetrical exchange, 103, 109–10, 119, 164, 177–78, 190, 262, 278–79; of life, 231; programmable image and, 119–20, 125–26

surveillance: algorithms for, 156–60; Babbage's calculating engines, 67; facial recognition, 156–57

sustainability, 39, 54, 87, 94; communism and, 132, 253, 282

symbolic structure, 77

synthetic finance, 5, 16, 21, 45, 107, 112, 114, 143, 212, 241, 251

Tabulating Machine Company, 90

Tadiar, Neferti, 30, 39, 47–48, 89, 133, 137, 141, 170, 204; *Things Fall Away*, 134

Taiwan, 198–99

Tarde, Gabriel, 112

targeting, 157

Taylor, Breonna, 215

techné, 36, 40, 46

technical form, 166–67

technical image, 60, 77, 79, 195–96, 264; alternative wagers within, 167–68; globalization of, 200; life as functionaries of, 164, 195–96; linear time and, 275; media ecology of, 187; music as, 197; as predatory, 196; as product of automated thought, 181–82; real abstractions created by, 154; universe of, 109, 123, 137, 164, 181, 258–59

technohumanist dehumanization, 89–97

technology, as white mythology, 81

Tegmark, Max, 73, 290n4

Tejaratchi, Sean, 175

telecommunications, system of, 5

"telecommunications" of price signal, 19, 64, 166, 209–10

Télécoms (France), 165–66

"10 Milliseconds of Trading in Merck" (Hunsader), 169

Thatcher, Margaret, 82

theft, of capital and labor, 122, 137, 141, 171, 175, 283

Things Fall Away (Tadiar), 134

thinking in numbers, 64, 79–81

Thomas Jefferson and Sally Hemings: An American Controversy (Gordon-Reed), 92

Thompson, Ken, 165

Three Times (Hou), 197–201

Through a Lens Darkly: Black Photographers and the Emergence of a People (Harris), 273

time: abstract universal labor time, 12, 17, 114, 115, 132, 178; alienation of, 42; concrete, 42; metabolic, 171, 176–77, 195, 204

Time, Labor and Social Domination (Postone), 31

"To Be Determined" (Chun), 161

totalitarianism, 40, 195, 247, 261, 283; informatic, 74, 256

totalizing practices, 69, 154, 195, 205, 217, 228, 261; images and, 109

Towards a Philosophy of Photography (Flusser), 79, 123, 258, 277

"Traces of Israel's Iron Dome Can Be Found in Tech Startups" (Coppola), 94

tradition, liquidation of, 71

tranches, 3–4, 27

transitional computing and economy, 217–18

Trotsky, Leon, 217

truth, regimes of, 179

tion of community by money, 211–12; humanism and, 84–86; photography and, 147–50; structural, 65, 104, 137

Virilio, Paul, 128, 170

Virno, Paolo, 65, 69, 128, 150, 152, 180, 189

Virtanen, Akseli, 282

virtual machine, 5–6, 9, 13, 27, 29–30, 186, 206, 264

"virtuosity," 65, 128, 150, 152, 180, 188–89, 251

vision machines, computerized, 162–63

Vismann, Cornelia, 89

visual culture, 32, 148, 151–52, 223, 267–68; "art" vs., 151; cybernetic role of, 127; older modes of, 106; screens as work-sites, 70, 101–2, 107–8, 123

visual economy, 195

visuality: feedback loop and, 79–81, 126–28, 146, 155, 159, 162–63; industri-alization of, 126–27, 225, 240, 270, 272, 277

Vitale, Chris, 93

volatility, 4–5, 20–21, 32, 36–37, 45, 49, 51–53, 142, 154, 212

Volatility Group seminar, 258

voltage differences, 161

von Neumann, John, 39, 78, 111–12, 115

wage labor, 17, 109–10; change in form, 178; remuneration, 171, 180, 196, 278–79, 283; remuneration of, 226–27, 230–31, 234, 251

Wages for Facebook, 168

Wales, Jimmy, 297–98n6

war: global, 133; "immaterial civil war," 155; metaphysics as medium of, 49, 131; semiotic, 155, 204

Wark, McKenzie, 123, 274, 295n18, 297n2

watching, labor of, 32, 66, 126, 127–38, 178

"we," 265; advertising and, 184–85; as computational, 83, 163; as conscripted, 65; cooptation of, 185–86; as simula-tion, 73; as unconscious of world computer, 69

wealth, sociality of, 38, 82, 178

W. E. B. Du Bois's Data Portraits Visualizing Black America (Battle-Baptiste and Rusert), 29, 288n11

welfare state, 209

Westworld, 168, 291–92n9

What Is Cybernetics? (Gilbaud), 77

whiteness, 95, 285n3; as referent, 93; technology as white mythology, 60, 81, 87; world spirit as Caucasian super-predation, 256–57

white supremacy, 24–26, 80, 92, 264

"white terror" (Taiwan), 198

Who Counts? (Nelson), 46

Wiener, Norbert, 12, 78, 94, 296n21; on low-level discrimination, 127, 169

Wiesel, Elie, 208

Wikileaks, 169

Wikipedia, 297–98n6

Wilson, Andrew Norman, 95–96, 168

Winant, Howard, 56

Wizeman, Eyal, 152

worker: as "ability machine," 33, 52; as "conscious organ," 66, 121, 129, 164, 213, 257, 286n7; as portfolio, 21, 39, 44, 46, 142

Workers Leaving the Googleplex (Wilson), 95–96

working day, 30–31

"working day," 71, 113

"Work of Art" (Benjamin), 123

work-sites: for data visualization, 136, 146; of the digital-visual, 154–72; photograph as image and code, com-modity and, 146–54; screens as, 70, 101–2, 107–8, 123

world, tranching of, 4

world computer: as abstraction, 33; avatars of, 215–16; computational racial capital as, 6, 35; defined, 5, 294n9; denizens of, 27–28, 32, 142, 171, 175, 259; futurity and, 35; Global South as product of, 96; material relations of, 152; operating system of, 65–66, 146,

world computer (*continued*)
165, 186, 196, 221, 222, 240, 252; as "super-intelligent," 121; as universal Turing machine, 70–71, 117, 121, 140, 290n2; as "vast automaton," 54, 66, 69, 129; as virtual machine, 186, 206, 264; "we" as unconscious of, 69

"world literature," postliterary, 104

world market, 15, 142–44, 170, 239, 241, 265

world spirit, 83, 90, 96; as Caucasian super-predation, 256–57

world system, 66, 102, 193; failure of, 4

Wynter, Sylvia, 8, 131, 197, 207–8, 211, 291n5

Yusoff, Kathryn, 33, 97

Zuckerberg, Mark, 53

Zuìhǎo de shíguāng (*Three Times*) (Hou), 197–201

www.ingramcontent.com/pod-product-compliance
Lightning Source LLC
Chambersburg PA
CBHW071014280326
41935CB00011B/1342